Walking the Gendered Tightrope

CAWP Series in Gender and American Politics

SERIES EDITORS:
Susan J. Carroll, Rutgers University
Kira Sanbonmatsu, Rutgers University

TITLES IN THE SERIES:

*Walking the Gendered Tightrope:
Theresa May and Nancy Pelosi as Legislative Leaders*
by Melissa Haussman and Karen M. Kedrowski

Gendered Pluralism
by Belinda Robnett and Katherine Tate

Who Runs? The Masculine Advantage in Candidate Emergence
by Sarah Oliver and Meredith Conroy

*When Protest Makes Policy: How Social Movements
Represent Disadvantaged Groups*
by S. Laurel Weldon

*The Paradox of Gender Equality:
How American Women's Groups Gained
and Lost Their Public Voice*
by Kristin A. Goss

*The Changing Face of Representation:
The Gender of U.S. Senators and Constituent Communications*
by Kim L. Fridkin and Patrick J. Kenney

The Political Consequences of Motherhood
by Jill S. Greenlee

Gender in Campaigns for the U.S. House of Representatives
by Barbara Burrell

Center for American Women and Politics
Eagleton Institute of Politics   Rutgers University
www.cawp.rutgers.edu

WALKING THE GENDERED TIGHTROPE

Theresa May and Nancy Pelosi as Legislative Leaders

Melissa Haussman and Karen M. Kedrowski

University of Michigan Press
Ann Arbor

Copyright © 2023 by Melissa Haussman and Karen M. Kedrowski
Some rights reserved

This work is licensed under a Creative Commons Attribution-NonCommercial 4.0 International License. *Note to users*: A Creative Commons license is only valid when it is applied by the person or entity that holds rights to the licensed work. Works may contain components (e.g., photographs, illustrations, or quotations) to which the rightsholder in the work cannot apply the license. It is ultimately your responsibility to independently evaluate the copyright status of any work or component part of a work you use, in light of your intended use. To view a copy of this license, visit http://creativecommons.org/licenses/by-nc/4.0/

For questions or permissions, please contact um.press.perms@umich.edu

Published in the United States of America by the
University of Michigan Press
Manufactured in the United States of America
Printed on acid-free paper
First published August 2023

A CIP catalog record for this book is available from the British Library.

Library of Congress Cataloging-in-Publication data has been applied for.

ISBN: 078-0-472-07634-5 (hardcover : alk. paper)
ISBN: 978-0-472-05634-7 (paper : alk. paper)
ISBN: 978-0-472-90372-6 (open access ebook)

DOI: https://doi.org/10.3998/mpub.12676438

Library of Congress Control Number: 2023937358

The University of Michigan Press's open access publishing program is made possible thanks to additional funding from the University of Michigan Office of the Provost and the generous support of contributing libraries.

With love to my son, Jonathan; my daughter, Suzanne; and my late husband, Tim
—Karen M. Kedrowski

For Linda, as always
—Melissa Haussman

Contents

Acknowledgments	ix
ONE Introduction	1
TWO How Female Leaders Get There: Party Workhorses but Not Party Animals	46
THREE Prime Minister May's Tightrope Walk between Brexiteers and Remainers	97
FOUR Pelosi's Tightropes	135
FIVE Staying On or Falling Off the Tightrope: Lessons Learned	183
Table 1	195
References	213
Index	265

Digital materials related to this title can be found on the Fulcrum platform via the following citable URL: https://doi.org/10.3998/mpub.12676438

Acknowledgments

We wish to acknowledge the work of change-oriented women politicians, namely, the two subjects of this book, Theresa May and Nancy Pelosi. Without their dedication to making politics more inclusive and workable, the political systems of the US and the UK would be poorer and less constructive. Obviously, much work remains to be done. We know that many feminists inside the US Congress and the UK Parliament work individually and in various caucuses to make politics more representative and functional, and while their work may be stymied at points, we know that in the long run their work is valuable and will produce more diverse leaders. Diverse leadership, supported by party caucuses, can only make the political institutions of both countries work better for the people who live there.

We are indebted to many people who, directly or indirectly, made this project a reality. First, we wish to thank the University of Michigan Press and the Center for American Women and Politics (CAWP) at Rutgers University for sharing our vision and publishing this book. CAWP and Rutgers were major actors in building the field of gender and politics into the vibrant subfield it is today. We build upon the work of fantastic scholars previously and currently affiliated with CAWP and Rutgers. We thank Sarah Childs for her support and willingness to share her expertise. We could not have pursued this work without the work of feminist giants in political science and other fields, all of whom are cited in the book. We have also benefited from the work and help of comparative politics scholars, who are also cited. We thank the many journalists who have written incisive and thoughtful articles on polarization and institutional cracks in the US, the UK, and Europe.

We wish to thank Ashley Montgomery and Sue Cloud of the Carrie Chapman Catt Center and Elizabeth Kidd and Amy Papineau of Carleton University, for research and preparations assistance on the manuscript. We also thank our editor at the University of Michigan Press, Elizabeth Demers. We are grateful to several reviewers who provided excellent feedback on earlier versions of this book. Our work is better because of you. Melissa also wishes to acknowledge the support of the Carleton University Political Science Department's research funds and of her chair, Professor Achim Hurrelmann.

Karen thanks Melissa for inviting her into this project, supporting her through some trying life events, and prodding her along. She is grateful to Melissa for being a great coauthor and a wonderful friend. Second, Karen gratefully acknowledges the unnamed Hill insiders whom the authors interviewed for their valuable insights into the Democratic Caucus. Finally, Karen sends a shout-out to her colleagues who participated in the "Smile and Write" writing group at Iowa State University and watched this project unfold. This group provided structure, accountability, and encouragement for many months. Melissa likewise acknowledges Karen for proving an invaluable coauthor through her work in puzzling through why the Conservative Party of the UK would select Theresa May as leader and then remove her rather shortly thereafter. Karen is a tremendously talented professional in mentoring students to achieve greatness in the political science field and was of incredible help and support to Melissa. Melissa also thanks the former and current MPs who provided enormous insights into the puzzle known as the UK Parliament and the electoral connections.

ONE

Introduction

In December 2018, two women leaders, Theresa May and Nancy Pelosi, separated by an ocean and different political systems, faced leadership challenges from within their own political parties, threatening their holds on power. Theresa May, leader of the Conservative Party of the United Kingdom (UK) and the country's prime minister (PM), had promised to negotiate an end to British participation in the European Union (EU). By December 2018, she had a deal on the table. Yet she faced a no-confidence vote from a faction within her own party. For her part, Nancy Pelosi, Speaker of the United States (US) House of Representatives, faced a leadership challenge from within her party even though she had fulfilled her responsibilities as the party's leading fundraiser and candidate recruiter and had led the Democrats to reclaim majority control in the US House. Yet, the 2018 challenge, undertaken as Pelosi was preparing to move into the Speaker's office, was just the latest in a more or less biennial ritual of direct or proxy challenges that began when she was first elected as Democratic whip in 2001.

In 2018, both women survived, but their victories were Pyrrhic ones. Pelosi won reelection as Speaker in 2018 by agreeing to stay in the position for only four more years. Theresa May conveyed to her cabinet and caucus more than once from December 2018 onward that she would give way to another leader after the caucus supported her Brexit bills. After three tries for support in 2019, May was forced to announce her resignation in May of that year, taking effect in July 2019. The accession of these women to leadership should be placed in the context of their parties' win-loss records and the "desirability" of their positions at the time. Nancy Pelosi became Democratic (minority whip) in 2001 and leader (in 2003) when the Democratic Party did not control Congress. Of course, she could only become Speaker when the Democrats controlled Congress, in 2007—under a Republican president but with large legislative numbers—the first time Democrats had controlled the House since 1994. No Democratic woman had been a committee chair in the House for decades. After Nancy Pelosi was elected Speaker in 2007, four ascended to this position. In 2016, Theresa May became prime minister one year after the Conservatives had won a majority for the first time since 1997. May served in the Osborne-Clegg coalition cabinet from 2010 to 2015 and continued in the Cameron cabinet after 2015 as an officeholder of one of the four "Great Offices of State," home secretary (the other three are chancellor of the exchequer, prime minister, and foreign secretary). May was one of the longest inhabitants of the home secretary portfolio and the first female Conservative MP to hold it.

The two women leaders oversaw historic achievements, dealing with two of the most complicated legislative packages each country had faced in decades. For Speaker Pelosi, this was the first comprehensive framework for noninsured people to access affordable health insurance in the history of the US in her first speakership and the oversight of two presidential impeachments in her second speakership. Prime Minister May did the heavy lifting on the EU withdrawal framework from 2017 to 2019. By the time her successor, Boris Johnson, came in as prime minister in July 2019, all that remained was to craft a deal with Northern Ireland, one that neither PM May nor the Northern Irish unionists had said they would accept. May also got pieces of the Withdrawal Act Bills through Parliament and helped confront social policy issues that had broken apart the Northern Ireland Stormont parliament in 2017.

Pelosi and May have walked a tightrope of gendered expectations in the context of inherited problems, masculinist adversarial institutions, and intraparty discord. Thus, representation by demographically diverse leaders is fraught. The types of representation most often discussed in the feminist political science literature, based on Pitkin's classic formulation, include descriptive, which is numbers based (i.e., when women are elected to office), and policy based, described as substantive. The third type recently discussed includes "symbolic," which would describe "legislators that people can relate to," that is, providing a symbol to voters that they are represented (Childs and Webb 2012, 19–20, 87). Unfortunately, even in 2021, our case studies show that male elites with disproportionate power pick women leaders based on descriptive representation to claim that the party is committed to change. Both Speaker Pelosi and former Prime Minister May worked to represent women in both substantive and symbolic fashion, but their party and institutional cultures still require more change away from the old male-driven adversarial mode and "traditional politics" to completely effectuate women's power as leaders.

Although the percentages of women in both the US House of Representatives and the UK House of Commons were at then-historic 23 percent in the US after the 2018 midterms and 32 percent after the 2017 UK election, it was clear that men were typically driving the defenestration efforts, as will be shown. Our book fits into the literature on political institutional and party systems and the debates over the importance of "critical mass" and "critical actors" (Childs and Krook 2009). The spoiler alert is that majoritarian systems with first-past-the-post voting are the most unfriendly to women's election and substantive leadership, and even in the face of reformed selection procedures, women's leadership is considered a secondary, temporary solution by many legislative caucus members.

What is also interesting about the two systems is that while Pelosi has functioned as House Speaker and May as leader of the House, neither post has full control over the legislative body. Each functions as the head of the majority party and, while responsible for getting bills through the entire House, does not control the opposition parties. In the US, this has been particularly evident since the late twentieth century. Thus, there is a built-in structural constraint to being both US House Speaker and UK Leader of the House. Our tightrope image is that of the leaders negotiating the various factions within her party as well as working to get the majority needed to pass bills. A fundamental question in this analysis is, Is loyalty gendered?—in terms of women leaders both securing the loyalty of their caucuses and demonstrating loyalty to their allies. Scholarship has shown that this has not been the case in the US (Green 2008), and we will show that it was not particularly the case with Theresa May; in other words, while these leaders helped other women get elected, they were not necessarily supported by them in legislative votes.

Justifying the Case Selection. Certainly, we recognize the important differences between the British Westminster system and the American presidential system of separate powers. However, we argue that the tales of these two leaders are similar in very important ways. First, their leadership positions are dependent upon the support of their party caucuses. Opposition and criticism from the opposing party or parties are expected. What we are looking at are primarily the gendered dynamics they faced in *intra*party challenges. Second, these leaders faced threats to their position when they proved they were skilled at the most difficult aspects of their jobs. Third, they both came into power and had to walk their gendered tightropes within divisive, male-dominated institutions that mirror equally divisive national political climates. They also inherited circumstances that shaped their leadership journey and the judgments of their leadership acumen, even though they had little control over these circumstances. In May's case, these were a complex history and an enduring national ambivalence about the European project within the UK. In Pelosi's case, they were institutional changes that changed the tone of the institution and undermined its ability to function. These similarities, we argue, override the differences.

Plan of the Book

The plan of our book is as follows. This introductory chapter forms the literature review, taking up the feminist literature on women's legislative and executive representation and other literatures on party and political institutional systems. Chapter 2 examines the criteria for leadership choices by parties and the long histories of both PM May and Speaker Pelosi in working for the betterment of their parties in and outside of the national legislature. It covers Theresa May in her pre-PM shadow cabinet and cabinet positions and Nancy Pelosi before her first election as Speaker in 2007. Themes introduced in chapter 2 include overall assessments of issue developments, intraparty discord, and interparty competition. Chapters 3 and 4 will add a fourth subheading, covering the appointment strategies each leader used, to manage discord and to get the majority vote required for policy delivery. Chapter 3 discusses Theresa May's history as prime minister and her work to implement the June 2016 "in or out" EU referendum results in the UK. May's decision to hold an election early in her mandate in June 2017 was consequential given that the Conservatives lost their overall majority in the House and she crafted a "confidence and supply" agreement with the socially conservative Democratic Unionist Party (DUP) from Northern Ireland, headed by Arlene Foster. The interests of Foster and the DUP were diametrically opposed to those of Prime Minister May with respect to the Brexit timetable—the DUP used a strategy of "running out the clock" since the Stormont Assembly had ceased functioning in January 2017. May needed the consent of the DUP to get her deal across the finish line, while issues central to the DUP had not yet been resolved, such as abortion and LGBT rights in Northern Ireland, and needed resolution before Stormont could resume power sharing. Within her Conservative caucus, May faced an ever-increasing percentage of "hard" Brexiteers, elected in the 2010, 2015, and 2017 UK general elections, who wanted to exit the EU so they could be free to strike trade deals with the US and other countries. This increase happened particularly after the global financial crash of 2008 and concomitant increases in low-skilled immigration. On the other side were Remainers, who just as unrealistically wanted a second EU referendum. May's interest in maintaining party unity and promoting Brexit was strongly hampered by those two sets of factors. The constellation of intraparty and opposition party forces, and those of the supposed "confidence and supply partner" after June 2017, were such that May was never going to be "allowed" to achieve Brexit.

Chapter 4 follows the plan of chapter 3 for Nancy Pelosi. It describes her ascension through House leadership in the twenty-first century, culminating in her first election as Speaker from 2007 to 2010 and then her second term when Democrats regained the majority in 2018. It covers Pelosi's large role in stickhandling the Affordable Care Act (ACA), particularly through the House in 2010. This would not have been possible without the large Democratic majorities in the House and Senate. In early 2009, the Democratic House majority was at around eighty members, and the Senate was at a nearly filibuster-proof fifty-eight members, with two Democratic-leaning Independents. Not a single Republican legislator voted for the ACA. Chapter 4 also deals with the Trump impeachments and the COVID and security protocols put in place in 2020 and 2021.

Both Pelosi and May were accused of taking the "progressive" wing of their party for granted. While the Congressional Progressive Caucus began in 1991 and was originally chaired by Senator Bernie Sanders, it increased its numbers after the 2018 election to just under half (ninety-six) of the House Democratic Caucus (Dayen 2021b). The other half of the caucus encompassed the centrist "New Democrat" Coalition, and influential issue caucuses included the bipartisan "Problem Solvers," the Congressional Black Caucus, and the Women's Caucus. While May had been known mostly as somewhere in the middle of the Remain-Leave divide during the Brexit referendum campaign in 2016, she identified as the Leave-supporting candidate in the leadership campaign of July 2016 in order to distinguish herself in part from other Leave supporters such as Boris Johnson and Andrea Leadsom. Historically, she had aligned herself with the "modernizing" wing of the party, eager to decontaminate it by supporting candidate diversity and a more up-to-date view of gender roles. The Conservative majority was lost in 2017, and thereafter majorities were denied to May for her various Brexit options. These events were due to Cabinet resignations and the movement of some Conservative Remainers to an independent group. Her successor, Boris Johnson, called another early election for December 2019. It increased the Conservative MP numbers to 365 and the majority required to pass the proposals May had negotiated with the EU along with some of the Johnson team's tweaks.

The concluding chapter discusses what these two case studies show us about whether female party animals can turn into respected party leaders and gain the support they need; unfortunately, the answer to this is often no. While May and Pelosi acted as leaders in the same fashion as men and had stronger credentials than many of the men they succeeded (and preceded in May's case), they faced continuous criticism of every option they pursued, in their parties, legislatures, and the press. The final chapter discusses what we think we know about women's descriptive, substantive, and symbolic representation in majoritarian legislatures and the vast spaces about which we still are uninformed. While our two case studies illustrate the nature of these two women's accession to party and legislative leadership and the bargains made along the way, they also show, in both cases, that men and women are actively plotting to undermine and replace them at nearly every turn. Women's leadership, according to Beckwith (2015), is contingent, awaiting the right crisis to occur in a party so they can make the case to be the perfect party savior. The problem with this formulation is that, as with Ginger Rogers, "doing it backwards and in high heels" still does not suffice for many masculinist politicians who continue to control the levers of power in these institutions and parties. Where each leader was able to make a dent in the prevailing ethos and practices, we will emphasize it. While the accession of these two women to high-profile positions was pathbreaking, their challenges are quite common.

Images of Women's Leadership and the Tightrope

Various studies have identified the barriers to women's leadership, often in private sector organizations, as "concrete walls" (Lupo 2017), "glass walls" (Comer and Drollinger 1997), the "glass ceiling" (US Commission on the Glass Ceiling 1995), or the "glass labyrinth" (Martin 2007). The term "concrete wall" was used in the 1970s to denote the outright "patriarchal ban on women's inclusion in the labour force or education" (Lupo 2017). While discriminatory practices have become seemingly more subtle since the 1980s, they persist. Glass ceiling studies of the private sector refer to barriers to advancement of diverse social groups. These groups will not achieve actual power, providing only descriptive diversity. The glass ceiling is based on "beliefs, attitudes and cultural norms" (Lupo 2017).

Business school academics have puzzled through the issues of why diversity has eluded private sector organizations. In 2007, Eagly and Carli described the glass labyrinth as the different weights that career choices have on women, particularly caregiving expectations and responsibilities. They showed that women working full time in 2007 spent as much time on childcare as the stay-at-home mother of 1975. As Martin, in her review of their work, stated, "To increase gender equality in the workplace, change must take place at the level of culture, the organization, the family and the individual" (2007, 90). While the labyrinth posits that women can have different ways of entering and progressing in an organization or institution, women must "blend the stereotypical male qualities of decisiveness and toughness" with the feminine-ascribed qualities of "warmth and inclusiveness." The shorthand for trying to maneuver this way is known as "smart power," when leaders know when to be firm versus gentle.

For business organizations, Eagly and Carli noted that members of marginalized groups are often brought in to lead an organization when it is at its lowest ebb and thus are likely doomed to fail (2007). Beckwith posited a similar finding for women leading political parties (2015). In 1977, Professor Rosabeth Moss Kanter wrote that a "critical mass" of 30 percent of women could start to "tilt" a corporate culture.

Responding to the business studies, we know that political organizations respond to different imperatives than the private sector and have different timetables. The US has regular congressional elections, while UK Westminster elections have to occur within every five years. These structure the work product of the legislature and the positioning of legislators, who are up for reelection in single member districts. Theoretically, every member of a legislative caucus is equal when it comes to their number of votes on the floor, with some holding positions of leadership. Corporate structures do not pretend to be equal, and each person within them is not necessarily subject to being fired at the same time (unless the business fails). Childs and Krook have been the leaders in showing the imperfect translation of the automatic assumptions of "critical mass" in a corporate culture (which don't often work) into legislatures with different pressure points and timeframes (2009).

In terms of architectural metaphors for women's power in legislatures, the "concrete floor" is addressed by Annesley, Beckwith, and Franceschet (2019, 2–3). They demonstrate the idea of descriptive representation and tokenism to show that once a woman has been appointed to a cabinet post, that minimum threshold must be continued or exceeded by following governments. We move away from these "construction design" analogies because, with the exception of the "concrete floor," they attempt to explain the reasons why few women reach the apex of power. Both May and Pelosi have shattered their glass or concrete ceilings, navigated their labyrinths, and walked around their glass walls to become their party caucus's legislative leader. The gendered tightrope explains the competing gendered expectations that they need to follow in order to remain in power. And like a real tightrope, it is very easy to fall off our symbolic one.

In the UK, holding a cabinet post is an important precursor to being able to vie for Conservative Party leadership. In their study of seven different political systems, Annesley, Beckwith, and Franceschet noted that typically fewer than 10 percent of MPs get into cabinet within their first term (2019, 125). However, Theresa May did exactly that in 2001, as the first of the 1997 elected Conservative MPs included in Opposition Leader William Hague's shadow cabinet in the typically female post of secretary of education and employment. May was appointed to six different shadow portfolios between 1999 and 2010 (221).

In the seven political systems they studied, Annesley, Beckwith, and Franceschet (2019) included three Westminster democracies (Australia, Canada, UK); the US presidential cabinet appointment process in its separation of powers system; the mixed-member proportional system of Germany; the presidential system of Chile using an open-list proportional representation (PR) system based on two-member congressional districts; and the PR parliamentary system of Spain. Their schematic identifies three sets of characteristics important to the selection of cabinet ministers (and future prime ministerial or presidential candidates). They included the *experiential*, which covered three subsets of factors: political experience, policy expertise, and educational credentials (111). Annesley, Beckwith, and Franceschet's framework follows Ostrom's 1986 work in describing institutional characteristics of "prescribing, prohibiting or permitting" institutional change (211). Their other two sets of criteria include *affiliational* and *representational*. The affiliational "refer to membership in the selector's personal network as a friend, political ally or contemporary" showing loyalty and trust (211). The authors note that in the US, UK, and Australia, affiliational criteria were the most strong and consistent (224). The third set of criteria, representational, may be based on "political, territorial or social groups" that have become "front-burner" qualifications in the party's selection process. The authors find that experiential and representational criteria are the most prescriptive, while affiliational are "permitted." While it is true that all potential cabinet ministers must meet experiential criteria, such that selectors can justify their choice on meritocratic principles, it is also the case that these criteria are "non-specific and flexible, allowing selectors considerable latitude in their application" (211).

Annesley, Beckwith, and Franceschet's criteria are related to those articulated by Escobar-Lemmon and Taylor-Robinson (2015, 2016). These authors restricted their comparative study to cabinet formation in presidential democracies in Latin America (Argentina, Chile, Colombia, Costa Rica) and the US, where, unlike in the UK, cabinet secretaries do not come from within the legislature (2016, 3, 16). Their three overall sets of criteria for how women get to cabinet, and whether they progress beyond it, are grouped into "political capital resources" (PCRs). One subset of PCRs is related to the experience and education credentials of cabinet aspirants; the second, which is hugely helpful for our purposes, specifically focuses on the *political party* experience of aspirants. This is relevant to Nancy Pelosi, who chaired the largest Democratic state committee in the US; functioned as the host committee chair for the 1984 Democratic National Convention in San Francisco and as finance chair in 1985–86 for the Democratic Senatorial Campaign Committee, and is credited with the only legislative flipping (of the Senate) that occurred during President Reagan's two terms (Page 2021). Similarly, Theresa May chaired the Conservative Party, the first woman in the post, from 2002 to 2003. Cabinet ministers (and government leaders) possessing these credentials are termed *organizational partisans* in Escobar-Lemmon and Taylor-Robinson's 2015 work (676). Escobar-Lemmon and Taylor-Robinson also include policy expertise in this second set of characteristics, unlike Annesley, Beckwith, and Franceschet (2019), who include it in their experiential characteristics. Escobar-Lemmon and Taylor-Robinson's third category, which makes sense for presidential cabinets, covers the links between cabinet ministers and "support resources," that is, links to outside groups. These were particularly relevant to the narrowing of May's options on Brexit in terms of outside links possessed not just by Eurosceptic cabinet ministers but also by others in the European Research Group.

In their 2015 article, Escobar-Lemmon and Taylor-Robinson identified four categories of ways in which cabinet members may leave: "survivors," who leave when the presidential term is over; "switchers," who move through different cabinet posts either during or after a presidential administration; "bad end," which is being fired or leaving in disgrace; and "retiring" (673–74). Slightly over 50 percent of the cabinet secretaries in their sample were in the first, or survivor, category, which was true for Theresa May's cabinet experience from 2001 to 2016. Also interesting for our discussion is the fact that organizational partisans such as May were more than 50 percent less likely to leave cabinet in a "bad end" (678).

Interestingly, Escobar-Lemmon and Taylor-Robinson found, as did Annesley, Beckwith, and Franceschet in 2019, that experiential qualifications did not necessarily mean that a cabinet secretary would be able to hold onto his or her job (2015, 686). Specifically, Escobar-Lemmon and Taylor-Robinson found both that women with policy expertise were more likely to meet a "bad end" than survive and that female organizational partisans were more likely to retire rather than meet a "bad end" (686). With respect to organizational partisans, their 2015 work suggested that people in this category have the know-how to manage party expectations by retiring rather than overstaying their welcome. It appears that both Pelosi and May performed the "expectation managing" function in accepting informal term limits in 2018, and again in 2019 for May, by claiming that they had "heard" their caucuses on leadership votes.

In the UK and US political institutions forming the core of this book and the experiences of Theresa May and Nancy Pelosi in leading them, we note that both Speaker Pelosi and PM May were put into hybrid roles. Unlike the workings of a Westminster system, the Speaker is both an organizational partisan and an administrator of the workings of the majority party and the House as a whole. Pelosi has accomplished all of these with relish, as the most successful congressional fundraiser ever at $1 billion and with her ability to get crucial pieces of legislation through (Page 2021). We have chosen to look at Theresa May as the "first legislator" in the UK House of Commons, since her key stumbling blocks were in trying to get iterations of the Brexit package through the House in 2018 (withdrawn) and in three instances in 2019. While she had been known as a quiet Remainer while in Prime Minister Cameron's cabinet, she undertook the task of trying to shepherd the implementation of legislation for the narrowly approved 2016 Brexit referendum through Parliament. Many in the Conservative Party and those in the DUP after the June 2017 election in the confidence and supply agreement with the Conservatives refused to support her proposals. Some in the party were trying to pay her back for not being Euroskeptic enough in the past, while others such as MPs Boris Johnson and Jacob Rees-Mogg were ready to launch their own Conservative leadership campaigns in 2018. While the prime minister is typically thought of as the executive, the task facing Prime Minister May in the Brexit proposals was mainly legislative.

While May was a "survivor" par excellence of the sort described in Escobar-Lemmon and Taylor-Robinson's 2015 study across cabinets and shadow cabinets under both rightist and progressive Conservative leaders, she simply could not transcend those divides in the party caucus when functioning as the prime minister, coming to a "bad end" in May 2019. Pelosi's role as first and foremost an organizational partisan, who was also a survivor of different leadership positions in the House, helped her to navigate leadership challenges, the most recent in 2018. For May, the institutional incentive structure shifted dramatically from her role as secretary in another prime minister's cabinet, where keeping a low public profile and not massaging party divisions were career-enabling features. May became the primary target of public and legislative feelings over Brexit after ascending to the leadership in 2016. She did not have the numbers on either side of the divide between Remain-supporting MPs who wished for another referendum and Euroskeptics who could not exit the EU quickly enough, especially in a bare-majority situation in 2016 and a confidence and supply one after 2017. One of her main strategies to try to contain the divide was through cabinet appointments, but both sides behaved badly, resigning when one iteration of the Withdrawal Act Bills did not meet their wishes.

Theories of Women's Political Presence

"Fresh Face" Leaders and Critical Mass Arguments. Many feminist political theorists and scientists, from Joni Lovenduski and Pippa Norris to Karen Beckwith, Sylvia Bashevkin, Claire Annesley, and Meryl Kenny, have noted the paradox of women's presence, particularly in "the higher the fewer" phenomenon in Anglo-American political systems. The paradox is that women are generally always viewed as "outsiders," only to be encouraged during "special" political times (Beckwith 2015) when the party has faced a series of crises, electoral or otherwise. Thus, while women are viewed as "fresh faces" to be encouraged as cardboard cutouts to help the party regain its electoral footing, the same credit is not given to them for having the gravitas and political experience to know how to actually perform as leaders.

Overall, feminist theories describe the nature of women as outsiders to the long-term history of political institutions and especially as leaders. We agree overall with the concept, identified by Annesley and Gains (2010), Kenny (2014), Lowndes (2014), and Beckwith (2015), that the structure of political opportunities is different for women and men. The problem, as all of these pieces illustrate, is describing how and why that is so and what the specifics of different political institutional configurations are in allowing for this—most specifically, for our purposes, why two of the most qualified representatives, according to the criteria set out by their respective institutions, faced untoward disrespect and removal attempts.

A prevalent theme in the literature is about women being seen as "new and different" leaders rather than what happens to them in their intraparty and intra-institutional settings. Karen Beckwith describes former prime minister Margaret Thatcher's successful challenge to Edward Heath in 1975 as a "crisis" situation when Heath "led the Conservatives into two election defeats" in 1974 (2015, 11, 731). At that time, male party elites stood back to let Thatcher lead the party out of crisis while planning to contend for the leadership in the future under renewed party strength. In related fashion, O'Brien (2015) found that parties in opposition were much more likely to pick women to lead them. In keeping with the literature, she finds that the parties, somewhat in desperation, turn toward a "new face" to project that they have learned the lessons of party defeat. We describe the interaction of the mechanisms used to promote and demote female leaders and May's and Pelosi's policy leadership in the following chapters.

We agree with Bale that "politics is a path-dependent activity . . . and so time, and timing, matter. So, too, do ideas, interests, institutions, and individuals" (2016, 22). Many crucial works have identified the particular difficulty of disrupting male dominance in "old" democracies (Dahlerup and Leyenaar 2013). The US and UK are certainly examples of such old democracies. As Dahlerup and Leyenaar note, democracies where women got the franchise around World War I have been viewed as promoting "incremental" inclusion of women in legislative bodies. Dahlerup and Leyenaar, as well as Hughes and Paxton (2008), describe the dynamic between "forces of change and forces of resistance" in political parties, women's organizations, and, we would add, legislatures (2013, 5). We also agree with the maxims of Lovenduski and Celis that "gender equality in descriptive and substantive representation should be analyzed as power struggles" and that "gender equality is actively resisted" (2018, 148).

Kelly and Duerst-Lahti note that the "image of the disembodied liberal individual ... has not aided women (or men of color) seeking equality and freedom as effectively as white men precisely because embedded notions require others to assimilate to assumptions given to us by those who see them as givens" (1995, 51, cited in Escobar-Lemmon and Taylor-Robinson 2015, 5). Characteristics attributed to white males become the norm for seeking cabinet and legislative leadership aspirants and for judging them while fulfilling their roles.

Hughes and Paxton have described the UK and the US as among the "low jump" countries, where an increase in women's representation in public life in education and the workforce produced a commensurate increase in national-level politics that was only in the 16–24 percent range (2008, 244). Part of the reason is the first-past-the-post electoral system used in both countries (247–48). In this framework, anything that seems "different" about a candidate, deviating from the white male norm, will be used by party selectorates to deny a woman's candidacy (Bashevkin 1993; Childs and Webb 2012, chap. 3). It is crucial to note that similar factors preventing the establishment of critical mass often also prevent the empowerment of women inside the legislature. Women are often described as "inferior" candidates and legislators (Childs and Webb 2012, chaps. 3 and 4). Once women reach some sort of group status in legislatures, including leadership, backlash against them continues (Lovenduski 2005, 5).

Among other theorists, Grey postulated that different critical masses are needed depending on the outcome sought (2006, 494). Unlike the "magic number" of 30 percent of a legislature that has often been proposed, following from Kanter's organizational behavior theories, the work of Studlar and McAllister in twenty OECD countries shows that the "impact of critical mass has been inflated" (2002, 248). Grey has suggested that while a legislature with 15 percent women may enable some changes to the political agenda, such as committee hearings on women-friendly legislation, "it may take proportions of 40% to have women-friendly policies introduced" (2006, 494). Citing Dahlerup, Grey also notes the paradox of women's legislative representation: "women have to prove they are just like male politicians ... [but] that they will make a difference when elected" (Dahlerup 1988, 279, cited in Grey 2006, 493). Grey has identified the "similar but different" expectations placed on women leaders when they navigate the political tightrope.

We are left with the idea that "critical mass" may be necessary but certainly not sufficient to explain the trajectories of female legislative and executive leaders. Studlar and McAllister cited Weldon's (2002) research claiming that a set number of female legislators is a mis-specified model and that instead the interactions that occur in a legislative body are more important (2002, 238). Unlike the "incrementalist" model described by Hughes and Paxton (2008) and Dahlerup and Leyenaar (2013), Studlar and McAllister state that "critical mass should . . . properly . . . refer to a threshold beyond which there is a change of behavior through acceleration ('chain reaction'), not just incrementalism" (2002, 238). Studlar and McAllister could not identify an operational threshold of "critical mass" in any of their twenty OECD legislatures surveyed at which intra-legislative behavior changed for the better. We will identify attempts made by both Pelosi and May to ensure such accelerations happened in their parties but in which they unfortunately could not control all the pertinent variables required to change members' behavior.

Studlar and McAllister noted that Dahlerup's 1988 study of six Nordic legislatures identified the conditions under which women's presence may promote a more positive functioning of legislatures, usually measured as the passage of women-friendly legislation. Her conditions envisioned changes related to "(1) the reaction to women politicians; (2) the performance and efficiency of the women politicians; (3) the social climate of political life (political culture); (4) the political discourse; (5) policy (the political decisions); and (6) women's empowerment (Studlar and McAllister 2002, 235, 249). Childs and Krook assessed Dahlerup's argument as emphasizing "critical acts" by which the position of the minority of women in a legislature could be changed (2009, 138). Phillips's argument about the "politics of presence" linked descriptive and substantive representation, claiming that more women would equal more consideration of women-friendly legislation (1995).

Dahlerup's sixth criterion of empowerment is crucial to our case studies. She states that "at the most fundamental level a concept of women's interest can only be derived from feminist theories about male dominance and patriarchy" (2014, 59–60). As she also notes, the concept of "substantive representation of women . . . only makes sense when embedded in feminist theory about changing male dominance" (66). We agree with her contention that "political life is a game of bargains, compromises, and mixed motives" (73). In our comparison, we note that male dominance has traveled well across two political systems. The first such political system, that of the US, is one without central party dominance over candidate nominations but with the highest threshold of fundraising requirements for individual national legislative candidates in the world, a hierarchical House with increased party polarization over the last few decades, and constitutional separation of powers across three coequal branches. The second, that of the UK, is one with increased central party dominance over nominations (although this is true mostly for Labour), a hierarchical House whose parties usually vote along the lines of "responsibility," and increased corporate electoral fundraising, especially for Conservatives.

Childs and Krook's formulation of "critical actors" as "acting for women" is a helpful concept, since it requires analysts to look both at the opportunity structures in legislatures and the intragroup dynamics in which critical actors are situated (2009). Throughout much of their careers, Nancy Pelosi and Theresa May functioned as "critical actors" seeking to modernize their parties and to increase the representation of diverse voices in the legislative caucus. While Pelosi was Speaker from 2006 to 2010, the House passed, among other things, the Lilly Ledbetter Fair Pay Act and the Affordable Care Act and repealed the noxious "Don't Ask Don't Tell" provision in the US military. While much of May's work to help women was under her home secretary portfolio, she introduced legislation on domestic violence that was passed by the House of Commons in July 2020 and remained in the House of Lords as of February 2021. May's and Pelosi's efforts to accelerate change in their respective parties and legislatures will be discussed in chapters 2–4. We will also show that they engaged with the six criteria described by Dahlerup (1988) for increasing women's empowerment.

Childs and Krook added a detailed set of criteria for the forces of "change and resistance" to women's political institutional empowerment. They provide specific examples of "constraining and enabling characteristics of legislative contexts" (2009, 128). In their discussion of the possibilities for substantive (policy outcome) representation, they identify five sets of relevant characteristics: "(1) anticipated effects of increased proportions of women; (2) constraining and enabling characteristics of legislative contexts; (3) identities and interests of female and male legislators; (4) feminist and non-feminist definitions of women's issues; and (5) stable and contingent features of policy-making processes" (2009, 128). In the "constraining and enabling characteristics," three of those factors are especially relevant to this study: "legislative institutional norms" (which in both Houses are adversarial and hierarchical); "positional power," described by Childs and Krook as legislative committee chairs but for our purposes also leadership posts in both Houses; and "legislative arenas, especially in terms of varying distributions of women and men in distinct legislative spaces" (128). With reference to legislative institutional norms, many US- and UK-based scholars have described the "bias toward men's experiences and authority"

(Childs and Krook 2009, 129; Kathlene 1995; Annesley and Gains 2014; Mackay 2008; Campbell, Childs, and Lovenduski 2006; Norris 1996). Childs and Krook note, correctly, that "critical mass" alone only focuses on actors and that embedding them in their political institutional context is a must (2009, 129). Masculinist practices often "undermine the ability (of women and men) to integrate women's concerns and perspectives into public policymaking" (130). As noted from Beckwith's (2015) research, positional power is granted to women typically by male leadership majorities to make themselves look more up to date and less fossilized in past practices. Childs and Krook's (2009) use of constraining and enabling characteristics is similar to Ostrom's typology of institutional rules, which "prescribe, prohibit or permit" change (1986).

Under the third category, "identities and interests of female and male legislators," Childs and Krook note that "gender is not a pre-political and fixed identity that women and men bring with them when they enter politics" but is rather "produced and reproduced within the context of particular legislatures" (2009, 131). Dahlerup has taken a similar stance, noting that it is far more helpful to consider gendering of legislative practices as a "historically and socially changing category," enabling us to use empirical analyses of "when, where, around which issues, and how women are mobilized on account of gender" (2014, 67). As Childs and Krook also state, "'gendering' processes may silence women by pressuring them to conform to positions taken by men on various political issues or blocking their opportunities to articulate freely their own views" (2009, 132). The interaction of such gendering processes with the requirement of party discipline in the Westminster Parliament was discussed by both Norris and Lovenduski (2001) and Annesley and Gains (2014). They showed that despite the record-breaking number of women elected as Labour MPs in 1997, they voted even more strongly than their male counterparts to cut funds to women social assistance recipients. Both sets of authors suggest that female MPs felt less empowered to buck party discipline and were required to show their "party-supporting" credentials.

Childs and Krook's fifth category, related to "policy-making processes," is also highly relevant. As they say, it is clear that some research finds that female legislators prioritize issues important to women. However, in a broader study such as our current volume, we agree that "an exclusive focus on enactment" is too narrow and that clearly more attention needs to be paid to the "entire legislative process" (2009, 134). As Childs and Krook note, "Policy cycles and demonstration effects strongly condition which issues enter and which are kept off legislative agendas" (134).

In reference to Childs and Krook's interest in showing when the substantive representation of women occurred, they wished to show "(1) not when women make a difference but on how the substantive representation of women occurs, and (2) not what 'women' do, but what specific actors do" (143).

We agree with Beckwith's view that the behavior of political party and legislative elites is still strongly conditioned by gender-biased socialization, in that "given nearly universal male dominance within party elites and in Prime Ministerships, female party elites face a different strategic context. Women ... are fully aware that on the basis of sex they are disadvantaged at the outset in intraparty contests" (2015, 728). In their five-country Westminster system comparison, Cross and Blais find that most often, due to the small number of female leaders in those systems, it is hard to discern an independent effect for gender (2012a, 7). This includes various types of party selection contests, whether parliamentary based or "primary based," involving the larger membership. While leaders in right-wing parties had shorter time spans, this is not necessarily true for female ones, again based on the small-N problem (120–27).

Cross and Blais tested the Mair hypothesis about the link between membership roles in choosing a leader and greater diversity in the leadership talent pool. In 2001 and 2005, the membership ballot chose male leaders Iain Duncan Smith and David Cameron, respectively. Cross and Blais found mixed evidence for the Mair hypothesis, showing that it did not always hold true for younger leaders and did not show a convincing relationship to gender (122–26). Again, this is due for Cross and Blais to the small number of women leaders in their sample.

Wauters and Pilet find a significant effect where parties in opposition and smaller in size select women to lead (2015, 84–86). Of course, these two sets of factors may also overlap. Their data set is 107 parties in fourteen countries from 1965 to 2012 (81). Their third finding includes the idea that more women in legislatures yields a stronger likelihood of picking a female leader. This last finding is contradicted by the bulk of the feminist literature, which finds that critical mass does not affect females' leadership chances (Childs and Krook 2009; Studlar and McAllister 2002).

Like Beckwith, O'Brien et al. describe political leadership as inherently "sexed and gendered," with "the archetypal leader being 'male in appearance and gender," as well as 'masculine in character traits' (2015, 698, citing Sjoberg 2014, 73). Annesley, Beckwith, and Franceschet (2019) cite Duerst-Lahti and Kelly (1995), who argue that the masculinist views of a credible leader include "assertiveness, competitiveness and objectivity."

Therefore, "social constructions of femininity mean that women struggle to be perceived as capable and steady leaders" (Annesley, Beckwith, and Franceschet 2019, 213).

While O'Brien et al. hypothesized in their fifteen-country study that female Prime Ministers and coalition party leaders in left-party governments would appoint more female cabinet members, they found that not to be the case. Their findings are ultimately that the presence of female Prime Ministers does not increase women's chances for cabinet posts; instead, male PMs on the left are the ones "who are making these pledges . . . since they can reap significant benefits from appointing women to their Cabinets" (2015b, 710).

In another 2015 article, O'Brien stated that "women are more likely to initially come to power in minor opposition parties and those that are losing seat share" (2015a, 1022). O'Brien's finding reinforces both Wauters and Pilet's and Beckwith's conclusions. On the other hand, O'Brien counters the "critical mass hypothesis" cited by Wauters and Pilet (2015, 84–86) that more women in legislatures leads to more women in leadership. O'Brien et al. find in their multi-country study that a high presence of women does not necessarily lead to more women in cabinet positions or even as PM (2015, 710). They suggest that their results are "a consequence of the opportunities and constraints facing male and female leaders in parliamentary and semi-presidential regimes" (691). To this we would add the constraints facing Speaker Pelosi in the US presidential regime. While O'Brien et al. (2015) hint at the fact that PR, closed-list, multiparty systems may be more friendly toward women's election and representation in cabinet and leadership positions, others make the statement more clearly. These include Sawer (2010, 207) and Dahlerup (2013).

In terms of women leaders, Jalalzai studied 108 female executives globally between 1960 and 2013 (2016, 40). Of these, "eighty-three were elected or appointed through normal procedures," while the remaining twenty-five served on an interim basis (32). Of the eighty-three presumably long-term (i.e., noninterim) officials, sixty-two were prime ministers and forty-six were presidents (32). Jalalzai's hypothesis, which follows from the "masculine" traits of hierarchical, top-down governing she gains from Duerst-Lahti's 1997 formulation, is that presidents generally have more power and thus will demonstrate more masculine traits. She also claims that prime ministers have fewer formal powers and are thus more "feminine" and open to accession by women based on "heightened vulnerability to ouster at any time, and bypassing of the public vote" (Jalalzai 2016, 43). However, we must identify Westminster prime ministers as a hybrid of the two types, since the Westminster system is extremely hierarchical and executive driven. The US House is quite hierarchical as well. Of the prime ministers, only twenty-three were "dominant" according to Jalalzai's formulation, that is, having at least four of seven requisite "power" characteristics; the maximum score reached was six, with some having zero.[1] Eight of the twenty-three dominant female PMs came from "unified" parliamentary systems, having a prime minister as the national executive, and nearly half of those were from Westminster parliamentary systems: New Zealand, Canada, and the UK (calculated from Jalalzai 2016, 69). Jalalzai shows that through 2015, female prime ministers did not serve significantly less time than males; in fact, female PMs served slightly longer on average, 3.69 years as opposed to 3.6 years for men (2016, 53). Theresa May serves as an interesting outlier to Jalalzai's findings, since she was the fifth-shortest sitting prime minister since the end of World War 2 (Sawe 2019). May's short tenure may be contrasted with that of Margaret Thatcher, the longest-serving prime minister of the twentieth century.

Intraparty Competition and Changes along the Ideological Continuum

The rest of this chapter describes the nature of the path-dependent party cleavages since the 1970s in the US and UK and relevant institutional changes affecting former PM May and Speaker Pelosi.

The United Kingdom. In the UK, regional divisions have caused a dealignment from the major two parties, Labour and Conservative, increasing support for nationally based parties. Citing H. Clarke et al. (2004) and Curtice (2010), Schleiter and Belu note the diminishing percentage of the vote gained by the two major parties. In the 1951 election, the two major parties gained 97 percent of the vote share; by 2010, their joint vote share was 65 percent (2016, 39). In part, they argue this is due to the UK's ability to send members to the European Parliament since 1973. Other issues clearly affecting the major parties' vote share since the 1960s and 1970s included the Northern Ireland sectarian battle and min-

---

1. Jalalzai (2016, 65–68) assigns prime ministers (and presidents) a power score based on whether they have formally granted jurisdiction among the following factors: presidential removal, discretionary appointment powers, cabinet meeting chair, emergency long-term or decree powers, central role in foreign policy, central role in defense, central role in government formation, or the ability to dissolve the legislature.

ers' strikes and coal shortages, In 1997, the Blair Labour government was elected in part on a promise to restore as many powers as constitutionally permissible to Northern Ireland, Scotland, and Wales. These "new" assemblies, built upon the attempts to devolve powers to the three countries since 1920, use variants of proportional electoral systems. Schleiter and Belu have argued that the Blair government's reforms accelerated the ease with which UK voters have been able to justify supporting parties other than the Conservatives or Labour and not feel they are "wasting" their vote (2016, 39).

The Interplay between Growth of the European Framework and Euroskepticism in the UK Conservative Party. Understanding Theresa May's Prime Ministership requires explaining the tortured history of the UK and the EU, as detailed in table 1. The ongoing schism in the UK and within certain parties over how much to align with Europe began after World War II. After the Declaration of Human Rights was ratified by the UN, then-Opposition Leader Winston Churchill helped formulate the European Convention on Human Rights (ECHR), a cause championed by the International Council of the European Movement, supported by both Churchill and future prime minister Harold Macmillan. The UK was the first to deposit its ratification of the ECHR in March 1951 (after the Conservative government had been elected). The Conservative Party was more likely to support the ECHR in the 1950s, and part of the reason why Churchill supported it was to "enshrine the rule of law in Europe." The ECHR is linked to the Council of Europe (COE), formed in London in 1949 and ultimately gaining forty-seven members. While not an EU instrument, the ECHR makes rulings that often regard EU members. While the European Court of Justice (ECJ) oversees EU member-state compliance with EU law, the ECHR is also relevant to its rulings since "the ECHR lies behind many of the general principles of EU law and its provisions have been used as a basis for the EU's Charter of Fundamental Rights" (Holder 2020).

Even under the COE's framework, objections were raised about the "supranational" character of the ECHR, particularly because Ireland and the UK have been the only members of the COE and later the EU with a common-law legal system. However, Ireland codified its constitution in 1937, whereas the UK has not. In earlier decades, the Labour Party objected to the COE and EU instruments as taking sovereignty away from the UK. This was viewed as mainly due to Labour's working-class core constituency and was only shifted under leaders Neil Kinnock and John

Smith in the late 1980s and accelerated by Tony Blair's accession to the leadership and the creation of "New Labour" starting in 1994.

As Smith has noted, the UK was only reluctantly converted to the idea of membership in a European community, based both on its political economy and the fact that it was never occupied during World War II. On the political economic front, the Labour government under Attlee had nationalized coal in 1946 and then steel and iron in 1949. Under Conservative governments, iron and steel were denationalized, and then they were renationalized under the Labour government of Harold Wilson in 1967. Thus, when the European Coal and Steel Community (ECSC) was formed in 1951 as an early version of a European framework (with six countries) and a nascent framework of supranationalism, the UK was not interested (Smith 2017). It could be said that there has always been a feeling in both the UK and the Continent that they were of separate histories and sensibilities. The ECSC was framed in part by French economist Jean Monnet, who wished to promote European unity. In 1957, through the Treaty of Rome, the European Economic Community (EEC) of the same members was formed. When the UK decided to request membership in the 1960s, it was turned down twice by French president De Gaulle. Under a third request, made under pro-European Conservative prime minister Ted Heath in 1974, De Gaulle's successor, Georges Pompidou, agreed. Unfortunately, before the UK joined, the EEC passed policies that the UK saw as aimed directly at hurting it, including the Common Agricultural Policy, the Common Fisheries Policy, and the Common Budget (Smith 2017). Some Conservatives later blamed Heath for rushing into a "bad deal" on these matters; British farming and fisheries policies were quite different from those of France, for example. Farming and fisheries came up quite strongly in the 2019–20 Brexit debates and negotiations. The potentially "supranationalist" architecture of the European project, including the ECJ and European Parliament were established in 1952 and the Council of the European Union and European Commission (the executive body) were created in 1967. Thus, when the UK signed up to the EEC in 1973, ratified in 1975 by domestic referendum, the "supranationalist" project was well on its way. We might infer that the objections against giving more power to the EU/ECJ have sometimes been about domestic political consumption and the standing of various leaders.

Margaret Thatcher supported the effort to make the UK part of the EEC in 1973 and campaigned for a yes vote in the British referendum on it in 1975. She also supported the single market through the Single European Act of 1985, to remove nontariff barriers to trade (Whitman

2013). While Thatcher approved of the single market, especially in the wake of the fall of Communism to bring in the Eastern European economies, she was strongly against the "federalization" of the European project through strengthening supranational political institutions. These objections responded to the project of Jacques Delors, the competence of the European Parliament, and the use of the ECJ in areas such as indirect taxation and social legislation (Moravcsik 1991, 30–32). As further noted, Thatcher "favored strengthening European political cooperation without creating an independent bureaucracy." Finally, she favored pan-European deregulation of services.

Thatcher also made a famous intervention to reduce the amount of value-added tax that the UK was paying the EEC in 1984 at a Paris meeting of the organization. There had been a long-running debate between the EEC and the UK over its contributions to the budget. As Vernasca notes, despite "being the third-poorest member" of the ten-country framework in the 1980s, the UK was paying a large portion of the EEC's budget, particularly to support what it viewed as less efficient European agriculture (2016). At the 1984 meeting, Thatcher secured the permanent lessening of the UK's share of the payments to 66 percent of the difference between what the UK contributed to the EEC and what the EEC contributed to it. As of 1985, it involved "the unblocking of Britain's 1983 budget rebate and £457 million, and a further cash payment of £600 million this year, with ultimately the EEC payments toward the UK potentially going up to £1 billion per year" (Brown 1984).

Thatcher's strong turn against Europe took place while Jacques Delors, the French president of the European Commission from 1985 to 1995, waxed publicly about adding social inclusion frameworks into the agency, since "nobody can fall in love with a common market." In his first mandate, Delors worked mainly to pioneer multiyear budgets and to pave the way for more comprehensive economic integration of the common market. In his second mandate, in his white paper, he began to lose some of the wealthier members by talking about extending the economic market from "economic solidarity and social cohesion" to the "environment, research and monetary cooperation." As Salm and Lehmann note, "He confirmed the suspicions of Thatcher and others that he intended to introduce strong supratritional regulatory policies in many areas" (2020, 7–9).

Opponents' fears were confirmed during the negotiations for the Maastricht Treaty, which created the EU, from 1990 to 1993. The treaty's central concepts included the idea of "European citizenship," allowing the free movement of people across borders, including residency; a common foreign and security policy; and closer cooperation between police and the judiciary in criminal cases. While the common currency, the euro, had been previously discussed, it had to be shelved in the 1970s due to the recessionary economic landscape. The euro plans were revitalized in the Maastricht framework in three stages: the first from July 1990 to December 1993, involving the free movement of capital between member states; the second from January 1994 to December 1998, emphasizing cooperation between national central banks and the "increased alignment of member states' economic policies"; and the third stage from January 1999 onward, which involved the gradual introduction of the euro (happening in 2002) and the implementation of a single monetary policy under the European Central Bank (European Central Bank 2020). The foundational pillars of Maastricht were the free movement of capital, people, goods, and services. The "pillar" structure was excised in the Lisbon Treaty, implemented in 2009.

Euroskeptics in the Conservative Party. One account of Margaret Thatcher's impact on the Brexit debate in the twenty-first century describes populist, anti-European supremacy, pro-market Conservative MPs elected in 1992 as "Thatcher's children," including Iain Duncan Smith, who became party leader in 2001, Alan Duncan, Nigel Lawson, Bernard Jenkin, and John Whittindale, joined by Liam Fox. Fox and Jenkin were early Euroskeptic leaders. Both Iain Duncan Smith and Liam Fox have also been strongly socially conservative. While Fontana and Parsons state that there was only a small coterie of Euroskeptics (ten or so) among the sixty-three new Conservatives elected in 1992, they joined previous skeptics from Thatcher's years, including Bill Cash, David Davis, Michael Portillo, and John Redwood (2015, 97). The latter two were identified as having been cultivated by Margaret Thatcher. The sixty-three new Conservatives replaced fifty incumbent pro-European Conservatives who did not stand that year. Some might also include Duncan Smith and Davis among the longest pot stirrers on the anti-Europe issue, since the former, for example, "attacked the Maastricht Treaty the minute he entered Parliament in his maiden speech in 1992" (*Politico EU*, 2001). Many of the prominent Euroskeptics, including David Davis, Steve Baker, and Liam Fox, were also former military members.

In trying to get the Maastricht Treaty through the House of Commons, Thatcher's successor, John Major, faced the same "parliamentary math" problem as that confronting Theresa May from 2016 to 2019 and Boris Johnson until after the December 12, 2019, election. After the April 1992 election, Major immediately tabled the Maastricht Treaty in the

House of Commons. He had a 21-seat majority (319 Conservative seats to Labour's 195 in the then 524-seat House), but 22 of the 319 were confirmed Euroskeptics. In 1991 at the EEC meetings, Major had won concessions including the UK's opt-out on the common currency, the social chapter on employment law, and the deletion of the word "federal" from the treaty. A related issue, the European exchange rate mechanism (ERM), under which the EU currencies were partially pegged to the European rate at the margins but allowed to fluctuate within those margins, was also on the Euroskeptics' minds. While Thatcher had allowed John Major as her chancellor to join the ERM in 1990, the UK had to withdraw in 1992 due to the pound falling below the lowest allowable limit. To placate the Euroskeptics, Major promised to allow a parliamentary vote on potentially rejoining the ERM and on the euro if the Conservatives won the next election (they did not). It took more than a year to get the proposal through the Commons (Berg 2018). PM Major faced "sixty-two rebellions over the bill, involving fifty MPs who cast eleven hundred dissenting votes" (Cowley and Stuart 2012, 403).

From the left, Labour tried to add a poison pill amendment in 1993 to include the adoption of the social chapter. Cabinet members Michael Portillo, Michael Howard, and Peter Lilley also supported it to defeat the whole package. Former PM Thatcher was vocally against her successor's Maastricht project from her new position in the House of Lords, objecting that the framework would "increase bureaucracy" and "diminish democracy" (Berg 2018). Former party chair Norman Tebbit added his voice to the opposition. Other Euroskeptics also voiced the tried-and-true objections that Maastricht would lead to a "centralized federal EU" and that the EU would get greater powers "at the expense of Westminster" (Berg 2018).

Major's bill was defeated on July 21–22, 1993. He then went back to the Commons and used a tactic that was ended by the Cameron-Clegg coalition under the Fixed Term Parliaments Act, that of daring the Commons to vote down his Maastricht bill again, tying it to a confidence vote, which would then precipitate an election. He thus won the vote on July 23 by 339 to 299 since nobody wanted an election at that time, having just held one the year before (Berg 2018). In paradoxical fashion, committed Euroskeptic Bill Cash instructed other Conservatives to support the government on this vote, claiming that since Labour was ahead in the polls, they did not want to hand over a Labour win. Jacob Rees-Mogg's father, a newspaper editor and writer, filed a suit against the Maastricht Treaty process in the House, claiming that it would take away sovereignty from Westminster. Rees-Mogg lost that case, with the judges deciding that the arguments did not have the merit to proceed. Other fallout from the increasing boldness of the Euroskeptics in the Conservative Party after the Maastricht vote was illustrated in a rebellion against Chancellor Ken Clarke's budget in November 1994. The budget included an increase in the UK's payments to the EU and an increased tax on fuel for UK households. Euroskeptics, including MP Christopher Gill, led a Conservative rebellion on the confidence measure. Eight Conservative MPs abstained, losing the Conservative "whip" in the process. While PM Major won the vote by 330 to 303, he lost his working majority in the House by withdrawing the whip from the eight MPs (MacIntyre 1994; Andrews 2019). As MacIntyre notes, the action to withdraw the whip was the first time a Conservative government had done so since World War II, with the Labour Party using this mechanism in 1961 (1994).

Fresh Start and the European Research Group in the Conservative Party Formed in Reaction to Maastricht. Following Fontana and Parson's 2015 categorization of Euroskeptics elected in the 1980s and 1990s as "Thatcher's children," we can denote the group elected from 2010 on, including women elected through May's "A-list" framework, as "Thatcher's grandchildren." Some of each group have participated in the main mechanisms to throw wrenches at any perceived Europhilia in the Conservative Party, including Fresh Start and and the European Research Group (ERG) respectivel. Fresh Start was formed by then-MP (later Lord) Michael Spicer as an attempt to delay the Maastricht vote in the House of Commons after the Danish referendum opposed the treaty in June 1992 (Whale 2018). Fresh Start got 110 signatures out of the Conservative majority of 319 on a nongovernmental "early day motion" to delay the Maastricht debate. Spicer attributes its influence to persuading PM Major to reject the euro, even though he had already promised to delay that vote until after the next election if the Conservatives won (Whale 2018). The Euroskeptics at the time were termed the "bastards" who were holding up Maastricht by John Major (Simons 2013).

Claiming that Fresh Start was the more militant group, Lord Spicer formed the ERG in 1994 from Fresh Start as a "slightly less aggressive group" (Whale 2018). A closer look at the campaign against May's Brexit proposals would belie that description of a "kinder gentler" Euroskeptic bunch. As a "parliamentary research group," the ERG did not have to publicize its list of members or individual members' contributions, which became crucial to its success after the parliamentary expenses scandal of 2009. Its first researcher, Daniel Hannan, was described as "wanting to take the EU down from the inside," which is why he got elected as a member of the European Parliament (MEP). He also provided the basis for Nigel Farage's anti-immigration, anti-ECJ campaign, which generally focused on the "illegitimate" role of EU institutions in British life (Geoghegan 2020, 107–10).

According to the accounts of the group, the ERG is similar to other parliamentary research groups in that it has members and subscribers. Whale states that its members "can join the Whats App group and express views at the weekly meetings." Subscribers, like other parliamentary groups, pay for the research and may share that research with others (Whale 2018). While the prevailing view expressed by Geoghegan (2020) and Whale (2018) is that the ERG did not become publicly rabid about Brexit until after the June 2016 referendum, the Fresh Start group, sharing some members with the ERG, was quite confrontational in the Liberal Democratic–Conservative Coalition years from 2010 to 2015. Geoghagan also details MP Steve Baker's "flair for organization that would be the envy of any Leninist sect" (2020, 109). Geoghegan has written extensively about the role of the ERG both in its push for the October 2011 vote inside the House of Commons to allow a referendum and then in the referendum campaign in spring 2016. While the ERG was officially "neutral" under previous chair Chris Heaton-Harris, this changed under Steve Baker's outsized presence. Geoghegan shows his oversized role in framing the conditions so as to favor the Leave side. Among the achievements credited to Baker and the ERG were the extension of the "purdah" period so that PM Cameron could not use the machinery of government in favor of Remain, the limiting of campaign finance during the referendum campaign, and finally the wording of the referendum question as two options. Baker himself had said that providing the two-option question rather than the usual one-option question increased the potential for a "leave the EU" answer by about 4 percent (Geoghegan 2020, 109–20). The ERG's insider knowledge and mobilization base inside the House of Commons clearly helped them to gain the upper hand in the referendum outcome and later to work to undo PM May's premiership in favor of a more friendly Brexiteer.

Some of Thatcher's "children" in Fresh Start and the ERG were Bill Cash, Iain Duncan Smith, Graham Brady, Bernard Jenkin, and John Redwood. The "grandchildren" in Fresh Start have included Sarah Wollaston, Andrea Leadsom, Dominic Raab, Martin Vickers, and Karen Brady. A "fresh start"–inspired letter to the editor of *The Telegraph* in February 2012 with more than one hundred signatures concerned the UK's role in EU policing and criminal justice procedures, to be discussed in chapter

2. These included those who joined the ERG, such as Priti Patel, Penny Mordaunt, Jacob Rees-Mogg, Christopher Heaton-Harris, and Steve Baker (Hope 2012; Whale 2018). One large difference between those who became the "Brexit ultras" driving the ERG, such as Rees-Mogg, Baker, and Johnson, and those who stuck with Fresh Start was that the latter favored a continued role in EU's single market (Craig 2013, 177). The Brexit ultras supported some or most of Baker's extreme libertarianism, in which he claimed that he not only wanted to undo the EU (like Daniel Hannan, the ERG researcher and MEP) but also was in favor of a "world trading system" with minimal regulation, which could create a depression on the scale of 1929 (Pegg, Lawrence, and Evans 2018). In 2017, it appeared that the harder Euroskeptics against both the single market and the customs union for goods had won over many of their softer Euroskeptic colleagues, who had supported some aspects of the single market.

While Lord Spicer had recounted that Fresh Start was formed in 1992–93, a newer iteration of its goals from the nonparliamentary website of Kwasi Kwarteng, secretary of state for business, energy, and industrial strategy, dated February 23, 2016, stated that "we initiated the Fresh Start Project in 2011" (Fresh Start Project 2012.). So it would seem that both Thatcher's children and her grandchildren were claiming credit for forming the group; what is more likely is that the post-2010 iteration was built on the efforts of the Euroskeptics elected under Thatcher or just after her premierships. In their "Options for Change" green paper, released in July 2012, the group still favored staying in the EU single market (Fresh Start Project 2012). On MP Kwarteng's website, eighteen members of Fresh Start claimed that "we have concluded that it is in the UK's long-term interests to leave" (Fresh Start 2012.). The website noted that some colleagues in the group "still believe the UK is better off remaining inside the EU," denoting denoting the softer Euroskeptics.

In 2014, Fresh Start held a jointly sponsored reception with the libertarian (and thus Euroskeptic) think tank Open Europe. Indeed, the 2013 green paper was jointly developed with Open Europe. The organization had been formed by "merchant-banker" Rodney Leach in 2005 and curiously had headquarters both in Brussels and in the buildings at 55 Tufton Street, London, the home of many Euroskeptic organizations. Open Europe was often scathingly described as using unrealistic economic premises and figures to promote Brexit. One example of their shallow thought was described by Professor Simon Usherwood of Surrey University, who wrote that the views of Open Europe and many Euroskeptics were based on a "myth of a static EU, a persistent misunderstanding of the nature of

European integration." He continued that "the legal and political reality of the process is that member states retain the primary control of the system. They own the treaties, they pay the bills, they chose to self-limit their power, even as they chose when and whether to implement legislative outputs" (Usherwood 2012). Similarly, Martin Sandbu in the *Financial Times* pointed out the group's faulty economic assumptions, particularly on the nature of the single market for goods and services, in that regulations in these frameworks are harmonized. Leaving such a framework and its attendant regulations does not automatically ensure prosperity (Sandbu 2016). An editorial in *The Economist* in 2010 discussed many of the same points as Sandbu, that Open Europe produced wildly inflated assertions about the "cost" of EU regulations and about how much of that cost was supposedly borne by UK businesses (*The Economist* 2010).

Another group of Thatcher's children and their followers in the Tory party overlapping with the anti-Maastricht skeptics and the newer skeptics was termed the "new bastards" by *The Guardian* (June 8, 2015). The label referred to PM Major's condemnation of some Tory Maastricht skeptics on a live microphone as "bastards." The "new bastards" were in a group of about fifty called "Conservatives for Britain," formed just after Cameron won the 2015 election with a slim majority. Like Fresh Start, the group had as its proclaimed purpose the idea of "fighting the referendum if the EU fails to allow fundamental change" (*The Guardian* 2015). In 2016, the group's cochair was the ERG wingman MP Steve Baker. Some of Thatcher's children in the group were Norman Lamont, Nigel Lawson (president), Liam Fox, John Redwood, Michael Ancram, Julian Lewis, Bill Cash, and Bernard Jenkin. Followers of Thatcher's children included MEPs Daniel Hannan and Emma McClarkin, United Kingdom Independence Party (UKIP) MEP David Bannerman, and MP Steve Baker. As with Fresh Start and the ERG, "Conservatives for Britain" was determined to hold the sitting PM's feet to the fire to ensure that there was no more slippage toward EU absorption.

By 2005, all three major parties in the UK—the Conservatives, Labour, and the Liberal Democrats—agreed on the need for an EU membership referendum (BBC 2015b). As Cowley and Stuart have noted, the "Europe" issue drove the Labour Party apart under the Single European Act referendum of 1975, "one of the largest shifts of sovereignty away from the UK," but Labour was allowed a free vote on the issue. However, at other times, such as in 1978 under whipped votes, Labour saw large rebellions over the European Assembly Elections bill (Cowley and Stuart 2012, 403). The largest rebellion through 2021 was the 2003 Labour MPs' rebellion on the

UK's entry into the Iraq War, with 139 MPs voting against their government (*The Independent*, 2019). As Cowley and Stuart note, Thatcher faced fewer rebellions on Europe in eleven years of governing than either Heath did in four years or Major in seven (2012, 402). However, David Cameron's rebellion over a backbench proposal to hold a referendum on European membership was almost twice that of what Major had seen in 1993; Major's was forty-one, while Cameron's was eighty-one (BBC 2011b).

As Cowley and Stuart also note, each Parliament since 2001 had become more "rebellious" than the next in terms of the number of backbenchers voting against the government (2012, 404). The percentage of Euroskeptics in the Conservative Party steadily increased, especially in the 2005 and 2015 general elections (Heppell, Crines, and Jeffery 2017, 767; Lynch and Whitaker 2018, 43). Heppell, Crines, and Jeffery have estimated that, between 2010 and 2015, 81 members of the Conservative caucus of 306 were "hard" Euroskeptics and 154 were "softer" ones who could perhaps be persuaded to stay if the EU were reformed; 11 Conservative MPs were identified as "agnostic" on the issue (771). Heppell, Crines, and Jeffery note that by the June 2016 EU referendum, of those publicly stating how they voted, Remain Conservatives numbered 172, while Brexit/Euro-rejectionists had nearly doubled from 81 to 144 (771). In part, this was due to a rejection of Cameron's (and later May's) "soft" Euroskepticism (772). The increase of "hard" Euroskepticism (Leavers) in the Conservative ranks mirrored the 2015 Conservative voters: 61 percent voting Leave and 39 percent voting Remain (775). After the June 2017 election, the 317 Conservative MPs included 138 who voted Leave versus 170 who voted Remain (with 9 MPs not disclosing their votes). This math would obviously not work for Brexit compromises in Parliament (Lynch and Whitaker 2018, 43).

Other issues of importance include the overlap between supporting a "hard" Brexit and being socially conservative against Cameron's support of same-sex marriage, which also increased across the Conservative caucus between the 2010 and 2015 elections. Heppell, Crines, and Jeffery identified 50 of these Conservative MPs (of 306) in the 2010 Parliament who were socially conservative Brexiteers and "implacable critics of Cameron," a number that increased to 82 of 330 after the election of 2015 (2017, 775).

Increasing EU Power through the 1990s. Consequential changes to the UK-EU relationship that would remain fodder for the Euroskeptics inside the Conservative Party and for voters included the following: The first was the switch to PR elections for the European Parliament in 1999, under which framework the far-right UKIP, which had been formed to pressure the Conservative Party on immigration, could gain seats. UKIP had come out of the Anti-Federalist League's framework, formed in 1993 by an anti-immigration Euroskeptic academic named Alan Sked (Merrick 2017b). In 1999, the party won two seats in the European Parliament, and in 2014 it became the "first party in more than a century other than Labour or Conservatives, to win the most votes in a UK-wide poll" (Merrick 2017b). At the time, it gained twenty-four of the UK's seventy-three seats and that same year two Westminster MPs when two Conservatives crossed over to UKIP. One was defeated in the 2015 general election. UKIP could certainly credit itself with helping to force the issue of a European referendum. In May 2019, UKIP did even better in the European Parliament elections, again winning the highest number of UK seats at twenty-nine.

Other shifts taking place at the EU level included the attempt to establish a European constitution in 2004, which was not ratified, but much of its content was included in the Lisbon Treaty, which Labour PM Gordon Brown shepherded through the House in 2009. It gave more powers to the European Parliament and included a permanent president of the EU Council, a new high representative for foreign affairs, and a new EU diplomatic service.

Finally, another major issue that ultimately fanned the anti-European flames was PM Blair's decision to open the UK's doors to immigration from the Eastern European "accession states" to the EU in 2001. As Consterdine notes, "The UK was one of only three member states along with Sweden and Ireland to open its labor market to these new EU citizens immediately" (2016). She also notes, "The number of migrants from Central and Eastern Europe into the UK was predicted to be in the region of five thousand to thirteen thousand on the assumption that other member states would also open their labour markets, [yet] most didn't." In 2004 and 2005, 129,000 migrants from the "A8" countries (the ten accession countries minus Cyprus and Malta) came to the UK (Consterdine 2016). In the early 2000s, Consterdine explains, the UK economy was doing well and could seem to integrate the influx of immigrants, a view that changed once the 2007–8 recession began. She also notes the irony of EU founding member countries' claims to "European citizenship" and "freedom of movement" when twelve of the fifteen "old" European states imposed restrictions on immigration, with Germany and Austria imposing the maximum seven-year waiting period on A8 country migrants, who could not freely work in those states until 2011.

Increasing UK Suspicion of the EU after Lisbon and the Financial Crisis. The renewed push toward European integration contained in the Lisbon Treaty (signed in 2007 and ratified in 2009) overlapped with the global financial crash, precipitating a eurozone crisis. Thus, the two events became even more intertwined in the minds of those who wished to protect the role of London as one of the world's preeminent financial centers. In the case of foreign exchange market turnover in currency markets, home to digital media and the location of foreign-owned banks, London has been the premier location for decades (Dsouza 2019; Bird 2014).

As Dsouza has noted, "Small British [financial] firms were bought off by international players and the culture of the country's financial sector changed forever" (2019). According to Bird, this was also aided by the light regulation and low taxation enjoyed by the financial sector (2014). Dsouza traced the inevitable schism between the interests of globalized financial interests and manufacturing interests, which were in many instances helped by EU accession: "The City of London developed at the heart of the British Empire, somewhat divorced from the UK's mainland economic needs. . . . The Bank of England consistently pursued policies that favored the City's position as a world financial center, even when such policies were harmful to the UK's mainland manufacturing interests" (2019).

In 2007 the Lisbon Treaty, which did not itself contain the "European constitution" but added it in an appendix, was signed by the European Council and delivered to member states for ratification. While former PM Tony Blair twice and Opposition Leader Cameron once had promised a UK referendum on the Lisbon Treaty, semantic measures were taken to evade it, such as "the Lisbon Treaty is not about implementing a European Constitution with supreme ECJ decisionmaking." However, that is exactly what a Commons committee found the appendix to mean. The treaty also "gave the EU full legal personality," including the ability to sign treaties "in the areas of its attributed powers." The treaty also included, for the first time, a withdrawal mechanism contained in Article 50, set into motion by PM May in March 2017. It specified different levels of EU competencies for the first time, ranging from EU-level-only through shared competence to state-only competencies (European Parliament 2020). Finally, it "completed the absorption of third-pillar aspects such as police and judicial cooperation in criminal matters into the first pillar" (European Parliament 2020). Sowing the seeds for legislation embodying an EU referendum, David Cameron gave a "cast-iron guarantee" in 2007 to "hold a referendum on any treaty emerging from the Lisbon process" if he were elected PM. The Liberal Democrats in 2008 called for an "in-out" Europe referendum. In 2011, the two parties got the European Union Act through Parliament, requiring a referendum on the "extension of an existing EU competence or conferral of a new one" (Craig 2013, 166). From at least 2007 onward it became the job of the Euroskeptics included in Fresh Start and the ERG to make sure that Cameron would keep his promise.

The Labour government got the Lisbon Treaty through the House of Commons in 2008. Both Labour and Conservative MPs voted against it. In October 2011, Euroskeptics in the Conservative Party, using a new committee established in the wake of the 2009 parliamentary expenses scandal, the Backbench Business Committee, were able to use the committee and a new e-petition procedure to add an EU referendum motion as an amendment to legislation then being considered (Cowley and Stuart 2012, 403). The new committee had been established to give backbenchers the ability to bring subjects to the floor for debate (D'Arcy 2016). At the same time as Euroskeptics were finding more fuel for their anti-federalist fire, they were learning to use newly available mechanisms to throw spanners into government legislation. The wording of the 2011 referendum question in the House was a three-pronged motion on whether the UK should stay or leave the EU or "renegotiate" its membership (BBC 2011b). Under PM Cameron, the coalition government defeated the measure 483–111, with 81 of the noes, that is, those voting in favor of the referendum, Conservative backbenchers. The vote saw strong words by Deputy PM Clegg against the Euroskeptic bunch: "They need to be a little bit careful about what they wish for" (BBC 2011b). Also, just before the May 2010 election, also using the e-petition procedure, one hundred thousand public signatures were delivered requesting a referendum on membership of the EU. After the government defeated the October 2011 vote on the referendum, nearly one hundred Tory MPs signed a letter to the PM backing the placement "on the Statute Book before the next general election a commitment to hold a referendum during the next Parliament on the nature of our relationship with the European Union" (D'Arcy 2016).

Two other sets of issues relating to financial services and the post-crash impact on globalization were the subject of EU-UK disagreement at the same time, which also ultimately made a referendum inevitable. The first was the EU's introduction of the "Tobin tax" in 2010 to levy taxes on financial transactions (bank trades). For the first time, the EU adopted a new tax "without the support of all its members," with eleven member states adopting it (Petroff and Thompson 2013). Given the importance of the London financial industry and of EU-owned banks there, the Tobin tax posed a large threat since it would be a double tax with "cascading impact" upon "each party in a trading change, except the central counterparty" (Johnson 2011). Financial centers including London, New York, Hong Kong, "and other major markets" wrote to the G20 in 2013, saying "the proposed tax would hurt the world economy at a time of significant uncertainty" (Petroff and Thompson 2013). The Cameron-Clegg coalition government launched a legal challenge at the ECJ in April 2013, arguing that the tax "would have extraterritorial effects and impose costs on non-participating member states." The ECJ rejected the challenge. It is easy to understand the sentiments in the Conservative party against the EU as a "lumbering federalist machine," working to stifle economic growth in London and viewing the ECJ as against the UK's economic interests. As of June 27, 2020, the EU, led by Germany, was reviving the idea of expanding the tax across countries to raise funds for COVID relief (Laurent 2020).

The second issue that further angered Euroskeptics was the December 2011 EU fiscal stability pact, which occurred two months after the record rebellion by backbenchers on holding an EU referendum. The twenty-six members agreed to join or consider joining the pact, under which caps and penalties on governments' spending and borrowing would be imposed (Adam 2011). Cameron exercised the UK veto to "protect the UK's financial sector from oppressive EU regulation," and 57 percent of the public polled approved of his move. The Labour opposition and even Deputy PM Clegg, a Liberal Democrat, expressed the usual concern that the UK's voice would be diminished in Europe by this action (Adam 2011). The 2011 Stability and Growth Pact was framed by Euroskeptics as a potential further loss of the UK's financial sovereignty. One of the distasteful measures to the UK was a new requirement to submit national budgets to the scrutiny of the European Commission and potentially be required to change them. Cameron had negotiated for a protocol to allow the London economic sector to opt out of proposed changes on financial services, which were decried as unacceptable by French president Nicolas Sarkozy (BBC 2011a). Sarkozy made a comparison between the "lack of global financial regulations and the worldwide consequences" and Britain's request for a waiver of requirements for its sector. At this point, London Mayor Boris Johnson approved of Cameron's actions, saying that "this was the only thing that it was really open for him to do" (BBC 2011a). Cameron faced a threatened rebellion in the House of Commons, with Euroskeptics pushing for a new referendum on either the treaty, if Cameron signed on, or an EU membership referendum (Faiola 2011). Twenty-five of the then twenty-seven EU members eventually signed onto the pact in 2012, excepting the UK and Hungary.

By 2013, PM Cameron decided that he could no longer hold the different Euroskeptic factions together in his party. At the same time, UKIP was running about 10 percent in the national polls. In January 2013, in his London "Bloomberg" speech, he promised that if his party won the next election, he would hold an "in and out" referendum by the end of 2017. He laid out a framework for potential compromises toward "defederalization" from the EU in the next four years, invoking many of the central themes of Euroskeptics' and financiers' views about the alienating turns the EU had taken. He also in essence cast aside the Liberal Democrats as future coalition partners since they were pro-EU. Cameron addressed five themes in his Bloomberg speech: (1) "Britain is at the heart of the single market, and must remain so. But when the Single Market remains incomplete in services, in energy and in digital—the very sectors that are the engines of a modern economy—it is only half the success that it could be"; (2) the second principle "is one of flexibility," so the EU could accommodate those desiring closer political and economic integration and those desiring less (the UK); (3) "that power must flow back to member states; it was put in the Treaty but never fulfilled"; (4) "there is not a European demos . . . it is national parliaments who are and will remain the source of democratic legitimacy and accountability"; (5) "fairness, that whatever new arrangements are enacted for the Eurozone, they must work fairly for those inside it our outside of it." With respect to the second criterion, Cameron specifically mentioned the euro (which the UK did not adopt but Ireland did); the Schengen "free movement zone," which neither the UK nor Ireland adopted; and the disagreement with the "European Court of Justice that has consistently supported greater centralization" (Craig 2013).

During the same month as Cameron's Bloomberg speech, the Fresh Start group released its "Manifesto for Change," claiming that PM Cameron must negotiate to change the Lisbon Treaty to include "an emergency brake for any Member state regarding future EU legislation that affects financial services," "repatriate competence in the area of social and employment law to member states, an opt-out of 'all existing EU policing and criminal justice measures not already covered by the Lisbon Treaty block opt-out,' and a new legal safeguard for all non-Eurozone countries to avoid discrimination," among other issues (cited in Craig 2013, 176–77). Curiously, as discussed with regard to the formation of Fresh Start, in 2013–14 the group acknowledged that "staying in the European single market and its benefits to UK exports and to Foreign Direct Investment are generally accepted to be the reason Britain entered the EU and the main reason for our remaining a member" (Craig 2013, 177). As is now known, by 2017, Fresh Start was working with the ERG to promote the complete exit of the UK from the single market and customs union.

In December 2015, the first EU summit after Cameron's May 2015 victory was held, but it was dominated by the crises of increased migration and Greek debt (BBC 2016b). In February 2016, PM Cameron and European Council president Donald Tusk negotiated on some of the issues brought up in the 2013 Bloomberg speech, including the issues of putting a stop to the "ever closer union" and allowing the UK Parliament greater say in political affairs. Cameron's achievement here was described in sports terms as a "red card," whereby if 55 percent of national parliaments agreed, they could block or veto a European Commission proposal (BBC 2016b). Other issues PM Cameron proposed, based on the 2015 Conservative manifesto, included a four-year "brake" (or waiting period for residency) on the ability of EU migrants to claim tax credits, child benefits, or publicly supported housing once they moved to the UK. Facing opposition by Poland and three other central European countries, Cameron got the four-year phase-in period to include in-work benefits, but tax credits would be phased in over the four years. Also, Cameron had wanted to guarantee this system to remain in place for thirteen years, but the EU offered seven. Changes to housing benefits were not negotiated. Obviously, this piece on immigration and the first part of the sovereignty of national parliaments were designed to deal with central claims of Euroskeptics. On a third issue, PM Cameron won guarantees that countries outside the eurozone would not be required to financially contribute to eurozone bailouts and would be reimbursed for any such funds used by the EU. On the other hand, Cameron again ran into opposition by France on the "freedom from EU regulation" issue for London banks and financial services, which he had encountered in 2011. France again insisted on a level playing field here with no opt-out from EU rules on financial services (BBC 2016b). The changes began to be debated in the House on February 20, 2016, and the June 23 date for the referendum was announced. As the BBC noted, if Cameron had not struck a deal with the EU, he would have had to return back to the EU to renegotiate. Cameron's then home secretary, Theresa May, said that the package offered the "basis for a deal," but Euroskeptics pooh-poohed it as usual. Had the June 2016 referendum won, Parliament would have continued to debate the package of reforms negotiated between PM Cameron and the EU.

The United States

The Changing National Context. In the US, the Great Depression led to the New Deal realignment, whereby the Democrats enjoyed being the majority party for decades. Their success relied, in part, on the "solid South." Those members and voters were politically conservative yet nominally Democratic, a holdover from the Civil War and Reconstruction. Yet because these Southern "Yellow Dog" Democrats, or "Boll Weevils," voted for the Democratic leader for Speaker, the Democrats were able to maintain uninterrupted control of the US House for four decades. However, President Lyndon Johnson (D-TX) predicted that by signing the Civil Rights Act of 1964, Democrats would lose the South. He was correct. The result was a realignment in the South, first at the presidential level and eventually in down-ballot races. Republicans now control most of the states in the Old Confederacy.

The Watergate scandal of the early 1970s led not only to the resignation of President Richard Nixon (R-CA) but also to lasting changes in American politics. First, public faith in government institutions fell dramatically after Watergate. Second, voters in states outside the South, which may lean Democratic or Republican, now often eschew party labels and adopt the "independent" moniker. Since the mid-1990s, a plurality of voters consider themselves political independents, a dealignment trend that is fairly durable and increasing (J. Jones 2022). The result is more instability in party control of Congress, which began with the Republican takeover after the 1994 midterm elections. Since then, partisan control of the House of Representatives has changed three times, and the vote margins are often slender (US House of Representatives n.d.).

Gerrymandering, the practice of drawing legislative districts to benefit one party or faction over another, is another contexual factor. In most states, the state legislature is responsible for drawing the district boundaries for its US House delegation. The parties in control of the state legislatures usually draw district maps that favor their party. When most state legislatures were Democratic, prior to 1992, the result was a number of majority white districts that elected (white) Democrats who owed their victories to minority voters that formed their base. After the Voting Rights Act amendments of 1990, many states were required to draw majority-minority districts to increase the descriptive representation of racial and ethnic minorities in the US House. This requirement successfully increased the number of Blacks and Hispanics in the House. At the same time, the districts surrounding the majority-minority districts became more homogenously white and Republican. Now, most members of the House of Representatives are elected in safe seats. Their most significant electoral threats are from primary challengers who hold more extreme positions. This threat pushes incumbents away from moderate positions and enhances the partisan divide within the US House.

In the last three decades, the cost of winning a seat in the US House of Representatives increased dramatically. According to Open Secrets (2021), the average House member spent $407,000 to secure her or his seat in 1990. By 2020, the average House member spent $2.3 million. That's a lot of money to raise every two years.

The House of Representatives. While the US House of Representatives is a constitutional body whose powers are defined in Article I of the Constitution, the body's traditions and rules have evolved over more than two centuries. Initially, the body was fairly informal, with dogs, spittoons, and acrimony that resulted, in 1856, in Representative Preston Brooks (D-SC) caning Senator Charles Sumner (R-MA) over his characterization of Brooks's cousin, Senator Andrew Butler (D-SC) (US Senate n.d.). As time passed, party caucuses evolved, and the House became more institutionalized with formal rules and procedures governing its business. The practices and rules incorporated the parties as a reality.

While there is greater homogeneity in parties today than in the past, both political parties still have groups of members who are ideologically outside the party's mainstream. For instance, the contemporary version of the Boll Weevils is the Blue Dogs, an informal group of moderate Democrats, primarily from the South and the Midwest, who seek to keep the party from going too far to the left. The House Democrats also include the Progressive Caucus, which attempts to move the party to the left and to adopt more activist policy. It boasts 101 members, nearly half of the Democratic Caucus (Congressional Progressive Caucus n.d.). On the Republican side, the Conservative Opportunity Society, founded in the 1980s, pushed the Republican Party to the right and became a vector for Newt Gingrich to move into the Republican Party leadership (Pearson 2015).

While the Blue Dogs worked within the party to successfully influence legislation and shape spending priorities (Pearson 2015, 49–51), other emboldened party caucuses decided to hold up their own majority's agenda. In 2015, a group of House Republicans established the Freedom Caucus. This group was dedicated to fiscal austerity and "an agenda of limited constitutional government in Congress" (cited in A. Clarke n.d.). Unlike other party and interest group caucuses, the Freedom Caucus's membership was by invitation only and was restricted to those who passed an ideological litmus test. The Freedom Caucus withheld its support from many pieces of legislation supported by the Republican leadership, including raising the debt ceiling, among other issues (Ball 2020, 236–37). While the Freedom Caucus is a Republican organization, it legitimated the idea that ideologically driven, junior backbenchers could criticize their own party leadership. Today, the four-member group of junior Democratic women nicknamed "The Squad" parlays their notoriety and their considerable public personas to pressure the Democratic leadership (Cruz Lera 2020).

Another change that scholars lament is the growing partisanship in US politics, where the leadership's primary goals are to capture or retain political power rather than to make good policy. The website Voteview, which monitors individual and party ideology using DW-NOMINATE scores, shows the increasing ideological distance between the two parties over time (Lewis et al. 2021). The ability and willingness to compromise, once considered an art form and a virtue, have become signs of weakness and a lack of principle. For example, as Jonathan Cohn notes in his book *The Ten Year War*, Republicans who favored health care reforms that were practically identical to the Obama package opposed the Affordable Care Act because Obama supported it (2021, 126–27). The result of partisanship has been increased gridlock, fewer laws enacted, and more government shutdowns (Mann and Ornstein 2008). In an attempt to recapture the bipartisanship of earlier years, the Problem Solvers Caucus formed in 2017 and in 2018. Its members sought to change the Democratic Caucus rules in 2019 to allow more bills and amendments to be brought to the floor for votes if they had sufficient bipartisan support. The effort largely failed (Lipinski 2021).

At the same time, Congress, of course, is a highly masculine environment. As Georgia Duhrst-Lahti (2002) notes, it has a hierarchical organization, an emphasis on formal rules and procedures, and a competitive nature, and men are the overwhelming majority of members. They are, quite literally, the face of power. Women House members frequently share stories of being mistaken for staff members or wives of House members. The physical space is even unfriendly to women. Women members did not have access to the House gym and pool until 1985 ("Members Only" 2017) or to a restroom near the House chamber until 2011 (McKoen 2011; see also Dittmar, Sanbonmatsu, and Carroll 2018, 64–69).

The language of politics and the language of leadership have violent overtones, another manifestation of the masculine nature of the institution. Candidates run *campaigns* with *strategies* designed for *victory* in *battleground* states or districts. Once elected, they *fight* for their constituents, party, or ideas. The very title "whip" refers to a "whipper in," a British term that refers to the person in a fox hunt who would whip the dogs back toward the hunting party. Within the partisan disputes, there are "winners" and "losers," suggesting a zero-sum game.

Within this context, the number of women in the House of Representatives slowly increased. Democratic women have outnumbered Republican women in most Congresses since 1955. However, the partisan disparity increased over time. Consequently, in 1955, when the Democrats started their four decades of uninterrupted control, 16 House members were women (10 Democrats, 6 Republicans). In 1975, 19 women served (14 Democrats, 5 Republicans). In 1995, the number had grown to 48 (31 Democrats, 17 Republicans), and in 2021, 119 women were serving (89 Democrats, 30 Republicans) (Center for American Women in Politics 2020).

The American Speaker and Institutional Power. The Speaker of the US House of Representatives is a constitutional officer and is third in line of succession to the presidency. This position has considerable power within the chamber and is responsible for general administration and the legislative agenda. The Speaker also has the ability to reward loyalty, punish opponents, and advance the majority party's agenda and/or compromise with the opposition. To use Celis and Lovenduski's (2018) terms, the Speaker has both positional and active power, with both "power to" legislate and "power over" other legislators. The speakership has evolved with the institution. According to Jenkins and Stewart (2013), the speakership was a relatively inconsequential position for the first half of the nineteenth century. Even after party caucuses evolved in the 1840s, they did not necessarily agree on a candidate for Speaker. By the early 1900s, however, the House had become a majoritarian institution, with the Speaker as its leader. According to Ron Peters (1990), Speaker Joe Cannon represented a period of heightened partisanship, and he successfully consolidated power in the speakership. After the revolt against Cannon, power gradually centered in the committee chairs, and the seniority system evolved. By the 1950s, the House was divided between three major groups: the Democrats, the Republicans, and the Southern Democrats. Given the Southern Democrats' long durations in office, they also occupied many committee and subcommittee chair positions. In this period, the Speaker's power was diminished, since committee chairs dominated the legislative agenda.

Cartels and Conditional Party Government. In the last twenty years, two theories have emerged to explain who holds and wields power in the House. Gary W. Cox and Matthew D. McCubbins (2005, 2007) argue that the majority party in the House has developed into a "procedural cartel," which tightly controls the institution's agenda in which the majority party controls key positions of power. In this framework, the subcommittee and committee chairs form the procedural cartel, since they can determine what pieces of legislation come to the floor for a vote, the content of that legislation, and what amendments will be offered. While the Speaker is not an inconsequential actor in the House, the primary power broker is the procedural cartel. The first attack on the procedural cartel came after the 1974 midterms when a large group of Democratic freshmen members was elected. These "Watergate babies" passed a subcommittee bill of rights that decentralized power away from committee chairs. This opened up many leadership positions to more junior members. They also deposed three long-standing committee chairs, undermining the established norm of seniority (Mann and Ornstein 2008, 60–64; Pearson 2015, 21–23).

John Aldrich and David Rohde pose an alternate (2011) theory, conditional party government (CPG). CPG predicts that when parties become more homogeneous, the leadership, including the Speaker, will become stronger. Arguably, this process began with the Republican revolution of 1995. Then-Speaker Newt Gingrich (R-GA) instituted a series of changes to the Republican Caucus rules that further altered the nature and character of the House. They included term limits for the Republican leadership and committee chairs; articulation of a national policy agenda, the "Contract with America"; creation of task forces to draft legislation, bypassing committees; fostering of a more partisan atmosphere in the body; and consolidation of power in the speakership (Mann and Ornstein 2008). Some of these changes carried over to the Democrats when they recaptured the majority in 2006, such as hyper-partisanship; others did not. In the next three decades, party control seesawed between the two parties, with the Democrats regaining control from 2007 to 2011 and again in 2019.

The Contemporary American Speakership. Jeffrey Jenkins and Charles Stewart (2013) augment both of these theories in their historical analysis of the speakership. They document how the American speakership evolved from a relatively nonpartisan race, elected in an ad hoc manner, into an "organizational cartel." In the organizational cartel, in place since 1860, the majority party monopolizes the distribution of perks and power. The Speaker's power grew and solidified in the early twentieth century under Speaker Joe Cannon (R-IL). Cannon had successfully concentrated power into the speakership, serving as a member of the Rules Committee and controlling committee appointments. The resulting revolt, led by progressive Republicans, decentralized power into the hands of committee chairs, removing the Speaker from the Rules Committee and undermining the Speaker's ability to make committee assignments (Jenkins and Stewart 2013, 280–81).

The revolt against Cannon ushered in a period in which power was decentralized and was held by committee chairs, who were usually the most senior members of Congress—what Cox and McCubbins would call the procedural cartel. Given the one-party domination of the American South, whose representatives easily accrued seniority, many committee chairs were conservative Southern Democrats. The chairs could dictate which bills would be considered in committee and brought to the floor for a vote. The Speaker had relatively little ability to influence committee chairs to consider legislation that they opposed, even if it was supported by a majority of the caucus.

After decades of little discipline within the Democratic Caucus, Speaker Jim Wright (D-TX), who became Speaker in 1987, began to consolidate power during his tenure, especially by using legislative maneuvers to stymie Republican legislation and to move Democratic bills. Under Speaker Newt Gingrich (R-GA), who became speaker in 1995, the Republican Party further weakened committee chairs' power by instituting term limits for chairs and undermining the seniority system in favor of loyalty to the caucus—and the Speaker. Moreover, the party leadership assumed control of the legislative agenda, wresting it away from committee chairs (Pearson 2015, 110–15; see also Palazzolo 1992).

When Democratic rule ended in 1995, the Republican leadership of the era introduced a more partisan tone, changing the collegial nature of the body. Lipinski (2021) argues that the Gingrich-led reforms started a trend where "members have increasingly ceded power in the legislative process to the party leaders," replacing "regular order" with the "Speaker's order." Speakers also had more control over committee appointments, especially committee chairs, and more control over what legislation will be considered on the floor.

Speaker Dennis Hastert further consolidated the major party rule by instituting the "Hastert Rule," whereby he would only bring legislation to the floor if a majority of Republicans supported it (Pearson and Schickler 2009, 171). The Republican Speakers so effectively controlled the Rules Committee that Pelosi had a difficult time filling all the Democratic seats for the 110th Congress, when the Democrats regained the majority, and the committee lost its exclusive status (Pearson and Schickler 2009).

In addition, an informal tool of the leadership is fundraising. According to Katherine Pearson (2015) the party leadership is increasingly important in party fundraising. For example, committee and subcommittee chairs are expected to donate to the congressional campaign coffers (65), leadership political action committees (PACs) are the norm, and candidates for leadership slots donate to their colleagues to secure votes from within the caucus (Kanthak 2007). Individual members, especially those from safe seats, may contribute to their colleagues' campaigns (Pearson 2015, 64–74). The Speaker also controls the leadership of the party's congressional campaign committee and has the final say on who will receive money. Loyalty is rewarded. Incumbents have priority, and challengers may go begging. Campaign donations then become a powerful means to incentivize and reward loyalty. This fact supports Jenkins and Stewart's (2013) organizational cartel theory as an important power for the Speaker.

Pelosi in the House. For her part, Nancy Pelosi entered the House in 1987, after the Watergate-era reforms were standard operating procedure, and she would have witnessed Speaker Gingrich's rise to power, the increasing partisan divide in the House, and the growth in the number of women elected to the House. (The internal Democratic Party leadership selection dynamics and Pelosi's rise to power will be covered in chapter 2.)

When Pelosi ascended to the speakership in 2007, she led an increasingly homogeneous party with disappearing numbers of moderate and conservative Democrats. By 2019, the story had changed somewhat with the rise of both the Progressive Caucus and centrist caucuses, along with the Congressional Black Caucus. Coupled with the institutional changes described above, Pelosi held the speakership at one of its most powerful points in history. Moreover, by all accounts, Pelosi was extremely good at the job, using a combination of political instincts, fundraising acumen, and the leader's rewards and punishments to maintain her position and the loyalty of her caucus (Pearson 2015, 30–33).

Conclusion

This introductory chapter describes the political environment and the ideological landscape confronting May and Pelosi when they stepped into their leadership roles in 2018–19. In each case, these legislators were faced with institutional changes and a tortured politics that was mostly not of their making but with which they had to contend. In Pelosi's case, it was the hyper-partisan atmosphere of the contemporary Congress and the instability resulting from relatively frequent changes in party control. In May's case, it was a nation long divided on whether and how the UK should participate in the EU. The fault lines were exacerbated by the 2008 global financial crisis, with London as the world's largest banking center heavily affected by it. As the EU faced financial stringency from 2008 onward, immigration crises followed.. These factors set the stage for the decisions that Pelosi and May made as they moved into positions of power and the choices they made once there.

We note the position of these two women leaders as, first, enormously competent *organizational partisans* (Escobar-Lemmon and Taylor-Robinson 2015). They had to walk various tightrope iterations to get to where they wished to be, which for both was to lead the party in their respective legislature. Numerous studies have shown that women in particular have to demonstrate a long history of party service to be considered even qualified candidates, let alone leaders. (Duerst-Lahti and Kelly, eds., 1995; Kittilson, 2006; Kenny 2014; Childs and Webb 2016).

To borrow other concepts from Escobar-Lemmon and Taylor-Robinson (2015), May had been a portfolio *switcher* in the shadow cabinets from 2001 to 2010 based on appointments by different Opposition leaders, but then one of the longest-term *survivors* in the home secretary portfolio under two different governments, the coalition government of 2010–15 and the short-lived Conservative Cameron government of 2015–16. Pelosi too was a *survivor*; while not in the presidential cabinet, of course, she steadily ascended the House ladder under an all-male leadership from 2001 onward, starting as minority whip in 2001 and then becoming minority leader one year later, the first woman to lead a US House party caucus.

The two women's "survivorship" qualities included working with parties and Houses that had historically privileged white male power, which did not facilitate the ability of others to gain and hold leadership positions. In her competencies to adapt to the right and center-left within the

Conservative Party, May was first brought in as shadow spokesperson for "Schools, Disabled People and Women" from 1998 to 1999 under Opposition Leader William Hague, and she then moved to shadow education and employment secretary in 1999. She was moved to shadow transport secretary under rightist Opposition Leader Iain Duncan Smith, who then made her the first woman Conservative Party chair from 2002 to 2003. May began a parallel set of efforts to modernize the Conservative Party in working with Baroness Anne Jenkin, whose Euroskeptic husband, Bernard Jenkin, was the party chair and leader of the Euroskeptics in the House. May's and Jenkin's work created the "Women 2 Win" group for nominating diverse candidates, which mainly came to fruition in the 2010 UK election. After that, the male power brokers in the party saw too many problems in terms of alienating the male local constituency leaders and stopped the practice.

From her first election to the House, Nancy Pelosi worked with Representative Steny Hoyer, a long-term Maryland adversary who clearly wanted her job. Over time, Pelosi balanced groups such as the Congressional Black Caucus, representatives of the most loyal group of Democratic voters, as well as the increasingly polarized Democratic Caucus.

Both women had to be extremely careful not to step on toes, another balancing act, to amass the political capital each needed for their leadership quest. As will be seen in chapters 2–4, when we deal with substantive issues each woman faced in her quest to reach the apex, each had to compromise on ideas that could open them to criticism from progressive feminists inside and outside the legislature. For both women, one such issue included reproductive choice, and for May, the issue of same-sex marriage as well.

As we discuss in chapter 2 how each woman gained her leadership credentials, we will use the "constraining and enabling" legislative features identified by Childs and Krook (2009) and the concepts used by Escobar-Lemmon and Taylor-Robinson (2015, 2016) and Annesley, Beckwith, and Franceschet (2019). Among the two last sets of authors, we reiterate that gaining the credentials and experience (educational, legislative, policy, and educational) is necessary but not always sufficient to be appointed to cabinet and thus as a potential leadership candidate in parliamentary systems. This holds true as well for ascension to the US House leadership structure, where there are many aspirants but few successes. It bears repeating that Annesley, Beckwith, and Franceschet found that affiliational criteria, being in selectors' networks of one sort or another, are most important in the US, Australia, and UK, which can help a leader's or a cabinet aspirant's career

(2019). We agree that in both the US and the UK, affiliational criteria are enormously gendered and that the question "Are you one of us?" is most often affirmatively answered for white men. Escobar-Lemmon and Taylor-Robinson note that, for presidential cabinets only, organizational partisans may have more ability to "soften" their exit by controlling the time frame in which they leave (2015). Both Pelosi and May, neither of whom were in presidential cabinets, used this strategy to signal to their intraparty opponents that they were open to leaving at a future certain date. When we discuss the concepts of intra- and interparty dissent in chapters 2–4, we will also be discussing the women's careers and status as organizational partisans.

TWO

How Female Leaders Get There

Party Workhorses but Not Party Animals

In our examination of the pre-speakership and pre–prime ministerial political careers of Theresa May and Nancy Pelosi, we explore the traps between formal criteria and informal practices in party and legislative management in the US House of Representatives and the British House of Commons.

This chapter demonstrates the salience of the parliamentary literature on the Pelosi case in the American House of Representatives. The American case is often left out of such analyses since the US has a presidential rather than a parliamentary system. Certainly, the relative dearth of women in high office also plays a role in its exclusion from gender-based analyses. While presidential and parliamentary systems have many important differences, they are less significant in this study than they may be elsewhere. The three case study chapters, starting with this one, draw on the importance of credentialing processes for leadership aspirants from diverse backgrounds—in our cases, two white women. The crucial existing studies of how female aspirants are identified, usually being included in cabinet in parliamentary systems and in presidential cabinets in the US or Latin America systems, include those that only looked at presidential cabinets (Escobar-Lemmon and Taylor-Robinson 2015, 2016) and those that looked at a variety of institutional systems (Annesley, Beckwith, and Franceschet 2019). While neither May nor Pelosi have served in presidential cabinets, their experiences of ascending to leadership are resonate with the Escobar-Lemmon and Taylor-Robinson studies.

In examining the necessary but not sufficient role of policy expertise, educational credentials, and political experience in reaching cabinet and thus in entering the "fast track" to potential leadership, Annesley, Beckwith, and Franceschet regroup some of Escobar-Lemmon and Taylor-Robinson's categories into these three aspects of "experiential criteria" (2019, 111). The Escobar-Lemmon and Taylor-Robinson studies identified the terms under which women would either be "Cabinet post switchers," which, of course, is typically not up to the individual but rather up to those with the power to make the switch (president), or survivors through the presidential term, who likely move on to another cabinet post. In their 2015 work, Escobar-Lemmon and Taylor-Robinson framed *policy expertise* as emanating from the private or public sector and requiring a significant number of years and responsibility. May had these credentials based on her banking experience prior to becoming elected first locally and then nationally. Pelosi gained them through her Democratic Party voluntarism in the 1970s and 1980s before becoming chair of the California Democratic Party in 1981.

Escobar-Lemmon and Taylor-Robinson's second criterion, *political experience*, was based on having built a career in national government through various elected or appointed posts and, importantly, included the concept of *organizational partisans*, referring to high party chair positions, which we apply to both Pelosi and May, with Pelosi as chair of the California Democratic Party from 1981 to 1984, chair of the host committee for the 1984 Democratic National Convention in San Francisco, and fundraising chair of the 1986 Democratic Senatorial Campaign Committee. Related to both the policy and the political credentials of Pelosi, Meyerson (2004) explained that "she was no amateur when she got to Congress," having grown up with a five-term congressman father and seeing how the political system worked and the issues troubling people. Meyerson also wrote that "Pelosi's greatest skill, however, is her ability to synthesize positions that reflect the various inclinations of her caucus and the political opportunities of the moment—and the period." Additionally, Congressman David Obey, then ranking member of the House Appropriations Committee, referred to Pelosi, a colleague on the committee, as "our Margaret Thatcher—she's tough as hell and has a very nice style to her." Obey also used the term "operational" for Pelosi, who was "able to understand other members' needs and able to put together deals to members' mutual satisfaction." Pelosi has since adopted the term "operational"—applying to those often inside but potentially also outside the party caucus—to her approved group of "bottom line" politicians who are willing to compromise to get legislation passed (Bzdek 2008, 50).

Pelosi started her first leadership PAC in the 1990s. Leadership PACs were begun by California congressman Henry Waxman in the 1970s to "leapfrog" over the seniority system in the House by contributing to other members' campaign war chests and to gain preferential committee assignments. Pelosi started a second PAC around 2000 as she climbed the leadership ranks, and, like she did in 1986 when she was credited with flipping the Senate during Reagan's second midterm election, she oversaw raising a large amount of money (although not enough to change Republican control) in the 2002 election when she was vying to become minority leader (Hickey et al. 2021; Bresnahan and Isenstadt 2011; Mullins 2004). Many of her potential leadership credentials were gained through the direct clientelistic relationship of fundraising and working on slating nominees in winnable seats as an organizational partisan.

Theresa May gained similar credentials as the first woman chair of the UK Conservative Party from 2002 to 2003. However, at that time, the party chair was not as directly responsible for fundraising, especially when compared with the US House and Senate leadership. May's influence as party chair was felt more in working to reform the nomination system, to centralize it, and to remove some local traditional male constituency influence in candidate slating. These reforms were found between 2005 and 2010 (Ashe et al. 2010, 455–80). In the UK system, the role of party chair is prestigious, especially for the first woman to hold it, and thus this contributed to May's quality credentials as a leadership challenger in 2016.

Another piece of the Escobar-Lemmon and Taylor-Robinson framework (2016) is in denoting cabinet "survivors," those who do not get forced out or quit before a government falls. Again, while their study was based on Latin American presidential systems, it is equally applicable to the Westminster parliamentary system. Theresa May was the second woman in the Home Office, one of the four Great Offices of State, and one of its longest occupants in history. On the other hand, as will be discussed, much of the policy in the cabinets of the Cameron-Clegg coalition, revolving around austerity, was in the hands of the all-male "Quad," including Prime Minister Cameron, Deputy PM Clegg, Chancellor of the Exchequer George Osborne, and Chief Secretary to the Treasury Danny Alexander.

The Annesley, Beckwith, and Franceschet 2019 study, comparing various types of political systems including Westminster, PR, and MMP parliamentary systems and the presidential systems of Chile and the US, splits the organizational partisanship criteria of chairing a party organization into experiential but the running of a campaign into affiliational (111, 137). Many of the experiential criteria are similar to those identified in the

Escobar-Lemmon and Taylor-Robinson studies of 2015 and 2016, that is, political experience, policy expertise, and relevant education.

In addition to experiential and affiliational criteria, Annesley, Beckwith, and Franceschet identify a third area of cabinet (and leadership) selector discrimination: deciding which representational criteria are important for the party to portray as being significant (2019, 154). In the cases of both the US Democratic and the UK Conservative Parties and governments, the interest has been in showing the "diversity friendly" nature of the parties by nominating and supporting candidates with a wide variety of backgrounds and in helping them gain legislative or cabinet leadership posts before contesting for the ultimate legislative or executive posts. Problematically for our study, the commitment often stops at descriptive representation, and then the traditional views crop up among the majority of male legislative members, this is, that the female leader is "just not up to it." Annesley, Beckwith, and Franceschet cite Ostrom's (1986) three-part framework in which characteristics prescribe, prohibit, or permit certain choices to be made in institutions. They concluded affiliational criteria to be *permissive* in terms of allowing selectors' various linkages to cabinet and leadership aspirants to be prioritized. This is especially true in the Westminster (particularly the British and Australian) and US systems, in which cabinet criteria are informally designated (2019, 134–35, 154). Representational criteria *prescribe* choices required of selectors to make the cabinet appear legitimate and representative (154). Relating the organizational partisanship criterion of Escobar-Lemmon and Taylor-Robinson to that of Annesley, Beckwith, and Franceschet's representational criterion, we will show that May's and Pelosi's high-profile histories in affecting the incentive structures by which candidates are nominated (May) and nominated and funded (Pelosi) brought them both support from those they helped and high antipathy from the white male club they worked to displace. Annesley, Beckwith, and Franceschet put experiential criteria into Ostrom's category of prescriptive rules as they did with representational (211). As with Escobar-Lemmon and Taylor-Robinson, however, they find that while all potential ministers (and we would add leaders drawn from legislative/executive leadership) must have relevant experiential credentials, these can be applied in a flexible and inconsistent manner (211). The bottom-line problem for female legislative/executive leaders then, applying to May and Pelosi, is that while certain parts of experiential criteria may be emphasized as a reason for picking the female leader, they can also be deemphasized, particularly if a majority male wishes to have that job in the future. While Pelosi has held the record for fundraising in Congress and won an enormous House majority in 2018, forty-one seats, as well as passed priority legislation through the House, she was still challenged for the leadership that year. While May helped to reform the local constituency discretion in picking candidates and to increase the descriptive and substantive diversity of them, as well as negotiating the bulk of the Brexit package with the EU, she was toppled from within by the opportunistic candidacy of Boris Johnson, who succeeded her, marshaling hardline anti-EU sentiment within the party.

We agree with Beckwith (2015) that the "structure of political opportunities" is different for female leadership candidates in that they are typically more qualified (and older) than males if they win their race. As Beckwith (2015) showed in her study of Margaret Thatcher and Angela Merkel, women leaders are often brought into leadership when the party is least powerful, in terms of previous elections or intraparty scandals. While the Speaker of the US House is always the leader of the majority party, Pelosi became the Democratic (minority) leader in 2003 after Richard Gephardt resigned the post due to the historic failure of the party to win midterm election seats in the House in 2002 and after she had raised significant funds in that election to forestall leadership challenges (Meyerson 2004). Theresa May became the Conservative Party leader and Prime Minister after David Cameron suddenly resigned after losing the European Brexit referendum in June 2016. While female leaders are not often able to wait to pick the optimal time to run for leadership, they also may have to force through issues based on a crowded agenda and a time frame limited by the next upcoming election. This was certainly true for Pelosi and Obama working on the Affordable Care Act in 2009–10. The time frame was also highly relevant to May's "quick" invocation of Article 50 of the Withdrawal Act in March 2017 (with an initial aspirational two-year time limit for the trade bill portion) and the decision to hold an election early in her mandate, in June 2017.

In addition to the different political opportunity structure for women leaders than their male counterparts and the outweighing of credentials and representational concerns by the affiliational ethos that "men are better suited to govern," we find that Childs and Krook's (2009) work on critical actors is relevant. As detailed in chapter 1, with the authors' five examples of "constraining and enabling" characteristics of legislatures, we look especially at their second criterion, which includes legislative institutional norms, positional power, and identities and interests of female and male legislators. On the last, we will detail the push-and-pull interaction between social conservatism and laissez-faire conservatism in the Conservative Party and the overlay with positions in the EU. In large part, the history of the Conservative Party since Margaret Thatcher's leadership has been the fights between the long-entrenched Thatcherites and their followers and the "modernizers" who wish to "decontaminate" Conservatism and broaden its appeal to younger metropolitan voters. The "modernizers," as described in the Bright Blue "Modernisers' Manifesto" of 2014, wished to show that the Conservative Party could be just as appealing as Labour on issues of social progressivism and could cut into Labour support, particularly after Tony Blair's 1997 first win (Shorthouse, Maltby, and Brenton 2014). That fight has crosscut the other cleavages that reference the UK's economic position in the world. With respect to varying affiliations of women in the US Democratic Party, as described by Childs and Krook (2009) as the interests of female and male legislators and the process of "gendering" issue positions taken by representatives, we will describe Pelosi's balancing work between centrists, often white men, and progressives, often women and men of color. The constraining and enabling factors referenced by Childs and Krook (2009) are also relevant to the concept of prescribing, prohibiting, and permitting institutional rules adopted from Ostrom(1986) by Annesley, Beckwith, and Franceschet (2019).

Theresa May

Early Credentials. After graduation from Oxford with a degree in geography, Theresa Brasier and Philip May were married in 1980. Philip and Theresa May were long-term Conservative Party supporters and participants, dating back from their time at Oxford. When they were married in 1980 and both chose early careers in finance, some thought Philip would become the politician in the family (Gimson 2019). Theresa May worked at the Bank of England from 1977 to 1983 and then at a payment clearinghouse agency, where as a consultant she successively served as head of European affairs and senior adviser on international affairs (Millington 2017). She was elected to the local council in the Durnsford ward of Merton in 1986. Her husband was a Conservative Party activist in the ward, and the council was majority Conservative at the time.

After running unsuccessfully in two Labour strongholds in 1992 and 1994, Theresa May was elected in the newly created Maidenhead district in 1997. May had been challenged for the nomination by David Cameron (*London Review of* Books 2017; Telegraph Reporters 2017). Cameron was declined by the local party association since he was neither a long-term party activist nor a previous local councillor. May was fast-tracked into shadow cabinet positions while Conservatives were in opposition. Under Opposition Leader William Hague (1997–2001), she became shadow education and employment secretary from 1999 to 2001, the first of the 1997 elected Conservative group to become a front-bencher in the shadow cabinet. She was then granted four other shadow portfolios between 2001 and 2005. David Cameron, however, was elected Opposition leader four years after becoming an MP, showing the disproportionate nature of male power in the party.

Issue Fault Lines within the Conservative Party and Affiliational Criteria. In addition to the issue of whether a member or MP was a "hard" (complete) or "soft" Euroskeptic, dividing issues have been along the lines of social versus economic conservatism, as well as, under Brexit, whether one's business interests lay within the EU or elsewhere. These lines overlay the issue of feminism in the party, with May viewing herself as a Conservative feminist (Bryson and Heppell 2010, 31–32, 45). As Bryson and Heppell have discussed, social conservatives tend to support hierarchy in the household, with women playing a traditional role. Economic and "modernizing" feminists in the Conservative Party can agree with liberal feminism that women should have the doors of all careers open to them, including the public sector. Conservatives have typically not supported state intervention, which was more the province of the Labour Party until 1997 and Tony Blair's and Gordon Brown's premierships. On the other hand, some "one nation Tories" such as Iain Duncan Smith and Theresa May support more state support for the disadvantaged than economic Conservatives of the right. As in the US Republican Party, libertarian economic conservatives tend to be mainly concerned about maintaining business confidence and keeping national deficits low. Social conservatives are less concerned with deficits but will often claim to be worried about "taxing and spending" by progressive parties. Phyllis Schlafly was a figure who, although keenly interested in getting elected to Congress herself, having run more than once, also was a premier organizer such that future president Ronald Reagan tapped her mailing lists (but not her) to help him win and hold office. Schlafly organized legions of followers from the Goldwater anti-communist movement through social conservative issues in the 1980s such as being opposed to abortion and the ERA. Schlafly could never really gain the ear of the "big male" players, having been ignored by both Goldwater and Reagan.

For those concerned with women's equality in the UK Conservative

Party, they would state that equality can be pursued without having to fundamentally change the workings of capitalism, perhaps just tinkering around the edges, such as in the case of childcare. Feminists in the Conservative Party can also square their beliefs that children up to a certain age are best cared for in the home, as can some liberal feminists. Theresa May identified herself as a Conservative feminist in the early 2000s, as part of the modernizing group that was mainly socially liberal.

Groups within the Conservative Party have been divided for decades along various spectra, including many intermediate positions on being "in or out" of the EU: economic conservatism (laissez-faire or libertarian), socially conservative, or more progressive. In terms of positioning progressivism in the Conservative Party, it is difficult for feminist Conservatives to be as strongly progressive as their Labour counterparts on issues, since the hierarchical party structure with strong constituency roles in nominations does not reward "outliers." The parliamentary wing also holds much more weight in removing leaders in the Conservative Party than in the Labour Party. The structural and cultural norms of the UK Conservative Party are shared by the US Republican Party, particularly as it has turned rightward on social issues since 1980. As with the Republican Party, issue bases have responded to geographic ones, with tried-and-true Conservative territory in southeast England added to London and its suburbs under David Cameron. The age demographic has favored those over sixty, and while the UK Conservative Party has been termed one of the most successful of its European counterparts in being able to move its position along the different issue spectrums and gain votes, it is also true that by 2000 the rank-and-file members were less than half of what they had previously been, around 250,000 subscribed members. Under economically rightist Conservative prime ministers, the Conservatives have tried to appeal to working-class voters, particularly in northern England, on a theme of aspiration to owning their own council (state-funded) houses and completing education to move to higher strata. As discussed, many of the Brexiteers occupy the more socially conservative end of the morality issue spectrum, so the two groups have become more highly represented among the Conservative intake over the past decades. In the US, the predominant base of the Republican Party in the South has made its voters and representatives more socially conservative.

Following the affiliational criteria of Annesley, Beckwith, and Franceschet (2019) and the framework of Childs and Krook (2009) concerning the constraining and enabling characteristics of legislative contexts, we note that both the US House and the UK House of Commons are highly hierarchical institutions, where power flows downward. The UK Conservative Party is like the US Republican Party where "whom you know" is the primary conduit to power, which fits perfectly with the idea of affiliational criteria. Freeman (1986) has noted that the "whom you know" ethos is counterbalanced by the US Democratic Party, in terms of "whom you represent," where demographic concerns such as those described by Annesley, Beckwith, and Franceschet can have structural power through party caucuses (2019). Neither May nor Pelosi originally had the power of her position, as described by Childs and Krook (2009) but they certainly had the credentials required to attain the position. Women have had to act as "strategic party actors" as described by Wineinger and Nugent (2020). The requirement of strategic acting is important in the UK case with respect to the tripartite issue spectrum that can shift, depending on which leader is in power and whether the government is in a majority, coalition or confidence and supply arrangement, as has happened with all three since 2015. As Childs and Krook noted regarding the constraining factors in legislative institutions, gendering processes can silence women legislators by requiring them to adhere to party positions. Childs and Krook specifically noted this about Labour and "Blair's Babes," but the process is clearly equally applicable to the Conservative Party when there were only specific times when May could be an avowed feminist (2009). As we will also discuss, while intersectionality has had a difficult time in the Labour Party, it has had a worse time being represented descriptively and substantively in the Conservative Party.

In terms of historical changes in the prominence of the three central issue fault lines within the parliamentary Conservative Party, John Major followed Thatcher as Prime Minister in 1992 until 1997. Major was of humble origins and a one-nation Tory, and he promoted further economic engagement with Europe through the passage of the Maastricht Treaty in 1993. In many respects as a Conservative, he was progressive for his time. The party has hewed back and forth between Euroskeptic and "modernizing" leaders. Modernizing leader William Hague followed Major as Opposition leader after the huge Labour win of 1997, but then the party shifted back to the Euroskeptic, right-wing leaders Iain Duncan Smith (2001–3) and Michael Howard (2003–5). After 2005, the leadership was primarily from the "modernizing" wing. The modernizers' positions were laid out in the "Bright Blue Modernisers' Manifesto" of 2014 (Shorthouse, Maltby, and Brenton 2014). As described in the manifesto, the Bright Blue organization was a "pressure group" designed to support social liberalism in the Conservative Party. Duncan Smith described their positions as "pashmina politics" (D'Ancona 2014, 20).

In October 2002 at the annual Conservative Conference, May separated herself from then-leader Duncan Smith with a speech partially crafted by the party's "modernizing Chief Executive, Mark MacGregor" (Bale 2016, 150). As she stated, "Twice (in 1997 and 2001) we went to the country unrepentant, unchanged, just plain unattractive. And twice we got slaughtered. . . . People call us 'the nasty party'" (Bale 2016, 150). While many people thought this was an unchecked tilt toward the modernizing wing of the party, May stayed on in the shadow cabinet of Euroskeptic Thatcherite Michael Howard, who followed Duncan Smith in 2003. May also alluded to the "one nation" theme of Duncan Smith when she described people as "just about managing." As was noted in 2011, "She understands both the right wing of the party and the branding problem Cameron has tried to tackle" (Stratton 2011).

It is unclear where to place Boris Johnson on the modernizing and social issues fault lines within the party. His personal life with multiple children with multiple partners, many of whom were not his wives, suggests he is not a social conservative, but neither does he have a particularly high regard for feminism. He rode the Euroskeptic wave to power and, while not known as a libertarian, was endorsed for leadership by the bankers and corporate leaders affiliated with the ERG. In the opportunistic fashion for which he is known, in 2019 he brought about the largest Conservative seat majority (80) since Thatcher won a 144-seat majority in 1983 by muddying the three fault lines both inside the party and with the voters. Ironically, despite the fact that Theresa May had negotiated more than 90 percent of Brexit before she was turfed out in May 2019 (resigning after Johnson had been chosen in July 2019), Johnson gained voters' trust as the person "best placed to deliver an 'oven-ready' Brexit." As an endorser of male sexual privilege and power, he was not a threat to the predominantly male Conservative Party as May had been. He also had never held party office and was thus not on the record on party reorganization toward the center as May had been.

Regarding the role of women in the party, one potential challenger for leadership in the early 2000s was social conservative MP Ann Widdecombe. She was antiabortion and an Anglican who left the church in favor of Roman Catholicism upon the Anglican Church's vote to ordain women. In their interviews with Conservative activists, Childs, Webb, and Marthaler found that respondents saw Widdecombe, first elected as MP in 1987 under Thatcher, as an example of the "old Conservative party," while others saw May, first elected ten years later, as an example of the "new one." The authors pointed to the ambiguity of party positions on candidates who disrupted the prevailing status quo of electing mostly upper-class white men. Some of the focus groups somehow equated May's election with that of women "who were not up to the job," even though May was elected without any affirmative action program in place (Childs, Webb, and Marthaler 2009, 208).

Intra-Party Politics and Theresa May as Party Chairman, 2002–3: Organizational Partisanship. Starting in 2001, May along with MP Andrew Lansley started on the idea of forming a "Priority List" of at least one hundred candidates for the next election. While May considered herself a modernizer within the party, she could not push the envelope under leader Duncan Smith. Much of her work on changing Conservative nomination practices would have to wait. While Duncan Smith was happy to appoint May for the purposes of descriptive representation, he was not prepared to let her work toward substantive representation of diverse interests. Regarding her work to nominate more women and BAME (Black, Asian, and minority ethnic) candidates, May was brought before the backbench 1922 Committee and told that "there was no way her proposals would see the light of day under Duncan Smith" (Bale 2016, 152). From then on, May had to argue for a more "neutral" proposal favoring a "business-like" set of selection criteria (152). These included the concept of a meritocracy, consistent with Conservative values.

At the same time, there was an uproar over the changes being proposed to the historic constituency-driven nominating contests by May as party chair. In his recollections, published as *The Spicer Diaries* in 2012, Sir Michael Spicer, a prominent Euroskeptic first elected in 1974, recalled how he and John Redwood, another charter Euroskeptic elected under Thatcher in 1987 (and former chair of her policy unit), found the Cameron-May A-list and the "centralization" of nominations under that procedure untenable (496, 503–4). Redwood was among those plotting to remove her as party chair in 2003. May has written that while she was chair of the party, she replaced the old "Parliamentary Selection Board" procedure, which reportedly followed the training procedures used at Sandhurst Military Academy, "with a new assessment process better-suited to transparency and fairness" (cited in Campbell and Childs 2014, 92). Other new candidate selection procedures involved interviews by those seemingly outside the party, such as a Conservative former MP who became a journalist (Ashe et al. 2010, 464). Also, the traditional "big speech" was replaced with a "question and answer" session for candidates, and a "selection" DVD was prepared for viewing by local constituency associations.

Most importantly, in Ashe et al.'s view, was changing the "selectorate" for candidates, to move away from the traditional party activists at the constituency level who could not update their views of what made a favorable candidate and include the general public (in intraparty primaries), the local party's executive committee, or "ordinary party members" (467–69).

May's intraparty power, while contingent, came considerably from her term as Conservative Party chair for a year. While she did not have the power of Nancy Pelosi to direct or withhold funds to specific candidates, her status as the first woman at the national party chair rank made her the public scapegoat for changes that Prime Minister Cameron was not always willing to own. It made her a lightning rod for the Euroskeptics and Thatcherite economic conservatives after 2016. Although Iain Duncan Smith had appointed her to the position, he was notorious for "appointing serious women to serious posts, then treating them badly." Another MP stated that "big beasts are men. [Duncan Smith] sees women in a secondary capacity. He wanted Theresa May to be a public face of the party on television but he wouldn't involve her in public policy" (*Sunday Times*, 2003).

According to the UK Conservative Party's website, the party chair is the highest-ranking member of the decision-making body of the party, the board. It is "responsible for all operational matters including fundraising, membership and candidates" and represents the three sections of the party—voluntary, political and professional" (Conservative Party 2021). The executive of the party exists as an administrative post to help the leadership and is appointed by the party's leaders, including the national board, which May headed as chair. The degree to which party chairs are required to be connected to the business and political communities is shown by the fact that Ben Elliot, the nephew of Camilla, then-Duchess of Cornwall, was appointed cochair of the party by Prime Minister Johnson in July 2019. Elliot runs a consulting business that has boasted on its website about his high-profile Russian clients and has since drawn opprobrium (Neilan 2022).

In 2003, Duncan Smith unilaterally fired the executive, Mark MacGregor, at which, according to Spicer, May was "much annoyed" (2012, 492). Duncan Smith then hired a replacement from the right wing of the party, Barry Legg. The board, chaired by May, overruled Duncan Smith on the appointment in May 2003 (*Sunday Times* 2003). Spicer noted that on May 18, 2003, the *Daily Mail* published a story about "power-crazed" Theresa May taking over constituency associations. Another member of Duncan Smith's shadow cabinet claimed,

"If she is allowed to succeed, I will not only resign from the Shadow Cabinet but will write you a letter calling for IDS to resign." [Spicer noted that on May 9], he had "had a tiff with May over restructuring of the party. I warn her publicly of major rows ahead if (the) board attacks associations' autonomy. She implies I am wrong and premature to raise the issue." (Spicer 2012, 502–3)

After Duncan Smith defended his unsustainable choice of executive Legg and the long-term employment of Duncan Smith's wife in his office, he was removed as Opposition leader in November 2003. As the *Sunday Times* (2003) noted, "To his allies, he is the victim of plotters, beset by scheming women who have fallen out with him at Conservative Central Office and are now taking unjustified revenge."

In 2005, May worked on a reset of the candidate nominations framework. A potential reason for this is that the Liberal Democrats had targeted her in the May election, and she wished to publicly amplify her "modernizing" credentials. She was part of the Liberal Democrats' failed "decapitation" electoral strategy of 2005. In addition to May, the "hit list" had included Michael Howard, Oliver Letwin, David Cameron, and David Davis (Woolf 2005).

May began working with Anne Jenkin, wife of the Euroskeptic then-party chair Bernard Jenkin, to create "Women2Win." Anne Jenkin was later appointed to the House of Lords. Jenkin was the fundraiser, and May was the parliamentary public face of the campaign. Both sponsored and appeared at training sessions. Prince cites May's former parliamentary staff as saying "there was no doubt that Women2Win and the wider project to modernize the Conservative party was her central priority" (2017, 173). Before the 2015 election, May told aspiring female candidates, "There is always a seat out there with your name on it" (Stamp 2016). May was obviously aware of the mechanics of well-credentialed diversity candidates being either passed over for nomination in Conservative constituencies or nominated in Opposition-held constituencies. MP Caroline Spelman, who followed May as the second female Conservative Party chair in 2007–9 and was, with May, in the shadow cabinets of Opposition Leaders Duncan Smith, Howard, and Cameron, had the difficult record of having run in twenty-seven constituencies before being nominated as the Conservative candidate (Reeves 2020, 211).

The idea of all-women shortlists (AWS) had first been suggested by the Liberal Democratic Party, formed in a merger between the Liberal and Social Democratic Parties in 1988. The Labour Party used the idea in 1997, initiating AWS in half of its winnable constituencies (defined as being within a 6 percent swing in the prior election) (Peake 1997). Labour was successful in vastly increasing its female MP membership in its landslide victory that year, electing 101 women to the Conservatives' 13. The Labour Party's AWS was challenged at a Labour tribunal, and PM Blair decried it as "not ideal at all" (Rentoul, Ward, and Macintyre 1996). The permission for AWS for half the winnable seats was ultimately enshrined into law by both the 2002 Sex Discrimination (Election Candidates) Act and the 2010 Equality Act, with the provisions extended until 2030 (Cutts, Childs, and Fieldhouse 2008).

After David Cameron was elected as Opposition leader in December 2005, he signed onto the Conservative version of the AWS, which was a "half male, half female" priority candidates' list, or the A-list of one hundred members (Reeves 2020, 210–13). Labour MP Rachel Reeves states that Cameron signed onto this plan within a week (213). The Conservative Party constituencies under Cameron "were expected, but not required, to select from the Priority List" (Childs and Webb 2012, 74–77). The diversity project also included an unspecified number of women and men from the BAME groups. Cameron adopted this list in 2005, and, according to Reeves, it was due to the Women2Win group and Theresa May. As Reeves recounted PM May saying in an interview with her, "Women2Win was an attempt to solve a situation in 'which women think they're in competition with other women—whereas men don't think they're in competition, the men all think they're the greatest'" (2020, 212). In 2007, the requirement for local associations to select from the priority list was dropped in Cameron's deference to the grass roots (Ashe et al. 2010, 467). However, Theresa May's work to increase viable women candidates continued.

After 2005, the Women2Win network promoted an "Ask Women to Stand" campaign, "with panel events targeted at talented women featuring MPs, candidates, councillors and party activists along with headhunters to provide support and explain the selection process" (Reeves 2020, 212). Amber Rudd, a George Osborne protege who was appointed by Theresa May as her home secretary in 2016, was elected through the A-list primaries. Andrea Leadsom, who ran against May for the leadership in 2016, was also elected through the A-list. She told Reeves that "it definitely made the difference, because it just gave female candidates the chance to be looked at" (2020, 213.) Many others who were A-list nominees in the 2010 primaries made it into Theresa May's cabinets, including Priti Patel, Esther

McVey, and Karen Bradley. A-lister Margot James was made a parliamentary secretary during May's premiership. Anna Soubry was another woman on the A-list but was not included in May's cabinet.

The 2010 election was the only one in which the A-list was used by the Conservatives, through which nineteen "star" candidates were elected and forty-nine female Conservative MPs overall. Because the practice was grafted onto a framework of historic male entitlement and decentralized candidate selection, one negative consequence was that "competition was created on the ground between 'local' [i.e., constituency-supported] men and A-list women" who were seen to be parachuted in from the central campaign and thus "undeserving" (Childs and Webb 2012, 82). Ashe et al. note the changing framework within UK parties' nominations after the parliamentary expenses scandal of 2009, in which an unusually high number of MPs decided to stand down for reelection (2010, 455–56). This could be compared in some ways with the US congressional "Year of the Woman" in 1992 in which, due in part to a congressional expenses scandal, a record number of white male incumbents retired. As Ashe et al. note, the overall number of female MPs did increase between 2005 and 2010, but only at an increase of 2.5 percent (456). However, the Conservative Party was quite successful in increasing its numbers of women in 2010, more than doubling them to forty-eight. Ashe et al. conclude that it is difficult to give one policy single causal credit for increasing the number of women MPs in the Conservative Party. On the one hand, they note that priority list women Conservatives were equally successful at getting selected for winnable seats and getting elected to Parliament. They caution that "without data on the timing of these individual selections we cannot be sure how candidates' 'A list' status intersected with the various other reforms of the selection process, adopted by the party between 2005–2010" (467–69). Also relevant is the fact that starting in 2010 and continuing after the 2015 UK general elections, in which the latter saw Conservative Europhile MPs stand down, the percentage of Euroskeptic MPs among white and BAME women and men has increased in the party.

Did the Nominations Changes Fundamentally Change the Conservative Party? To this question, the answer would have to be "no," but the work of May and others provided a lightning rod to galvanize the older Thatcherites such as Spicer, Redwood, and Duncan Smith as well as their newer counterparts elected in the twenty-first century. On the one hand, entitled white men were not completely shut out, as the example of MP Gavin Barwell shows. Barwell became PM May's chief of staff after the 2017 election and was on the 2010 A-list not because of his descriptively representative credentials but because he was a former aide to the extremely wealthy and powerful Conservative Party treasurer (1998–2001), deputy chair (2005–10), and mega-donor Lord Michael Ashcroft. Ashcroft was in the House of Lords from 2000 to 2010. Barwell had also served as a Conservative Research Department member and consultant as well as a special adviser to the Cameron shadow cabinet position of secretary of state for the environment and was considerably involved in the 2010 election campaign.

Barwell's connection to Lord Ashcroft was important, as Ashcroft had been termed the financial "savior" of the Conservative Party since the 1997 Labour landslide. He contributed millions of pounds to the party, with a hiatus after the 2010 election (until 2017) since he fell out with PM David Cameron over Cameron's "liberal conservatism" (aka "modernizer" credentials). Ashcroft set up a fund to target thirty-three marginal seats in the 2005 UK election and was "involved in a private consortium funding 93 constituency campaigns" (Siddique 2010). The Target Seats and Marginal Seats Fighting Fund, as it was called, gave money in the preelection writ period "when it could not be limited or regulated by electoral law" (Bale 2016, 318). The "Ashcroft marginals" strategy was to elect MPs in 2005 or weaken potential opponents in marginal seats so that Conservatives could win them in 2010 (Stratton 2010; Helm, Doward, and Syal 2010).

In 2009, Lord Ashcroft bought a controlling stake in the blog PoliticsHome, the owner of the website ConservativeHome. The latter urged a Leave vote in 2016, since it was set up by pro-Leave researchers. Ashcroft has retained ownership of ConservativeHome. As journalists have noted, Ashcroft's stake in the e-journalism world has enabled him to have a "large megaphone" with which to tout his opinions (Gimson 2013). He has done so against sitting PMs when they did not act as he wished, including PM Cameron in 2012 and PM May in 2019. Ashcroft's issue with Cameron was that the PM worked too closely with the Liberal Democrats in coalition, for Ashcroft's basic wish was to keep the Conservative Party "true to its principles." He was against Cameron's pro-gay marriage policy and attempts to reform the EU and, as a Thatcherite, favored lower taxes, which the coalition government did not deliver.

Other women who were connected to Cameron found themselves on the A-list, with mixed consequences. On the negative side, lawyer Joanne Cash was an A-lister who ran in 2010 against the Conservative local association chair Amanda Sayers. The seat was a plum one since it was Westminster North and was held by a slim three thousand Labour vote majority (Kite 2010). Cash was accused of spending more of her time on the "social action projects favored by Cameron's right-hand man, Steve Hilton" than on the grueling door knocking of retail politics. She earned the designation "fluffy bunny candidate" (Kite 2010). The fight between the constituency chair and the candidate became a proxy war between the party chair, Eric Pickles, who agreed with Cash, and the party leader in the House of Lords and president of the local party association, Lord Strathclyde. First MP Pickles agreed with Cash that the chair, Amanda Sayers, should leave. However, Sayers enlisted Lord Strathclyde's help and then was reinstated. In response, Cash abandoned her candidacy but was almost immediately reenrolled as the constituency candidate after enlisting the help of Conservative headquarters and the PM (Kite 2010). Cash did not go on to win the seat from Labour in the election.

Another Cameron-inspired move to highlight diversity among Conservatives lay in his appointment of the youngest-ever member of the House of Lords and the first Muslim to a shadow cabinet position in 2007, Sayeedi Warsi, a criminal defense lawyer who had tried to win a House seat in 2003. The newly created position was shadow minister for community cohesion and social action (Saner 2016). Warsi, who cochaired the Conservative Party from 2010 to 2012, was described as "one of the most controversial and outspoken cabinet ministers" (Saner 2016). Warsi was moved to minister of state for foreign affairs and minister for faith and communities in the Cameron cabinet reshuffle of 2012, but she quit the cabinet in 2014 over the Conservative Party's position on Gaza.

By 2012, the cochair of the Conservative Party, Grant Shapps, announced the end of the A-list program. The party association revolts, stoked by party traditionalists against the A-list candidates, were more than the party leadership was willing to deal with at the time. In 2012, after her replacement by Shapps, Warsi publicly named his protégé, Mark Clarke, as a tyrant. Clarke was named by many Conservative activists as a verbal and physical bully, whose behavior led to the suicide of a young Conservative, Elliott Johnson (Saner 2016). The Conservative Party claimed not to know of Clarke's misdeeds, which was publicly contradicted by Warsi. In 2015, David Cameron authorized the Conservative youth campaign called "Road Trip," which bused young volunteers around the country; Clarke led the program. More rumors emerged of bullying and underage drinking on that tour, and after the death of Elliott Johnson, Shapps resigned as party cochair and as Cameron's international development secretary (BBC 2015a). In addition, Clarke was dismissed from the Conservative Party. In October 2017, Shapps was identified by Conservative Party whips as the lead plotter to unseat May as Prime Minister (Grierson 2017).

The campaign for the 2015 election, unveiled by campaign director Stephen Gilbert in 2012, focused on eighty crucial seats for the fixed-term election, called the "40/40" campaign, where forty marginal seats were to be held and another forty flipped (Howker and Basnett 2017). As Howker and Basnett stated, the plan for the campaign was to be centrally controlled from the Conservative campaign headquarters, and candidates for the seats "would be selected early and full-time campaign managers, heavily-subsidized by CCHQ, would be appointed in every 40/40 seat" (2017). Australian political consultant Lynton Crosby, who helped deliver Boris Johnson's two London mayoral victories, and Jim Messina, chair of President Obama's 2012 reelection campaign (and previous Obama White House deputy chief of staff), were brought into the campaign. Messina was known for his data-savvy operations, which enabled micro-targeting of each desired potential voter (UK Conservatives). As Howker and Basnett noted, "The 2015 Conservative campaign was the most complex in British history . . . with warehouses of telephone pollsters put to work a year ahead of the election to track the views of undecided voters in key marginal seats."

Part of the issue with the 2015 campaign spending was the conflation of two levels of campaign finance that, as in the US, are supposed to be clearly segregated. Constituency associations have low spending limits and are required by law to adhere to them; the idea behind this is that "anyone" can run for office. National party funds are to be used for the national campaign. In the 2015 campaign, which actually began in by-elections in 2014, many, including UKIP leader Nigel Farage, began to note the presence of paid personnel from the central Conservative campaign headquarters, including Stephen Gilbert and campaign specialist Marion Little, as well as many volunteers who were housed long-term at local hotels. One such campaign was in the constituency of Newark in Nottinghamshire to help the local Conservative candidate, Robert Jenrick. Free transportation from various points in London was promised, as was a dinner with former Conservative chair Eric Pickles (Howker and Basnett 2017). The same framework occurred in another 2014 by-election where Conservative MP Douglas Carswell had shifted to UKIP. A return filed by the constituency treasurer did not include the costs for campaigners staying more than three hundred nights at hotels. Volunteers for that campaign were promised free attendance at a dinner with a talk by a "special guest," Theresa May (Howker and Basnett 2017). Such was the anxiety over UKIP by the Conservative Party in the 2014 by-elections and the 2015 campaign that many national figures, including Chancellor George Osborne, Home Secretary Theresa May, Prime Minister David Cameron, and candidate (and former two-term London mayor) Boris Johnson, made local appearances.

In addition to the "Road Trip" campaign, the Conservatives sent out a "battle bus" into many of the constituencies. While candidates were told that the national party was paying for the costs, the expenses of sending national party employees to work on campaigns centered in MPs' districts were ambiguous at best.

One particularly problematic constituency example from 2015 was South Thanet in Kent, where resources were directed to elect the Conservative nominee Craig Mackinlay, who was opposed by UKIP leader Nigel Farage. May's special adviser at the Home Office, Nick Timothy, worked on that constituency-level campaign, against the prescriptions of election law, which said that no national civil service appointee could work in a constituency election campaign (Channel 4 News 2017). Timothy disputed the rules, claiming that special advisors were not covered under civil service rules. May's political secretary, Stephen Parkinson, was also working in that constituency (Howker and Basnett 2017). There was much interest in Timothy's role, given that he became the policy director of Theresa May's Downing Street office when she was elected Prime Minister in July 2016 and a major driving force behind her government's 2017 campaign frame of "One Nation Conservatism" to try to broaden the party's appeal. The Conservative candidate, Craig Mackinlay, who was a chartered accountant, won the South Thanet seat. He played a role in trying to quash the constituency-based inquiry announced after the election (Chakelian 2021).

After the 2015 campaign, in which the Conservatives narrowly won a five-seat majority in the House (330 of 650 seats), the Electoral Commission inquired into the reports of overspending and incorrect uploading of constituency spending to the national level (Syal 2019). The inquiries were based both on constituency-level irregularities and on the national party's wrongful accounting and reporting. Ultimately, the Liberal Democrats were fined the maximum amount of £20,000 for overspending in 2015, while the Conservatives were fined £70,000. Marion Little, the campaign specialist sent to various constituencies, was fined £5,000 for her role in South Thanet and given a nine-month suspended sentence. The judge in the case "accused [national] Conservative party headquarters of 'a culture of convenient self-deception' and 'inadequate supervision'" (Syal 2019; Mason 2016).

An enormous dilemma existed for Theresa May by 2017. Some press reports have suggested that the problems of overspending on the 2015 election were the chief reason she called the election early into her mandate in 2015. By 2015, after a one-year extension on the inquiry, twelve police forces had forwarded files to the Crown Prosecutorial Service (CPS) on a number of MPs, up to twenty (Howker and Basnett, 2017; Mason 2017b). As was confirmed on the date of the April 18, 2017, election call by a source at the CPS, any charges against the MPs would have to be announced by the date of the election on June 8 (Stone 2017b). Ultimately, only MP Craig Mackinlay was charged, and he was found not guilty for overspending while Marion Little, the campaign worker, was. The importance of the election-timing calculation was that while many Conservative MPs later criticized May for the early election, the Conservative majority would have been lost if even five of the charged MPs were forced out of office and by-elections were to occur. Thus, a no-win situation was in place, where May could either wait to see if MPs would be charged and by-elections would occur or call a general election. Also, some of May's senior aides, including Nick Timothy, could have faced fines and prison time. Ultimately, May "threw the dice" and quashed the CPS inquiry by calling the election.

Theresa May had been successful at moving back and forth on the three central fault lines of the Conservative Party since her election as MP in 1997—the modernization of candidate selection procedures, the EU and Brexit, and social conservatism versus the liberal conservatism of the modernizers. This was reflected in the 2016 leadership race. Shortly after ascending to the top of the party as Prime Minister, she was outmaneuvered by Boris Johnson, who was able to combine his positions, particularly as an ardent Brexiteer (a position he never held before the referendum), to open the wedge between the ever-increasing number of Brexiteers in the parliamentary party and those who wished to remain in the EU on a modified basis.

Leadership Selection in the British Conservative Party and Assessment of Expertise and Credentials versus a "Fresh Face." Quinn describes a "revolt" in the British Conservative membership after the party's landslide loss in 1997. The response of the party was to change leadership selection to a two-step contest, in which the membership would be involved at the second step. As before, two MPs would nominate leadership candidates. If three or more candidates were nominated, a series of parliamentary winnowing votes would ensue. This process would continue until only two candidates were left, and then the second round would be opened up to members through a postal ballot (Quinn 2015, 99–102). The postal ballot system was used most recently in 2019 for Boris Johnson.

While it appeared that in 2016 open Euroskeptic and social conservative Andrea Leadsom was going to stay in and force a postal ballot against Theresa May, she seemingly was convinced to drop out at the last minute.

As Quinn discusses, while the party seemed to open up a way for the membership to have a vote, MPs were still firmly in control from start to finish. Part of this, he surmises, is that MPs did not want to have the membership foist an extreme leader on the parliamentary party. He also states that "it was suggested that one purpose behind the new system was to make it difficult for pro-Europeans to become party leaders as they would be unacceptable to the Euroskeptic mass membership" (102). Thus, the game that potential leaders have had to play is to show that they are Euroskeptics to appease the membership and the hard right of the parliamentary bloc while also showing they have the unifying credentials necessary to become leader.

Quinn also refers to the criterion of "divisiveness" in terms of leadership choices, but it seems at times that this refers to issue stances, while at other times it is regarding would-be challengers' openness in touting their potential challenges. Quinn acknowledges that "divisiveness" can be a label applied either to organizational challengers or to those who are seen as outside the mainstream on the party's central issues. It is easier to see how somebody could be cast as "divisive" if they are either a stalking horse or an open contender for leadership, but it is harder to understand the term given that it is operationalized ideologically by Quinn as "when one faction is larger than the other" (2015, 14).

Quinn's description of David Davis, longtime Euroskeptic party chair before May, who quit as her secretary for exiting the EU in July 2018, is an example of the different ways to measure the criterion of "divisiveness." Davis campaigned in the leadership election of 2005 as anti-Cameron, trying to establish himself early on as the chief anti-EU candidate and thus the potential "uniter" of the party (116). He also campaigned in 2001 and 2003, clearly having been interested in the position. Quinn notes that Davis's opponents saw him as divisive and unable to unite the party (128, 163). Clearly, those who have the power in the party (mostly MPs in the British Conservative Party) get to decide who is too "divisive" on issues and out of sync with the party majority.

Stark's Criteria of Acceptability, Electability, and Competence. Annesley, Beckwith, and Franceschet's (2019) experiential criteria seem to fall in between the two criteria of acceptability and competence, first developed by Stark (1999) and discussed by Quinn (2019). Stark's and

Quinn's works are about picking party leaders, but since many come from the ranks of cabinet it is easy to relate the criteria in the Annesley, Beckwith, and Franceschet work to those discussed by Stark and Quinn (1999, 2015). In both the UK and the US Houses, seniority is an important criterion in picking leaders.

Quinn (2019) cited Stark's 1999 criteria of "acceptability," "electability," and "competence," in that order, as reasons for choosing party leaders. As Quinn notes, Stark's is "one of the most frequently-used frameworks for analyzing leadership elections" (2019, 65). In Stark's framework, party leadership contests employ a "hierarchy of party needs," with "unifying the party ("acceptability") as number one, followed by electability (ability to win future elections), and finally governing competence (ability to implement policy). In his 2015 book, Quinn cites Stark's framework regarding potential party leader calculations as follows: "When parties are divided, they select the candidate most acceptable to a broad range of opinion and therefore most likely to unite the party" (159). If parties are not divided, they use either the "electability" criterion or "perceived competence in government" (159). In 2016, both the majority of the Conservative MPs and cabinet were for the Remain option (67, 75). As Quinn notes, "May had long been considered a Eurosceptic and after siding with Remain, she took a backseat role in the referendum, not criticizing colleagues or making controversial claims" (68). Just as she had been fluid between having "one nation" views toward improving the lot of those on the lower end of the economic scale and being in the modernizer camp, which aimed at attracting higher-income voters to the Conservative tent, May had moved slightly along the Brexiteer-Remainer fault line over the years.

Leadership candidates during the short leadership campaign talked about their preferred dates for triggering the Article 50 withdrawal process, with Theresa May and Michael Gove supporting a 2017 date and Andrea Leadsom supporting 2016 (Quinn 2019, 70). While Gove and Leadsom stressed the guarantee that EU citizens living in the UK could remain, May stressed the importance of the rights of UK citizens in the EU post-Brexit. The three were on the same side regarding ending the free movement of labor (70). May had initially entered the leadership contest of 2005, along with David Davis and Liam Fox (who ran in 2016, too). May dropped out early, after the party conference in October (109). Leadsom had also established her "ultra Brexiteer" status in 2016, after having been with Fresh Start since 2011, which had claimed it could live with the EU single market as long as reforms were made. The month before the June 2016 referendum, Leadsom wrote on ConservativeHome that "in 2011, the Fresh Start group shared the presumption that we would remain in the EU" but that by 2016 "there is simply no recognition that the democratic deficit at the heart of the EU is potentially a fatal weakness," urging a "yes" vote for Leave on June 23 (Leadsom 2016).

While George Osborne, Cameron's chancellor, was a Remainer and thus a competitor to May in that issue space, he became tagged by the Brexiteers with the "Project Fear" label during the campaign. That campaign emphasized the likely economic costs of Brexit. There were four chief Leave campaigners: Boris Johnson, Michael Gove, Andrea Leadsom, and Liam Fox, former defense secretary. While Johnson had been considered the main "Leave" candidate for leadership, Michael Gove stabbed him in the back, stating that he did not have leadership qualities, and entered the race himself. Leadsom entered the race against Johnson when he reneged on a promise to give her one of the Great Offices of State in the cabinet if he won (Booth 2016). Also, as Quinn shows, the Remainers preferred May by a wider majority than the Leavers preferred Johnson (Quinn 2019, 70). Johnson (and Fox) quickly lost support, with only Gove and Leadsom left as the main Leave alternatives. By the second ballot, it was down to May versus Leadsom, and Leadsom had been widely panned in the press for having stopped at junior minister status and for exaggerating her financial policy credentials. The majority of MPs, including many Leavers and Cameron's cabinet, gravitated toward May (70). By July 11, 2016, Leadsom dropped out after making an ill-considered public statement, based on her social conservative credentials, comparing the fact that she had children and May did not, which would somehow make her a more "sensitive" leader. As expected, given that the modernizers had strength in the party at that point, the comment redounded on Leadsom. At that point, May became the consensus candidate, ending the necessity of going to the party membership for a second-level vote.

Quinn states that his findings for the 2016 Conservative leadership election contest "modify" Stark's framework in that future electability was considered third, not second, in the selectors' criteria. He also shows that by the referendum's aftermath, May, not Johnson, was seen as "best able to unite the party" (Quinn 2015, 73). Additionally, he shows that during the referendum campaign from February to June 2016, "the most important criterion was who would make the most competent Prime Minister" (73). In February 2016, at the beginning of the referendum campaign, May was tied with Osborne on "who would be able to handle a crisis and take the tough decisions," while those two plus Johnson were about the same on evaluations of "who would make the strongest leader" (78). However, after the referendum, May was the clear leader on competence as well, including "being the leader best able to negotiate Brexit" (78). Nearly all of May's competitors ended up being appointed to her cabinet in 2016 (Leadsom, Fox, and Johnson) with the exception of George Osborne, who was sacked as chancellor, and Michael Gove, who had to wait until after the 2017 election to be appointed secretary of state for environment, food, and rural affairs.

Interparty Issues (May in the Coalition Cabinet) 2010–15 and Intraparty Issues after 2015 (May as a "Cabinet Survivor" in Escobar-Lemmon and Taylor-Robinson's terms). The first postwar coalition government, crafted after the May 6, 2010, election did not return a majority party, was formed of the Conservatives under David Cameron and the Liberal Democrats under Nick Clegg. This was, in part, because David Cameron did not wish to head a minority government (Bennister and Heffernan 2012, 781). Heppell noted that the choices after the 2010 election were a Labour–Liberal Democratic minority government, a Conservative minority government, and a coalition with the Conservatives (who had won 306 seats); the Liberal Democrats had won 57 seats. As he stated, "The new government was going to implement economic reforms," given the 2008 global financial crash and specifically the Eurozone problems. Heppell found that Cameron's choice to go with the coalition gave him the time to implement a "long-term economic agenda" (2015, 4). On the other hand, according to Heppell, the preference of many parliamentary Conservatives was to go with the minority Conservative government option (6).

Scholars have noted that Cameron, representing the party with the most votes, took control of framing the coalition, particularly since the Liberal Democrats had no governing experience. The Liberal Democrats emerged with five cabinet seats but only three secretary of state positions, which are the most senior positions in the British cabinet with the automatic right to attend cabinet meetings. Ministers and parliamentary secretaries may or may not be invited to attend cabinet meetings. Bennister and Heffernan note that the allocation of portfolios was not part of the formal coalition agreement but rather negotiated directly between Clegg and Cameron. The Liberal Democrats ended up with the three department heads of business, energy, and climate change and the Scottish Office (2012, 781). The other cabinet-level positions were chief secretary to the treasury and deputy Prime Minister, which under the coalition agreement gave Clegg an independent base of power, one that could not be altered by

Cameron (McEnhill 2015, 102; Bennister and Heffernan 2012, 780). All of the Liberal Democratic positions were awarded to white men. The Liberal Democrats received 22 percent of ministerial posts compared to 16 percent of parliamentary seats (McEnhill 2015, 102). The Liberal Democrats' strategy was to aim for breadth over depth in portfolio allocation, yielding Conservative control over the "big spending departments" and twenty-four ministerial posts across departments. The Liberal Democrats had to rely on junior ministers to be "their voice in most departments" (Bennister and Heffernan 2012, 781). Heppell states that the five Liberal Democrat cabinet posts were "either peripheral or advantageous to the Conservatives" (2015, 6).

The Conservatives' "'red lines'—on deficit reduction, defense, immigration and Europe—were protected" (Heppell 2015, 5). In related fashion, "any perceived gains that the Liberal Democrats had secured on social policy terms were nullified . . . [because] the need to reduce the deficit would be the overall framework applied by the Cameron Conservatives (5). The coalition status in effect meant that the Liberal Democrats would not be able to implement their free university tuition electoral pledges of 2005 and 2010 (which Labour leader Jeremy Corbyn would steal in 2017 and 2019). In terms of the representation of the Liberal Democrats as secretary of the treasury, Heppell notes its utility in spreading the blame for the coalition's austerity policy. Indeed, previous Liberal Democratic pledges were scuppered, including those where secretaries promoted and the government passed proposals to raise university tuition fees and increase nuclear power stations (6). According to Heppell, the Conservatives' goal was to work on the economic questions to put themselves in a better position for 2015, letting the Liberal Democrats work on political questions such as the proposed Alternative Vote. On the other side, the Liberal Democrats tried to avoid being tarred by the austerity label that the coalition manifesto would inevitably bring and that would ultimately hurt them in 2015. The austerity issue was handled mainly by the all-male "Quad," consisting of PM Cameron, Deputy PM Clegg, Chancellor Osborne, and Chief Secretary to the Treasury Danny Alexander. As Montgomerie wrote, "The Quad's power helps explain why this government feels as if it's run as much by the Liberal Democrats as the Conservatives. . . . The Cabinet doesn't matter" since the Liberal Democrats had half the representation in the "Coalition's sovereign chamber" (2012).

Minister for Equalities, 2010–12. In the UK, as in Canada, the minister for equalities position has not traditionally been appointed as a stand-alone cabinet-level position. May occupied the equalities ministership position in combination with her secretary of state for home affairs (home secretary) portfolio. Liberal Democrat MP Lynne Featherstone became parliamentary undersecretary of state for equalities and minister in the Home Office and parliamentary undersecretary of state for criminal information and equalitie. Featherstone served as May's parliamentary secretary during this period., until the Cabinet was shuffled in 2012. May had specifically requested that Featherstone work with her on the issue of violence against women and girls overseas, a role Featherstone retained until the 2015 election (Featherstone 2016, 5). In 2012, Maria Miller, secretary of state for culture, media, and sport, was given the minister for women and equalities portfolio, with Liberal Democrat MP Jo Swinson and Conservative MP Helen Grant as parliamentary undersecretaries of state for equalities. From 2014 to 2016, the minister for women and equalities post was held by MP Nicky Morgan, but due to her vote against Cameron's gay marriage legislation in 2013, the "equalities" component was stripped out and given to MP Nick Boles to administer marriage equality.

Like Bill Clinton and Barack Obama once they were elected president, May acknowledged a change of heart toward supporting LGBT rights more fully (Prince 2017, 224–25; Featherstone 2016, 31–32). Under the pre-Cameron days, especially under socially conservative Catholic leader Iain Duncan Smith, support for LGBT rights was a nonstarter for the opposition frontbench, with a three-line whip imposed on the issue. Featherstone also names Philip Hammond, May's chancellor from 2016 to 2019, as another opponent of LGBT rights (2016, 102–3). On six of seven proposals to come up before the House of Commons from 1998 until 2013, May either voted the Conservative line (against the Labour government) or was absent. The only exception was to vote for civil partnerships legislation in 2004 (Mortimer 2017). Two of the votes, one to allow lesbian and gay couples to adopt in 2002 and the other on the question of repealing Section 28 of the Local Governments Act prohibiting the "promotion of homosexuality" in 2003, passed the Labour government with Conservative opposition. The more progressive Conservative MPs on the LGBT issue before 2015 included Theresa Villiers and George Osborne.

Since leaving the House in 2015, Baroness Featherstone has spoken and written about her work to pass equal marriage legislation, which made it through the House of Commons in February 2013 under the coalition government. Featherstone details how she began working with Liberal Democrats, specifically leader Nick Clegg, on the issue and then started to discuss the potential proposal with Minister of Equalities and Home Secretary Theresa May in 2011. She notes that May's office signed on to the proposal in 2011 and did a "write round" to cabinet colleagues to roundtable the proposed policy. Part of the wording was that "it has become clear that there is a genuine desire on the part of some to move forward to equal civil marriage and equal civil partnerships. The government will work with those with a key interest in this to examine how we might move forward to legislation" (Featherstone 2016, 101–2). Featherstone also describes how former Conservative leader of the Opposition William Hague (1997–2001), a staunch human rights advocate, published a letter supporting the bill in *The Telegraph* with George Osborne and Theresa May on February 5, 2013, the date of its second reading in the House of Commons, stating in part that "attitudes toward gay people have changed. A substantial majority of the public now favor allowing same-sex couples to marry, and support has increased rapidly" (115–16). May also wrote a *Times* editorial in March 2012 supporting gay marriage, stating, with an unusual openness about her history with the Church of England, that the legislation "has nothing to do with telling the Church—or any religious group—what to do" (cited in Prince 2017, 225). There was a strong public push for the bill by the Conservative leadership, including David Cameron, both because he had long been a supporter and because he wanted the Conservatives to be seen as the lead on the legislation. Also, to head off the naysayers, Cameron hosted faith leaders at Number 10 for his Easter speech that year (Featherstone 2016, 128). He also told prominent skeptics in his cabinet such as Philip Hammond and Iain Duncan Smith that the legislation would go ahead. However, local Conservative associations, some Conservative MPs, and a conservative religious coalition were publicly opposed. This came to a head for Conservative associations after the May 2012 local elections, in which the Conservatives suffered large losses (113–15).

On February 5, 2013, the bill, which did not require religious organizations to conduct LGBT marriages, passed with a minority of Conservative support under a free vote. The Conservative vote was 136 against and 126 for, with 35 abstentions. The "yes" majority came from the Liberal Democratic and Labour ranks (124). Ultimately, because he was assured that no faith tradition would have to perform such ceremonies (including the Roman Catholic and Anglican Churches), Iain Duncan Smith voted in favor, while Hammond remained opposed (104).

Strategically, the vote for full marriage equality helped UKIP and ultimately the socially conservative anti-EU wing of the Conservative Party. Featherstone notes that UKIP head Nigel Farage pledged to use an anti–gay marriage theme for the (PR) elections to the European Parliament in

2014. It worked, giving UKIP the highest number of seats from the UK, twenty-four of seventy-three, the first time neither Labour nor the Conservatives had won. While party management within the Conservatives would become more difficult since many anti-EU MPs were also socially conservative, the move toward LGBT marriage could not be contained forever. In 2015 the Republic of Ireland approved it by an enormous majority.

Home Secretary, 2010–16. In 2010, David Cameron and George Osborne decided to promote Theresa May, as the senior woman in the shadow cabinet, to secretary of state for the Home Office. This was due in part to her presence as the most senior female Conservative MP and in part to Cameron's promise to increase the number of women on the Conservative front bench. Seldon and Newell believe Osborne supported her in this highly difficult and broad cabinet portfolio to see her fail and wash out as a potential leadership contender (2020, chap. 2). A positive account of the choice mentions May's "pitch perfect and unflagging performance" during the 2010 campaign as a reason for being chosen for one of the four Great Offices of State (Annesley, Beckwith, and Franceschet 2019, 129). Annesley, Beckwith, and Franceschet note that upon being chosen as home secretary, "May's political credentials were systematically downplayed, trivialized, or disregarded by the press" (221). May's historic ability to move across the fault lines of the Conservative Party was on display in her various cabinet posts in the coalition and Cameron governments.

The home secretary portfolio was made more contentious under the coalition agreement because of the cabinet committee structure; Deputy PM Nick Clegg chaired the Home Affairs Committee, which had a "broad remit covering constitutional, education, health, welfare and immigration issues" (Bennister and Heffernan 2012, 784). The relationship between the more permissive Liberal Democratic policies on immigration and the historic Conservative tough lines on immigration in their election manifestos meant that Home Secretary May would have her mettle tested in working with Deputy PM Clegg. The PM did not have direct involvement in the committee (784). Thus, Home Secretary May was the main decider but also the main lightning rod for opposition. She consistently took a hard line on immigration, which, as will be discussed, put her in direct conflict with other potential leadership contenders, including George Osborne and Michael Gove. Her strong stand on lowering immigration, both unskilled workers from EU countries and education "overstays" from Asian countries, continued to give her the necessary credibility with the party's right wing. While she and Clegg often butted heads, the Home Affairs Committee also included Conservative secretaries of state, including Justice Secretary Kenneth Clarke between 2010 and 2012 (and then Chris Grayling, long-term colleague and friend of both Theresa and Philip May, between 2012 and 2015); Secretary for Education Michael Gove from 2010 to 2015; Andrew Lansley, May's previous colleague on the all-women shortlist issue, who was secretary for health until 2012; and Secretary of State for Work and Pensions Iain Duncan Smith from 2010 to 2015.

Home Secretary May had many early successes in her tenure. She was only the second female home secretary. The first was Jacqui Smith under the Labour government of Gordon Brown, serving from 2007 to 2009. May was the longest-serving home secretary in sixty years, just a few months shy of the six years and six months served by James Ede from 1945 to 1951. Minister May's third year in her portfolio (from spring 2012 onward) gained her even more praise from the media and others, "having earned a reputation as a 'safe pair of hands'" (Prince 2017, 251). Long-term Conservative members agree that she had earned this reputation among the party's MPs and members (personal interview, July 22, 2020). One of her successes in this position was in overseeing the 2012 London Olympics.

Other successes included the passage of "Clare's Law" in 2014, which enabled the police to give those experiencing domestic abuse background information on their abusers, which had previously been denied (Home Office, Government of the UK 2014a). In February 2017, the PM began a consultation on a comprehensive national domestic violence bill, introduced into Parliament in 2018. It was finally enacted into law by the Johnson government in 2021. In addition, Home Secretary May announced funding for a national female genital mutilation (FGM) prevention program, working in partnership with the National Health Service, at the 2014 "Girl Summit" between the national government and UNICEF (Home Office, Government of the UK 2014b). For this policy, she worked with cross-party alliances and Justice Secretary Chris Grayling to introduce civil protection orders and with Education Secretary Michael Gove to commission curricula for schools on forced marriage and FGM. Also included in the package of reforms was a "cross government specialist FGM unit" to train police officers and border services personnel about unearthing the practice. On the downside, some believed that the mandatory reporting by doctors to police could deter girls and women from accessing medical care, especially if they feared deportation (Boffey 2015).

Two big reforms the home secretary undertook were splitting up the UK Border Agency and devolving some functions of the police service to locally elected commissioners. For the first, she took on the previous Labour governments, stating that their creation of the UK Border Agency in 2008 had not functioned as planned, especially on securing borders. When creating the agency, the Labour government had stated that the Home Office's immigration policy implementation "was not fit for purpose" (BBC 2012b). It seems analogous to the creation of the Department of Homeland Security in the US after the 2001 attacks. The Border Agency had combined immigration, taxation, and customs and had worked with the Foreign Office. May split off the Border Force to deal with immigration, stating that immigration checks had become too lax and that the Border Force would "be directly accountable to ministers" (BBC 2012b).

Home Secretary May was on the hawkish end of immigration policy, seeking to reduce net immigration to fewer than 100,000 persons per year. This target was seen as unrealistic by most, since the EU framework required workers' freedom of movement. However, the commitment had been included in the 2010 Conservative manifesto (Prince 2017, 242). May included foreign students in the targeted reduction (Seldon and Newell 2020, chap. 1). The BBC reported that in 2016, the year of the Brexit referendum, immigration from EU and non-EU sources was at 248,000, which was about 84,000 persons lower than the previous year (BBC 2017a). More than two-thirds of the people came from the EU. In her work to fulfill her mandate and that of PM Cameron to reduce immigration, Secretary May had clashes with other members of cabinet, including the deputy PM from 2010 to 2015, Nick Clegg (McKeever 2020, 61).

May also clashed with Chancellor Osborne and Education Secretary Michael Gove on immigration. Osborne wished to entice more wealthy Chinese investors to come to the UK, whereas the Border Agency was heavily scrutinizing the applications (Prince 2017, 241–49, 259). As May's public acknowledgments grew, others around her who aspired to replace David Cameron as PM became uneasy. Chief among them was George Osborne. May survived Cameron's cabinet reshuffle of 2012, a sign that he approved of her performance thus far (292). Michael Gove, who was backing Osborne, "began to view May with suspicion" (279). Another of May's hallmarks that continued when she was PM was her low tolerance for what might be called boys playing the games of politics or playing games for their own sake (249). Gove and May clashed as well, since May would not separate foreign students from the immigration targets, affecting Gove's Education Department.

One former Liberal Democrat cabinet minister in the coalition government, David Laws, noted that May was not "one of the boys" and that there "was a distinct frostiness between the Home Secretary on the one hand and David Cameron, George Osborne, Michael Gove and their inner circle on the other" (Prince 2017, 220, 288). Lynne Featherstone also noted that "men often found her difficult to deal with. . . . They just weren't used to someone who stood their ground the way that she did" (213, 222–23, 229, 255). By 2013, based on her accomplishments as home secretary, one voter poll found May to be the most favorably viewed government member, just behind then-London mayor Boris Johnson (271).

Police Reform. The police service changes were part of the coalition agreement hammered out in 2010, with language stating that the police would be made more accountable through oversight by a directly elected official" (BBC 2016)c. In her address concerning the white paper for the proposed law on police structure reform of August 16, 2011, Home Secretary May referred to the austerity policy following the global 2008 economic crisis as one reason for devolving parts of local police function (Home Office, Government of the UK 2011). In her speech, she addressed the sources of the police force's funding from both national and local funds and responded to the claim that she was cutting 20 percent off the top of the central police force budget. She explained that 80 percent of police costs were for salary and that salaries were to be frozen for the next two years, thus bringing the reductions to about 6 percent in total over four years (Home Office, Government of the UK 2011). In her goal to return many policing decisions to local concerns, Secretary May announced that "the responsibility for policing local communities will be kept local." To that end, she introduced elections in the forty-one police areas in England and Wales for police and crime commissioners (PCCs). Some believed that there was a partisan edge to this, to drive out Labour-appointed police authority and to replace them with Conservatives, elected by the local councils. It is true that more Conservative than Labour PCCs were elected starting in 2012 (Dempsey, Strickland, and Moses, 2016).

The Police Reform and Social Responsibility Act of 2011, shepherded by May, "provided for the most radical transformation and constitutional shake-up in the governance and accountability of the police in England and Wales for almost fifty years" (Bainbridge 2021, 3). Bainbridge explains that the act removed the home secretary from overseeing local police affairs (3). As the BBC noted, the plan was to "give people a say in how they are policed" (2012a). The home secretary could still intervene in cases of national emergency, but otherwise it was a new "hands off" policy on local policing decisions. Similarly, "many of the governance and executive functions that previously fell within the remit of Police Authorities [had] been assumed" by the newly directly elected local PCCs to include "setting the local police force budget and producing a Police and Crime plan that details local policing priorities and strategic objectives" (Bainbridge 2021, 3).

The home secretary's reforms contained in the 2011 act also included setting up a "National Crime Agency, charged with taking on serious and organized crime, economic crime, border policing and child protection" (Home Office, Government of the UK 2011). The locally elected chief constables were also to work with the agency to "make sure that localized policing doesn't come at the expense of regional, national, and international crime-fighting." In her August 2011 speech, the home secretary also noted the expensive patchwork nature of police procurement, "buying the same things in 43 different ways from different suppliers," and the rationalization of buying procedures for the future (Home Office, Government of the UK 2011).

While the coalition government promised to undertake the police reforms, Liberal Democrat leader Nick Clegg rowed back from the reforms at an early opportunity. A child abuse scandal in Rotherham, South Yorkshire, was reported to have happened between 1997 and 2013. Shaun Wright was the head of children's services in that town between 2005 and 2010 and then became elected as a PCC in 2012. After the report was made public, Home Secretary May called for his resignation. Liberal Democrat Nick Clegg made the sweeping pronouncement that the reform his government had supported (elected PCCs) should be scrapped (BBC 2016c).

Clegg was not the only male politician to run away from the significant reforms Home Secretary May brought to the police services of England and Wales. In 2014, the home secretary fought for compulsory changes to the Section 60 powers allowing police officers to stop and search members of the public in a "no suspicion search" without any evidence of a crime being committed (Barrett 2014). The Inspectorate of Constabulary had found that 27 percent of searches were being carried out without reasonable grounds (i.e., under Section 60). Also, the Equality and Human Rights Commission found in 2013 that Black people were between six and twenty-nine times more likely to be stopped than whites (Chakelian 2014). As Chakelian noted, many blamed the disproportionate stop and search history for the 2011 London riots. While the home secretary had pushed hard for the reforms to be made compulsory as early as 2013 (and included in the Throne Speech opening Parliament in 2014), she was blocked by

Prime Minister Cameron, who feared the loss of the "law and order" image of the Conservatives (Barrett 2014; Chakelian 2014).

Home Secretary May referred to the Article 60 practice as an "affront to justice": "I want to make myself absolutely clear: if the numbers do not come down . . . the government will return with primary legislation to make these things happen. . . . Nobody wins when stop and search is misapplied. It is a waste of police time. It is unfair, especially to young, black men" (Chakelian 2014).

As of August 2014, "all 43 police forces in England and Wales had signed up and 24 would implement two key aspects immediately." The immediate changes would be that "an officer of chief superintendent rank" would have to sign off on a Section 60 authorizing search based on the belief that "violence would take place," with a reduced time frame in which to search to fifteen hours (Barrett 2014; Hymas and Swinford 2019). Previously, junior officers could use the "no suspicion" search powers. Under the reforms, officers who carried out a stop and search would henceforth be required to note the outcome as to whether the search resulted in an arrest, caution, or no further action. By November 2014, the changes were mandatory, including "others which allowed community groups to observe stop and search in action" (Barrett 2014). While unfortunately Cameron and Clegg and senior cabinet ministers had backed away from supporting the home secretary in her determination to put forth the promised police reforms, the chief constable of the College of Policing supported her. He stated that "stop and search procedures are necessary to help us tackle crime but it is clear that they are being misused too often" (Barrett 2014).

It is clear that May displayed a great deal of "tenacity on stop and search" (Chakelian 2014). It is fitting, since she faced down many of the worst aspects of the policing profession, including its bloated, top-down nature and overuse of stop and search, to apply an admiring comment by a former colleague that she is "as tough as boots" (personal interview, July 14, 2020). It is hard to imagine a more masculinist institution than policing, and the fact that both leaders of the coalition government shied away from the necessary reforms is testament to her leadership. Men responded that she had "emasculated" police powers in her reform of stop and search came, including a former home secretary regional officer, who lamented "Theresa May's war on the police" (Acheson 2019).

Opting Out of EU Policing Procedures—Surviving Fresh Start's Wrath—in the Short Term. Just as the potential Brexit referendum had been central to David Cameron's ability to remain Conservative leader, with his work subject to various rebellions by members of Fresh Start, the ERG, Conservatives for Britain, and other groups, Theresa May got a foreshadowing of her future when Fresh Start zeroed in on her work relating to EU criminal justice and policing matters. In 2009, in negotiating the Lisbon Treaty, Prime Minister Blair had continued John Major's practices under the Maastricht process by securing potential UK opt-outs with regard to about 140 policing and criminal justice instruments. The national veto was given to all EU members at the time, with a decision end date to stay or remain in 2014. In October 2012, Home Secretary May made a statement in the House of Commons regarding her plans to opt out of most of the EU framework in the justice and policing areas. On this issue, as on so many others in her remit, Home Secretary May clashed with coalition deputy PM Nick Clegg, "who wanted the decision to be based on fighting crime and not for the Tories to burnish their Euroskeptic credentials." Clegg and the Liberal Democrats wished to retain, at a minimum, the European Arrest Warrant (EAW), which had been instrumental in helping to prevent terrorism, and Europol, "which helped uncover the world's largest pedophile network." While May wished to use the second part of Blair's framework, to opt back into selected elements of the EU framework, it was noted that "Clegg was playing hardball" on the issue. The fight between the Conservative home secretary's position and that of the Liberal Democrat deputy PM was portrayed by Liberal Democrat peer Matthew Oakeshott as "throwing toys out of the pram on the European arrest warrant and then try[ing] to put them back in one by one" (Watt 2012).

Deputy PM Nick Clegg and the Liberal Democrats were not the only ones Home Secretary May had to fight, however. Around thirty Conservative members of the various Euroskeptic groups, with Fresh Start the most vocal, took the opposite point of view, that remaining in any European measures was "bowing" to Europe and getting rid of British sovereignty. The one hundred Euroskeptics who sent the letter to *The Telegraph* in October 2012 to "repatriate powers on crime and policing" listed many ways in which they wished the UK to regain its sovereignty in the crime and policing areas. These included "not being subordinated to a pan-European public prosecutor, the European Investigation Order, and the European arrest warrant." As they stated, "We want the UK Supreme Court to have the last word on UK crime and policing, not the European Court of Justice." The group also noted that they preferred "practical co-operation across borders" to "control" (Hope 2012).

As with so much of the anti-EU rhetoric promoted by Fresh Start, the ERG, and Conservatives for Britain, there was much exaggeration and hyperbole in their 2012 letter to *The Telegraph* and their 2013 "Manifesto for Change." A report prepared by the nonpartisan Institute for Government in December 2017 compared the UK's experiences with the European Court of Justice (ECJ) with the other fourteen members that had joined before 2000. In every case, the UK came out either at the mean or more favorably. Regarding the formal procedures by which member states are notified by the ECJ of potential cases against them, the first step is a "letter of formal notice" sent to the country with a period given for reply. As the Institute for Government's study noted, "Between 2003 and 2016, the Commission made 753 decisions to send letters of formal notice to the UK. This put the UK at the mean number of such notices received, at 7th out of 15 states" (Hogarth and Lloyd 2017, 5–15). The authors noted that the UK had been consistently close to the mean every year since 2003. Overall, they pointed out, the numbers of such formal letters sent out by the EU had declined vastly over time, at a rate of nearly 50 percent, "probably reflecting a growing preference at the Commission for cases to be resolved using domestic legal remedies and informal dispute resolution procedures" (7, 10). In more than two-thirds of the instances where they received the formal letters, the UK had already resolved the issue but not transposed the result to the European Commission, "which was typical across the bloc" (10).

The second step in formal adjudication procedures between the ECJ and member states is the "reasoned opinion," undertaken when a "member state fails to explain itself satisfactorily" and the commission sends further detail of the infringement to the member state, setting a completion deadline (Hogarth and Lloyd 2017, 4). The number of cases in this category regarding the UK was far below average, "as the UK devotes considerable resources to resolving disputes informally as soon as it receives a letter of formal notice and even more once it receives a reasoned opinion" (8). The third and final level, where referral to the ECJ is undertaken, was shown to be fairly minimal for the UK, which was at the lowest end of cases in this category, with more cases only than the Scandinavian members (9).

Hogarth and Lloyd's (2017) study for the Institute for Government made several other important points about the UK's relative success rate at the ECJ, something that clearly did not impress the Euroskeptics. When involved at the ECJ, the authors noted, the UK "won" 25 percent of the time between 2003 and 2016, a good record given that typically the ECJ would issue findings against member states. As noted, "This is by far the highest success rate of any member state in our study" (10). While countries do not always present defenses against cases at the ECJ (with the

UK choosing to do so only half the time in the period of study), its win rate among those cases more than doubled to 53 percent (12). Finally, the authors noted that the areas of criminal justice and policing made up a very small portion of the UK's interactions with the ECJ at all three stages of the process (formal notice, reasoned opinion, and court referral). The vast majority of the cases were about the UK's internal market, health and consumers, and the environment (13–14).

In an editorial in *The Telegraph* on November 9, 2014, Home Secretary May summed up her position as "Fight Europe by all means, but not over this Arrest Warrant." She addressed many of the points made by the Euroskeptics in their various manifestos and letters to the editor. She started by noting that she had cut immigration from outside Europe (over which she had control) back to the levels of the 1990s but that the issue of free movement within the EU, one of the EU pillars, remained. As she stated in terms of her notification to the EU of the plan to opt out of about 130 criminal justice and policing matters, "Our guiding principle was and remains that if there is no clear purpose for a European law, there shouldn't be a European law. But where we need to co-operate with other member states to fight crime, prevent terrorism and protect the public, we will do so" (May 2014a). Among the thirty-five measures she planned to opt back into, "in the national interest," were the European Criminal Records Information System, the Financial Intelligence Units, and the Prisoner Transfer Framework.

In addressing the publicly aired grievances of Fresh Start and others on the EAW, May noted that "extradition is always an emotive subject." At first, as introduced by the Blair government in 2002, the EAW allowed extradition of British citizens for "minor and trivial offences" (May 2014a). May noted that she had gotten that law changed to bring in a proportionality standard that had to be met in order to begin extradition proceedings. Under proportionality, only British citizens who were going to be charged and tried in other countries would be extradited. This was different from the previous system, where countries could request extradition and not actually try the people extradited. Another change was to tighten up extradition proceedings, so that if an offense were not illegal in Britain, British citizens could not be extradited for the offense elsewhere. At the time, twenty-two member states could refuse to extradite their citizens for trial in Britain (May 2014a). Since Brexit took effect at the end of 2020, ten member states notified the UK that they would not extradite their nationals to the UK; however, they already had that power to refuse as part of their national laws (Riley-Smith 2021).

On November 10, 2014, the House held its vote on reentering parts of the European Union's criminal justice and policing framework (after the initial opt-out). As Swinford notes, the government chose to bypass a fulsome debate and instrument by including only ten of the measures, not the total package of thirty-five, which the UK government sought to rejoin. The motion presented was a secondary piece of legislation, a statutory instrument, and it also did not include the EAW, despite the coalition government's promise of a parliamentary vote specifically on it. The Labour shadow home secretary, Yvette Cooper, formed an atypical alliance with the Fresh Start rebels and others and tried to get the vote on the EAW pushed until the next day, November 11. The Speaker, John Bercow, castigated both the coalition government and its ministers. On the night of November 10, more members were called back in, and the final vote to pass the secondary legislation, which Home Secretary May said "the government would treat as a vote ([confirming)] the arrest warrant," was held, with the government winning the vote against holding debate on all thirty-five measures the next day. Swinford noted Labour's response that "Theresa May handled the matter 'dreadfully'" (2014). While the parliamentary maneuver won at the time (the UK left the EAW when Brexit was finalized at the end of 2020), it also likely confirmed the skepticism of Fresh Start MPs, among others, about May's commitment to Brexit. On the other hand, given the Institute for Government's analysis and the changes made by Home Secretary May to make the European criminal justice measures less onerous to UK citizens and political institutions, it is clear that no amount of "red meat" thrown to the Euroskeptics would suffice.

Nancy Pelosi

The Early Years. Nancy D'Alesandro Pelosi was born on March 26, 1940, to Thomas D'Alesandro Jr. and Annunciata (Big Nancy) Lombardi D'Alesandro. She was the youngest of seven children, six of whom survived into adulthood, and the only daughter. Pelosi was born into a political family. Her father, Tommy, entered politics at age twenty-five when he was elected to the Maryland State House; he was first elected to the US House of Representatives in 1938. In 1947, when Pelosi was seven years old, her father was elected mayor of Baltimore, a position he held until he was defeated in 1959 (Ball 2020; Peters and Rosenthal 2010).

Pelosi was socialized in the urban, ethnic machine politics of midcentury Baltimore. While her father was mayor, young Nancy worked with her mother to greet visitors, host dignitaries, and help with constituent services. Pelosi's brothers were groomed to enter politics; her oldest brother, Thomas III, was elected mayor of Baltimore in 1967. Pelosi, by her own account, was raised to "be holy" (Ball 2020, 5), not to enter politics. She was educated in Baltimore Catholic primary and high schools and then bucked family tradition by leaving the city to attend Trinity College, an all-women's Catholic institution in nearby Washington, DC. While there, she met her future husband, Paul Pelosi, then a student at Georgetown, and they eventually settled in San Francisco. It was there that Pelosi raised her five children (Ball 2020; Peters and Rosenthal 2010).

Before running for the US House, Pelosi had been a party activist and a public commission member. Yet she had not held elective office at either the local or state level when she was elected to Congress in a special election in 1987. Instead, Pelosi had served as the California Democratic Party chair—arguably with a constituency of millions—and was responsible for bringing the 1984 Democratic National Convention to San Francisco. Nonetheless, her resume did not help her secure election as the Democratic National Committee chair in 1985, where she was called an "airhead" by one detractor and an "overbearing player of feminist politics" by another (Tumulty 2020). Shortly thereafter, Senator George Mitchell (D-ME) named her finance chair for the Democratic Senate Campaign Committee. Her fundraising success helped the Democrats win control of the Senate in 1986 (Meyerson 2004).

As a local political activist and prodigious fundraiser, Pelosi was close to Representative Phil Burton, a Democrat who represented San Francisco, and his wife, Sala Burton. When Phil Burton died suddenly in 1983, Sala Burton was elected to fill his seat that same year. Four years later, while suffering from cancer, Sala Burton asked Pelosi to run for her seat in Congress. By this time, only the youngest of Pelosi's five children, Alexandra, remained at home. Pelosi wanted Alexandra's support before declaring her candidacy. Alexandra's response was, "Mother, get a life" (Ball 2020, 31; C. Pelosi 2019, 31).

Despite Sala Burton's endorsement shortly before her death, Pelosi faced a difficult primary challenge from Harry Britt, a gay activist and former staff member to the assassinated supervisor Harvey Milk (Ball 2020, 33). The campaign was hard fought, and Pelosi was attacked on sexist grounds. As Pelosi's daughter Christine recalls,

> People attacked her for "only being a mom"—one columnist said Nancy couldn't "hold the clipboard" of a supervisor on the issues—as

if stay-at-home moms don't read the paper or help with homework or engage in children's education and learn new things. . . . Another candidate had called her a dilettante for being a party leader, even though as a party leader, she raised the money needed to register one million voters in the 1982 election. . . . She was attacked for having a wealthy husband and a big home by the very people who spent countless hours in our family home. . . . She was attacked for raising money from a national base—although that national base of voters had funded the 1984 Democratic National Convention in San Francisco. . . . She was attacked for receiving "Sala Burton's deathbed endorsement"—a rather ghoulish way to attack the endorsement of a congresswoman endorsing a woman as her successor. (C. Pelosi 2019, 41–42)

Pelosi was elected handily and was sworn in, with her father proudly watching, in June 1987. At this point, she began the slow process of accruing seniority, learning the issues, and carving her areas of influence. Like other House members, Pelosi worked on local issues that carried national significance. One was to preserve the Presidio, a historic site and military base just outside San Francisco. This opportunity helped her build relationships with John Murtha (D-PA), who sat on the House Appropriations Committee, and Senator Frank Murkowski (R-AK), who became an advocate in the Senate (Ball 2020, 53–54).

Pelosi eventually acquired a seat on the powerful Appropriations Committee, serving alongside her friend Murtha. She also served on the House Intelligence Committee and was the lead Democrat on the House Ethics Committee, which investigated then-Speaker Newt Gingrich in 1996, who was eventually censured and fined. Pelosi was most vocal on AIDS and human rights issues, especially with respect to China (Peters and Rosenthal 2010, 39–45).

As Escobar-Lemmon and Taylor-Robinson (2019, 105–7) note, cabinet ministers need to bring assets to the administration. The same can be said for party leaders. Pelosi had a lifetime of experience to build her political skills, defined by Escobar-Lemmon and Taylor-Robinson as political experience and personal connections. Pelosi began to develop her political skills and experience in childhood, learning about the importance of personal relationships and constituency service. Her personal friendships with Phil and Sala Burton led to Sala's encouragement to run for office and her eventual endorsement. As a party volunteer in San Francisco, Pelosi polished her fundraising skills, and as California Democratic Party chair she expanded her personal network and accrued formal leadership and management experience. However, Pelosi's unsuccessful bid for the Democratic National Committee chair also demonstrates how women's credentials are often discounted. As she said in response to the "airhead" insult, "Everywhere I go, they tell me, 'if you were a man this would have been over a long time ago—slam dunk.' . . . I have all the credentials" (Ball 2020, 26).

Escobar-Lemmon and Taylor-Robinson (2016) also discuss how policy expertise is an important resource for cabinet appointees; the same is true in leadership selection. Pelosi gained her policy experience through her work on the Appropriations, Ethics, and Intelligence Committees. The latter would provide the future Speaker with foreign policy credentials that are difficult to accrue in the House of Representatives. This lends Pelosi legitimacy when dealing with administration officials focusing on affairs of state. Similarly, service on the Appropriations Committee, which funds the federal government each fiscal year, provides its members professional acquaintance with the broad scope of federal government programs and personal acquaintance with the bureaucratic officials and the interest groups invested in the various policies. The Ethics Committee experience would also ensure that Pelosi understands the laws, institutional rules, and norms of behavior expected of members, also important knowledge for a future Speaker. Annesley, Beckwith, and Franceschet (2019, 90-107) build on Escobar-Lemmon and Taylor-Robinson's work. They define "ministrable" candidates as those having the "experiential," "affiliational," or "representational" qualities needed in government. These same criteria can also be applied to leadership selection within Congress or political parties. Annesley, Beckwith, and Franceschet's experiential and affiliational qualifications are roughly analogous to Escobar-Lemmon and Taylor-Robinson's political skills and policy expertise resources. Annesley, Beckwith, and Franceschet's representational qualification introduces a new element—diversity, broadly defined—into the mix. Pelosi used representational arguments in her unsuccessful bid for national party chair, emphasizing that she was a Westerner outside the Washington establishment. In her first race for Congress, however, Pelosi depended upon her affiliational credentials, as "a voice that will be heard," as she ran against an openly gay opponent (Ball 2020, 26, 32–33).

Running for the Leadership. The Speaker is the leader of the entire House of Representatives and has power over its general administration and legislation. To use Celis and Lovenduski's (2018) terms, the Speaker has both positional and active power, with both "power to" legislate and "power over" other legislators. Even so, the Speaker is also the leader of the majority party, and the nomination process is an intraparty matter. During the forty years of uninterrupted Democratic control of the US House (1955–95), a leadership ladder evolved in practice: majority whip—majority leader—Speaker, plus an array of deputy whips, caucus chair, and caucus secretary, with committee and subcommittee chairs also supporting these leaders. The majority whips and majority leaders were considered the heirs apparent to the Speaker. As Robert Peabody noted in 1976, "When a vacancy exists in a top leadership position, a clear pattern of succession exists, and the next ranking member in the party leadership is elevated without challenge" (278).

The Democratic leadership in the House of Representatives has historically been male dominated. While Nancy Pelosi is not the first Democratic woman to hold a leadership position in the House, prior to her ascension to the whip position, women were clustered in the lower rungs of the ladder, principally as deputy whip, chief deputy whip, and caucus secretary (Center for American Women in Politics [CAWP] 2020). An apparent glass ceiling existed between these lower rung positions and the top three positions, with no clear path to ascend to the higher positions from the lower ones. When Pelosi entered the 100th Congress, only two women held leadership positions: Mary Rose Oakar (D-OH) was Democratic Caucus secretary and Lynn Martin (R-IL) was Republican Caucus vice chair. No women served as full committee chairs since the 94th Congress (1975–77), a situation that did not change until 1995, when the Republicans won the House majority. Since 2007, the Democrats have consistently elected at least three women as full committee chairs and at least four to party leadership positions (CAWP 2021), suggesting that a "concrete floor" is in place, at least informally.

Leadership Races and Gender Dynamics in the US House. So how did aspiring Democratic leaders step onto the ladder in the first place? Green and Harris (2019) describe both *nascent* and *expressive* ambition to run for leadership posts. Nascent ambition may be intrinsic, a product of a desire to accrue power or to play a role in legislative negotiation that may be more interesting than the tedium of committee work and case work. Nascent ambition may also be nurtured by others who encourage a member to run for a leadership post or by a mentor who nurtures and grooms protégés for future leadership roles. By contrast, members who show *expressive ambition* by running for a leadership post must overcome some strong disincentives:

the time, energy, and money that is required to build a winning coalition; the risk of losing a prized committee position; the power of incumbency (if there is no vacancy); and/or opponents' strength within the caucus (34–41).

Given all these factors, Green and Harris note that certain House members are better suited to enter the leadership ladder than others. One factor is to be elected to the House at a young age, giving one more time to build the resume and relationships necessary to be elected to the leadership. A second is to be from a safe seat. Members representing competitive districts need to spend more time on reelection and have less time to fundraise for fellow caucus members. A third factor is to be appointed to one of the major committees, especially Rules, Appropriations, or Ways and Means, which allows a member an opportunity to make connections and to build a record of achievements (2019, 30–31).

It is worth noting that the Republican Party's leadership history is rather different from that of the Democratic Party. There is less of a career ladder, and the GOP Caucus historically has been far more likely to replace its leaders, especially during its forty-year period in the minority (Connelly and Pitney 1994; Green and Harris 2019; Nelson 1977; Peabody 1976). This instability has been attributed to ongoing frustration with perpetual defeats.

Campaigns for the House leadership are candidate centered, just as campaigns for election to the House itself. Candidates declare their intentions to run, develop a strategy, appoint campaign managers, develop messaging, and solicit votes from among caucus members. Competitive elections usually arise when there is an opening on the leadership ladder. Given the risks of challenging an incumbent, most leadership races occur for an open seat. As Green and Harris (2019) note, unsuccessfully challenging an incumbent leader or an heir apparent could result in, at a minimum, embarrassment and, more seriously, retribution from the victor and her or his allies (36–41).

Candidate Qualifications. Scholars of the House leadership have not defined a set of qualifications for office, akin to Stark's "acceptability, electability, and competence" or the experience in ministerial (or, analogously, committee or subcommittee chair) positions that was so vital to Theresa May's rise. Indeed, the word "qualifications" does not appear in the indices of more than a dozen works on the House leadership (Bond and Fleisher 2000; Connelly and Pitney 1994; Green 2010, 2015; Green and Harris 2019; Jenkins and Stewart 2013; Palazzolo 1992; Pearson 2015; Peters 1990, 1994; Peters and Rosenthal 2010; Polsby 2004; Rae and Campbell 1999; Rohde 1991).

Nonetheless, there is a rich literature that focuses on gendered dynamics in candidate emergence, which can be applied to House leadership contests. First, women candidates discount their qualifications to run for public office, even when they are clearly well qualified to hold office. Thus, when they do run for office, they tend to be more qualified than their male counterparts (Dolan 2014; Lawless 2012; Lawless and Fox 2005, 2010). Women candidates are also more likely to have primary challengers, while being just as likely to be elected as similarly situated men. This also implies that women candidates are more qualified (Lawless and Pearson 2008).

Moreover, women's motivation to enter public life is often driven by issues rather than personal ambition. Thus, women are more likely to run for office at the local level, especially school board, and are less likely to use these positions as stepping stones to higher-level office (Lawless and Fox 2010).

In addition, family responsibilities pose a greater barrier to women's candidacies than men's. Women are more likely to postpone seeking public office until their children are grown (Lawless and Fox 2010). Since they are older when they enter public life, women have less time to move to higher-level offices or to seek leadership position.

Finally, sexism, whether implicit or explicit, plays a role. Sanbonmatsu (2006) found that political party leaders, who are primarily men, recruit from within their personal networks, which are also primarily men, thus leaving women out. Lawless and Fox (2010) concur. The women in their study were less likely to report that they had been recruited to run for office by local political leaders. Their interviewees also note that politics is such a masculine world that they may be reluctant to enter it and to face the sexism inherent there.

Even if they have not focused on the qualifications for office, scholars of the speakership have examined Democratic House members' paths to leadership and concluded that they require a combination of mentorship and ambition. Tony Coehlo (D-CA) and Richard Gephardt are examples (D-MO) of the latter—leaders who made their ambitions explicit and sought to move onto the leadership ladder. By contrast, Sam Rayburn (D-TX), Carl Albert (D-OK), and Thomas P. "Tip" O'Neill (D-MA) are examples of those who are products of mentoring.

Indeed, the successful leadership candidate's characteristics, or "qualifications," are more pedestrian than those found in the parliamentary systems. Green and Harris, for instance, break down their analysis into the "3 Cs . . . candidates, campaigns, and context" (2019, 11). As they describe it:

> Once candidates emerge, their professional relationships are likely to translate into electoral support, and just as in elections more generally, their distinctive characteristics and prior records serve as cues to voters.... Characteristics that are potentially salient to legislator goals include age, seniority, gender, region, electoral cohort, and ideology, while prior records may include specific political positions, votes on salient matters, and past service to lawmakers. (11–12)

Former Speaker Newt Gingrich is a notable exception to the choice of moderate, amiable, and low-key leaders. Indeed, Gingrich's ultimate demise is a cautionary tale to the bombastic. Today we see that, while many leaders occupy the center of the ideological spectrum, some leaders have come from the ideological extremes of their parties, although it is unclear whether this is a product of partisan polarization or a contributor to it (Harris and Nelson 2008).

The only "skill" that appears to be necessary for modern speakers is to communicate effectively in the news media. As Barbara Sinclair notes, "Unlike Speakers of the past, the contemporary Speaker is also expected to play a prominent role in the legislative agenda setting and in national political discourse" (1995, 41).

Nancy Pelosi and Steny Hoyer. How well does Nancy Pelosi's case fit into the scholarly literature on leadership selection in the US and in presidential and parliamentary systems, and where do we see gender dynamics at play? To answer those questions, we can look at the careers of Speaker Pelosi and former Majority Leader Steny Hoyer. The two provide an interesting comparison since they both are Maryland natives who simultaneously worked for Senator Daniel Brewster (D-MD) as young adults. Hoyer was assigned to policy matters, while Pelosi worked as a receptionist (Peters and Rosenthal 2010, 214–15). Moreover, they have both served in Congress for more than three decades; Hoyer was elected in 1981 and Pelosi in 1987, both in special elections.

Hoyer's path to power is a rather conventional one. After attending law school, he was elected to the Maryland State Senate, where he served for fifteen years, gradually working his way into the state senate leadership. After his election to the US House, Hoyer followed a rather standard leadership path, working his way up the leadership ladder: deputy majority whip (1987–89), Democratic Caucus chair (1989–95), Democratic Steering Committee cochair (1995–2000), Democratic whip (2003–7 and 2013–17), and majority leader (2007–11 and 2019–2023). He moved down from the majority leader to the Democratic whip position only when the Republicans won control of the House in 2013 ("Biography of Steny Hoyer" 2020).

Pelosi, by contrast, did not seek an advanced degree but moved across the country and became a wife, mother, and party activist, rising as far as state party chair. Pelosi was forty-seven years old when she was elected to her first position, compared to age twenty-seven for Hoyer, a gender difference that is very typical. This is consistent with Escobar-Lemmon and Taylor-Robinson's finding that male cabinet ministers are more likely to hold graduate degrees than female ones (2016, 85).

However, titles notwithstanding, holding state-level office in California is quite different from holding state-level office in Maryland. In 1980, Hoyer's last year in the Maryland Senate, 4.2 million people resided in Maryland. Thus, the forty-seven members of the Maryland Senate each represented about 89,000 residents. By contrast, in 1980, California was home to 23.7 million people. The forty members of the California State Senate each represented constituencies of nearly 600,000 people, larger than the constituencies represented by each of the forty-five members of the California US House delegation, which was about 592,000 (US Census 1983).

Pelosi meets many of Green and Harris's (2019) preconditions for moving onto the leadership ladder. First, she represents a safe Democratic seat. After her initial election, Pelosi has won reelection handily every two years. Electoral security allowed her to become a chief fundraiser and candidate recruiter for the party (Peters and Rosenthal 2010, 41–42; see also Ball 2020). Second, Pelosi got started on the Democratic leadership ladder after serving on the powerful Appropriations and Intelligence Committees and on the Ethics Committee when it investigated Speaker Newt Gingrich's ethics violations in 1996. Yet, she used these committee assignments to move into the upper ranks of the leadership rather than stepping onto the lower rungs. Pelosi also raised money for the Democratic Congressional Campaign Committee (Peters and Rosenthal 2010, 41–42).

At the same time, Pelosi characterized her approach to her service in a typically female way—by denying any personal ambitions—and, instead, was focused on her issues and constituents. In her own words, "I didn't set out to be Speaker of the House" (N. Pelosi 2008, 1), although she recounts that some colleagues recruited her to run for Speaker as early as 1994 (100). At the same time, others did not see her as a leader, either, as this description by Peters and Rosenthal illustrates:

> Yet in 1998, few would have put her [Pelosi] on any list of future Speakers. She had made it from the kitchen to the House, but she

had not made the more difficult transition from rank-in-file member to party leader. . . .

. . . As her star rose in the Democratic Caucus, Pelosi was sometimes asked about her aspirations. She consistently denied leadership ambitions. Her commitments, she would say, were to her constituents and her issues. In the House, other California members such as George Miller and Vic Fazio stood ahead of her in line for party leadership. (Peters and Rosenthal 2010, 42–43)

In 1997, with Representative Vic Fazio's (D-CA) retirement, Pelosi's California colleagues encouraged her to consider running for a leadership position. In July 1998, Pelosi announced her candidacy for the Democratic whip position. Her announcement was remarkable for several reasons. First, there was no opening. David Bonior (D-MI) and Richard Gephardt were still the Democratic leaders with no expressed intentions to leave. Second, as noted above, Pelosi proposed to skip the lower rungs of the Democratic leadership ladder, such as caucus vice chair and chair, and move directly into a senior leadership position (assuming that the Democrats would capture the majority and hold the speakership). Women had previously held these lower-rung positions, yet they never led to a senior leadership position. Third, the heir apparent was Steny Hoyer, who had dutifully climbed the leadership ladder and had unsuccessfully challenged Whip David Bonior (D-MI) in 1994 (Peters and Rosenthal 2010, 43–45). Finally, in 1998, Pelosi was decidedly more liberal than Hoyer, who was a centrist. To use Harris and Nelson's (2008) terminology, Hoyer was a "middleman" and Pelosi, by contrast, was neither in the middle nor a man.[1]

The noncampaign campaign continued for three more years. Pelosi's expressive ambition intensified after the 2000 election. The Democrats needed only a net gain of seven seats to win the majority. Pelosi promised five from California and asked Democratic (minority) Leader Richard Gephardt (D-MO) to find two more. Pelosi did her part, prodigiously fundraising and traveling nonstop (Ball 2020, 93). In the end, Democrats picked up five Republican seats in California. Elsewhere, the Democrats lost seven and one Democrat became an Independent, for a net loss of three seats. Pelosi was angry and frustrated. "I don't think these boys know how to win," she said to her friend George Miller (Page 2021, 172). Typi-

---

1. Notably, these ideological differences, which were stark in the early 2000s, had disappeared nearly two decades later. In the 115th Congress, under a Republican majority (2017–19), Pelosi's and Hoyer's D-NOMINATE scores were nearly identical (Lewis et al. 2021).

cal of many female politicians, Pelosi was not motivated to accrue power for herself. Rather, it was other directed. She sought a leadership role to ensure the future of the party to enact progressive policies for the nation.

Pelosi's race for the Democratic whip position was going to be an uphill climb. First, she had not been mentored for the leadership ranks. Green and Harris recognize the importance of mentoring in their analysis of the paucity of women, African Americans, and Latinos who have sought leadership positions in the House. As they note:

> Women and minorities have been historically underrepresented in Congress, reducing the number available to run for leadership, but the same factors that shape nascent ambition may have discouraged those already in the House from running. For instance, the mentor-protégé relationships tend to develop among colleagues with similar personal and political backgrounds, putting more junior lawmakers from smaller, nonmajority demographic categories at a disadvantage when the chamber's senior members and leaders are white-male dominated. Minority lawmakers may thus feel discouraged from considering a run for leadership when denied the preferment given to others who fit the mold of past patterns of succession. (2019, 32)

By contrast, Hoyer had been groomed to rise up the leadership ranks. When Pelosi was elected in 1987, Hoyer was already deputy whip. Keep in mind that Pelosi and Hoyer are practically the same age. If Pelosi harbored any nascent ambition for leadership (which she denies) prior to the 2000 election, she was *already* behind in the competition to attract mentors, accrue seniority, and build her leadership resume—challenges that were further complicated by her gender—if she sought a conventional route to the leadership.

There is ample evidence that Pelosi was not mentored for leadership. Her announcement that she was running for whip was met with both skepticism and incredulity. Some Democratic Caucus members reportedly asked, "Who said she could run?" As her daughter Christine recounts in her memoir, Pelosi's reaction was, "'Oh really? I have to have your permission to run? You have really stoked my fire—now I'm definitely running if you think I have to have your permission'" (C. Pelosi 2019, 4–5). Christine then recounts that "party elders" came to Pelosi and asked for "a list" of agenda items supported by women members of Congress that they would pass in exchange for Pelosi's withdrawal (5). The future Speaker refused. Christine also notes that the first time her mother entered the inner Speaker's office was as Speaker (5).

Pelosi may not have had mentors in the House, but she had many friends, or, in Annesley, Beckwith, and Franceschet's (2019) term, "affiliational credentials." One was her relationship with John Murtha. She also built relationships within the California delegation and with Democratic colleagues who met for weekly dinners (Peters and Rosenthal 2010, 41).

In Annesley, Beckwith, and Franceschet's (2019) terms, Pelosi would have gained her experiential credentials through her committee service, like other House members. Because she was not entering the leadership via the traditional ladder, Pelosi used other means to gain her affiliational credentials. As reporter Harold Meyerson wrote:

> Accounts of her girlhood home sound like something out of *The Last Hurrah*—in particular, her father's daily habit of receiving constituents in his living room. Even today, married to wealth (her husband, Paul, is an investor), she is clearly at home in the world of cigar-chomping ward heelers—so at ease that the old bulls of the Democratic Party, including such pragmatic blue-collar Democrats as Pennsylvania's John Murtha, have always felt comfortable with her. (2004)

As Peters and Rosenthal (2010) recount, Pelosi methodically campaigned for the whip position through a series of dinners in which she presented her argument for leadership: a combination of gender, geography, and vision—combined with prodigious fundraising—making, at least in part, a representational case for her candidacy. While she does not appear to have made ideology a part of her argument, Pelosi's left-of-center rather than centrist voting record also may have added to her representational case.

Specifically, Pelosi argued that the time had come for a woman to enter the leadership ranks. In addition, she argued that the Democratic leadership needed representation from the West, the home of innovation and new ideas. Finally, her vision to retake the House was not to compromise with the Republican leadership, which would only help the Republicans retain power, but to craft an alternative agenda to put before the American public. This was, in effect, a call to eschew compromise in favor of partisanship—with the two parties having starkly different visions for the country. Through it all, she raised money for Democratic candidates. She also began to shift away from her "issues and constituents" focus to express a more typically masculine trait—personal ambition. As she told a reporter in 1998, "Think of me in terms of a majority whip or whatever comes after that" (Peters and Rosenthal 2010, 44).

After David Bonior announced his retirement from the House, Pelosi was elected in 2001 as Democratic minority whip against Steny Hoyer. In Green and Harris's (2019) terms, Pelosi had met the "three c's"—she was a candidate; she had the characteristics that a majority of the Democratic Caucus wanted (Western or California roots and female); and the context was favorable, in terms of both service to the party (fundraising) and vision for the party.

In another parallel to Annesley, Beckwith, and Franceschet's (2019) analysis, Pelosi's appointment to the Appropriations Committee is analogous to the Great Offices of State in the British system. Appropriations, Rules, and Ways and Means are the three most powerful and prestigious committees in the House of Representatives. Appointments to these committees are very competitive and highly sought after by members of both parties. In addition, the Intelligence Committee is also a prestigious committee, both for its oversight function and because it is one of the few ways that members of the US House can influence foreign policy.

Pelosi's rise does mirror patterns associated with the rise of female leaders in parliamentary systems. She was elected whip after Republicans retained control of the House, even though her strategy had assumed a Democratic House majority after the 2000 election. Although Pelosi was a well-established House member, she was something of a "fresh face," coming into the leadership through an unconventional path. Finally, the Pelosi-Hoyer race highlighted a schism within the Democratic Party between the moderates and liberals over the future of the caucus that continues to the present day.

Conclusion

Due to women's continued lack of social power in politics, particularly in long-established majoritarian systems, the combination of the Annesley, Beckwith, and Franceschet (2019) criteria of "experience," "affiliation," and "representation" often does not work in their favor. While women and racially diverse candidates may be chosen for a leadership role to demonstrate that a party "gets it" about the need to change its image (and, in fact, those candidates have long-storied credentials), they are not necessarily viewed as deserving of holding that power, and backroom machinations will begin to undermine them almost as soon as the new leader is chosen. The irony is that while representational criteria (new faces) and experience (credentials) line up together to promote these candidates, at the end of the day, for whatever reason, they are not considered "affiliates" of the old boys' club and find their tenures at the top precarious.

With respect to the UK Conservatives, while May has been portrayed as having a modernizing goal for the party since almost the day she joined it, she also had to take a back seat to Opposition Leader Iain Duncan Smith's opposition to social policy reforms while Labour was in power. Not until David Cameron became the modernizing PM in 2010 was it considered acceptable for frontbench members to support same-sex rights. Similarly, as was shown, May's long-term interest in changing the nomination rules of the Conservative Party, which depended so much on party fiefdoms in the local party associations, had to wait until Cameron was elected PM. However, as was discussed, local party associations had a lot of distaste for the "A-list" program and ensured it ended a premature death, in conjunction with Cameron's top-down interventions, which were likely well meant but viewed as corrupt. Many local associations told Cameron after the 2012 local council losses to shelve the gay marriage plan, but he went on ahead with it, along with Theresa May (who had left the equalities portfolio by then and left it to her successor Maria Miller to implement), and Liberal Democrats Nick Clegg and Lynne Featherstone.

As home secretary, May amplified her "traditional" Conservative credentials, namely, on restricting immigration and implementing austerity programs on the police force. Additionally, she did implement gender-based reforms, including domestic violence protections in police procedures and the anti-FGM program. On the other hand, while her work on remaining parts of the EU framework on criminal justice and home affairs made lots of sense to the Conservative moderates, given the need to fight international crime with international tools, it earned her the strong enmity of those who had chosen to die on the hill of the EAW, which would resurface when she was leader.

Escobar-Lemmon and Taylor-Robinson's criteria relating to women's inclusion in and success in presidential cabinets (2015, 2016) are similar to and complemented by those of Annesley, Beckwith, and Franceschet for both presidential and parliamentary cabinets (2019). The former authors identified that while policy expertise and political experience, notably as organizational partisans, which apply to both May and Pelosi, were necessary to being included in cabinets, they did not necessarily guarantee successful survivorship. However, in May's case, the combination of these factors did guarantee her status as both a survivor of "cabinet switching" when the Conservatives were in opposition until 2010 and a long-term survivor of one of the most difficult of the four Great Offices of State, the home secretary portfolio, from 2010 until 2016. Unfortunately, as will be shown in chapter 3, the long-standing divisions in the Conservative Party that were exacerbated before, during, and after the Brexit referendum vote of June 23, 2016, meant that her status as party leader and Prime Minister from July 13, 2016, through July 24, 2019, was never secure. The more difficult status she faced as Prime Minister was based both on personal desires of certain male politicians (Grant Shapps, Jacob Rees-Mogg, Boris Johnson, and Iain Duncan Smith) to get rid of her and on their ability to tap into the growing Euroskepticism of the Conservative MPs after the 2015 election intake. As will be shown in the next chapter, May tried to navigate the tightrope between two polar opposites—the Remainers, who consistently held out hope for another Brexit referendum, and the ERG and other Euroskeptics, who refused to vote for any of May's proposals committing the UK to continued membership in the EU for Northern Ireland, even though that membership continues in 2022.

In terms of the qualities defined by both Annesley, Beckwith, and Franceschet (2019) and Escobar-Lemmon and Taylor-Robinson (2016), Nancy Pelosi was well qualified to move into a leadership position and had a lot of resources to offer the Democratic Caucus. First, Pelosi brought significant policy expertise, not only in the broad sweep of the federal government and foreign affairs but also in the administrative rules and procedures of the House (experiential qualification; policy expertise resources). Second, her personal connections in the House and nationally helped her both get elected in 1987 and fundraise successfully (affiliational qualification; political and support resources). Third, she has extensive political skills, which help to develop national messages, secure legislative bargains, and advance the party's agenda (experiential qualification; political skills). Finally, Pelosi argued that she would enhance the representativeness of the party leadership as both a woman and a Westerner.

However, one should not downplay the unusual and risky move that Pelosi took to challenge Hoyer for the Democratic whip position. Pelosi was not on the leadership ladder, and had she played by the unofficial rules of the caucus, she was not likely to end up on the ladder. Instead, she demonstrated expressive ambition in the most methodical, nonthreatening, and feminine way: by hosting dinners to campaign for an opening that didn't even exist. This might explain her willingness to discount the norm of seniority, as we will see in chapter 4.

THREE

Prime Minister May's Tightrope Walk between Brexiteers and Remainers

This chapter continues to cover the four major substantive subheadings of this book, including the major issues concerning Brexit that Prime Minister May worked on, intra- and interparty contestation in UK elections and in the legislature, and May's ability to appoint sympathetic cabinet secretaries and ministers. The frameworks of Escobar-Lemmon and Taylor-Robinson (2015, 2016) and Annesley, Beckwith, and Franceschet (2019) continue to guide this discussion. In particular, the differences between the ability of Theresa May to be the Home Secretary "cabinet survivor" across the Cameron-Clegg (2010–15) and Cameron (2015–16) governments versus her ability to lead a fractious Conservative Party without a majority for any one Brexit option after 2016 form an important part of the discussion. So, too, do her policy expertise and political credentials in administering the Home Office. As Home Secretary, May's remit included the immigration issue, which had been a key hot button prompting the Brexit referendum outcome. May's history of walking the gendered tightrope in the Conservative Party from her first election in 1997 and of aligning herself at various times with modernizers (electing more diverse MPs), Remainers, and Brexiteers (after 2016) showed her innate understanding of different party groups and how to ascend through the party structure. Her history as a high-profile organizational partisan as party chair in 2002–3, based on the Escobar-Lemmon and Taylor-Robinson concept, had made her suspect in the eyes of many hard-right anti-modernizing Brexiteers and helped sow the seeds of the challenges to her leadership after 2016. Finally, as the Escobar-Lemmon and Taylor-Robinson and Annesley, Beckwith, and Franceschet studies have shown, possessing political experience, policy expertise, and educational credentials—in short, "experiential" criteria—is necessary but not sufficient for either being a "cabinet survivor," as Escobar-Lemmon and Taylor-Robinson show, although the criteria worked in May's case, or getting appointed to cabinet in the first place, as Annesley, Beckwith, and Franceschet discuss (2019, 111). As Annesley, Beckwith, and Franceschet have summed up with regard to Ostrom's 1986 tripartite framework of rules permitting, prescribing, or prohibiting various behaviors by party and legislative leadership, the experiential criteria are prescriptive and need to be there to justify a cabinet minister's selection, although the criteria themselves can be interchangeable and flexible (210). In our case studies, we find that while both Theresa May and Nancy Pelosi were considered the strongest candidates at the time of their selection for executive/legislative leader and legislative leader, respectively, challengers routinely decried the women's levels of expertise while not possessing similar backgrounds themselves. Annesley, Beckwith, and Franceschet (2019) also state that affiliational criteria, including campaign work but not party chairmanship roles, fulfilled by both Pelosi and May are "permissive" in Ostrom's formulation. Finally, they find that representational criteria based on "party identities or territorial or social" backgrounds desired by cabinet selectors, and in our instances the Democratic and Conservative legislative caucuses, are the most prescriptive. Again, signposting the choices of May and Pelosi as the most qualified candidates based on experiential, organizational partisanship, and representational criteria did not make them immune to challenges once they attained the pinnacle of leadership—but it did give selectors a justification for choosing them.

Many in her own party and in the Opposition Labour Party described May's position as weakened after the June 8, 2017, election canceled the Conservatives' bare majority they had gained in 2015. After the election, the previous Conservative majority of 330 went down to 317 (not including Speaker Bercow), and the confidence and supply agreement with the Democratic Unionist Party (DUP) brought the Conservatives up to a bare (+1) majority over the 326 required. Since neither Labour nor the Liberal Democrats would pair up with the Brexit-supporting Conservatives, May could not form a coalition as Cameron could in 2010. The DUP was a difficult partner to work with on many fronts. The position of Prime Minister May and her party's hardening views on Brexit after 2016 will also be discussed with reference to the three central fault lines in the Conservative Party, one of which was the type of economic conservatism supported. Economic positions varied from libertarian at the rightist extreme to laissez-faire in the middle to "one nation" conservatism espousing some state support for those below the poverty line on the economic "left" of the party. The second major fault line was Brexit and which aspects of the EU the UK should leave. The third issue division was that of social conservatism versus social liberalism, with the latter espoused by the "Bright Blue" modernisers and the former found more often among the ERG and Fresh Start, in which Brexiteers were located.

Ultimately, this chapter's discussion concerns the virtually unwinnable situation posed by the 2016 European Union Referendum and the requirement of working with the DUP, the putative "confidence and supply" partners, after the June 2017 election. While the DUP initially claimed it might support a short-term customs agreement with the EU in support of May's early 2018 proposals, it changed its tune drastically after the ERG's saber-rattling in July 2018 over the Chequers proposal.

Cabinet Appointments in 2016

After PM Cameron's resignation and May's confirmation as party leader and PM on July 11, 2016, she announced her new cabinet. In that shuffle, most (nine) of the "Notting Hill" inner circle of "Cameroonians" were dropped. Both Osborne and Gove were excluded. A *Telegraph* story referred to it as the "most brutal cull in British modern political history" (Hughes and Henderson 2016). The number of Brexiteers was changed to seven of the twenty-three cabinet ministers, instead of eight of the twenty-two under Cameron. The number of women increased slightly, to seven (30 percent of the cabinet). While Boris Johnson, a competitor, was made foreign secretary, that department was carved up into a new Department for Exiting the EU headed by David Davis. Kuenssberg had noted previously that Davis was a man "difficult to placate" (BBC.com, July 13, 2016.). According to the BBC, May's cabinet was more diverse on racial and gender equality and gave women more senior roles (2016d). While nearly two-thirds (64 percent) of Cameron's cabinet had been "Oxbridge" educated, this applied to less than half of May's cabinet. Of the women on the 2010 A-list, five of them were in May's 2016 cabinet: Andrea Leadsom, Amber Rudd, Liz Truss, Karen Bradley, and

Priti Patel. Others were added in the post-2017 election reshuffle. Notably excluded from May's cabinets were Nicky Morgan, who had been in Cameron's cabinet, and the Remainer Anna Soubry. May's top aides from the Home Office, who had been nicknamed the "evil Tory Spads," returned to be by her side as PM until June 2017.

Issues before the 2017 Election

To demonstrate that she could be both a "modernizer" and a "one nation Tory," May pledged to be the PM for "those just about managing and those working around the clock" and to work for uniting the Conservative Party post-Brexit (Kuenssberg 2016). May's policy adviser from both the Home Office and Downing Street until after the June 8, 2017, election, Nick Timothy, was a socially conservative, "one nation" Brexiteer Tory in the mold of Iain Duncan Smith. He had a significant influence on the 2017 Conservative election platform.

There are many questions and just as many potential answers as to where the early election call of 2017 came from. Chapter 2 covered the argument that it was called to derail the Crown Prosecutorial Service's inquiry into many MPs for not declaring their over-the-limit constituency spending. Another suggestion is that it was done to give May the maximum time, once Article 50 of the Lisbon Treaty had been invoked, to start the two-year clock to achieve as many parts of the withdrawal process as possible. The poll numbers were certainly in the Conservatives' favor in 2017, with May and the Conservatives far ahead in the polls for months prior to the election call (Tonge, Leston-Bandeira, and Wilks-Heeg 2018a, 1–2; Bale and Webb 2018, 46). However, Tonge, Leston-Bandeira, and Wilks-Heeg also note the ambiguity of some preelection polls in 2017, where Lord Ashcroft's YouGov poll model was predicting a hung Parliament, which few believed (2018a, 2).

The majority of UK elections since World War II have been called before the usual end of the parliamentary mandate; including that of 2017, the number is thirteen of eighteen (Schleiter and Belu 2016, 44). Until the Fixed Term Parliaments Act of 2011, the executive had controlled the ability to decide election dates rather than having to seek a two-thirds majority of MPs. The fixed term was set at five years and only affected the 2015 election. However, the requirement of two-thirds of MPs assenting held in the 2017 and 2019 UK general elections. In March 2022, the Johnson government repealed the act.

Issues in the 2017 Conservative Manifesto

While PM May wished to contest for her own mandate, she also needed to deal with certain promises made by the previous governments, particularly with respect to older voters, the Conservatives' core constituency. The time frame on these policies, and the hits to the public budget, would impact Theresa May's election framework, whether it took place in 2017 or 2020. The first example was the Care Act of 2014, which on the one hand increased the amounts individuals had to put toward their own social care in old age. On the other hand, the act promised a cap on lifetime expenditures at £72,000, but in July 2015, two months after he won reelection, PM Cameron put off the implementation of the cap until April 2020 (Jarrett 2015). April 2020 fell one month before the next fixed general election date. The act made consistent the provisions for social/elderly care across England, not affecting other countries (Snell 2015). The cap's provisions were that, if a family included their home's value in their assets for the means test, the value would be extracted only to the last £72,000. Also, the fees would only be assessed after the client's death. Social care is a devolved policy in the UK, and England had the least generous benefits levels (Schraer 2017). The means tests for social care as implemented in 2010–11 contained the requirement to include one's house in the capital assets test if one were to move to a residential care home. However, there are numerous ways to avoid selling a home if one moves into residential care, such as if a spouse/partner or disabled dependent lives there, and there are various deferred payment schemes available through the local council (National Health Service n.d.). If care were to be provided in one's home, then the home's value would not be included in the assets test (Watt and Varrow 2018).

Cameron's successor would have to address the 2020 start date of the proposed lifetime cap on social care costs. The second action taken by the coalition government to appeal to elderly voters in 2010 was to enshrine the "triple lock" pension guarantee on the basic State Pension and the component of the new State Pension to take place in April 2016. The triple lock said that the affected part of the pension would rise by the largest of the following three components: a flat 2.5 percent increase, the rate of inflation, or average earnings growth (Inman 2017; Curry 2017). The triple lock program was set to expire during the next fixed election year of 2020, but it was still in place after that time. After he won a slim majority in 2015, PM David Cameron undertook a third social policy change with a 2020 sunset time frame. He imposed a five-year freeze on income tax, value-added (or "point-of-sale") tax (VAT), and national insurance costs (Travis 2017).

The 2017 Conservative manifesto stated that both "Corbyn" and "Thatcher" values were to be rejected, no further privatizations were expected and dropped the Cameron commitment to implementing 12 billion pounds of welfare savings. The manifesto also promoted increasing the number of exam-requirement grammar schools, something the Cameron government had refused to do (Travis 2017).

The Conservative platform addressed the contents of the 2014 Care Act, noting that by 2040 the number of those over the age of seventy-five in the UK was expected to double to ten million (Mayhew 2017, 501). The Care Act had also adopted a Reagan-style "new federalism" approach, off-loading the responsibilities of assessing and funding the national "substantial need" standard onto municipal councils (Mayhew 2017, 501). However, in 2015, the Cameron government had also taken the step of waiting to implement a good part of the Care Act until 2020, including the 72,000-pound spending cap placed on the care costs of the eligible elderly. As Mayhew notes, "The cap is not particularly easy to implement because it requires new administrative machinery . . . and the hoped development of insurance products has not happened in practice" (2017, 504). On its first public release on May 17, 2017, the manifesto stated that the lifetime cap on social care costs, which still had not actually been implemented in law, would require home values to be included in means tests for in-home care. At that point, the lifetime cap was purely a hypothetical, due to start in 2020. On the one hand, this was seen as a new, potentially threatening development to the elderly. On the other hand, as has been discussed, the calculation of a person's means to pay for a residential care home had already envisioned the potential for a home's value to be included since the 2014 Care Act. Similarly, there were numerous exceptions made to councils' ability to include the home's value in a means test, including the ability to put off the sale of the home until the occupants had passed on or moved out. The same type of delay for including a home's value for the means test for in-home care was in the manifesto. While the manifesto did not promote an overall cap on costs to be borne by a family for residential care as the as-yet unimplemented portion of the 2014 Care Act promised, the potential inclusion of a home's value as part of the means test for paying for residential care followed what was already in law.

The second social policy change in the 2017 manifesto that caused a great public outcry was that of changing the triple lock on pensions to a double one after 2020. By 2017, it was clear that the value of the part of the State Pension subject to the triple lock was booming far and away more than expected; "between April 2010 and April 2016 the value of the state pension has been increased by 22.2%, compared to growth earnings of 7.6% and growth in prices of 12.3% over the same period." The bottom line was that pensioners saw their incomes rise at "almost double the pace of the average worker" (Emmerson 2017, cited in Inman 2017). The economic analysis of this policy showed increasing intergenerational inequality, since those still working did not see their incomes rise as fast, and losses of billions of pounds of income to the national budget (Dunn 2017; Inman 2017).

On pensions, as originally framed by May's policy adviser Nick Timothy, the proposal was that as of 2020, prices and earnings would be factored into the basic State Pension and the new State Pension, the latter for individuals reaching pensionable age after April 2016. The preexisting flat 2.5 percent component would be removed (Curry 2017; Dunn 2017). Both Labour and Liberal Democrats supported the continuation of the triple lock policy. Since May's administrations, the triple lock still has not been changed by Conservative governments, likely given the importance of older voters to the party.

With respect to Prime Minister Cameron's policy of freezing VAT, income taxes, and national insurance contributions until 2020, the 2017 manifesto committed to keeping the first two and to raising the personal allowance levels for exemptions to income taxes. The manifesto also committed to lowering corporate tax levels from 19 percent to 17 percent after 2020 (Dunn 2017). The other major social policy change was implementing what "David Cameron had never dared to," which was lowering the fuel subsidy for the wealthiest pensioners by up to £300 (Merrick 2017a). A European Commission report showed that the UK was the bloc's leader in subsidizing fossil fuels, mainly through rebates to individual customers (Carrington 2019). This issue was thus another potential red flag.

The Conservatives' poll numbers started dropping after May 17, 2017 (Ross and McTague 2017, 263–80). By May 22, the Conservative campaign had backed off of the anticipated 2020 change from the triple pension lock, removed the provision for potentially allowing local councils to include a home's value in a means test for providing in-home elderly care, and changed the maximum "spend down" limit to a lifetime cap on residential care costs to be borne by individuals (273).

While Ross and McTague effectively ridiculed PM May for stating on May 22 that "nothing has changed," as of that date, she was right. Given that none of the potential changes had yet been implemented, nothing had been changed in law. As Mayhew has noted, the reason the Cameron government abandoned the cap on lifetime costs for social care in a residential care home was due to the expense to the government and the complicated, difficult nature of implementing the cap (Mayhew 2017, 500–507). However, the newspapers had a field day describing "May's U-turn" on social care.

On Brexit, the manifesto stated in rather general fashion that there would be a mostly "hard" Brexit (in terms of the EU common market and customs union). There was also language about the UK staying in the European Convention on Human Rights of 1950 (Travis 2017). Interestingly, May's hard-line stance on immigration while home secretary was not completely consistent with remaining in the Council of Europe's supranational framework. One academic account noted that Brexit actually mattered very little in the campaign (Goes 2018, 68). The manifesto did allude to the demands that the EU had by that point made en bloc to the UK, including the rights of EU nationals in the UK and British nationals in the EU and the continuation of the 1998 Good Friday (Belfast) Agreement, preventing the return of a hard border between the Republic of Ireland and Northern Ireland. The manifesto, yielding to Brexit opinion and following previous Conservative manifestos, also mentioned immigration control.

Ross and McTague's (2017) narrative of the campaign is that Corbyn was an unexpectedly strong campaigner against May. Ironically, an issue used against May was related to her previous home secretary portfolio from 2010 to 2016, when both Opposition Leader Jeremy Corbyn and former Cameron policy adviser Steve Hilton attacked her for cutting police budgets from 2010 to 2015. On March 22 and May 22, 2017, two high-profile terrorist attacks occurred, on Westminster Bridge and in Manchester, respectively, with loss of life. A third attack took place on June 3, 2017, just before the election. Hilton and Corbyn spoke in the media about the need for May to "resign" on June 5, 2017 (three days before the election), because she had supposedly not kept the UK secure enough while home secretary. To anybody with a careful review of her record, this was an opportunistic attack (Watts 2017). While police numbers were cut under the austerity budget of the coalition government, the cuts were stopped after the Cameron government took office (Warrell 2017). Twenty thousand police members were cut from 2010 to 2014. However, funding for counterterrorism operations was increased in line with inflation (Warrell 2017). The Labour manifesto of May 2017 called for an increase of ten thousand police officers (Syal and Topping 2017). In any event, it is unclear whether more police officers would have stopped the terror attacks of March 22 and May 22, 2017. Under May's watch as home secretary, and later through March 2017, the BBC noted, thirteen planned terrorist attacks in the UK had been thwarted (2017b).

Hypermasculinity was on display in the 2017 campaign, both by former Cameron operatives Hilton and Oliver and by the Labour leadership, especially during the waning days of the campaign. Flinders states that Corbyn grabbed the populist mantle early and heavily massaged his image as an "anti-political cult hero" (2018, 228–30).

Attacks on May from Prime Minister Cameron's former staff claimed that she had not been publicly campaigning for Brexit as strongly as she should have and that she hid her prior Remain credentials in order to become the next leader after Cameron. That argument does not hold up to strong scrutiny since most expected the Remain side to prevail in June 2016. However, the attacks by Cameroonian staff show a distrust of the strongest, most capable female cabinet secretary in the Cameron and Cameron-Clegg governments.

Labour leader Jeremy Corbyn was also given a lot of "wiggle room" in the campaign to be the boyish outsider, despite the fact that he was seven years older than May. Many younger voters liked his claim of being an "outsider" capable of shaking up the practices at Westminster, although he had first been elected as an MP three decades prior (Flinders 2018, 228). Theresa May, the first woman in British history to hold two of the Great Offices of State, was defined by Corbyn as the "establishment insider." His use of the term was ironic, given that May's achievements in this regard were hard-fought and that she was elected to Parliament a decade after Corbyn. The Cameroonian staffer–Labour Party nexus of attacks on Theresa May continued throughout the 2017 campaign.

2017 Voting Blocs. The turnout increased in 2017 over that of 2015, particularly among young voters (Denver 2018, 24). While young voters largely stayed home during the 2016 referendum, they did turn out more in 2017, likely due in part to Corbyn's perceived charisma and in part to the Labour promise of free university tuition, stolen from the Liberal Democrats' 2010 manifesto. They also opposed a "hard Brexit," which was one of May's publicly stated options in 2016 and 2017. In 2014, only 70 percent of twenty- to twenty-four-year-old potential voters were registered versus more than 95 percent of the over-sixty-five group (Harrison 2018, 256). In the 2017 election, the vote direction was one where young voters (ages eighteen to twenty-four) voted 23 percentage points higher than the overall population for Labour—63 percent to 40 percent—and much less for the overall population of the Conservative Party—24 percent to 42 percent (258). Turnout increased for the age group eighteen to twenty-four but declined for the over-sixty-five group (259). However, those over the age of fifty-four increased their votes for the Conservatives in 2017 over 2015, likely due to supporting both Brexit and Theresa May, who had understood the need to appeal to the right wing of the party, over David Cameron, who led the party as an overt modernizer in 2015 (Holder, Barr, and Kommenda 2017).

Denver noted that a higher percentage of 2016 Leave votes in a constituency meant a lowered turnout in 2017; the more Remainers in a constituency, the higher the 2017 turnout (2018, 25–26). This would fit with the Labour Party's campaigning on Remain in 2017. Denver also noted that Conservatives did better in the Leave areas than in Remain (22).

There has also been a long-term inversion between social class, occupation, and educational levels, with Conservatives picking up more working-class votes in 2017 and among their traditional elderly constituency, while losing among women age fifty-five and under, those with graduate degrees, and those with managerial or professional jobs (Denver 2018, 22; Flinders 2018, 226–27). Flinders adds to this that the two "new tribes" of "backwaters and cosmopolitans" have shifted across elections; the cosmopolitans went for Conservatives in 2015 but for Labour in 2017.

Geographically, the cosmopolitan cities are the growing metropoles of southern English cities, while the backwaters are northern areas of postindustrial England and the English seaside towns, where Brexit was strongest (Flinders 2018, 226–27). Flinders also notes the overlay of a "millennial, multi-faceted axis" over the traditional postwar class bifurcation of UK politics. Within the Conservatives, Bale, Webb, and Poletti point to the unifying socially conservative axis on which both strong Brexiteers and weaker Euroskeptics find themselves (2020). Another paradox of the election, as noted by Denver, is that the YouGov polls showed May's approval rating plunging from +17 in April to −5 in early June, while Corbyn's went from −52 to −2. However, "on the eve of the election, the incumbent PM was the preferred person for the post" (2018, 27–28). As is also known, the Conservatives won the highest vote share since 1992, at 42 percent.

In 2017, the DUP increased its seats at Westminster, with the party adding two more MPs, including Emma Little-Pengelly, to its previously eight-male complement. In Scotland, the Scottish National Party lost twenty-one seats, going from fifty-six to thirty-five, and the Conservatives gained seventeen seats. The United Kingdom Independence Party lost its

Westminster representation, likely due to both the referendum in 2016 and May's early strong statements that "Brexit meant Brexit," going down to a vote share of less than 2 percent.

Prime Minister May's 2017 Cabinet Shuffle Appointments

In 2016, May's cabinet contained seven women and seven Leavers versus Cameron's 2015 cabinet of seven women and four Leavers. In 2017, May's cabinet went down to six women after Andrea Leadsom, House leader, was removed, and up to at least nine Brexit supporters after two previous Remainers, Liz Truss and Gavin Williamson, changed their Brexit stances (Crerar 2018b). May balanced Leave cabinet secretaries with Remain ministers just under them and vice versa (Duncan 2021, 7–10). While her model might recall Lincoln's "Team of Rivals," it ultimately became difficult to sustain once the two poles in the parliamentary party, Brexiteers versus Remainers, decided to dig in their heels and prevent any solution from occurring during the Prime Minister's term.

Interparty Alignments and the Confidence and Supply Agreement with the Democratic Unionist Party after 2017

As McTague has noted, "The European Union set the train in motion [on Brexit] even before the results officially had been announced" (2019). Early on the morning after the referendum, EU Council president Donald Tusk sent a five-paragraph memo to the twenty-seven bloc members urging them to speak with one voice in the upcoming negotiations with the UK. "This means settling the divorce first and the future relationship second." The three "red lines" set out by the EU included the amount of money to be paid by the UK to the EU, the status of EU citizens in the UK and vice versa, and, most importantly for Brexit, the upholding of the Good Friday Agreement of 1998 for free movement of people between Northern Ireland and the Republic of Ireland (McTague 2019). While the bent of many was to criticize May for acceding to the will of the EU on the "two step" process (three red lines to be dealt with first, before trade issues) no previous UK PM had succeeded in dislodging a twenty-seven-member united EU once it had come to a common position. Cameron had vetoed the UK's participation in the EU stability pact in December 2011, and twenty-five of the twenty-seven remaining EU members, except the Czech Republic, went on to implement the stability pact aimed at rescuing the euro and the eurozone. Given Cameron's previous veto of an EU accord, it was clear that the position of the EU under Michel Barnier, "who had lobbied hard for the job" after losing the European Commission's presidency to Jean-Claude Juncker in 2014, was to be hard-core (Crisp and Capurro 2021).

Prime Minister May recognized the importance of keeping the supply chain in place between the UK and Ireland. The UK imports much of its food from Ireland and the EU generally, and farm products are the number one component of its manufacturing exports, larger than the aerospace and car industries (F. Lawrence 2017). In related fashion, the ties between the EU and Northern Ireland were important to Northern Ireland's farm industry. The EU's common agricultural policy had the biggest impact on Northern Ireland within the UK. Another potential hit to the Northern Ireland economy was the 2015 agreement within the Stormont Executive to lower the corporate tax to 12.5 percent to make it more competitive with the Irish Republic (de Mars et al. 2018).

Northern Ireland and its relationship with the Republic of Ireland and the UK were to require the most creativity on the part of PM May and her negotiating team. Most parties wanted to see the Good Friday Agreement of 1998 preserved. The agreement in 1998 had reinstated the Stormont Executive, which had been in periodic abeyance for previous decades, and added the power-sharing requirement on the executive to represent both nationalist and unionist votes and parties. Another crucial part of the infrastructure was the creation of the North-South Ministerial Council, representing the two countries on the island. The council covers twelve areas of sectoral cooperation, with half of them implemented separately by each country and half implemented on a joint basis. Separately implemented areas included agriculture, education, environment, health, tourism, and transport. Jointly administered areas included inland waterways, food safety, EU programs such as the National Development Plan in the Republic of Ireland and the Northern Ireland Structural Funds Plan, the North-South Language Body, trade and business development between the two countries, and coastal lights (Sargeant 2020).

The DUP was formed in 1971 by the Reverend Ian Paisley and was strongly against the Irish Republic and forces of Irish nationalism. Paisley led the party from 1971 until 2008, when Peter Robinson was selected as party leader. The Stormont multiparty executive was in place from 2007 onward. Robinson led the party and the Stormont government as head of the majority party until the legislature dissolved itself in September 2015 over the killing of a former IRA member. The nationalist parties

Sinn Fein and the Social Democratic and Labour Party (SDLP) refused to uphold Robinson's request for the legislature to suspend its business while an inquiry was held (Dalby 2015). Robinson resigned as first minister, and all DUP cabinet members resigned along with him, except for Arlene Foster. She thus ran unopposed as the party's next leader. In the May 2016 Northern Ireland elections, with each of eighteen constituencies electing six members of the legislative assembly on a proportional basis, the DUP won thirty-eight seats and Sinn Fein took twenty-eight. Foster became the first minister, and Martin McGuinness of Sinn Fein became the deputy first minister. It is interesting to note that both Arlene Foster as the head of the DUP and Theresa May as the head of the Conservative Party came to power after male leaders had essentially "broken" the parties.

Less than a year after the May 2016 elections, the practice of power sharing at Stormont cracked again in January 2017. The presenting issues this time were the public costs of a renewable energy scheme, implemented by Arlene Foster in 2012 when she was the minister for enterprise, trade, and development; but by 2016 when she was first minister, the costs of the plan remained. Other intractable issues included the proposed official role for the Gaelic language in Northern Ireland and the fact that Stormont had had five votes on same-sex marriage between 2012 and 2015, sponsored through a Sinn Fein–Green partnership. On the question of a unified island government, most Sinn Fein adherents supported it, while the DUP was clearly against it. Restarting the power-sharing agreement and keeping the North-South Ministerial Council in working order under Brexit were key priorities related to the island. The DUP was pro-Brexit, although the majority of Northern Ireland voted to remain in Europe in June 2016 (Paun and Cheung 2017, 7–8). Much of the DUP's caucus at Westminster, especially in the confidence and supply agreement with the Conservatives after June 2017, was pro-Brexit as well and often leaned on the party's chair, Arlene Foster (Emerson 2018).

The political issue space in Northern Ireland by the twenty-first century included two polarized wings (nationalist and unionist) with opposition parties in the middle. This did not reflect the majority of popular sentiment, where polls showed that 40 percent of Northern Irish voters saw themselves as neither unionist nor nationalist (Paun and Cheung 2017, 7). The bulk of party allegiances were between the moderate SDLP, historically affiliated with the UK Labour Party, and the Ulster Unionist Party (UUP), historically affiliated with the UK Conservative Party (Paun and Cheung 2017). The UUP supported the Good Friday Agreement and since 1998 had been locked in a battle with the DUP for the unionist vote in Northern Ireland. By 2007, the harder-line unionist (DUP) and nationalist (Sinn Fein) parties dominated, which made it much harder to pass legislation through the assembly. Paun and Cheung note that party financing changes in 2016, allowing opposition parties to become funded for the first time, had the consequence of cementing the DUP–Sinn Fein polarization, with the more centrist parties moving into an opposition coalition. They also note the reduction in constituency size for elections from 2017 onward, from 6 in each of the 18 constituencies to 5 (108 to 90).

In the Republic of Ireland, Fine Gael, under which Leo Varadkar led the Irish parliament (Oireachtas) from June 2017 to June 2020 as Prime Minister, or Taoiseach, is slightly to the right of Fianna Fail. It has a more pronounced pro-market liberalization stance. Ireland voted to stay in the EU, and Sinn Fein is a pro-EU party.

Social Issues and the DUP

On November 2, 2015, a coalition of nationalist and other parties had voted to legalize gay marriage in Northern Ireland, but they only won by one vote (53–52), and, more importantly, only four of the forty-one unionists supported it. The DUP used the power of a "petition of concern," a mechanism included in the Good Friday Agreement, to block the law. The mechanism had been included to allow parties representing either Protestants or Catholics in Northern Ireland to claim that legislation should not pass due to insufficient community support (McDonald 2015). Many found it ironic that many Catholic members of the legislature were willing to support it but that the fundamentalist Protestants in the DUP were not. Yvonne Galligan has discussed the overwhelmingly male leadership and framing of issues in Sinn Fein, the DUP, and the UUP during "the Troubles" in Northern Ireland. The opportunity structure for female leaders did not open up significantly until after the Good Friday Agreement (Galligan 2020, 10–13, 17).

In Ireland, Sinn Fein was sometimes ambivalent on gay marriage but campaigned for it in the 2015 referendum (Hayes and Nagle 2019, 457–62). It also saw it as a lever against the DUP in Northern Ireland, proposing it numerous times after 2012. In 2017, the Sinn Fein president, Gerry Adams, and the deputy first minister, Martin McGuinness, called on First Minister Arlene Foster (DUP) to step down, but she refused, saying that "if Sinn Fein are playing a game of chicken, in terms of me stepping aside, they are wrong" (McDonald 2017). When Foster would not stand down, McGuinness did, and Sinn Fein refused to nominate a successor and withdrew from the legislature. In the March 2017 elections, a resurgent nationalist vote took away many seats from the DUP, bringing it down to just a one-seat lead over Sinn Fein (twenty-eight seats for the DUP to Sinn Fein's twenty-seven). The unionists would have thirty-eight seats in Stormont, including the UUP's ten. Nationalist-supporting parties, including Sinn Fein and the SDLP, were up to thirty-nine seats after the March 2, 2017, election. Thus, Foster at the head of an imperiled DUP was even more hard-line during the Brexit negotiations, since any softening of the unionist position would be seen to aid Sinn Fein and the drive toward Irish nationalism.

There was a fair amount of work required by PM May and her cabinet from 2017 to 2019 to be able to move the parties in the Stormont power-sharing executive toward resolving their differences. On the one hand, after the March 2017 impasse at Stormont, Northern Ireland secretary James Brokenshire tried to get the two sides to agree to resume power sharing in the executive, with no luck. On the other hand, the Conservatives at Westminster did not want to impose direct rule on Northern Ireland. Ultimately, during the three-year hiatus of the Stormont assembly, Westminster did pass a budget for the country, but civil servants there were the ones administering the financial details.

The Conservatives had stated after the June 2017 election that the DUP "would have no influence over social issues," but it was clear that the relevance of the Stormont impasse and the need to get the DUP on board for Brexit and ultimately the resumption of the executive would involve social issues. To this end, the government accepted in its Queen's Speech on June 21, 2017, a Labour amendment, brought by frequent pro-choice campaigner Labour MP Stella Creasey, to allow Northern Irish women to travel to England to access publicly insured abortion services (Kuenssberg 2017). This action was necessary to avoid defeat on the Queen's Speech, a confidence measure, which was likely given the backbench and opposition support. This policy was an early work-around for the illegality of abortion in Northern Ireland at that time.

The next step in the PM May–First Minister Arlene Foster pas de deux came in February 2018, when the Northern Ireland secretary Karen Bradley worked on negotiating the return of the power-sharing agreement at Stormont. Despite Sinn Fein previously campaigning for same-sex marriage in Northern Ireland and the Republic of Ireland, it did not include the issue in its proposal to restart power sharing (*News Letter* 2018). The negotiations failed particularly over the issue of Scots versus Irish Gaelic speakers in Northern Ireland. At that point, Foster "urged the UK government to start making policy decisions," which some viewed as a call to Westminster to restore direct rule but was intolerable to Sinn Fein (Sayer 2018). Bradley stated after the failed negotiations that PM May's government would likely allow a conscience vote for MPs on the issue of same-sex marriage. On another front, Labour MP Conor McGinn and openly gay Lord Robert Hayward were working separately in their houses to put forth such legislation. The concern of the Conservative government was to find a way to both keep the DUP's proverbial hands clean on same-sex marriage and abortion decriminalization and keep the DUP in its confidence arrangement with the Conservative Party over Brexit. Had the May government acted in heavy-handed fashion on either social issue, it is unlikely the DUP would have gone along with a return to power sharing at Stormont and it would have carried out its threat to topple May's slim governing majority.

As with decriminalizing abortion in Northern Ireland, the same-sex marriage issue had to undergo several delicate steps. Legislation was introduced in both houses in March 2018 yet blocked in later months by Conservative MP Christopher Chope (*Belfast Telegraph* 2018). In November 2018, the Northern Ireland Executive and Exercise of Functions Act was passed, which had sections describing the criminality of abortion and same-sex marriage as human rights violations. It also received royal assent and enabled the Westminster government to issue guidance to civil servants on the incompatibility of the Northern Irish laws with international human rights. The bill was originally designed in more limited format to enable civil servants in Northern Ireland to administer departments, but the amendments were added by Labour MPs Stella Creasy and Peter McGinn and voted in. Bradley opposed the social issues language, as she viewed it as an attempt to achieve through direct rule what the Stormont legislature had not yet approved (Duffy 2018).

In July 2019, Conor McGinn again introduced an amendment to an upcoming Northern Ireland administrative bill, to legalize same-sex marriage three months after passage of the legislation if the Stormont assembly were still suspended. The House of Lords' version, shepherded by Robert Hayward, required the secretary of state to issue regulations extending same-sex marriage to Northern Ireland if the executive power sharing were not restored by October 21, 2019. The rights would take effect on January 13, 2020. Lord Hayward's amendment and the legislation passed in the House of Commons on July 18, receiving royal assent on July 24, 2019.

The same-sex marriage amendment was passed by a 383-member majority. Labour MPs Stella Creasy and Conor McGinn added an amendment on abortion rights to take place if Stormont's power-sharing executive was not operational by October 21, 2019. This amendment passed with a 332-member majority. Theresa May, Karen Bradley, and Boris Johnson abstained, to continue the emphasis that they were not interested in direct rule in this matter (Baynes 2019). Thus, the two social issues of abortion and LGBTQ marriage were taken off the table for the DUP and Sinn Fein as potential obstacles to renewing the power-sharing agreement, leaving the Gaelic language and use of the "petition of concern" issues, which were temporarily resolved by January 2020.

Negotiations with the EU in 2017. With respect to triggering Brexit, the PM had argued through 2016 that she had the prerogative power, enjoyed by the head of government, to trigger the withdrawal from the Treaty on the European Union (TEU) under Article 50. There was no clarity offered through either TEU Article 50 (which was being used for the first time) or the British unwritten constitution (Raitio and Raulus 2017, 29). Since the challenge to the Executive's unilateral action was brought by lawyer Gina Miller, the UK Supreme Court ruled in January 2017 in the *Miller* case that acts of Parliament were needed to trigger Article 50, as this would have impacts on UK domestic law and the rights of UK residents. In response, the May Government submitted two measures to Parliament (32). The first component, triggering Article 50 of the TEU, which started the two-year clock, was put before the House in January 2017 and was implemented on March 29, 2017.

In December 2017, PM May went to Brussels to meet with European Commission president Juncker, having negotiated with the governments of Ireland and Northern Ireland. This trip and the preceding negotiations were part of demonstrating to the EU that the UK had met the EU's red line of "sufficient progress" in internal UK negotiations on the Republic of Ireland–Northern Ireland border so that phase 2 of Brexit could start (McTague, Cooper, and Dickson 2017). While May had reached an agreement with Irish Taoiseach Leo Varadkar that Northern Ireland would remain aligned with Ireland on major regulatory matters, including farming, agriculture, energy, and transport, she had also negotiated with the DUP over the weekend. In exchange, Ireland would drop its requirement for Northern Ireland to remain in the single market and customs union. However, during May's meeting with Juncker on December 4, Arlene Foster made a televised appearance claiming that the DUP had never agreed to any form of regulatory alignment continuing under Brexit and that any divergence from the UK was unacceptable.

Affiliational, Experiential, and Representational Criteria. Until the Brexit negotiations began in earnest in 2017, Theresa May was widely seen as the most competent leader to deliver the results of a 2016 referendum she had not fully supported. May was widely seen in the months just after the June 2016 referendum in Ipsos/MORI polls in September 2016 as a much more capable leader than Labour's Corbyn (68 percent to 24 percent), good in a crisis (52 percent to 18 percent), and of sound judgment (56 percent to 30 percent). Denver notes that "her ratings were consistently and strongly positive while Corbyn stayed in the negative territory." Her predecessor, David Cameron, was "regularly believed to be more 'style than substance' by 40 to 50 percent of respondents, whereas only 25 percent viewed May in this manner" (2018, 12). These results were true across ages, genders, and social groups (Ross and McTeague 2017, 92).

There is no question that in 2016 May was also picked as someone who presented as mostly inoffensive to both the Brexiteer and Remain camps, unlike George Osborne (Remain) and Boris Johnson or Andrea Leadsom (Leave). The goal of the Brexiteers after the 2017 election in both the Westminster DUP and for the hard-core and conditional Euroskeptics in the Conservative Party was to throw many monkey wrenches into her attempts at moving ahead on the Withdrawal Agreement Bill (WAB) contained in the Brexit package so as to enable one of their own to take over and claim the credit for Brexit. May was also the clear winner on the experiential criteria, having served longer in Parliament than most of her challengers in 2016 and those who worked to undermine her after 2016. As previously discussed, she was not given the credit by Brexiteers for her experience. Instead, they tended to treat her as a cutout figurehead, possessed of only descriptive characteristics to make the party seem kinder and gentler. May had been elected thirteen years prior to Andrea Leadsom, her main female challenger, and thus possessed experience in dealing with both the modernizers and the right wing of the party. Unfortunately, the ethos of both the Euroskeptic wing of the Conservatives and the DUP did not validate representational criteria, instead being concerned with the financial bottom line under Brexit. While Prime Minister May tried to contend with the post-Brexit finances in the fairest manner possible given her "whole UK backstop" proposal, it was simply used as an excuse by the ERG-DUP alliance to reject her Brexit deal. The nature of the cross-party alliance became clear in 2018.

Intraparty and Interparty Issues: Getting from Lancaster House in January 2017 to the passage of the Withdrawal Act of June 2018

In her 2017 speech on her "Plan for Britain," PM May noted that the UK would leave the single market but that also she had an "open mind" about future customs arrangements with the EU, with various options on the table, including a "new customs agreement, becoming an associate member of the Customs Union or remain a signatory to some elements of it" (May 2017). These sentences alluded to the various trade arrangements some of the Scandinavian countries and Switzerland had established with the EU over time. May also noted the importance of trade to the UK economy and that "since joining the EU, trade as a percentage of GDP has broadly stagnated in the UK." She noted that she had created the Department of International Trade. Liam Fox, one of "Thatcher's children" elected in 1992 and a confirmed Euroskeptic with ties to the US Republican Party and the Atlas Institute, was appointed as secretary of that department and retained that position throughout May's terms. In a nod to the Brexiteer ultras in her cabinet and caucus, PM May also mentioned that "we want to get out into the wider world, to trade and do business all around the globe" (May 2017). Also, importantly, the January 2017 speech articulated the historic importance of the Common Travel Area between the UK and the Republic of Ireland, predating the UK's accession to the EU, and the need to "deliver a practical solution as soon as we can," since "nobody wants to return to the borders of the past." The Prime Minister also noted something that some of her cabinet members at times forgot: that "this is not a game or a time for opposition for opposition's sake. . . . It is vital that we maintain our discipline . . . [with regard to] every stray word and every hyped-up media report [that make] it harder for us to get the right deal for Britain" (May 2017). In 2017, the joint agreement between the UK and the EU acknowledged the need for a "legally watertight" solution to the border question, not something postponed until future negotiations (Institute for Government 2020b).

Intraparty Issues: Remainers. By early 2018, both wings of the Conservative Party (Remain and Leave) and their relevant interest group supporters outside Parliament were making public statements to try to sway parliamentary votes. Newspaper stories disclosed a meeting held by financier and progressive interest group patron George Soros, who in 1992 had "broken the Bank of England" by betting against the pound before the UK withdrew from the exchange rate mechanism, at his London flat of key members of Best for Britain. The spokesperson for this group was

Gina Miller, who had successfully brought suit against the Conservative government for claiming it had the unilateral authority to withdraw from Article 50 of the Lisbon Treaty in 2016–17. Nick Timothy, former chief of staff and policy adviser to Prime Minister May, also wrote an article about this meeting. Clearly, Remain forces wished to make sure that at the very least a customs union including the UK would be part of the Brexit package (Blanchard 2018; Timothy, McCann, and Newell 2018). If pressed, Remainers would often espouse the need for a second referendum, since the first iteration was poorly worded and gained only a slight majority. It was estimated that by January 2018, Soros had funneled £400 million to the Remain cause represented by the Best for Britain group.

Toward the end of requiring some form of customs union upon Brexit, in April and May 2018, the government lost key votes on Remainer-sponsored amendments, first in the House of Lords and then in the House of Commons, respectively. The House of Lords' amendment to the government's WAB (Withdrawal Agreement Bill) supported remaining in the customs union after Brexit until arrangements that satisfied the EU and the UK were negotiated (Wilkinson and Cullen 2018). At the time, the DUP surprisingly claimed that it supported the Remainers' strategy, with public statements both by leader Arlene Foster and by Nigel Dodds, the DUP Westminster leader, that they would prefer remaining in the customs union involving seamless trade with the rest of the UK, to an "Irish sea border" (Emerson 2018). The DUP spokespersons were also clear on the fact that they primarily wished to leave the EU's customs union (Emerson 2018). The Conservative government reiterated that it had no plans to stay in the customs union after Brexit, since staying in the EU customs union prevented the UK from striking bilateral trade deals outside the EU. What the Remainer amendment's success showed was that there was no discrete majority to be found within the Conservative Party and its confidence and supply partner on Brexit, a point reiterated many times over the following year.

The second set of negotiations was with Dominic Grieve, Remainer former attorney general under David Cameron until he was fired from that position. Grieve's amendment, number 19, was ultimately proposed in the House of Lords by Viscount Hailsham. The first part of the amendment required a parliamentary vote to approve the Withdrawal Agreement and any "transitional measures," if possible, before the European Parliament debated and voted on these issues (Institute for Government 2020a). The goal was to ensure Parliament would have a vote if either the House had rejected the Withdrawal Agreement or if no agreement had been reached with the EU by November 30, 2018 (Perkins 2018). The amendment would avert a "no deal" scenario by which the UK would move to World Trade Organization (WTO) terms with Europe. It required a vote by Parliament on the next steps.

The compromise the government reached with the backbench on this question was language stating that if Parliament did not approve the bill, a minister would make a statement setting out the framework for "how the government would propose to proceed" within twenty-eight days. It also stated that the House of Commons would be able to vote on a motion framed "in neutral terms" to consider the ministerial statement and again if no deal had been reached with the EU by January 21, 2019. As an Institute for Government explainer pointed out, "the big debate" was whether the "neutrally framed" motion would be amendable since normally they are not. As the explainer states, the government essentially pushed the issue to the House Speaker, "confirming it is the role of the Speaker to determine whether it is or not" (Institute for Government 2020a).

The third consequential amendment in 2018 for the future proceedings, number 25, was submitted by Conservative Lord Patten, who had chaired the 1998–99 Commission on Independent Policing in Northern Ireland. The government responded with an "amendment in lieu," accepted by both Houses as amendments 1, 2, and 19 had been. The government's language stated that instead of referring to specific areas of North-South cooperation, it would use the language in the Good Friday (Belfast) Agreement of 1998. Importantly, the government's proposed and accepted language stated that any new border arrangements would have to be negotiated between the EU and the UK and could only pertain to "physical infrastructure including border posts or checks and controls."

These amendments were included in the Withdrawal Act Bill enacted in June 2018. By then, Brexiteers in the Conservative Party were busily plotting their next move.

Intraparty and Interparty Issues: Brexiteer Alliances. The next major iteration in the Brexit withdrawal agreement formulation took place over the weekend of July 6–7, 2018, between the PM and her cabinet at the PM's country residence, Chequers. As with the Lancaster House speech, the Chequers draft framework contained twelve points, most of which either had been already dealt with in the Withdrawal Act, had passed the previous month, or had been agreed on in negotiations with the EU. One element was aimed at appealing to the group of Euroskeptics in Fresh Start who had signed the 2012 letter to *The Telegraph* against the EU's Criminal Justice and Policing Framework, including the European Arrest Warrant

(EAW). Language in the Chequers agreement promised "restoring the supremacy of British courts by ending the jurisdiction of the ECJ in the UK." This language was a bit of "fudging" toward Euroskeptics since the UK retains some trading agreements with EU countries, and law that was made under the EU framework pre-Brexit continues to be applicable, and the ECJ will be able to hear challenges in these areas (Library of Parliament 2017).

Later in July 2018, the government (under the name of Secretary for Exiting the EU David Davis) was about to release its white paper on Brexit to Parliament for a vote that month on how to keep the basics of the Good Friday Agreement in operation. It would include some alignment by Northern Ireland with Ireland and the EU in terms of customs checks and trade so as not to reinstate hard borders yet move forward with exiting the EU as much as possible. Also, importantly, in July 2018 the EU had not yet moved on its stance about how to deal with the Good Friday Agreement in terms of the required "backstop" of keeping Northern Ireland aligned with EU protocols on the single market and customs until a new free trade agreement or deal between the EU and the UK emerged (Herszenhorn and Barigazzi 2018).

The Chequers language that was roundtabled to the cabinet reiterated the Withdrawal Act regarding future customs arrangements with the EU as needing to be voted on by the House, in response to a ministerial statement on the matter by October 2018. The included language stated that the UK would "commit the UK to 'continued harmonisation' with EU rules" on all goods, including agriculture but not services trade after Brexit (BBC 2018a). The right of Parliament to oversee the trade policy and to choose to diverge from EU rules was also included.

The other elements concerning the border in the Chequers framework were as follows: "the borders between the UK and EU would be treated as a combined customs territory" (for goods trade, including agriculture); the UK would apply domestic tariffs and trade policies for goods intended for the UK but charge EU tariffs and their equivalents for goods going to the EU; and "a post-Brexit UK would be able to control its own tariffs for trade with the rest of the world." The UK-wide customs union with the EU would be temporary. The Chequers agreement (framework for the white paper) argued that the existence of these arrangements would get rid of the need for the default backstop proposed by the EU, "keeping Northern Ireland within the EU customs territory and 'common regulatory area' covering goods and sanitary and phytosanitary regulations" (Institute for Government 2020a). In other words, Chequers proposed a UK-wide backstop so as not to single out Northern Ireland and separate it from the UK, which was anathema to the DUP.

Secretary for Exiting the EU David Davis had argued for a version of the Canada-EU Comprehensive Economic and Trade Agreement (CETA), which was negotiated from 2009 to 2014 and by the end of 2020 had only been approved by sixteen of the required twenty-seven EU national parliaments. His argument was that the CETA allowed for "greater flexibility" for Canada as a non-EU member to pursue other trade agreements around the world. He also argued that electronic arrangements could be used to facilitate trade between Northern Ireland and the EU post-Brexit or to achieve a "max fac" solution. The consensus at the time was that such an electronic mechanism to suit those requirements did not exist. Also, of course, May's 2017 Lancaster House speech and the 2018 Withdrawal Agreement only argued for continued customs and single-market arrangements for Northern Ireland as long as they would be necessary, that is, until Stormont resumed its power-sharing executive and the UK and the EU would be able to agree to end the differential treatment of Northern Ireland.

The Chequers summit and its immediate aftermath provided a Kabuki-style stage for the ERG Brexiteers to signal to the DUP that they would work together to defeat Theresa May's proposals from then on. Both Davis and his department minister, Steve Baker, previous head of the ERG who quickly followed him out the door, claimed they did not trust the EU to ever "let" the UK leave the backstop. In an unrealistic fashion, they held out for the "unilateral" power for the UK to make that decision, ignoring the fact that Northern Ireland would still be part of the EU single market during the transition term. There was no viable option whereby the UK would be able to have that power and observe previously agreed frameworks such as the Good Friday Agreement and the Common Travel Area.

Not to be outdone, Boris Johnson quit as foreign secretary the next day. He clearly harbored leadership ambitions of his own and was not about to let David Davis be the poster boy for a hard Brexit in lining up potential MPs. Like Davis, Johnson was said to oppose the Chequers language, which seemingly involved a trial balloon for the UK to participate in a "European Economic Area" (EEA)—like arrangement as some of the Nordic countries, who had access to the EU single market but were not members. Thus, they could not vote on rules and were instead "rule takers." Both Davis and Johnson wished to plant their swords in the ground of being against "EU rule taking." Johnson went even further than Davis in clearly setting out his leadership plans, putting forth a "Chuck Chequers" event at the Conservative Party conference on October 1–2, 2018.

Issues: Revisiting the Customs Legislation in July 2018. David Davis was replaced as Brexit secretary by libertarian Brexiteer Dominic Raab. Raab had been prominent in the 2013 Open Europe–Fresh Start "Manifesto for Change" and had signed the 2012 *Telegraph* letter to withdraw the UK completely from the EU's Criminal Justice and Policing Framework. On July 16, 2018, the government put the customs parts of the Chequers agreement/white paper to the House of Commons for a vote. As she had compromised with the Remainers to get the Withdrawal Act of 2018 through in June of that year, so PM May compromised with the ERG on amendments to the customs legislation. Thus, the parts of the Chequers agreement with the UK collecting taxes on behalf of the EU and vice versa (unless all member states agreed) were excised at the group's behest. Another ERG amendment on removing the UK from the EU's VAT regime under Brexit was included. The fourth amendment, cosponsored by the DUP, the ERG, and Labour MP Kate Hoey, stated that after Brexit, there would be no customs border in the Irish Sea, preventing a border between Northern Ireland and the rest of the UK (BBC 2018a). Some attacked the successful amendment, "new Clause 37," as violating the EU's envisioned backstop for Northern Ireland. Acceptance of the ERG/DUP amendment was also important as a signal to be sent to the EU that there could be a potential way forward on the Northern Ireland trade and popular movement issue. While the July and fall 2018 movement was helpful to the minority DUP, the conditions for reinvigoration of the Stormont Executive would not be finally in place until summer and fall of 2019, based on the work of May's government on social issue legislation.

The customs legislation narrowly passed on July 16, 2018. On July 17, the second element, the trade bill to include "some 40 trade agreements signed by the EU with third countries and place them in UK law," passed. Remainers had also proposed an amendment to keep the UK in a customs union if a deal had not been reached by January 2019 (Kuenssberg 2018; Crerar 2018a; Sabbagh 2018b). The latter was a rehash of one of the defeated amendments from the June Withdrawal Act. According to Crerar, "Government whips threatened to pull the third reading of the bill and table a no-confidence motion in May themselves if the vote was lost, raising the spectre of a general election" (2018a). Minister for Defence Procurement Guto Bebb resigned from the government over the compromises made by PM May to the ERG on the taxation issues. On the other hand, he had signed the Fresh Start letter to *The Telegraph* in 2012, demonstrating a previous willingness to play ball with the Brexit faction. The events of July 2018 showed the tenuousness of a majority on any Brexit customs union bill.

Libertarian Think Tank Pressure in September 2018. In what could be viewed as a carefully choreographed set of exits from PM May's cabinet after the Chequers framework was unveiled in early July 2018, the Atlas Network, including its US member, the Cato Institute, and its London affiliates, the Institute of Economic Affairs (IEA) and the Free Trade Institute (which changed its name for a while to the Free Trade Initiative), formulated their "alternatives." The time frame of these supposedly viable alternatives to what PM May was working toward on the ground is also instructive. The IEA/Cato/Free Trade Initiative document was released in September 2018—a month before the Conservative Party annual conference and a month before PM May was due to report to both Parliament and the EU about the progress on the customs "arrangements" post-Brexit.

The set of proposals was unrealistic in the extreme: "zero tariffs on all goods; zero non-tariff trade barriers; zero restrictions on competition for government procurement and on foreign direct investment; rules to make mutual recognition of potentially protectionist product standards and regulations more feasible; prohibition on the use of anti-dumping measures; and prohibitions against restrictions based on scientifically-unsubstantiated public health and safety concerns and national security concerns that do not meet certain minimum standards" (Ikenson, Lestor, and Hannan 2018). Daniel Hannan's presence in the document should be noted, as he was one of the prime reconveners of the ERG (from Maastricht Euroskpetics of the Major era), a leader of Vote Leave, and the first research director of the ERG (Knight 2016). Hannan was a member of the European Parliament from 1999 to 2020 and was able to work against the EU from within it, using EU funding for office expenses and communications. In what could only be described as an ultimate irony for somebody spending their life claiming to be against privilege and bureaucracy, he was placed in the House of Lords by PM Boris Johnson in 2021.

On September 24, 2018, the IEA released another part of the fantasy framework, pushing for a "clean break with Europe," known as Plan A+ for Brexit. It was branded as a "plan of idiocy" by *The Guardian* (Crace 2018). Essentially, Plan A+ said that PM May's Chequers framework was unnecessary and that all the UK needed to do was to accomplish a "no deal" Brexit on WTO terms. Apparently, none of the panelists (five MPs) understood that the WTO differentiates between those countries that have "most favored nation status" and those that do not in terms of tariffs. Also, joining the WTO does not automatically eliminate protectionism. This is perhaps not surprising given that David Davis, when he was the secretary of state for the Department for Exiting the EU, alleged in a press interview that the "no deal" (WTO) option would magically absolve the UK of its payment obligations to the EU.

More problematic was that the ERG/IEA nexus was actively involving government MPs, including Davis and Johnson, who inappropriately arranged a free launch of Plan A+ using Westminster facilities in publicly opposing the PM and in essence promoting itself as a "shadow government" on Brexit. As the summary of Plan A+ noted:

> In her Mansion House speech, then Prime Minister Theresa May stated that the UK's regulations need not be identical to the EU's, even if they would achieve the same outcomes. But the government White Paper, *The future relationship between the United Kingdom and the European Union*, proposed that the UK would have substantively harmonised regulations with the EU, which, with the customs arrangement it outlined, would mean it is hard to see how any independent trade policy is possible. It also described a swathe of other ways in which the UK would be unable to determine its regulations. (Singham and Tylecote 2018, 16)

It is clear that the IEA's pro-Brexit activity galvanized the ERG to act in ever-more extreme fashion. Geoghegan reports that in October 2018, IEA employee Shanker Singham, Lord David Trimble of Northern Ireland (of the UUP), and Euroskeptic MPs Iain Duncan Smith and Owen Paterson traveled to Brussels of their own accord to present their pro-Brexit alternative to the government's backstop plan to the EU negotiator, Michel Barnier. Barnier did not meet with them since they did not represent a government, instead sending his deputy to deliver that message (2020, 175).

In November 2018, the EU agreed to PM May's 585-page Withdrawal Agreement, which then needed to be voted on by Parliament. By that time, the EU had also moved on the issue of permitting a temporary "all UK" backstop with the EU rather than a Northern Ireland one. Michel Barnier, chief negotiator, had also reduced the number of goods being checked upon arrival in Northern Ireland to "sanitary," that is, live animals (Herszenhorn and Barigazzi 2018). These EU changes were consistent with the ERG–DUP–Labour amendment of July 2018, which had outlawed the border down the Irish Sea. The time-constrained backstop for the UK to remain in a limited customs and single-market arrangement so as to give time to solve the Northern Ireland–Republic of Ireland relationship under Brexit was too much for the Brexiteer ultras, who unrealistically believed that as of March 2019 they would be free to strike new trade deals all over the world. In a November 2018 repeat of the July 2018 resignations of David Davis and Steve Baker, their replacements, Dominic Raab and Suella Braverman did the same. Another cabinet minister, Esther McVey, who had been elected through the A-list and was a staunch Brexiteer, quit at the same time. The November 2018 resignations over issues that had not significantly changed since July 2018 except for the better (the backstop) were choreographed by the ERG. As they had consistently stated, the Brexiteer ultras claimed they "did not believe" that the EU "could be trusted" to deliver only a temporary backstop. They also did not wish the UK to have to negotiate with the EU, but on this latter point they betrayed their misunderstanding of what unilateral Westminster negotiations would mean for Northern Ireland. Again, the Northern Ireland Executive issue had to be addressed, and Theresa May's government ended up largely doing so before she stepped down in July 2019. Many of those stepping down from cabinet positions with Theresa May were later rewarded by Boris Johnson with cabinet positions (or offers, in Baker's case), including MPs Raab, McVey, and Braverman.

Theresa May's Leadership Challenge(s) of 2018

In September 2018, the ERG met to start plotting how to get rid of Theresa May as PM and basically never looked back. As Conservative MP Guto Bebb stated, "There was never any intention to support May's deal" (Geoghegan 2020, 113). Even beginning at the time of the customs bill in July 2018, the ERG was counting opposition votes to see if it had enough (forty-eight) to start a no-confidence vote (it did not). By September 2018, former ERG chair (and Brexit minister) Steve Baker claimed it did (*The Economist* 2018b). As described at the time of the Chequers framework in early July 2018, Boris Johnson was eagerly campaigning for the job to replace her. By October 2018, the DUP's Brexit spokesperson, Sammy

Wilson, stated that "the PM could not push the DUP around" in terms of potentially accepting a single-market continuation for Northern Ireland but not the rest of the UK. Part of its reasoning was that Northern Ireland could not then sign on to new free trade deals, as the UK would be able to after Brexit, if it were still in the EU's ambit, as it currently remains. The DUP showed its displeasure by abstaining on a Labour amendment to an agriculture bill in October 2018 and signaled it would not support the government's budget bill. Prior to the Fixed-Term Parliaments Act, that would have meant an automatic no-confidence vote in the PM and an election (Payne 2018). By November 2018, the DUP told the PM that it would not support her Withdrawal Bill vote, scheduled for December 2018, based on the single market issue. While the Withdrawal Bill at that point envisioned a UK-wide customs union after Brexit until the UK and EU negotiated an exit, the DUP opposed the single-market aspect applying only to itself. Thus, the DUP became basically a confidence and supply partner essentially with the ERG only rather than the Conservative government, which it had pledged to support (Sabbagh 2018a). In early December, the party told the ERG that it would support a no-confidence motion against May if her Withdrawal Agreement Bill (WAB) were voted down (Wearmouth 2018). On December 10, PM May knew she did not have the support for her Withdrawal Agreement Bill, given the DUP-ERG nexus, and pulled the vote.

In response, Jacob Rees-Mogg and the ERG got the signatures required to hold a Conservative Party leadership vote on May. Before that happened, she went to the Conservative backbench caucus committee, the 1922 Committee, and urged them to support her, indicating she would not contest another general election as PM. While Lord Ashcroft had donated to the Conservative Party in 2017 due to his belief that PM May would bring about Brexit, by December 2018 his e-journal, *Conservative Home*, publicly urged the party MPs to drop her as leader on the day of the party's confidence vote, December 12. May survived the vote, 200–117, despite some Brexiteers' hopes that she would resign. Starting in December 2018, May kept trying to negotiate with the EU a proposal that the Northern Irish backstop would at most last for a year after the transition ended.

Interconnections between Economic Interest and Euroskepticism. None of the ERG "ultra" thinking on economic freedom for the UK was new, especially not after the referendum results of 2016. In 2013, Baker wrote on his website, countering former Bank of Canada chair Mark Carney's "easy money" policy as Bank of England head, that "we now live in a world of extensive explicit discretionary power over both money and the financial system which ought to allocate real capital to the most productive uses" (S. Baker 2013). In 2017 and 2018, Jacob Rees-Mogg called Carney both an "enemy of Brexit for intervening in British politics with his speculations" and a "second-tier Canadian politician" (Withers 2018; Stewart 2017). Both Baker and Rees-Mogg have been ardent opponents of government bailouts and central banks.

Then-MP Liz Truss formed a similar group to the ERG in 2011 shortly after her election. The Free Enterprise Group, as it is known, contains many of the same members as the ERG. Although she claimed to have voted Remain in the 2016 referendum, Truss has since claimed that "Margaret Thatcher was her favorite Prime Minister" (*Politics.co.uk* 2022). The Free Enterprise Group put on joint events with the IEA, such as the Growth Forum of 2012, which included many ERG and Fresh Start members such as Priti Patel, Kwasi Kwarteng, and Dominic Raab, as well as Liz Truss and Sajiv Rajid (IEA 2012). Also in 2012, MPs Kwarteng, Patel, Raab, and Skidmore published an argument calling for as much deregulation in Britain's trade universe as possible and the ability to do trade deals around the world, including in the Commonwealth and emerging markets (Kwarteng et al. 2012).

In January 2018, the City of London had tried to broker an EU deal to allow London's financial services market continued access to the EU market after Brexit. This was similar to former PM Cameron's attempted negotiations on the issue of financial market divergence, and it got virtually nowhere as he had (*Irish Times* 2018). The plan proposed by the financial services sector of the city would have allowed cross-border trade in financial services "on the condition that each side preserve regulatory standards in line with the best international standards." Predictably, the EU response was that if the UK were leaving the single market, no "similar" level of market access would be allowed. These attempted negotiations left a bad taste in the mouth of the ERG, some of whom were bankers or hedge fund entrepreneurs, and virtually ensured their noncooperation on the Brexit proposals put forth by PM May. The Brexiteer ultras centered in the ERG were much more interested in the fact that the number one component of the UK economy (80 percent) and of each component state is financial services. As one member of the Johnson government noted, "There is no agriculture in Singapore," alluding to the fact that many see the goal of the Brexiteer ultras as making London into a deregulated "Singapore on Thames" (McGleenon 2020).

Within months of quitting the cabinet, David Davis became a consultant for JCB, a construction giant whose head, Baron Bamford, is an ardent Brexiteer and funder of that cause (Geoghegan 2020, 180). In the three-month preelection period, in 2017, the largest corporate contribution to the Conservatives came from JCB (Mason 2017b). By 2019, JCB was funding Boris Johnson's leadership campaign (Colson and Bienkov 2019).

Davis is believed to have come to his pro-Brexit opinions in his seventeen-year executive career with the Tate & Lyle Sugar Company (Geoghegan 2020, 168). One source of the sugar refined by Tate & Lyle was the Caribbean, specifically Belize, of which former Conservative Deputy Chair Michael Ashcroft is a citizen. Tate & Lyle's product has thus been in direct competition to the sugar derived from sugar beets grown on the English coast, as noted by Roberts in *The Guardian* in March 2017:

> Tate and Lyle was one of the only large employers to campaign openly for Brexit during the referendum and, after Theresa May invokes Article 50 on 29 March, sugar will be on the frontline of the upcoming battle over Britain's economic future. The reason lies in the EU protection afforded to Tate & Lyle's company's arch-rival British Sugar, which uses a very different technique to make a chemically identical product. Its brand of white crystal, Silver Spoon, is made not from imported sugar cane, but from sugar beet grown on farms in the east of England.

Tate & Lyle was identified as one of the few "big firms to support Leave in the Referendum" (Geoghegan 2020, 167–68). Davis wrote a 1988 book about restructuring Tate & Lyle's Canadian sugar subsidy, Redpath, in *How to Turn Round a Company*. In 2010, Tate & Lyle was bought by American Sugar Refineries Inc. Davis's experience in turning around a Canadian subsidiary could well have underlined his enthusiasm for a "Canada plus" free trade deal instead of May's carefully formulated one.

To state the obvious, those with experience earning their fortunes outside the UK-EU framework were among the most ardent Brexiteers. These parliamentarians and Conservative Party funders (Ashcroft) could afford to be rather singular in their views that "Brexit meant a hard Brexit," since they had no qualms about earning income from outside the EU. Another account identified many Brexiteers who held vast offshore portfolios. In addition to former Conservative deputy chair Ashcroft, they included another major funder of the Conservative Party and the Vote Leave campaign, former lord Robert Edmiston. One source of his wealth was from aviation, headquartered in the British Virgin Islands until it moved to Malta, an EU member, in 2016 (Garside, Osborne, and MacAskill 2017).

For truth in advertising, PM May's husband had been working for a US-owned investment firm (Capital Group) since 2005 but had also previously worked for German-owned Deutsche Asset Management (2000–2005). The Capital Group is the seventh largest money manager in the world (Mooney, Newlands, and Williams 2016). PM May's job was to try to hold the whole Conservative Party together, walking the tightrope between various singular economic interests, but also to deliver a Brexit framework that could still work for smaller producers in Northern Ireland and other UK countries.

The Withdrawal Agreeement Bill (WAB) Votes of 2019. The three votes on the Withdrawal Agreement took place on January 15, 2019, and then on March 12, 2019, by which time the EU had agreed to add an appendix to the agreement stating that it was unlikely, if the backstop had to be implemented, it would be in place for more than a year after the transition. Nonetheless, May's three votes, the first two on the Withdrawal Agreement and the Political Declaration and the last on the Withdrawal Agreement alone on March 29, 2019, were all defeated, with Conservative Brexiteers providing a significant "no" margin (Aidt, Gray, and Savu 2019, 592). The ultimate futility of having votes on the Withdrawal Agreement under the parliamentary math of 2017–March 2019 was shown in the "Letwin Amendment," whereby various alternatives were submitted to be debated on March 27 and April 1, 2019. "No" majorities, some quite slim, came in for every single possible choice, running from no deal through a new common market proposal to the European Free Trade Area to a confirmatory public vote on what the government agreed. In addition to the backstop, the necessary transition for the UK to remain aligned with EU rules for at least a year after the Withdrawal Agreement was concluded through the end of 2020, with "many arrangements staying in place," was in the Withdrawal Agreement. While the ERG and other Brexiteer ultras bristled at this set of arrangements, the positive aspect was that it would give more time to reach a final deal and not crash out of the EU on WTO minimalist terms (Sandford 2020). Of course, the latter was exactly what many in the ERG saw as beneficial to their business interests.

The vote on January 15, 2019 was 432 against and 202 in favor, including 118 rebellious Conservatives of both Remainer and Leaver stripes

(Aidt, Gray, and Savu 2019, 587). This included Remainers who hoped for a second referendum.

Not to be outdone, on January 16, 2019, Jeremy Corbyn, who saw power in his grasp, put forth a no-confidence motion across the House, one day after May's defeat on the first vote. She barely survived this vote, 325–306, with all opposition parties voting against her. This was the only vote on which May got the support of the DUP.

Remainer Remorse: Cabinet Exits. In January 2019, a pro-Remain group of MPs and House of Lords members formed another parliamentary group, called Right to Vote. It was formed to advance the proposal for a second Brexit referendum, a position to which PM May moved in April 2019 after it was clear the Brexiteers were not to be placated. The group also existed to raise (and spend) money for a second referendum, having spent £40,000 by the end of its first month in operation (Colson 2019). In February 2019, Conservative MPs Heidi Allen, Sarah Wollaston, and Anna Soubry left the Conservative Party, denying May a Conservative majority in her future votes. The Conservative Remainers who left the party had been part of the All-Party Parliamentary Group on European Relations since 2018 and aligned with the Peoples' Vote Campaign begun in 2018 for a second referendum vote (Elgot 2018b). The DUP did not support May's March proposals since the Stormont issue had not been solved, and thus it was clear that the three MPs who left in February 2019 were the second step in the breaking of any hope of support for May's deal.

By early 2019 Prime Minister May was also facing financial pressure from the business community, some of which was withdrawing donations to the Conservative Party (Colson 2019). Colson notes that the coffers of the Conservative Party were quite low, with the then chair having to help pay bills from his considerable finances. A trend of "donors deserting the party in favour of explicitly anti-Brexit or pro-Brexit vehicles" was in place in early 2019, including the JCB support of Johnson's developing leadership bid (Colson 2019). By 2019, former leader Iain Duncan Smith, who had appointed May to the chair position of the Conservative Party in 2002, was openly helping Boris Johnson's campaign to replace her (Tominey 2019b).

March 2019 Votes. In between January and March 2019, PM May negotiated further movement from the EU on the Northern Ireland backstop. These actions included the establishment of a "joint interpretative instrument" in the case of deliberate foot dragging by the EU on the backstop, so that the UK could unilaterally enter into arbitration. Another piece added was a joint EU-UK statement to the Political Declaration, "committing both sides to seeking alternative arrangements for the Irish border so as to end the backstop by December 2020 (Sandford 2020). Third, the potential power to unilaterally leave the backstop was approved by the EU, again in the case that EU-UK negotiations broke down. While the majority against this bill was smaller than in January 2019, nearly 100 less than in January (149 nays on March 12 versus 230 in January), it still did not pass. By then, the ERG-DUP alliance was firmly entrenched.

Between the March 12 and March 29 "meaningful votes" on the Withdrawal Agreement, the PM got the EU to agree to delay the operative date of Brexit from March 29 to May 22 if Parliament approved the deal during the week of March 24. If that did not happen, the EU would give the UK until April 12 to decide whether to cancel Brexit and leave the EU on a "no deal" basis (with no withdrawal agreement in place), or or request a longer delay. The last option ultimately happened. While May threw herself on her sword again and told Conservative MPs she would resign if they passed the agreement on March 29, that did not happen. On May 22, 2019, Ashcroft's *Conservative Home* again dipped its weighty oar into electoral politics, rather spectacularly urging voters not to support Conservatives in the May 23, 2019, European Parliament elections if "May was not on her way out by the end of today" (Goodman 2019). After Nigel Farage's supposedly new and different "Brexit party" gained the highest percentage of UK votes and seats in the May 23 European Parliament elections, May announced on May 24 that she would step down as PM on June 7.

What Was Different about Johnson's Agreement? The bulk of Boris Johnson's agreement with the EU of December 24, 2020, did not differ significantly from the Withdrawal Agreement negotiated by PM May. What was different was that the UK-wide customs union with the EU was dropped, with the UK leaving in January 2021. The ability of Scotland, Wales, and England to leave the single market was in May's proposal. Northern Ireland would remain aligned with the EU as part of the single market for four years, until 2024. At that time and at four-year intervals thereafter, the Stormont Parliament would be invited to legislate on its future, but a 60 percent majority would be required. The Stormont Executive had been rendered inoperable by dissolution over an allegation of corruption against the DUP. After both the UK election of December 2019, where Boris Johnson gained his eighty-seat Conservative majority at Westminster, and the Northern Ireland election of that same year in which the DUP and Sinn Fein lost seats to the centrist Labour and Social Democratic Parties and the nonaligned Alliance, Westminster started applying pressure on the DUP and Sinn Fein to restart the executive power-sharing agreement. The Conservative Northern Irish secretary, Julian Smith, gave the DUP and Sinn Fein an ultimatum to restore the Stormont Executive by January 13, 2020, or face an assembly election (Carroll 2019; S. Jones 2020). The DUP and Sinn Fein complied with the ultimatum. Northern Ireland would continue to apply the EU's customs regulations to goods coming from the UK and Ireland at its ports; but goods going into the Republic of Ireland or the rest of the EU would face no new checks or controls (Campbell 2020). Until Stormont decides otherwise, Northern Ireland remains in the EU single market and subject to the European Court of Justice as its final arbiter.

Also to appeal to the Brexit ultra or "Spartans" crowd, Boris Johnson dropped a key line from the 2019 Political Declaration in December 2020. While it confirmed that the UK (including Northern Ireland) was free to pursue trade deals; the sentence "the United Kingdom will consider aligning with [European] union rules in relevant areas" in any future trade talks was deleted (O'Carroll 2019). As former PM Theresa May stated in the House of Commons on December 30 when it voted to support the trade deal struck between the EU and the UK, "In 2018 in Mansion house, I said that we wanted to work to get a financial services deal in the future treaty arrangement and that it would be truly groundbreaking. . . . It would have been, but sadly it has not been achieved. We have a deal in trade which benefits the EU, but not a deal in services that would have benefited the UK" (Boscia 2020). While PM May set out goals for EU trade in financial services in her March 2, 2018, Mansion House speech, the financial services were eventually put aside, primarily since the EU refused to negotiate.

The key strategy for the ERG was to get rid of Theresa May before March 2019, when the two-year Withdrawal Agreement (Article 50) deadline would originally expire. As a Deloitte report (2016) noted, "The two-year deadline under Article 50, which could be extended by unanimous agreement, does not apply to trade negotiations. The UK could continue in negotiations on EU trade agreements for many years after Brexit" (2016). This perfectly describes the situation after 2020; the EU and the UK will need to negotiate financial services "equivalence" in terms of how to sell services in EU markets, now that the UK is not part of the single market or customs union. Similarly, the agreement on fishing rights signed in December 2018 will hold the UK to the status quo for five and a half years (*Financial*

Post 2020). In other words, the ERG and Conservative Brexit donors need not have been in such a hurry to drop Theresa May. She was trying to sell an ambiguous concept, Brexit, supported by England and Wales.

Conclusion

Theresa May's ability to negotiate between hard and fast poles of opinion within the Conservative Party on Brexit was minimal, yet she tried valiantly. As a creature of her party who wanted to save it at all costs (and avoid electing a Corbyn-led government), there was nobody who worked harder to try to find a wedge of majority opinion within a restive caucus.

As has been discussed throughout this book, May's task had the most constraints and yet the broadest remit. Margaret Thatcher was thrown overboard by her caucus in 1990 due to disagreements over which parts of the European framework the UK should join, and most Conservative PMs since her time have had to perform a related balancing act. The balancing act was most pronounced under Thatcher's successor, John Major, and then under Conservative PM David Cameron from 2010 to 2016. Major had the tool of threatening an election due to the framework then in place in the Conservative Party, so he was able to use this to hold the rebels to heel and get the Maastricht Treaty passed by the House in 1993. Cameron faced high-profile rebellions within his party, which only paled in comparison with May in post-referendum 2016. Cameron and May worked on a similar trajectory, which was to try to find some core of majority opinion within the Conservative Party on some facet of EU membership, while assuring the Euroskeptics that they were not secretly plotting more integration. PM May, of course, had the hardest task of all, trying to deliver a vote that asked people in June 2016 only if they wanted to leave the EU, not the shape it should take. May, her advisers, and the cabinet ministers loyal to her tried to work through ways to get her divided caucus to deliver the results of the referendum, but with a bare majority of the Commons after June 2017, it could not be done. Those voting against the government and quitting their cabinet posts at times included those from both Fresh Start, who had been against her project to withdraw from only parts of the EU Criminal Justice and Policing Framework in 2012, and the ERG, who were mostly concerned with striking new deals around the globe and had no patience for the time frame of extending Brexit, particularly where the fate of Northern Ireland was concerned. Euroskeptics in the party have included both those known as "Thatcher's children," who were mainly in agreement with Thatcher's privatization medicine for the UK but also often against "more" EU in their lives. Some of them were also social conservatives and thus against modernization of the Conservative Party, a project with which May had aligned herself early in her career. Those in Fresh Start and particularly the ERG, who mainly identified themselves with "buccaneering" global capitalism, such as Steve Baker and Jacob Rees-Mogg, and who would not tolerate anybody telling them they could not go out and strike as many economic deals around the globe as they wished. David Davis was a long-term flamboyant Euroskeptic first elected under Thatcher who proved unworthy of leadership posts. He also did not support May's proposals since he believed in unrealistic fashion that the UK could strike a Canada-type "free trade" deal with the EU in two years, something that still has not completely been implemented in Canada despite having begun in 2009. Finally, there were Remainers who clung to the hope that they could force a second referendum and quit May's cabinet yet did not quite seem to understand that voting down May's proposals led them closer to a "no deal" option (and chaos between Northern Ireland and its trading partners).

First elected in 1997, Theresa May understood where both the right and liberal wings of the Conservative caucus came from and tried to steer a middle ground. Unfortunately, the Brexit referendum and those trying to effect Brexit were not in the middle ground; they only lived in "yes" or "no" camps. While working on Brexit, May also had to contend with the age-old power imbalance in Westminster as expressed through MPs' ignorance of the notion of sexual consent and to work to get a framework in place to help staff report and deal with inappropriate contact. While she also made great strides in electing a more diverse Conservative caucus through the A-list, some of those MPs decided not to support her Brexit proposals in the end, either throwing their weight behind the very overt challenger Boris Johnson, such as Priti Patel and Theresa McVey, or leaving to be part of an "independent" group, such as Sarah Wollaston.

Finally, there was no way that Boris Johnson could have produced Brexit without the heavy lifting PM May did, including but definitely not limited to her cabinet's role (and some members of the House of Lords) in getting the DUP and Sinn Fein governing again in Stormont. While Johnson's Northern Ireland Protocol violated the previous Withdrawal Agreement and is still problematic, it was the final chink in the work May had done to get rid of the backstop and get the Brexiteers and the DUP on board in 2020.

In terms of the criteria identified by Annesley, Beckwith, and Franceschet in 2019, Theresa May was the strongest in terms of being able to act as a representative of modernizers, Remainers, and Brexiteers in trying to achieve a workable Brexit. However, neither the ERG nor in the end their confidence and supply partners, the DUP, wanted her proposal due to their professed desires to strike trade deals outside the EU immediately upon the end of the Brexit process, including the transition. While the DUP in 2018 had professed to support May's proposal of an all-UK customs union with the EU (which did not take place on Brexit) since it did not want a border down the Irish Sea, a border down the Irish Sea is what it got in Boris Johnson's Northern Ireland Protocol of 2020. While the DUP purported to play along with the May government's attempts to move Northern Ireland forward on social issues, as of 2022 the issue of abortion access was still problematic there. In May 2022, the unionist parties lost the majority in Northern Ireland elections for the first time, with Sinn Fein winning. In aligning itself with the ERG part of the Conservative Party in 2018, and with Boris Johnson's leadership bid, the DUP effectively ensured that a less satisfactory outcome to Northern Ireland's trade issues would occur. In May 2022, the DUP refused to enter government formation talks with Sinn Fein, ostensibly due to its hatred of the Northern Ireland Protocol, which its support helped produce.

May was not one of the "Cameroonian" elites. She has been a standard-bearer for the Conservative Party. She clearly is not part of the libertarian economic thinkers allied with the ERG either. Thus, in keeping with Annesley, Beckwith, and Franceschet's framework, the affiliational "you're not one of us" refrain is used particularly in the single-member district, majoritarian systems of the UK, US, and Australian lower house. In experiential credentials, she was selected party leader by her MP colleagues in 2016 because she was at the top, having been the senior woman in the Clegg-Cameron coalition and the Cameron governments. Despite her work on both "modernizing" and issue fronts to appeal to the right wing of the party, especially immigration, May fell prey to the DUP's worst instincts of working against the people of Northern Ireland and the ERG's embrace of a policy that has in fact kept part of the UK in the EU for longer than May's plan would have done. While PM May used every tactic at her disposal to walk a tightrope of ever-diminishing cabinet numbers on both the Remain and Leave sides, and a tightrope of constant intra- and interparty negotiating on the Brexit Withdrawal Agreement Bill, Prime Minister May was not given the credit she deserved for actually negotiating the bulk of the Brexit agreement. The UK-wide customs union with the EU dropped out, with the UK leaving the EU's customs union and with

England, Wales, and Scotland leaving the single market in January 2021. She is not to be blamed for her tears of frustration at the end of her leaving announcement on May 24, 2019, that would seem to be the mildest expression possible of the intra- and interparty treachery that she experienced. Finally, the skills May displayed in being a "cabinet survivor" and organizational partisan as per Escobar-Lemmon and Taylor-Robinson's work (2015, 2016) helped her get to the leadership, particularly in her ability to appeal to different stripes of the Remain-Brexit divide. When push came to shove and a majority of votes was needed to get the withdrawal bills of 2019 through, the long-surviving masculinist ethos of the Conservative parliamentary party grouped together to deny her the required number of votes to effect Brexit.

FOUR

Pelosi's Tightropes

This chapter discusses how Nancy Pelosi successfully engaged with some of the greatest challenges of her leadership career. Even though Pelosi was uncontested in her historic election as Speaker in 2007, she has faced direct or proxy challenges to her leadership since 2002 (keeping in mind that she was first elected to the leadership in 2001). Thus, despite the fact that she has been the Democratic leader for nearly two decades, these repeated challenges to Pelosi's leadership indicate that others in her caucus see her as either vulnerable or a liability—or both.

This chapter also explores several case studies that document Pelosi's political acumen and also demonstrate the tightrope that she had to walk as a frequently demonized woman exercising considerable political power. The first case study is Pelosi's success in engineering the enactment of the Patient Protection and Affordable Care Act (ACA), in spite of unified Republican opposition and Democratic shenanigans in the Senate. The second case study is Pelosi's repeated clashes with Republican president Donald Trump, which resulted in two presidential impeachments. The third and fourth case studies include Pelosi's responses to the global COVID-19 pandemic and the January 6, 2021, attack on the US Capitol. The chapter ends with Pelosi's decision to step away from the leadership after the 2022 election.

The events recounted here took place within the changing contexts of American politics, the House of Representatives, and the power of the leadership within the institution. Thus, Pelosi became Speaker when power had been consolidated again into the office. The Republicans' rules changes influenced the Democrats' rules. Seniority, while important, was no longer sacred. Ambitious Democrats faced pressure to create leadership political action committees (PACs) and to donate generously to their colleagues. Party members worried that any move to oppose the leadership would lead to punishment from the Speaker, including a loss of campaign donations. Moreover, an individual member's ability to shape the legislative agenda was curtailed by the increasing power of the party leadership. Yet, even though she "knows her power," as the title of her autobiography suggests (N. Pelosi 2008), we argue that Pelosi is constrained in how she can use her power because of the gender dynamics she faces.

Escobar-Lemmon and Taylor-Robinson (2016, 104–26), in their analyses of women in presidential cabinets, note that cabinet positions are scarce and that prime ministers need to appoint individuals who can bring assets to the administration. Much the same can be said for party leadership in the US House: few positions are open, and leaders must bring many assets to the table to benefit the party, including political skills. This chapter demonstrates how Pelosi's political skills have helped her remain on the tightrope even when she wobbled.

Walking a Tightrope: The Early Years as Democratic Leader, 2002–10

According to Green and Bee (2016), intraparty leadership challenges have become more frequent since the 1990s, leaving leaders to campaign and dole out favors to ensure they retain their positions. Nancy Pelosi is no exception and may, in fact, face such challenges more frequently. Since she was first elected Democratic whip in 2001, she has faced direct challenges in 2002, 2010–11, 2016–17, and 2018–19. Pelosi also faced proxy challenges, where a candidate she openly supported for another leadership post faced opposition from within the caucus, in 2006–7 and 2014. Given the frequency of these challenges—approximately one every three or four years—challenging Pelosi is almost regular business. At the same time, the American speakership as an institution has become more powerful. This section will recount her early challenges and identify the gendered dynamics within them.

The 2002 Democratic Leader Race. Only eight months after Pelosi secured the Democratic whip position, Richard Gephardt retired from the House of Representatives. As they prepared for another Congress as the minority party, Democrats set about the task of choosing their leader. Pelosi was poised to move up the leadership ladder from Democratic whip to Democratic leader. Steny Hoyer, who challenged her for whip the previous year, declared his candidacy for Democratic whip and quickly secured enough supporters to secure the position. Pelosi, however, faced two challengers in her race, both representatives who promoted themselves as moderates in comparison to the "San Francisco liberal" Pelosi.

The first challenger to declare his candidacy was Martin Frost of Texas. His supporters believed he was the "shrewder" politician and more likely to keep moderate and conservative Democrats from leaving the party. Frost and his supporters were concerned that the Democratic Party, dominated even then by urban progressives, would position itself too far to the left and be punished by voters. Frost, however, failed to secure enough support from the caucus, dropped out of the race in early November, and backed Pelosi (Hulse 2002; V. and eHei 2002).

On the same day, however, Representative Harold Ford Jr. announced his intent to challenge Pelosi in a 6:00 a.m. phone call to radio personality Don Imus. Ford was an interesting character. Just thirty-two years old and in his third term, Ford was a member of both the moderate Blue Dogs and the Congressional Black Caucus (CBC). Ford attempted to define Pelosi as old and out of touch, saying that he was "new and different" and she was "a throwback." Pelosi responded with an age-related retort: "Well, I've been in office eight months. I guess when you're very young, eight months is a long time" (York 2002).

Pelosi handily won election as Democratic leader. In a prescient op-ed, columnist Cal Thomas predicted that the Republicans would use Nancy Pelosi and her liberal voting record as a bludgeon in future elections:

> [Pelosi's election] will allow Republicans to again invoke the image of Democrats as the big-government, high-taxing, over-regulating, entitlement-establishing, unaccountable, irresponsible, gun-confiscating, totalitarian-coddling, peace-at-any-price, ACLU card-carrying, same-sex-marrying, unrestricted aborting, anything-goes philosophy of the Dukakis-Mondale-McGovern extreme left wing of their party. (Thomas 2002)

Congressional scholar Ross K. Baker (2002) had a more charitable view. Baker points to the increasing polarization of the House. For a party of liberals, Pelosi, as a liberal, was an appropriate choice. Baker points out that her predecessor, Gephardt, steadily moved to the left as he fulfilled his leadership ambitions. While Pelosi's election did open the Democrats up to attacks from the right, she is "as authentic a representative as anyone of where the Democratic Party stands."

But were Frost and Ford really moderates? According to the Voteview Congressional Roll Call Votes Database (Lewis et al. 201), no. Instead, these three were not far apart ideologically. Pelosi's first dimension DW-NOMINATE score[1] in the 106th Congress (1999–2000) was –0.49, decidedly liberal. However, Ford's was –0.359 and Frost's was –0.316. They were more moderate but not dramatically so (Lewis et al. 2021).

Gender dynamics in these two examples are subtle yet present. The first harkens to the ageist claims in Ford's coded language. He implied that Pelosi, at age sixty-two, was old and out of touch. While these attacks are used against both men and women *d'un certain âge*, they carry a stronger negative connotation against women, who face a double standard because women's social value is predicated so strongly on their youth and attractiveness (Deutsch, Zalenski, and Clark 1986). Thus, Ford's critiques have a potency for Pelosi that they would not carry for a male leader. The second is the characterization of Martin Frost as "shrewd." Again, by framing Frost as shrewd, Pelosi is, by contrast, naive, harkening to stereotypes of feminine helplessness, despite the fact that Pelosi was known for her political acumen.

The 2002 challenges preview, just eight months after she stepped onto the leadership ladder, many of the themes that would appear in later leadership challenges: Pelosi is too old. Pelosi is too liberal. Pelosi is a target, and she gets in the way of younger members' ambitions.

Election as Speaker, 2007. Nancy Pelosi was officially elected Speaker of the House on January 3, 2007. She ran unopposed within the caucus, and there were no Democratic defectors in the House floor vote. Even as Pelosi made history as the first woman elected Speaker of the US House and the highest-ranking woman in the US government, there were ample gender dynamics at play.

First, as noted in chapter 2, Pelosi did not enter Congress with the intention of moving into the leadership. Rather, she came to work on issues, such as human rights in China and AIDS. This is typical of women

---

1. First dimension DW-NOMINATE scores are a measure of ideology on a liberal (-1.0) to conservative (1.0) continuum. The closer a member's score is to -1.0, the more liberal he or she is. Conversely, the closer to 1.0, the more conservative. Members with a score of 0.0 are moderates. (Lewis et al. 2021).

candidates for office, who never envision seeking elective office but are motivated by an issue or cause.

Second, Pelosi harkened to feminine tropes as Speaker. For instance, when she ascended into the speakership, Pelosi famously asked her grandchildren and the other children in the chamber to join her at the podium—in defiance of the House parliamentarian (Lawrence 2023, 28–29). There she announced that the Democrats' purpose was to build a better future for America's children (Cunningham 2012). Her own news interviews were rife with references to motherhood, saying that her organizational skills and her "mother of five" voice would be valuable when organizing and corralling the Democratic Caucus members (Kedrowski and Gower 2009). Similarly, Dabbous and Ladley (2010) found that Pelosi's news coverage in her first one hundred days used numerous feminine, and even sexist, tropes. In her biography, written for a young adult audience, Pelosi reframes motherhood and housekeeping from being "just a housewife" to taking pride in the work of raising children and "saving the world, one child at a time" (N. Pelosi 2008, 129). While she reminisces that she loved being a stay-at-home mom, Pelosi also notes that getting elected to Congress when her children were mostly grown came at a cost—that of entering positions of power at an older age than many of her younger colleagues (128).

Third, as Speaker, Pelosi sought to promote other women into leadership positions. According to the Center for American Women in Politics, the last Democratic woman committee chair to serve prior to Pelosi's speakership was Representative Leonor Sullivan (D-MO), who chaired the Committee on Merchant Marine and Fisheries from 1973 to 1977. Pelosi immediately appointed four women as committee chairs, including Louise Slaughter (D-NY) as chair of the Rules Committee. Three of these women continued in their leadership positions through the 111th Congress. In addition, Representative Rosa DeLauro (D-CT) chaired the Democratic Steering Committee, which makes committee appointments for the caucus, a position she still holds (CAWP 2021).

Finally, Pelosi remembers her first meeting at the White House as Speaker for its historic nature:

> I had no apprehension about going to this meeting. Still I felt different. I walked into the room, and then as I went into the room and the door closed behind me, in this small room at a small table with those people, I realized this was unlike any other meeting I'd ever been

to in the White House. In fact, it was unlike any meeting that any woman had ever been to at the White House. I was there, not with derivative power as an appointee or staff person of the president. I was there elected by the Democrats in the Congress of the United States to represent a coequal branch of government. As President Bush graciously welcomed me to the meeting, I was feeling really closed-in in my chair. I mean, I've never had that sensation before or since. I was really crowded on my chair. And there was Susan B. Anthony, Lucretia Mott, Elizabeth Cady Stanton, Sojourner Truth, Alice Paul. They were all on the chair—you name more—they were all on the chair. And I could hear them say: "At last, we have a seat at the table." (C. Pelosi 2019, 53–54)

The Majority Leader Race, 2006–2007. Although Pelosi ascended to the speakership without opposition, Pelosi faced opposition in other ways. The first was the contest for majority leader. Steny Hoyer, as Democratic whip, was expected to ascend the leadership ladder to majority leader. Hoyer, however, faced opposition from Pelosi's friend and mentor John Murtha, the moderate and hawkish Pennsylvanian. While Pelosi asked Murtha to refrain from actively campaigning for the majority leader position during the summer and fall election season, he continued to meet quietly with members of the Democratic Caucus and seek their support. The race heated up after the election, with both candidates actively campaigning through personal meetings, whip counts, "Dear Colleague" letters, and campaign contributions from the candidates' PACs (Green and Harris 2019, 147–55).

Pelosi was initially neutral in the race; however, a few days before the caucus vote, she endorsed Murtha, again defying the leadership ladder. She and her surrogates immediately began to lobby uncommitted Democrats. Her fellow Californians Anna Eshoo and George Miller were reportedly "really beating up on people to back Jack or else" (Green and Harris 2019, 151). Because of Pelosi's endorsement of Murtha, the majority leadership race was framed as another Pelosi versus Hoyer contest. This one did not end up with a Pelosi victory. Whip counts recorded 114 votes for Murtha plus 6 "leaners." In the end, Murtha (and Pelosi) lost by 63 votes (149 for Hoyer; 86 for Murtha). This was a defeat for Pelosi early in her speakership and threatened to undermine her ability to effectively lead the Democratic Caucus.

The postmortem analyses of the Hoyer-Murtha race agree that Pelosi erred in publicly backing Murtha rather than remaining neutral. Their explanations for Murtha's defeat vary. Green and Harris (2019, 152–56) note that Murtha's backers had committee or geographic ties to him or Pelosi or were freshmen who might have been swayed by the Speaker's support. Hoyer, on the other hand, received support from senior Democrats, older members, and those in the leadership. Hoyer also gave more generously to his colleagues' campaign funds, and this also won him many votes. Hoyer was also personally popular and brought leadership experience to the race. Murtha, by contrast, carried baggage as a champion of earmarks, narrowly focused on defense policy, and a tarnished survivor of the ABSCAM scandal of the 1980s (Ball 2020; Green and Harris 2019; Peters and Rosenthal 2010).

Yet, what was Pelosi's motivation for backing Murtha in the first place? Peters and Rosenthal (2010, 67–68) and Green (2008) attribute this support to the value she places on personal loyalty and her determination. Molly Ball also noted that Pelosi's usual optimism did not allow her to realize the futility of Murtha's bid (2020, 126).

The gender dynamics of the race and of the postmortems are just under the surface. The first is the characterization of the race itself. Ball notes that some in the caucus saw the contest as "Mommy and Daddy are fighting" (2020, 127). Norman Ornstein said that Pelosi's "tenaciousness became stubbornness" (Peters and Rosenthal 2010, 67), reframing a positive trait into a negative one, which often happens to women. Others thought that Pelosi and her surrogates used "strong arm tactics" to recruit supporters to Murtha by threatening them with demotions. Green (2008) quotes a reporter who commented that Pelosi "nursed grudges." Note that doling out rewards and punishments is clearly the prerogative of the Speaker and one that is routinely used to inspire loyalty within the party caucus (Pearson 2015), yet when Pelosi attempted to use these levers of power, she was criticized in gendered terms.

A related question is the concept of loyalty. Is this a gendered concept—one, like ambition, that is positively constructed for men and negatively constructed for women? Military commanders, for example, are praised when they enjoy the loyalty of their troops and are seen as weak when faced with mutiny. Yet, in Pelosi's case, observers say she is "loyal to a fault" (Peters and Rosenthal 2010, 68) or, less flatteringly, "grudge holding and vindictive" (Ball 2020, 127). Ball also points to this double standard: "Some also contended that if a man had supported his long-time friend, it might have been seen as tough and impressive rather than petty and personal" (127).

After the caucus meeting where Hoyer was elected comfortably, Pelosi proclaimed, "Let the healing begin" (Peters and Rosenthal 2010, 67). Interestingly, with this statement, Pelosi herself used gendered language to indicate that the party is pulling together. She implied that the contest had led to some sort of injury—an injury that she probably worsened by getting involved in the majority leadership race—and thus she was now responsible for its repair. Arguably, Pelosi could have said something like "Competition shows our strength" or "All factions of our diverse party are united in our goals" to communicate an optimistic future. Rather, by using the healing metaphor, Pelosi comes across as nurturing, maternal, reassuring, and nonthreatening.

Commentators agree that Pelosi's loss signaled a potentially serious weakness and called into question her ability to lead the Democrats. Was she wobbling on the tightrope? Certainly, it was practically impossible for Pelosi to punish all 149 Democrats who voted for Hoyer, even if she could accurately identify all of them. Moreover, attempting to do so would be at odds with her call for "healing," and it would have undermined her ability to work with Hoyer effectively and to achieve legislative goals. Yet, the lack of consequences for defectors may have set up Pelosi for future leadership challenges.

Constraining the Power of Committee Chairs. Pelosi's attempt to term-limit committee chairs shows both her political skills and the gendered tightrope she walked. In 2007, Pelosi wanted to maintain the Republicans' rule, instituted by Speaker Gingrich, that limited the terms of committee chairs. Term limits for committee chairs, of course, strengthen the organizational cartel. Not surprisingly, this effort was opposed by the CBC and several powerful chairs at the time, especially David Obey (D-WI), presumptive chair of Appropriations; John Dingell (D-MI), presumptive chair of Energy and Commerce; and Henry Waxman (D-CA), presumptive chair of Oversight and Government Reform. Other members of the Democratic Caucus were loath to limit the power of committee chairs given that the presumptive chairs had been waiting so long to take their gavels and had worked so hard to win back the majority. For her part, Pelosi justified the term limits by stating, "Fresh blood needs to circulate through the committees" (Weisman 2007; see also Whittington 2007). Term limits were dropped from the Democratic Caucus Rules in the 111th Congress (2009–10), reinstated under the Republican majority from 2011 to 2018, and dropped again when Democrats regained the majority after the 2018 election (Hudiburg 2019). While there is no term limit for committee chairs, the current Democratic Rule 21 states that the "Steering and Policy [Committee] need not necessarily follow seniority in making nominations for Chair" (Rules of the Democratic Caucus 2021, 20).

Contrast Pelosi's apparent capitulation with Newt Gingrich's experience. Arguably, the Republican ranking members had waited a long time for their gavels and had worked hard to gain the majority. Yet, Gingrich was able to ignore seniority, install loyalists, and impose term limits. Of course, no members of the GOP Caucus in 1995 had ever served in the majority, unlike many senior members of the Democratic Caucus in 2007 who remembered being in the majority before the 1994 elections. Another variable is gender. Gingrich could aggressively consolidate power in the organizational cartel without worrying about gendered expectations that would lead to a backlash. Similarly, senior (male) members of the Democratic Caucus were willing to challenge Pelosi, a woman, in spite of her political skills and the power of her office. They prevailed in the short run at least.

Nonetheless, Pelosi successfully asserted her authority over committees in other ways, allowing her to sidestep seniority without provoking a dispute within the caucus. For instance, the current language of Rule 21 gives a head nod to seniority yet clearly communicates that it is not a deciding factor. Similarly, in one well-publicized episode, Pelosi sidestepped the authority of John Dingell, who opposed any efforts to limit emissions from automobiles to protect his home state's automotive industry, by creating a Select Committee on Climate Change. Dingell had publicly ridiculed the body as "the committee on world travel and junkets" (*Detroit News* 2007) and a "glorified task force" (Lawrence 2023, 25–26). In another, committee chairs found that the leadership, especially the Speaker's office, was involved in details of drafting legislation, a responsibility that was traditionally the purview of the committee staff, leading one reporter to note that "gavels just aren't what they used to be" (Yachnin 2007). While committee chairs chafed at this intrusion, the Speaker prevailed and continued to be engaged in both strategy and details of legislation (Personal interview, July 8, 2021). Arguably, Pelosi secured as much power over the majority as bombastic Gingrich did, yet she did so in quiet, noncombative, and subtle ways.

Walking a Tightrope to Pass the Affordable Care Act, 2009

The beginning of the 111th Congress in 2009 was an optimistic time for Democrats. In the preceding election, Democrats had maintained control of the House of Representatives, they had a sixty-vote, filibuster-proof majority in the US Senate, and Barack Obama was coming into the White House. Pelosi looked forward to helping the president enact his ambitious agenda, which included health care reform. Pelosi's victory was due in part to the changes in the leadership rules, which concentrated power in the speakership, and in part to her own understanding of legislative rules and process. Pelosi's political skills carried the day.

The ACA, also known as "Obamacare," is the latest step in the US's century-old, tortured, and so far incomplete effort to provide medical insurance to all Americans (for a complete history, see Starr 1982, 2013). In 2007, approximately forty-four million Americans, primarily unemployed adults between the ages of eighteen and sixty-four, lacked health insurance (Cohen and Martinez 2009). The ACA is a sweeping piece of legislation, with nearly one thousand pages and ten titles. According to Obama adviser Ezekiel Emmanuel, only the first two titles dealt with coverage. Title I specified the benefits package, subsidies, exchanges, employer and individual mandates, and consumer protections. Title II included the Medicaid expansion and public option. The remainder of the bill addressed taxation, emphasized prevention, included Medicare reforms and cost savings, reauthorized the Indian Health Care Improvement Act, and enacted reporting requirements. Title VII, which provided for a long-term care insurance program, was repealed (Emmanuel 2014, 201–3).

Because the ACA included new taxes, the Constitution's Origination Clause applied, requiring the House to pass the bill before the Senate.[2] Because of the sweeping nature of the policy and committee jurisdictions, three House committees had jurisdiction over the legislation: Ways and Means, Energy and Commerce, and Education and Workforce. Speaker Pelosi had been a member of the House during the last major health reform debate during the Clinton administration. Then the reform was bottled up in committees, which could not agree on final language. Pelosi wanted to make sure history did not repeat itself.

Energy and Commerce Chair, 2009. Pelosi's first task in working to enact the ACA was to ensure that the committee chairs would work with her and together to pass a bill. One sticking point was John Dingell, the senior Democrat on the Energy and Commerce Committee. Ensuring that a cooperative chair was on this committee boiled down to another proxy fight between Pelosi and Hoyer. Dingell, the incumbent chair, was a Hoyer

---

2. Article I of the US Constitution, which defines the powers of Congress, requires that all revenue (i.e., tax) bills must be passed first by the House of Representatives.

ally who had clashed with Pelosi previously on climate issues (Ball 2020, 159; Lawrence 2023, 25–27). While Dingell had long supported health care reform, he had failed to report the Clinton health reform plan out of committee in 1993–94 (Nather 2014), and there was little assurance that he would back the Obama administration's bill over his own.

Pelosi's ally and fellow Californian Henry Waxman, next in seniority, challenged Dingell to become chair. Dingell refused an offer from Majority Leader Steny Hoyer to consider stepping down in two years. While Pelosi was officially neutral, the Steering and Policy Committee, considered a Pelosi proxy, recommended Waxman for the top post, so Dingell took the dispute to the full caucus. While he enjoyed the support of moderates and the CBC—because of both Dingell's seniority and his support of civil rights—Dingell lost by a vote of 137–122 (Broder and Hulse 2008; Cohn 2010; Emmanuel 2014, 162; O'Connor 2008).

The "Tri-Com." Pelosi's next task was to ensure that the three committees with major jurisdiction reported out a bill and quickly. To meet Pelosi's deadlines, the three chairs decided to divide the legislation and work together on a single bill. Called the "tri-com," for "tri-committee," the staff members even had their own logo and tote bags (Cohn 2010).

According to a top Pelosi aide, the key to Pelosi's success as leader was that she "understands her Caucus." She knew that the legislation had to have a financing mechanism to appease the moderates. She also knew that the bill needed to have universal coverage to appeal to Progressives. Pelosi herself worked to ensure that the minimum benefits package was generous and included significant consumer protections such as community rating and guaranteed issue (Kirsch 2011, 271; personal interview, July 8, 2021). Pelosi's political skills were on display again. She also had sufficient *policy expertise*, à la Escobar-Lemmon and Taylor-Robinson (2016, 81–103), to know what the legislation needed to include.

The Abortion Debate. Pelosi's third task was to pass the bill through the House so it could be taken up in the Senate. Here she ran into trouble in the guise of Bart Stupak (D-MI). Stupak, like Pelosi, is Roman Catholic. Unlike Pelosi, he opposes abortion.

The House version of the ACA included several provisions in which the federal government would be paying for health care. The first was the Medicaid expansion, in which the federal government would pay for most of the costs to cover qualified Americans, with little state liability. The second was the insurance premium subsidies, which would make purchasing individual health insurance on the marketplaces affordable for many Americans of moderate income. The third was the public option, whereby consumers could choose between purchasing private health insurance or buying into an enhanced Medicare program (Emmanuel 2014; Kirsch 2011, 34–36).

Given that the ACA also covered abortion services, by implication, federal tax dollars could be used to pay for these services. This realization did not sit well with Bart Stupak and a few other antiabortion Democrats. It also would have undermined the Hyde Amendment, which prohibited using federal funds for abortion services and had been policy for over three decades. Stupak and his allies introduced an amendment to extend this ban to ACA (H. Con. Res. 254). Abortion services and their administrative costs could be purchased as a rider or included in private plans. Yet, in either case, these costs could be paid only through private sources (Llanera 2013).

The Republican Party was unified against the ACA, so Pelosi would need to achieve a majority with Democratic votes. With the Democrats' majority of 255 seats, there could only be 37 defectors. Of course, other Democrats had reservations about the bill unrelated to the abortion question, especially about the public option (Brill 2015, 172). Pelosi did everything possible to win over these undecided members. However, even when this horse trading was complete, she was short. The only option was to agree to the Stupak Amendment. Pelosi's next job was to sell this to the Pro-Choice Caucus, of which she was a member. As Molly Ball recounts:

> Pelosi listened patiently as the women vented about how unfair it was. The vast majority of House Democrats were among the 190 members of the Pro-Choice Caucus, and yet they were being told that they were the ones who had to give in to a stubborn, unreasonable minority. This, [Representative Louise] Slaughter said, was a betrayal—not just of the women in Congress, but the women of America.
>
> Pelosi pushed some papers across the table: her tally sheets. The story they told was more powerful than any argument she could make. Without the [Stupak] amendment, she said, "I don't have the votes." (2020, 180)

Support for the Stupak Amendment, which was included in the House version of the ACA, reflects a deep schism within the Catholic Church on the issue of abortion. The United States Conference of Catholic Bishops, representing the governing hierarchy of the church, supported the Stupak

Amendment and even urged that it go further to exclude abortion services from all insurance plans sold on the exchanges. Yet, on the other hand, the Catholic Health Association, the trade group representing Catholic hospitals, supported the bill with or without the abortion provision (Kirsch 2011, 272–73, 313). This disagreement was also evident in the vote on the Stupak Amendment. Many Catholic Democrats like Stupak were more likely to support the Stupak Amendment (Llanera 2013), while others such as Pelosi, who is deeply devout, were not.

Securing a Vote on the Senate Version. After the House passed the ACA, the Senate took up the legislation. In 2009, the Democrats had a sixty-vote majority. However, because of solid Republican opposition to any reform, Majority Leader Harry Reid (D-NV) could not afford even one Democratic defection. To fall short of sixty votes would mean that the Republicans could successfully filibuster and kill any reform. The result was that wavering Democrats were in powerful positions to exact favorable provisions in exchange for supporting the legislation. To secure Blanche Lincoln's (D-AR) vote, Reid included a provision that allowed employers to delay offering health insurance to their employees for up to a total of four months, put in place to reassure Walmart. The public option was eliminated to placate Joe Lieberman (D-CT), whose state was home to many insurance companies. Ben Nelson (D-NE) secured a provision stipulating that the federal government would cover 100 percent of the Medicaid expansion costs for Nebraska in perpetuity, a provision derisively called the "Cornhusker Kickback." Al Franken (D-MN) and Evan Bayh (D-IN) both benefited from a provision to reduce taxes on medical devices. Mary Landrieu (D-LA) negotiated for increased federal aid for her state, a provision nicknamed the "Louisiana Purchase." To please advocates of federalism, a single federal marketplace was replaced with fifty state-level exchanges. Other important differences included a tax on very generous health insurance plans, like those enjoyed by autoworkers, called the "Cadillac tax," and the absence of a provision comparable to the Stupak Amendment (Brill 2015, 172–85).

After Senator Edward Kennedy's death in August 2009, Massachusetts held a special election to fill his seat in January 2010. To everyone's surprise, the Democratic nominee, Attorney General Martha Coakley, lost to the Republican nominee, Scott Brown. This election cost Reid his sixty-vote, filibuster-proof majority, meaning that the conference report, which would reconcile the differences in the House and Senate versions, would likely be filibustered and fail to be passed by the Senate.

The Obama administration proposed that the Democrats use a Senate rule known as "reconciliation," which permits the Senate to pass the budget-related provisions with just fifty votes (with the vice president casting the tiebreaker). However, the House would have to pass the Senate version of the bill in its entirety with a "sidecar" that would tweak a few budget-related provisions (Ball 2020, 190–91; Brill 2015, 188). If the House failed to pass the Senate bill, the legislation would go to a conference committee. The conference report, no matter its final language, was sure to face a fatal filibuster in the Senate.

Pelosi was then faced with a difficult and unpleasant task: getting a majority of her caucus to support the Senate version, which many loathed. The most controversial provisions included the Cornhusker Kickback, the Louisiana Purchase, the missing public option, the Cadillac tax, and weak abortion language. However, Pelosi set about to convince the Democratic Caucus to move forward with supporting the Senate language, perceived flaws and all. She was determined, as she told a group of reporters:

> You have to go through the gate. If the gate's closed, you go over the fence. If the fence is too high, we'll pole-vault in. If that doesn't work, we'll parachute in. But we're going to get health care reform passed for the American people. (Ball 2020, 190)

With the White House's assistance, Pelosi worked out funding compromises, reassured liberals, and secured a promise from the White House to limit abortion coverage via executive order. The Cadillac tax was reduced and postponed, and the Cornhusker Kickback and the Louisiana Purchase were eliminated in the reconciliation sidecar. In addition, Pelosi demanded, and received, a letter signed by every Democratic senator promising to vote for the bill when it came up under reconciliation. The House passed the Senate bill on March 21, 2010, by a 219–212, majority, with thirty-four Democrats voting against it (Ball 2020, 192; Brill 2015, 192). While the White House's support helped, Pelosi personally worked the phones and met with members to secure all the votes needed to pass the legislation (personal interview with former member of Congress, March 8, 2021).

By March 2010, the ACA was extremely unpopular, successfully framed by its opponents as a job killer, government overreach, and full of "death panels." At the same time, individual provisions, including community rating, preexisting condition protections, and the ability to keep adult children covered until age twenty-six, were very popular (Brodie et al. 2019). Pelosi was referring to this apparent paradox when she said, "We have to pass the bill so you can find out what's in it" (Brill 2015, 190). In the decade since it passed, the ACA has remained fairly unpopular, with 30–40 percent of Americans, and over 80 percent of Republicans, holding unfavorable opinions of the law. Ten contentious years later, the ACA is still law, although weakened by some court decisions and Trump administration executive orders, with some 15.5 million people having health insurance coverage as a result (Cohn 2021; Finegold et al. 2021).

One brief analysis of Pelosi's media coverage from the health care debate describes the news coverage in both masculine and feminine terms. In the first case, she was "stalwart, imposing, formidable, arm-twisting, pressure maker, and threatening." At the same time, she was maternal, with health care being "personal," making gendered appeals such as "being a woman will no longer be a pre-existing condition," and mentioning family and shared cultural values. This allowed Pelosi to overcome the media's negative bias against women officeholders (Taylor 2012).

This historic case once again showcases Pelosi's political skills and her willingness to use the power of the organizational cartel. First, she knew that she needed a skilled and sympathetic chair leading the Energy and Commerce Committee and saw her choice successfully elected by the Democratic Caucus, overriding seniority in the process. Second, she undermined the authority of the individual committee chairs by ensuring that they worked together as the "tri-com" to pass a single version of the legislation. Third, she ensured the bill had all the provisions needed to appeal to the factions in the Democratic Caucus. Fourth, Pelosi persuaded the Democratic Caucus to pass a problematic Senate bill, despite many members' misgivings, by exacting commitments from senators in advance and ensuring the most contentious elements were eliminated. Finally, fueled by her policy expertise, Pelosi was not willing to settle for anything less than sweeping, comprehensive reform that would provide Americans with significant financial protection and a generous benefit plan. She was willing to stand up to the leadership of her own church and to negotiate with abortion opponents to get the legislation passed. Recognizing her crucial role, some of her supporters dubbed the legislation "PelosiCare" (Page 2021, 243).

Walking a Tightrope in the Minority: 2010–14

The Democratic Leader Race, 2010–11. After two years of unified government under President Obama, the Democrats fared poorly in the

2010 midterm election, losing sixty-four House seats and the majority. While midterm elections are usually a referendum on the incumbent president—and in this case, the ACA—the national Republican Party also made Speaker Pelosi the focus of the election. The Republican Party and candidates spent over $65 million to run more than one hundred thousand negative ads featuring Pelosi (Jones and McDermott 2011).

The ads had an impact. According to the Gallup Poll, in 2007, when Pelosi was first elected Speaker, 44 percent of Americans had a favorable view of her compared to 22 percent who had an unfavorable opinion. Thirteen percent reported they had never heard of Pelosi, and 21 percent had no opinion. By January 2011, Pelosi's favorability rating had dropped to 33 percent, and those with an unfavorable opinion rose to 54 percent (Gallup Poll n.d.).

As Speaker, Pelosi could be blamed for all the perceived ills of Congress, and as a Californian, she could be depicted as out of step with ordinary Americans (Ball 2020, 205). The National Republican Congressional Committee (NRCC) made the race a national one by tying Pelosi to vulnerable Democrats all over the country. They focused on the candidates' voting records or even their support for Pelosi as Democratic leader (Bendavid 2009). The NRCC even posted a "Fire Pelosi" banner on its headquarters prior to the election. During the campaign, two dozen Democrats announced that they would not support Pelosi's next bid for Speaker (Jenkins and Stewart 2013, 305).

Given the Democrats' "shellacking," as President Obama described it (Halloran 2010), there was speculation that Pelosi would step down as Democratic leader. As one commentator noted, Pelosi was seventy years old and a grandmother who had already served twenty-three years in office (Bresnahan 2010; Ball 2020, 208). (Hoyer and Clyburn were also septuagenarian grandparents, yet this fact was not mentioned.) A group of House Democrats allegedly circulated a letter addressed to Pelosi reading, in part:

> Madam Speaker, fairly or unfairly, Republicans made you the face of resentment and disagreement in our races. While we commend your years of service to our party and your leadership through many tough times, we respectfully ask that you step aside as the top Democrat in the House. (Taranto 2010)

One member who was willing to make the case to Pelosi directly was Representative Heath Shuler, a moderate Democrat[3] from western North

---

3. Unlike Frost and Ford, who challenged Pelosi in 2002, there was significant ideological

Carolina whom Pelosi had recruited to run in 2006. Shuler had expressed reservations about Pelosi's leadership during the 2010 election campaign. After the election, Shuler called Pelosi to ask her to step down. As Molly Ball recounts:

> He told her he understood. In high school and college, he'd been the champion football player everybody loved, but then he got to the NFL and flamed out. "They replaced me as starting quarterback," he said. "And I had two options. I could say, 'I'm not the problem—it's everyone else.' Or I could support the other guy taking my place. I decided to be a team player. And I'm asking you to be a team player." (2020, 207)

Shuler's football analogy was not persuasive, and the next day Pelosi notified the caucus of her candidacy for Democratic leader. Shuler then lodged a quixotic campaign against Pelosi. Shuler himself admitted he wasn't really expecting to win but was running to "make a point" (O'Connor 2010). Pelosi's detractors were primarily centrists who, like Shuler, argued that keeping Pelosi at the helm would result in further Democratic losses. "She is the face that defeated us in this last election," one was quoted as saying to the Associated Press (Abrams et al. 2010). The moderate Blue Dogs also expressed concern for the economy and deficit spending (Chaddock 2010).

In addition, Pelosi's decision to stay once again put her at odds with Steny Hoyer, who apparently briefly considered running against her for the Democratic leader position. Then Hoyer was placed in the awkward position of opposing Jim Clyburn (D-SC), the highest-ranking African American in the Democratic leadership, for the position of Democratic whip. Pelosi then created a new position for Clyburn, "assistant leader," to maintain her support within the CBC (Allen 2010).

Shuler's challenge was ultimately unsuccessful. He lost two key votes in the caucus. The first was to delay the election so that members would have more time to consider alternatives. The second was the leadership vote itself, which Shuler lost 150–43. Even though Shuler only received 22 percent of the vote in the caucus, this outcome "marked a significant challenge" to Pelosi's leadership (Chaddock 2010). Eventually, nineteen Democrats, again mostly Blue Dogs, voted for Shuler on the House floor, another embarrassment to Pelosi (Jenkins and Stewart 2013, 305).

---

distance between Shuler and Pelosi. Shuler's DW-NOMINATE score for the 111th Congress (2009–11, immediately before his challenge) was -0.07. Pelosi's was -0.49 (Lewis et al. 2021).

In his postmortem, Billy House of the *National Journal* analyzes Pelosi's victory in terms of her prodigious political skill as a party leader and fundraiser—two key functions of congressional leaders (Pearson 2015):

> Her reputation as a strategist and disciplinarian has helped keep her afloat, but more than anything else, Pelosi, 71, is a monster fundraiser. For all of the criticism that she polarizes voters, she is a bigger rain-maker than any other member of Congress. Her nearest competitor is probably Speaker John Boehner, who raised less than half of what Pelosi racked up in the first quarter [$10.9 million]. And she has helped equip Democrats to contest the airwaves in many crucial elections. (House 2011)

It is not surprising that Pelosi faced a leadership challenge after a devastating midterm loss. Her predecessor, Richard Gephardt, also faced a challenge when he ran for the position of Democratic leader in the wake of the devastating 1994 midterm election (Clymer 1994; Harris and Green 2018). Yet, we can see signs of sexism in the 2010 election, its postmortems, and Shuler's challenge to Pelosi. First, the ads that demonized Pelosi were sexist. For instance, one depicted her as the Wicked Witch from the *Wizard of Oz* (CNN 2010). In another, Pelosi is shown against a backdrop of flames, with clenched fists held aloft in a bellicose position (Weiner 2010). Celinda Lake also notes that the attack ads show Pelosi talking rather than listening (Beinart 2018). In his fascinating study of Google search terms of several political leaders in 2010, Justin Buchler analyzes Google's suggestions to attach the epithets "crazy," "insane," "idiot," "stupid," and "moron" to Pelosi's name. Only Representatives Michele Bachmann (R-MN) and Ron Paul (R-TX) had more epithets attached to their names, and only Senator Al Franken matched the same number as Pelosi.

Second, like a high school principal who sends a girl home to change her clothes so she won't be a distraction to male students, the unhappy Democrats asked their woman leader to accept punishment for the bad behavior of others (Republicans) rather than hold the perpetrators responsible for their actions. Third, in his unsuccessful effort to persuade Pelosi to step down, Shuler used a sports analogy, perhaps because Pelosi is a devoted fan of the San Francisco 49ers. Nonetheless, this argument may not have been terribly persuasive to a woman born in 1940 and educated long before Title IX provided athletic opportunities to girls. Fourth, neither the White House nor the Democratic National Committee made many efforts to defend Pelosi against the attack ads (Ball 2020, 206), yet after the election, the Democrats sought to rehabilitate Pelosi's image through an "extreme makeover" with a new message: "This woman's work isn't done" (Davis 2010).

The gender dynamics do not end there. Pelosi's reactions are feminine, gracious, and telling. As Molly Ball notes, Pelosi did not complain about the ad campaign and continued to donate funds to Democratic congressional candidates, even if they voted against Democratic legislation or stated their opposition to her (2020, 206–7). Juli Weiner of *The Atlantic* reported that Pelosi "spoke mournfully about the dozens of Democrats who would not be returning to Washington" (2010). Moreover, Pelosi did not punish the nineteen Democrats who voted against her on the House floor. Jenkins and Stewart, in their historical account of the rise of the partisan "organizational cartel," or majority-party domination of the House, state:

> The fact that this display of disloyalty had no material consequences means that it was viewed as an act of position-taking by electorally vulnerable members, not a body blow to the principle of party organization of the chamber. In other words, it was an accepted form of highly visible dissent meant for public consumption, not a serious assault on the organizational cartel itself. (2013, 305)

We posit another explanation. Had Pelosi exercised her powers to punish these members, she would have been considered petty and vindictive. This would be even more unseemly in an era where Americans expect their women leaders to be "Nice," that is, polite and likeable (Lakoff 2005). Therefore, even though Pelosi held the power to impose consequences for this disloyalty, doing so would have come at a high cost because of her gender. Female leaders are expected to be warm, self-effacing, and concerned with community rather than competitive, ambitious, and visible or aggressive in exercising power (see, e.g., Netchaeva, Kouchaki, and Sheppard 2015; Beinart 2018). When they do so, they are punished, while male leaders are perceived as decisive. Pelosi walked that gendered tightrope by ignoring the ads, mourning the defeat of her Democratic colleagues, and not punishing the detractors.

For all of the Republicans' negative stereotyping, Pelosi often frames her service as Speaker in terms of care work—a traditionally woman's domain—carried out on the largest scale, the nation. As noted earlier, Pelosi called the children attending the 2007 swearing-in ceremony to join her at the podium as she called upon Congress to do its business on behalf of future generations (Cunningham 2012). Similarly, Pelosi framed the question of whether to run for the Democratic leader post in terms of protection:

> Somebody had to stand up for liberal values, not just against the GOP, but against a Democratic White House and Senate that would sell them out without a second thought. Somebody had to protect the president from his own worst instincts and meager negotiating skills. Somebody had to protect the Affordable Care Act from the Republicans who had vowed to repeal it. Somebody had to protect Medicare and Social Security and all the other Democratic accomplishments of the last century from being negotiated away. (Ball 2020, 209)

Nonetheless, as Cunningham (2012) notes, maternal frames, and by extension other gendered feminine frames, can also be interpreted as weakness. Coupled with her reluctance to punish defectors, walking this tightrope could make Pelosi appear weak and vulnerable to repeated leadership challenges.

Energy and Commerce Committee Ranking Member, 2014. As Matthew Green (2015) states, the minority party has three goals and four strategies to achieve them. The goals are to regain majority status, make policy, and win the presidency. The strategies to support these goals are electioneering (fundraising, campaigning, and recruiting candidates), message development, obstructing (engaging in deleterious actions to stymie the majority party's initiatives), and, finally, legislating. After her leadership challenge of 2011, Pelosi launched into all of these tasks, including obstruction and a refusal to engage in too much bipartisan legislation. Providing the majority Republicans with too many victories would undercut the Democrats' goal of recapturing the House majority.

In this environment, Pelosi remained as Democratic leader after the 2012 and 2014 elections, in spite of the party's failure to regain the majority. By contrast, when the Republicans found themselves in the minority for the long term, they had significant turnover in their party leadership (Peabody 1976; Green and Harris 2019). Yet Pelosi did not face a significant challenge to her leadership, in spite of the party's losses. However, after the 2014 midterm election, Pelosi did face a proxy challenge that pitted her against Steny Hoyer. Again.

California Democrat Henry Waxman, the ranking member and former chair of the powerful Energy and Commerce Committee, and John Dingell, the second highest ranking Democrat, both retired from the House in 2014. Moderate Representative Frank Pallone (D-NJ) was the next senior member of the committee and, by traditional norms of the House, should step into Waxman's position. This would place Pallone in line to take over the position of committee chair when and if the Democrats recapture control of the House.

Committee chairs and ranking members are elected by the Democratic Caucus. Party leaders normally remain neutral in these races, and the Democratic Caucus often defers to seniority. Nonetheless, Pelosi endorsed her best friend, Californian Anna Eshoo, who was fifth in seniority on the committee (or third, after Waxman's and Dingell's retirements).[4] In any case, Eshoo had less seniority than Pallone, who was backed by Steny Hoyer. Pelosi's support was more than symbolic. She lent the resources of her office to Eshoo and even functioned as her campaign manager (Cillizza 2014).

The race came down to two issues: seniority and money. One little known fact of American politics is that committee leaders are expected to raise money for the party, either as donations to the national committee or through their own leadership PACs. In the latter case, the member controls where the donations go, which are a means to secure votes and reward loyalty (Pearson 2015, 122–26). In this case, both Pallone and Eshoo built coalitions through donations to their colleagues' campaigns. In February 2014, in the earliest days of the leadership race, *Politico* reported that Pallone had donated only $1,000 through his leadership PAC. Eshoo, at that point, had not yet formed a leadership PAC but had donated $100,000 to the Democratic Congressional Campaign Committee (DCCC) (Haberkorn and Goode 2014). By August, Eshoo had formed a leadership PAC (Currinder n.d.), and Pallone and Eshoo had donated $274,000 and nearly $300,000, respectively, to their colleagues (French 2014).

Pelosi's willingness to discount seniority should not have been a surprise, given her 2007 attempt to impose term limits on committee chairs. Yet Eshoo's and Pelosi's disregard for the norm of seniority met with skepticism, if not outright opposition, from the CBC. The CBC supports the seniority system because it is a way to protect their members from being passed over for these leadership slots. Pelosi responded with a letter to the Democratic Caucus stating that seniority should be "a consideration" and not "a determination" (Dumain 2014a). CBC member Emanuel Cleaver

---

4. Immediately ahead of Eshoo in seniority was Bobby Rush (D-IL), a member of the CBC, who was not a candidate for Chair (Dumain 2014b).

II (D-MO) predicted that all CBC members would back Pallone. Charles Rangel, another CBC member, opined that Pelosi, in her endorsement of Eshoo, "officially buried seniority" (Dumain 2014c).

Anna Eshoo received the support of the Democratic Steering and Policy Committee, the group that places Democrats on committees and makes recommendations on leadership. The Steering and Policy Committee typically works hand-in-glove with the Speaker in making these decisions. Frank Pallone then had to secure the public support of 50 members of the caucus in order to force a vote of the full Democratic membership. Pallone presented a letter signed by 53 of his Democratic colleagues, which represented more than a quarter of the 199 Democrats (plus nonvoting delegates) in the caucus (Dumain 2014d; French and Bresnahan 2014).

Even though both Eshoo and Pallone claimed to have commitments from over 100 Democrats, Pallone prevailed in the caucus vote, winning 100–90. As one observer noted, "There just wasn't a good reason to replace Pallone" (personal interview, July 8, 2021). While neither Eshoo nor Pallone would interpret Pallone's victory as a repudiation of Pelosi's leadership, others did. Bill Pascrell (D-NJ), for example, said, "One may make the argument that she overdid in terms of the letter she sent out, on the other hand, she had every right to do it. She didn't break any laws"[5] (Dumain 2014d; see also House 2014).

Chris Cillizza, then commentator for the *Washington Post*, was less charitable. Calling Eshoo's loss "a major setback," Cillizza opined that this repudiation was due, in part, to young members who are not "necessarily willing to watch as Pelosi dictates her will to the caucus nor wait until she decides it's time to leave to make some noise about how she runs things" (2014).

Notably, Eshoo and Pelosi were being held to a double standard on the issue of seniority. Eshoo's challenge came when the norm of seniority was already weakened by the rule changes put in place by the Democratic majority elected in 1974 and the Republican majority in 1995. These changes enhanced the power of the Speaker by ensuring his or her allies were in these key roles. While each party makes its own rules for leadership selection, the majority party's practices influence the climate and culture of the institution. Moreover, retiring chair Henry Waxman became Energy and Commerce chair when he successfully challenged the long-standing chair, John Dingell. While the CBC opposed Waxman because of its support for the seniority system, that was not enough to undermine

---

5. This comment is a little curious, given that the Democratic Caucus's leadership selection rituals are determined by the Caucus's rules, not by law. Perhaps Pascrell meant that Pelosi ignored tradition and norms but not Caucus rules.

Waxman's candidacy (P. O'Connor 2008). Yet the seniority debate was enough to defeat Eshoo and, by extension, undermine Pelosi's prerogatives as Speaker.

While Nancy Pelosi was still targeted by the Republican Party's negative ads in the 2012 and 2014 election cycles, she was not directly challenged for her position as Democratic leader and she was not an issue in the Energy and Commerce race. However, nearly half the caucus felt comfortable in backing Pallone over Pelosi's endorsed candidate. Again, punishing half of the caucus for their breach of loyalty would not be feasible. Nonetheless, given Pelosi's record of not imposing consequences and letting bygones be bygones, members may have felt more comfortable in defying her.

One might argue that Eshoo's campaign was as much a challenge to Hoyer's leadership as it was a proxy challenge to Pelosi. However, Hoyer was Pelosi's subordinate and wielded less power in the organizational cartel. Once Pelosi endorsed Eshoo, the question became whether one was comfortable in defying the Speaker, not defying the majority leader.

Why did Pelosi back Eshoo over Pallone when there was ideologically little difference between them?[6] The contemporaneous news coverage of the race does not address this question. However, we do know that Pelosi is fiercely loyal and will stand by her friends. As in the case of backing her friend John Murtha in 2007, Pelosi's personal loyalty is considered a weakness, not a strength. Moreover, given her political skills, Pelosi would not be surprised by the CBC's opposition to or others' loyalty to Pallone. Yet Pelosi demonstrated again that she was not wedded to the norm of seniority, and the language of her endorsement letter is very similar to Rule 21.

Leadership Challenges and More, 2016–19

Despite her skills and successes, Pelosi faced challenges to her position as Democratic leader in 2016–17 and 2018–19. Was this just more of the same, or was something else at play? Both, we argue.

The 2016–17 Leadership Race. The 2016 election cycle was dominated by the presidential contest between Donald J. Trump and former secretary of state Hillary Clinton. For her part, Pelosi remained very unpopular—

---

6. In the 113th Congress (2013–15), Eshoo's DW-NOMINATE score was -0.381 and Pallone's was -0.404. By comparison, Pelosi's was -0.49 and Hoyer's was -0.38 (Lewis et al. 2021).

her unfavorable rating hovered between 45 and 50 percent (Gallup Poll n.d.)—and she continued to be a feature in GOP ads that ran in various congressional districts. However, after the presidential election, in the days preceding the leadership contest, the Democrats were in disarray. They had failed to win the presidency and failed to win a majority in the House.

Moreover, the Democrats were now in a Congress whose climate had been changed by a new development: the rise of the restive caucus. The Freedom Caucus, formed in 2015, caused endless headaches for three Republican Speakers and successfully unseated one, John Boehner. Paradoxically, the Republicans' turmoil actually allowed Pelosi to accrue power as minority leader. If Pelosi delivered a block of Democratic votes, Boehner could pass legislation, even without the Freedom Caucus members. However, doing so came at a cost to Boehner. He had to grant Pelosi concessions, making the legislation more moderate and further incurring the wrath of the Freedom Caucus members. The Freedom Caucus, however, set the stage for junior Democratic members to voice their opposition with the caucus leadership in the future.

In 2016, Pelosi continued with her prodigious fundraising as well, contributing to candidates across the country. Nonetheless, these skills seemed to matter little as the Democrats organized themselves for the 115th Congress. Representative Jim Crowley (D-NY) considered challenging Pelosi, at the behest of several members of the caucus, but could not find a path to victory. There were few others interested in running. As Ball describes it:

> The insurrectionists had to be careful: an unsuccessful coup would put them in Pelosi's doghouse, consigned to congressional Siberia. Just as she had with her children, Pelosi generally didn't punish members of her caucus; she didn't have to. They feared her too much to test her patience. The withdrawal of her usual graces, the chill of guilt and disapproval, was enough to keep people in line. (2020, 242)

Eventually, Representative Tim Ryan entered the race. Representing Youngstown, Ohio, a waning Midwestern industrial city, Ryan was concerned that the Republicans' continued demonization of Pelosi made it impossible for the Democrats to win in the heartland. Without a "fresh face" (Berman 2016), Ryan was concerned that the Democrats were becoming a party of major cities on the two coasts and ignoring the vast middle of the country. One example Ryan cited was Pelosi's effort to make the Zika virus threat a major issue in the midterm election. "It's very important, but that's not a national message. That's in New Orleans and South Florida. People here [in Ohio] say, 'I've never been to South Florida.' That could be Venezuela to them. Or the North Pole" (Hohmann and Deppisch 2016).

In addition, Ryan's campaign pointed to the "stagnation" at the top of the Democratic leadership, with three septuagenarians who had held their positions for years. There was little opportunity to develop leadership skills among the next generation of members, and some were eager to do so. Others were leaving the House in pursuit of different opportunities. By contrast, the top three Republican leaders at the time, Speaker Paul Ryan (R-WI), Majority Leader Kevin McCarthy (R-CA), and Whip Steve Scalise (R-LA), were all under the age of fifty-five (Cottle 2016).

Ryan did not deny that Pelosi was good at her job. In fact, he acknowledged that he could not match her negotiating skills or her fundraising success. Ryan admitted, "I'm a Nancy guy" (Hohmann and Deppisch 2016), but "I personally don't believe that we can win the House back with the current leadership" (Lillis 2016).

Pelosi won reelection by a two-thirds majority of the caucus, 134–63 (Cottle 2016). Again, it's not a surprise that Pelosi faced a challenge after another electoral loss, especially one coupled with the shock of President Trump's election.[7] Yet, there were gender dynamics at play as well. First, while the age of the three Democratic leaders—Pelosi, Hoyer, and Clyburn—was cited as a problem, only Pelosi drew a challenger. If the Democratic Party leadership's image is too old, too "coastal," and too entrenched, these critiques could apply to Hoyer and Clyburn just as easily as to Pelosi. And rather than challenging the top of the ladder, one might have more success with a lower-level post. One observer used a sports analogy to explain why Hoyer and Clyburn escaped scrutiny: "It's about the head coach. When you're losing, you don't worry about the assistants" (personal interview, July 8, 2021).

In addition, Tim Ryan, like Heath Shuler before him, was a former football player, and his identity was very much wrapped up in this chapter of his story, contributing to the gender dynamics of his challenge. According to Russell Berman (2016):

> [Ryan's] week-long candidacy has been an explosion of sports metaphors. Democrats, he has said, are akin to a losing football team that must "change quarterbacks." Another more complicated example

---

7. Hillary Clinton was predicted to win the popular vote, which she did. However, the polls did not capture a surge in Trump support in the Upper Midwest (Ad Hoc Committee 2017).

involved the Boston Red Sox returning to the World Series in 2013, a year after dumping their manager, Terry Francona, who then returned to the Series himself with the Cleveland Indians. (How this differentiates Ryan from Pelosi, known to be a passionate fan of the San Francisco Giants and the 49ers, is less clear.)

Similarly, if Ryan was a "fresh face," Pelosi, by implication, had crossed that invisible line to where she was no longer "fresh." Not only does this play into the ageist stereotypes that are more damning to women than to men, it also again blames Pelosi for the Republicans' attacks that caricatured her in sexist ways. Instead of defending Pelosi or attempting to rehabilitate her national image, the answer is to replace her with a white male, who is a more conventional image of a high-ranking leader. Again, Pelosi's political skills, especially her ability to use the organizational cartel to her advantage, allowed her to survive this challenge. She wobbled on the tightrope but did not fall.

#MeToo Reaches the US Congress. The global #MeToo movement reached the US Congress in October 2017. The scandal first touched Tim Murphy (R-PA), who resigned after reports surfaced that he had an extramarital affair and encouraged his paramour to have an abortion. Eight more members of Congress were implicated and eventually resigned or decided not to run for reelection. The nine included one senator, Al Franken, and five Republican House members. The first of three House Democrats to be implicated was Representative John Conyers (D-MI), then the longest serving member of the House of Representatives and a respected leader in the CBC. Several former staffers accused Conyers of inappropriate touching, sexual propositions, and other improprieties. Eventually, Conyers's office acknowledged that it used congressional funds to pay a $27,000 settlement to a former employee (*Daily Beast* 2017). Conyers was not alone. From 2003 to 2017, public dollars were used to pay about $300,000 in settlements against thirteen members of Congress (Linderman 2018).

By all accounts, Pelosi botched her initial response to the Conyers revelations. In a *Meet the Press* interview a few days after the first story was released, Pelosi defended him, calling him "an icon" and asserting that he was entitled to due process. Moreover, Pelosi stated that she did not know the women involved and thus could not judge their veracity (Tamborrino 2017). Given that Pelosi is loyal to her friends, such a response is in character. However, Pelosi was criticized for her reaction, which appeared out of touch with the moment. Pelosi then released a statement calling for an Ethics Committee investigation, "no matter how great an individual's legacy" (Office of the Speaker 2017a). Finally, after meeting with one of the women who accused Conyers, Pelosi issued a statement of support: "I believe what Ms. Sloan has told me" (Office of the Speaker 2017b). In her analysis of Pelosi's responses, journalist Megan Garber opined,

> It was a surprisingly tone-deaf response for a politician who is not only a veteran of *Meet the Press*, who thus had to expect that a question like this would be coming, but for someone who has previously—and validly—celebrated herself and her fellow women in Congress for breaking "the marble ceiling." Pelosi was, by valorizing her colleague and dismissing the women making accusations against him, aligning herself with a longstanding instinct to mistrust women who come forward to share their experiences and disrupt the status quo. (2017)

Garber concludes that Pelosi ended on the right side of history with her public support for Melanie Sloan. Moreover, Pelosi expressed her support for congressional reforms that would tighten Congress's sexual harassment policies. Congress, which normally exempts itself from employment regulations that it imposes on other employers, accomplished this on the eve of Pelosi's return to the Speaker's chair. In December 2018, it passed the Congressional Accountability Act of 1995 Reform Act (S. 3749). This law eliminated the waiting period and mandatory counseling for individuals filing complaints, required that members be personally liable for settlement costs, added protections for interns and fellows, and required the House and Senate to publish an annual report of sexual harassment complaints filed (Zhou 2018). The bill passed with bipartisan support; its principal sponsor in the House was Representative Jackie Speier, another Californian.

Speaker's Race, 2018–19. The 2018 midterm election seemed similar to previous House elections. The Republicans continued to spend freely on ads demonizing Nancy Pelosi (DeBonis 2018b). She continued to be unpopular, with 53 percent of Americans having an unfavorable opinion of her (Gallup n.d.). Pelosi continued to pay little attention to her approval ratings and continued to raise huge sums to support Democratic congressional candidates; the DCCC raised nearly $300 million in the 2018 election cycle, and Democratic leadership PACs donated another $28 million (Open Secrets 2020). The outcome, however, was different. The Democrats won 235 races, a majority of seventeen seats, and control of the House of Representatives. This victory was aided by the unpopularity of President Trump and a record voter turnout for a midterm election.

Nancy Pelosi accomplished everything that a modern US congressional leader is supposed to do and that she had promised to do: recruit good candidates, provide ample financial support, and win the majority. Moreover, she was the first presumptive Speaker since Sam Rayburn in 1955 to return to the speakership after having lost the House majority. Critical elections theory would predict that this resounding success would solidify Pelosi's standing in the Democratic Caucus and cement her leadership position in the House. Yet, in spite of this obvious success, another factor remained unchanged: Pelosi faced a leadership challenge from within her own party. Pelosi's supporters were "incredulous." "It was like winning the World Series and firing the manager. It just didn't make a lot of sense to replace her" (personal interview, July 8, 2021).

The seeds of this challenge to Pelosi, however, were planted two years earlier. Representative Tim Ryan and his allies led the charge. Other leaders included Kathleen Rice (D-NY), Ed Perlmutter (D-CO), and Seth Moulton (D-MA). In Molly Ball's words, Moulton was "a square-jawed, Harvard-educated, forty-year-old marine veteran. . . . Moulton had just been elected to his third term in Congress, but what he lacked in experience he made up for in self-assurance" (2020, 277).

In addition, nine Democrats in the Problem Solvers Caucus withheld their support to gain leverage for rules changes (personal interview, March 8, 2021; Landers and Raju 2018).[8] The Problem Solvers Caucus was founded in 2017 as a bipartisan group "committed to finding common ground on many of the key issues facing the nation" (Problem Solvers Caucus n.d.). Their proposed changes would empower rank-and-file members to bring legislation to the floor, a power that was the purview of the Speaker.

In 2017, one criticism of Ryan and his supporters was that a group of white men were seeking to replace the only female in the House leadership. In response, Pelosi's opponents courted Marcia Fudge (D-OH), an African American liberal from Cleveland, to run against Pelosi. In November 2018, Pelosi's challengers circulated a letter signed by Democratic members who pledged that they would not support Pelosi for Speaker. The challengers needed seventeen Democrats to vote for someone other than Pelosi to deny her the speakership (McPherson 2018c).

---

8. The nine members who signed this letter are Jim Costa (CA), Vicente Gonzalez (TX), Josh Gottheimer (NJ), Dan Lipinski (IL), Stephanie Murphy (FL), Tom O'Halleran (AZ), Kurt Schrader (OR), Darren Soto (FL), and Tom Suozzi (NY) (DeBonis 2018a).

A total of sixteen Democrats eventually signed the letter, including two whose races were still being contested when they signed.[9] In addition, several more announced they would not vote for Pelosi although they did not sign, including Fudge; Rashida Tlaib (D-MI), who had signaled in August that she "probably" would not support Pelosi; Conor Lamb (D-PA); and Abigail Spanberger (D-VA) (Aupperlee 2019; McPherson 2018c; Raju, Grayer, and Killough 2018; Spangler 2018). The arguments against Pelosi were remarkably similar to those in the past: she was too unpopular; she was the subject of many negative ads targeting Democrats in conservative districts; and the House leadership was too old. As Ed Perlmutter (D-CO) stated:

> For me—and I'm even more emphatic about it than I was two years ago—this is about change. You look in the middle of the country, at the districts we picked up—a lot of candidates said they wouldn't support her, or avoided the question. Hundreds of millions of dollars have been spent demonizing her, and it's permeated the public's view of her. That's not her fault. But what she hasn't done is have a succession plan. And that's an element of being a leader. (Draper 2018)

Altogether, without double counting Kurt Schrader (D-OR), who signed both letters, thirty members had pledged at some point that they would not support Pelosi for Speaker, more than enough to defeat her in the House floor vote. They were, as a group, noticeably more moderate than Pelosi. Their average DW-NOMINATE score is −0.259 (with a range of −0.069 to −0.581) compared to −0.49 for Pelosi (calculated by author for the 116th Congress using data from Lewis et al. 2021). Of the thirty, 20 percent (six) were women, a proportion slightly less than in the House (23 percent). Green and Harris (2020) found that members from more moderate districts, younger members, less senior members, and moderate members were more likely to declare their opposition to Pelosi.

In response, Pelosi and her staff embraced an all-out leadership campaign, calling in favors, securing endorsements, engaging surrogates, and contacting members of the caucus. Her choices were strategic. She

---

9. The sixteen signatories were Anthony Brindisi (NY), Jim Cooper (TE), Joe Cunningham (SC), Bill Foster (IL), Brian Higgins (NY), Stephen Lynch (MA), Ben McAdams (UT), Seth Moulton (MA), Ed Perlmutter (CO), Kathleen Rice (NY), Max Rose (NY), Tim Ryan (OH), Linda Sanchez (CA), Kurt Schrader (OR), Jeff Van Drew (NJ), and Filemon Vela (TX) (McPherson 2018d).

targeted those most likely to flip first (Green and Harris 2020; Pearson 2019). Pelosi's allies noted the implicit sexism in the challenge, derisively referring to the leading opponents as "#fivewhiteguys" (Green and Harris 2020). Pelosi had secured an electoral victory, and her leadership was challenged when three male Democratic leaders—Hoyer, Clymer, and Senator Chuck Schumer—were unchallenged. Moulton himself was especially criticized, as Molly Ball notes:

> The grassroots backlash against Moulton was particularly brutal. Many women looked at him and saw a familiar archetype: the younger male know-it-all who steamrolled them in meetings and got promoted over their heads. Could you even imagine, Pelosi's allies whispered, what people would say about a forty-year-old woman who thought she could single-handedly take out an accomplished male leader in the twilight of his career? (For that matter, could you imagine anyone crusading to get rid of a distinguished older man, who was scandal-free and still in command of his faculties, on the grounds that he wasn't likeable?) (Ball 2020, 281)

Pelosi survived the leadership challenge. In part, her strategy was the stuff of the organizational cartel: talking about legislation, doling out perks, agreeing to minor revisions to House rules to placate the Problem Solvers Caucus, and, for Fudge, guaranteeing a subcommittee chair position. She also agreed to allow the Democratic Caucus to vote on term limits for committee chairs, although she did not take a position on this potential rule (McPherson 2018d). When the Democratic Caucus vote for Speaker came, Pelosi distributed a ballot that included her name with the options of "yes" and "no." This allowed those who promised to vote against her to keep their promises while still supporting her on the House floor (Ball 2020, 282–83).

Yet, in a major concession, Pelosi agreed to term limits for the top three Democratic leadership posts. The compromise included the Democratic leader and the Democratic whip positions, as well as the speakership, and limited these officeholders to three terms (or four terms with sufficient support in the caucus). However, in this compromise, Pelosi's tenure (and presumably Hoyer's and Clyburn's) would be limited to four more years. With this deal, seven members who signed the letter agreed to support Pelosi on the floor (McPherson 2018a). Eventually, Pelosi was elected Speaker, with twelve Democrats voting for other members and three voting "present" (Aupperlee 2019).

In January 2019, *The Hill* reported that "Speaker Pelosi sent rank-and-file Democrats an unmistakable message this week: Stick with the team and you will be rewarded, oppose the team and you could be punished" (Wong 2019). This opening line should have read, "Speaker Pelosi sent rank-and-file Democrats an unmistakable message, oppose the team and you'll be okay." Wong reports that the Democratic Steering and Policy Committee, which determines committee assignments, denied Kathleen Rice a position on the Judiciary Committee and that Anthony Brindisi (D-NY) was denied a seat on Armed Services. Yet, a half dozen others who opposed her, including Ryan and Moulton, were awarded plum positions; in Ryan's case, he became chair of an Appropriations subcommittee (Wong 2019).

Even after she was elected Speaker, Pelosi faced public criticism of her leadership from another faction: a foursome of young, newly elected women of color called "the Squad": Alexandra Ocasio-Cortez (D-NY), Ayanna Pressley (D-MA), Ilhan Omar (D-MN), and Tlaib. The four rose to prominence in part because of the historic nature of their elections. Both Ocasio-Cortez and Pressley defeated Democratic incumbents in primaries. Pressley became the first African American woman elected to Congress from Massachusetts. Tlaib and Omar are the first Muslim women elected to Congress. Ocasio-Cortez, who unexpectedly unseated Joe Crowley, a member of the House leadership and a Pelosi ally, has eleven million Twitter followers and a national media profile. Tlaib gained notoriety when she called for President Trump's impeachment using profanity (Stolberg 2019). President Trump also called for the four members of the Squad to "go back" to the countries they came from. All four are American citizens, and three were born in the US (Rogers and Fandos 2019). They were among the most outspoken members of the Progressive Caucus, critical of Pelosi's leadership.

The moderate and progressive factions both claimed credit for the 2018 Democratic victory. Moderates claimed that the Democrats won the majority because they were competitive in rural and working-class swing districts. The Progressives argued that their message brought legions of energized voters to the polls, leading to record voter turnout rates nationwide. Pelosi, they charged, did not have the "energy"—an ageist trope—to move forward the Progressives' agenda on climate change and health care. In fact, Ocasio-Cortez led a protest outside Speaker Pelosi's office before she was sworn in (Adragna and Colman 2018). The Squad also broke with the Democratic majority on an immigration bill, and other Democrats worried that the Squad would support progressive challengers to some moderate members in Democratic primaries (Stolberg 2019). The relationship further chilled when Pelosi brushed off criticisms by noting that the Squad only constituted four votes in the House and Ocasio-Cortez criticized her for attacking four women of color (Bade and DeBonis 2019).

For her part, Pelosi was keenly aware that the Democratic majority was fragile and that she needed to help the vulnerable moderates to keep their seats. Therefore, she was careful to make sure that the Democratic agenda was moderate so that the moderate Democrats would not be asked to vote on legislation that would be difficult to defend in their districts (see, e.g., Fairbanks 2007). This strategy was widely recognized yet vilified by the left, called "machine politics" and "strangulation" (Heer 2019).

Interestingly, there is little ideological difference between the moderates who opposed to Pelosi's leadership and the progressive members of the Squad, based on the congresswomen's DW-NOMINATE scores (an average of −0.267 compared to −0.259) (calculated by author with data from Lewis et al. 2021). The Squad's voting records are indistinguishable from the moderates' because, in the final analysis, there are just very few issues that divide the Democratic Caucus (see Lewis 2019a, 2019b). Similarly, Cruz Lera (2020), in her comparison of the Squad and four "establishment" women members, including Pelosi, found that there were few differences in fundraising success, roll call votes, and bill sponsorships. In short, Democrats have far more commonalities than differences. Moreover, Pelosi, the consummate vote counter, was careful to bring up legislation that will pass, meaning that the moderates would vote for it.

A Cannon Revolt Redux? Critical elections theory might predict a sea change in Pelosi's prospects after winning the House majority in 2018. Yet, one can make the case that 2018 was further indication of dealignment and the resulting rapid changes in partisan control. In 2019, the Senate remained in Republican control, and, of course, there was no change in the White House. The country remained divided. The Democrats' majority was small and divided internally. Pelosi maintained a high unfavorable rating; the Republicans continued to use her as a cudgel in their attack ads, and, by asserting her lack of "energy," detractors used coded language to make an ageist attack.

As in 2016, the challengers once again sought to punish Pelosi for the Republicans' unfair negative attacks. Once again, Pelosi was lenient with her detractors, choosing to risk inviting further resistance because she was soft on dissention rather than being seen as vindictive for fully exercising her powers as Speaker. Once again, Pelosi was the only one of the three highest-ranking leaders to draw a challenger. Hoyer and Clyburn retained their positions without any hint of opposition.

Another way to understand this is to revisit Speaker Joe Cannon. As mentioned in chapter 1, Cannon exercised considerable power as Speaker in the early 1900s, serving on the Rules Committee and appointing all of its members. The Rules Committee had grown in significance with the adoption of the "Reed Rules," put in place by Cannon's predecessor, Thomas Reed (R-ME), which solidified the House as a majoritarian institution. Consequently, Cannon was able to dictate what legislation came to the floor, to cut off dilatory motions, and to write the rules under which legislation would be debated and brought to the floor. Cannon used this power to maintain the tariff, in spite of the opposition of the Democrats, many progressive Republicans, and news reporters (Peters 1990, 75–91).

Compare Cannon's power with the assessment by Dan Lipinski (2021), who is both a political scientist and a former member of the House of Representatives. He notes that the "regular order"—the usual legislative process that emphasizes committee work and bipartisanship—has been replaced with the "Speaker's order." Under "Speaker's order," the Speaker plays a significant role in directing the legislative process, which limits members' ability to engage in independent policy making through the committee process. Bipartisan policymaking, likewise, is curtailed by the hyper-partisanship and the straight party-line votes of the contemporary Congress. Committee chairs may be punished and others can be shut out of leadership roles for disagreeing with the Speaker. The Problem Solvers Caucus's proposed rule changes would have allowed for more measures with bipartisan backing to be brought up for a floor vote. The result would have been, in Lipinski's formulation, a move back toward "regular order" and away from "Speaker's order." Pelosi did keep tight control on the legislative process. As Susan Page writes:

> [Pelosi] generally had a low regard for symbolic gestures. Once she became Speaker of the House, she almost never scheduled votes unless she knew that she had a majority in hand. She would roll her eyes when Republican Speakers John Boehner and Paul Ryan would bring up bills for a vote without being sure they would pass, risking humiliation at the hands of the Tea Party and the Freedom Caucus. (2021, 305–6)

When Pelosi did not bring up legislation that may not pass, she curtailed the powers of individual committees and members, much like Cannon did. The ACA and the impeachment case study (see discussion below) demonstrate how she is willing to bypass the traditional committee structure and bring legislation forward only when she is certain she has the votes.

Moreover, even as early as 2007, Pelosi was not afraid to manipulate the rules to ensure that the Democratic agenda would pass through the House (Wolfensberger 2018, 28).

Also as described in chapter 1, Speaker Pelosi is one, but not the only, architect of this consolidation of power. Nonetheless, it made her a target. Moreover, there is a crucial difference between the Cannon revolt and the 2018–19 challenge. The Cannon revolt occurred as a *result* of how he used his powers. By contrast, Pelosi became a target *before* she started *to exercise these powers* during her second speakership. Of the (more or less) thirty opponents she faced in 2018–19, only eight—including two members of the Problem Solvers Caucus—were in Congress when Pelosi was Speaker from 2007 to 2011, where they would have experienced Pelosi as Speaker firsthand.

As one Democratic House member noted, recent changes in the House have so successfully consolidated power into the speakership that other leadership positions are less desirable. Moreover, given the symbolic importance of having an African American in the leadership, no Democrat was likely to challenge Representative Clyburn (personal interview, March 8, 2021). However, this same symbolic importance, apparently, is not attached to having a woman in the leadership.

So, how did the Cannon revolt succeed while the Pelosi challenge did not? Cannon, like Boehner and Paul Ryan, lost his position due to a deeply divided caucus. In Cannon's case, progressive Republicans, who opposed high tariffs, partnered with Democrats who voted to change the House rules so that the Speaker no longer chaired the Rules Committee and could not appoint all its members. At the same time, the progressive Republicans still supported Cannon's election to the speakership. In response to the rules change, Cannon stepped down (Peters 1990, 84–86; Jenkins and Stewart 2013, 280–82).

As Aldrich and Rohde (2011) describe in their "conditional party government" theory, when the majority party is divided, as it was for much of the twentieth century, then the power of the Speaker is reduced. However, when the majority party is largely unified and ideologically distinct from the minority, then power becomes concentrated into the party leadership (Rohde 2013). Appeasing an unhappy faction is not necessary to stay in leadership.

The House Democratic Caucus was certainly divided. The unhappy Progressives, with the Squad as their public face, thought Pelosi was too moderate. The moderates, like Ryan and Moulton, believed Pelosi was a drag on the party because the Republicans successfully defined her as a crazy liberal. The unhappy Problem Solvers Caucus members thought the speakership—and Pelosi—was too powerful. The unhappy ambitious felt locked out of leadership positions because the octogenarians at the top refused to retire. Nonetheless, these divisions paled in comparison with the ideological schism with the Republicans. Therefore, creating an alliance with members of the minority party was out of the question. For all their frustrations, grumbling, and worries, the Democratic malcontents were unable to successfully unseat Pelosi.

Speaker Pelosi is a target not only because she is a woman—subject to sexist attacks from the opposition—but also because she was powerful, savvy, and enduring. Pelosi walked a tightrope that is all too common for women leaders, especially those who have to manage male subordinates. If women adopt masculine, agentic traits as leaders, they risk being perceived as lacking interpersonal skills, even if they are successful in their jobs. Meanwhile, men who demonstrate these same behaviors are considered competent leaders and good managers (Rudman and Glick 1999). Moreover, men who answer to female managers are more likely to engage in assertive and even insubordinate behaviors with female managers than with males (Netchaeva, Kouchaki, and Sheppard 2015). Finally, male subordinates are more likely to rank the performance of female transformational leaders lower than male transformational leaders (Ayman, Korabick, and Morris 2009). In short, as former *Boston Globe* reporter Martin Nolan wrote in 2011, "Nancy Pelosi is 'controversial' because she is effective."

The final question though is this: was Pelosi's victory in 2019 a Pyrrhic one? To survive the latest challenge, she did have to agree to step down after four more years as leader. Even though the Democrats retained their majority after the 2020 election, it was trimmed to just seven votes. Pelosi was reelected without opposition during a tumultuous period in which the outcome of the presidential race was contested at the highest levels. By early 2021, Democrats were already looking to a post-Pelosi leadership, although she had no plan to choose a successor (Caygle and Ferris 2021). Pelosi's term limit was not written in the House rules, and in January 2022, she announced that she would run for reelection in Congress (Walsh 2022). While Theresa May returned to the "backbenches" of Parliament, no US Speaker had done so.

Pelosi's Tightrope Walk with President Trump

Just as Theresa May had to walk a tightrope between the "hard" and "soft" Brexiteers, as discussed in chapter 3, Pelosi found herself walking a tightrope between factions of her caucus on the issue of impeaching President

Donald Trump. While these events occurred after the leadership challenges of 2016–17 and 2018–19, they demonstrate Pelosi's understanding of the political environment and of knowing when and whether to act. They are, thus, an excellent case study to illustrate Pelosi's political acumen and its intersection with her institutional role.

From the outset, the Trump administration broke a number of political conventions and possibly laws. As Susan Page recounts, the list of possible impeachable offenses was long: violations of the emoluments clause, the family separation immigration policy that grossly violated human rights, the firing of FBI director James Comey, and the evidence of illegal activity unearthed by Special Counsel Robert Mueller's investigation of Russian influence in the 2016 election (2021, 299).

Trump and Pelosi had an uneasy relationship. Trump was a notorious womanizer who was elected despite a devastating audio tape in which he bragged about sexually assaulting women and his belittling treatment of political opponents with derisive nicknames. As Pelosi recounts, in her first meeting with Trump after his inauguration, he disregarded the prepared remarks that included calls for unity and bipartisanship and instead erroneously claimed that he had won the 2016 popular vote. Pelosi broke with protocol to respond, while her male colleagues sat silently. She disputed the claim and concluded, "You can't negotiate unless you stipulate to a fact. And what you're saying has no basis in fact. So, if we're going to do anything together, we have to have the truth on the table" (Page 2021, 262).

Pelosi also famously showed her mettle in 2017 at a White House dinner when the administration and congressional leaders were discussing protections for undocumented immigrants who arrived as children, known as "Dreamers." Pelosi, the only woman at the table, was interrupted and talked over—a well-documented gender dynamic (Tannen 1994). Pelosi finally interjected, "Do the women get to talk around here?," which put an end to the interruptions (Parker 2017).

Similarly, Pelosi met with President Trump in December 2018, when she was facing her most recent leadership challenge. Before a group of reporters, they publicly disagreed over Trump's threat to shut down the government. The disagreement escalated to this exchange:

"You know, Nancy is in a situation where it's not easy for her to talk right now. I understand that," the president told reporters, raising a question about whether she was really able to speak for House Democrats because of those who were challenging her election as Speaker. "Mr. President," she responded icily, "Please don't characterize the strength I bring to this meeting as the leader of the House Democrats, who just won a big victory." (Page 2021, 274–75; see also C. Pelosi 2019, vii–viii)

The image of Pelosi leaving the White House, donning her sunglasses and wearing her red winter coat, became an instant meme.

The First Impeachment. When Pelosi ascended to the speakership in 2019, she faced significant pressure from the Progressive wing of the Democratic Caucus to immediately bring impeachment charges against President Trump, especially as Mueller's investigation began to yield indictments. For her part, Pelosi demurred. She had several reasons to do so. First, Pelosi had a healthy respect for impeachment and believed that it should not be used for partisan purposes. She thought the House's impeachment of Bill Clinton in 1999 was "ridiculous" (Page 2021, 299), and she refused to agree to impeachment proceedings against George W. Bush in 2007 (205). Pelosi sought to avoid turning impeachment into a divisive tit for tat.

Second, Pelosi favored using congressional oversight rather than impeachment to hold the administration accountable. As calls for impeachment increased at the end of the Mueller investigation, Pelosi continued to demur. In her words, "He's just not worth it" (Page 2021, 300). Moreover, the Russian interference story was complicated, and the Trump administration claimed that Mueller had exonerated Trump because he was not indicted.

Third, Pelosi understood that maintaining a Democratic majority depended upon keeping moderate Democrats from swing districts in office. A lengthy, divisive impeachment fight would weaken them going into the 2020 election cycle and potentially jeopardize their reelections. Finally, Pelosi does not like to lose, and if the House impeached Trump—at the cost of time and money—the Senate was sure to acquit Trump and the president would remain in office.

Circumstances changed in August 2019, when *Politico* reported that the US was withholding military aid to Ukraine, which was at war with Russia over its annexation of the Crimea. By September 9, the House Intelligence Committee had a readout of President Trump's telephone call with Ukrainian president Volodymyr Zelensky, in which Trump asked the Ukrainian government to investigate former vice president Joe Biden and his son Hunter for corruption (Sullivan and Jordan 2020). Revelations mounted: overtly meddling in the US election; undermining a long-time, well-respected foreign service employee; dispatching the president's personal attorney on government business; and illegally withholding congressionally appropriated funds. They all pointed to irrefutable abuses of power and criminal activity. A group of moderate Democrats from swing districts, anchored by five women with military or intelligence experience dubbed "the Women Who Kill," wrote an op-ed that appeared in the *Washington Post* calling for Trump's impeachment (Cisneros et al. 2019; Sullivan and Jordan 2020).

On September 24, 2019, Speaker Pelosi announced that the House would undertake an impeachment inquiry. At this point, she needed to make some strategic decisions. The first was to define the scope of the impeachment inquiry. Would it include any findings from the Mueller report or any other of the myriad possible impeachable offenses? Pelosi declined. She opted to focus the impeachment only on the abuse-of-power issues emanating from the telephone call with the Ukrainian president. This strategy was clean and simple and would be easier for vulnerable Democrats to defend (Sullivan and Jordan 2020, 185–86; Page 2021, 313).

The second was to decide which committee chair would take the lead on investigating the charges. The choice was between Jerrold Nadler (D-NY), chair of the House Judiciary Committee, and Adam Schiff (D-CA), chair of the House Intelligence Committee. Normally, impeachment proceedings are in the jurisdiction of the Judiciary Committee. However, Nadler's "audition," a frustrating and unproductive hearing with former Trump campaign manager Cory Lewandowski, demonstrated to Pelosi that Nadler would not be able to manage a high-stakes impeachment inquiry (Sullivan and Jordan 2020, 160–66). Thus, the task fell to Schiff, a longtime Pelosi ally, and the Intelligence Committee.

While the Intelligence Committee would take the lead on the investigative hearings, the Judiciary Committee was still responsible for reporting out the articles of impeachment. On December 13, 2019, when the Judiciary Committee was scheduled to vote, and Pelosi was out of the country, the Republicans engaged in numerous delay tactics, attempting to force a late-night impeachment vote and to gain a critical talking point. In a third strategic decision, Pelosi advised Nadler to recess the Judiciary Committee immediately before the vote and to reconvene in the morning to take the vote. Thus Pelosi—and Nadler—robbed the Republicans of their talking point (Page 2021, 312–13).

The House of Representatives impeached President Trump on December 18, 2019 (Page 2021, 314). While Pelosi knew that the Senate would probably acquit President Trump, she did want to ensure that the Senate trial was fair, especially since Senate Majority Leader Mitch McConnell

(R-KY) said publicly that he was going to coordinate with the president's defense team. In her fourth strategic decision, in December 2019, Pelosi announced that she would delay sending the articles of impeachment to the Senate until she had details on how McConnell would conduct the trial. Pelosi took what was considered a housekeeping matter—delivery of the impeachment articles—and used it for leverage. She put pressure on McConnell to call witnesses, pressure that he ultimately resisted (Sullivan and Jordan 2020, 386–93; Page 2021, 314–16). While the Senate voted to acquit President Trump on February 5, 2020, he was only the third president in US history to be impeached.

The Second Impeachment. Only four US Speakers—Schuyler Colfax, Carl Albert, Newt Gingrich, and Nancy Pelosi—had led a House that was considering articles of impeachment, and only three—Colfax, Gingrich, and Pelosi—had presided over an impeachment floor vote. These facts alone place Pelosi apart from most other House Speakers. Yet in early 2021, Speaker Pelosi found herself in the unique position of managing a second impeachment inquiry and vote against President Donald Trump.

Pelosi's relationship with Trump had steadily deteriorated as Pelosi—accidentally or on purpose—created compelling visuals that became instant memes and visual symbols of Democrats' disdain and opposition to the president. The "red coat" photo and meme mentioned above was joined by the 2019 State of the Union "clapping" photo and meme, in which Pelosi appeared to mock the president (Hayes 2019); the "ripping speech" photo and meme from the 2020 State of the Union (Plank 2020); and the "standing and pointing" photo and meme, which was eventually used in a DCCC fundraising drive (DCCC n.d.). The latter occurred at a White House meeting on October 16, 2019, during the House's impeachment investigation. Congressional leaders clashed with Trump over his decision to remove troops from Syria. Pelosi, the only woman in the room, is standing opposite President Trump and pointing her finger at him. By all accounts, the meeting was a disaster and marked the last time that Pelosi spoke to President Trump (Jacobs 2020; Marcos 2020; Page 2021, 308–9, 352).

Against this backdrop, the Democratic nominee, Joe Biden, won the November 3, 2020, presidential election with decisive victories in the popular vote and the Electoral College. President Trump, however, refused to acknowledge Biden's victory, making erroneous claims of widespread vote fraud and charging that the election was "stolen" from him. Trump's claims continued unabated, despite a lack of evidence to support his assertions. Many of Trump's supporters, including members of Congress, accepted the president's narrative. In a December 2020 survey, only 24 percent of Republicans believed that Biden had won the election (Montenaro 2020).

On January 6, 2021, the House and Senate met in joint session to certify the Electoral College vote count and, with it, Joe Biden's victory. At the same time, thousands of President Trump's supporters rallied in Washington, DC, to express their support of the president's claims. President Trump spoke to the assembled crowd on the Ellipse outside the White House, calling upon them to "fight like hell" (Naylor 2021a; Restuccia and Mann 2021). Less than an hour later, while President Trump was still speaking, protesters broke down the first barriers to the Capitol. Hundreds of protesters then swarmed the Capitol building, verbally threatening Vice President Pence and Speaker Pelosi; breaking into the House and Senate chambers and the Speaker's office, forcing members of Congress to take shelter; and destroying property. Five people died in the melee, and more than one hundred were injured (Cameron 2022; Jackman 2021). In addition, the architect of the Capitol estimated the cost of the riot was $30 million for repairs, cleaning, and additional security (Chappell 2021).

This time, Pelosi moved quickly. Pelosi chose to forego a lengthy investigation, given that the evidence was weighty, the events were televised, and members of Congress themselves were witnesses to—and victims of—the violence. Instead, the House voted on a single article of impeachment, incitement of insurrection, on January 14, 2021. It passed by a 232–197 margin, with ten Republicans voting to impeach. Pelosi called impeachment "a constitutional remedy that will ensure the republic will be safe from this man who is so resolutely determined to tear down things that we hold dear and that hold us together" (Fandos 2021a). The article of impeachment was delivered on January 25 (Office of the Speaker 2021b). On February 13, the Senate again voted to acquit the now former president by a 57–43 margin, short of the two-thirds majority needed. Seven Republicans joined the Democrats in a vote to convict (Sprunt 2021).

Not Acting Like a Lame Duck: During the Trump presidency, Pelosi often found herself surrounded by men and had to overcome the implicit—and even explicit—biases of those she dealt with. One might expect that after Pelosi agreed to term limits in 2019 her influence in the House and with the administration might be compromised. However, Pelosi acted like neither a deferential female nor a lame duck. Instead, she used her considerable political skills to articulate the Democrats' priorities and to criticize the administration. She also understood the need to rise to the occasion and use the constitutional prerogatives of the House to impeach President

Trump. Pelosi also skillfully used the organizational cartel to make the case most effectively. For instance, she chose Schiff over Nadler and, in so doing, bypassed the Judiciary Committee's traditional jurisdiction over impeachment proceedings. Similarly, she made the most of a housekeeping task, delivering articles of impeachment to the Senate, to exact some assurance of a fair trial in the Senate. This is a person who "knows her power" and may have teetered on the tightrope but then found her footing.

Walking the Tightrope while Doing Institutional Care Work

The years 2020 and 2021 posted some unique challenges to the nation: a global pandemic followed by an insurrection. The previous case studies—engineering legislative victories and leading impeachment inquiries—are noteworthy. Yet they came with some recent precedents and established procedures to follow. However, Pelosi found herself in two unprecedented situations in 2020 and 2021: establishing COVID-19 protocols and dealing with the aftermath of the January 6 riots. Moreover, both are forms of what we can call "institutional care work," with the institutions being American democracy and the House of Representatives. As Speaker, Pelosi was responsible for understanding what caused the events of January 6 and for protecting the House of Representatives from the twin threats of a global pandemic and possible violence between members of the House themselves.

January 6 Investigation. After the dust cleared from the second impeachment proceedings, Pelosi turned her attention to investigating the January 6 insurrection. Again, this became a partisan battle. Some Republican lawmakers sought to downplay the severity of the events by claiming the rioters were Antifa (short for "anti-fascist," a violent left-wing faction), "peaceful patriots," or people on "a normal tourist visit" (Itkowitz 2021). Some House Republicans continued to claim, erroneously, that there was widespread election fraud and that President Trump was rightfully elected. As late as May 2021, a majority (53 percent) of Republican voters bought into the claims that the election was fraudulent and that President Trump was elected (Reuters 2021).

Against this backdrop, Speaker Pelosi began to determine how to investigate the events of January 6, 2021. The first proposal was to create a ten-person independent commission, composed of outside experts, Democratic and Republican members, and House members and senators. The proposed commission failed, with numerous Republicans claiming that Pelosi had partisan motivations. The House supported the creation of the independent commission. However, the Democrats in the Senate could not secure enough Republican votes to overcome a filibuster (Naylor 2021b). Pelosi then proposed creating a House Select Committee to investigate the January 6 events. Republicans attempted to undermine this effort as well, saying it had partisan motivations. The House voted to create this committee on June 30, 2021, by a vote of 222–190, with only two Republicans voting with the Democratic majority (Demirjian 2021). Minority Leader Kevin McCarthy proposed five members for the committee: Kelly Armstrong (R-ND), Jim Banks (R-IN), Rodney Davis (R-IL), Jim Jordan (R-OH), and Troy Nehls (R-TX). Pelosi took the unprecedented step of refusing to appoint Banks and Jordan because they repeated Trump's election lies or maligned the committee (Fandos 2021b; Office of the Speaker 2021c). McCarthy then responded by stating that no Republicans would serve on the committee. This allowed Pelosi to bypass the House Republican Conference and appoint two Republicans who were outspoken critics of President Trump and who had voted to impeach him in January: Liz Cheney (R-WY) and Adam Kitzinger (D-OH) (Select Committee 2022, ii). The committee then could claim to be bipartisan without contending with members who might strive to undermine the committee's work.

This situation again demonstrates Pelosi's ability to walk the gendered tightrope. First, she attempted to create a bipartisan, bicameral commission that would have public legitimacy. In Pelosi's words in a floor speech in May:

> My colleagues, the press says to me, "Why don't you just go do your own task force, your own Select Committee to investigate this? You have the votes, you have the subpoena power. You have this or that." I said I don't want to do that. We want this to be as it is shaped, bipartisan, with shared responsibility, shared staff, in a way that the public will have respect for the outcome. (Office of the Speaker 2021a)

Gendered themes permeate the entire speech; this passage is particularly telling. In a stereotypically feminine way, Pelosi chooses not to exercise her powers in order to share—another feminine and selfless act—staff, responsibility, and legitimacy.

However, when this opportunity is denied, Pelosi then assertively uses her institutional power to create the January 6 committee. Since the effort to create an independent, bipartisan commission failed, Pelosi had the ability to create and fund the committee; determine its size and composition; define its agenda; and enable it to hire staff, subpoena and depose witnesses, levy contempt charges against those who refused to cooperate, and schedule private and public hearings. These are considerable powers, and Pelosi did not shy away from vigorously exercising them once a more "feminine" approach failed.

Protecting the House from the Pandemic and Violence. The last deadly, global pandemic prior to COVID-19 was the 1918 influenza epidemic. At the time, Congress attempted to continue to do business as usual. However, this became increasingly difficult as the epidemic spread. It struck Washington, DC, in October 1918. That month, the House and Senate closed their public galleries. Yet, Congress could not recess. It needed to meet to conduct the business of government as well as to pass legislation strengthening the public health system. The House began to operate on "unanimous consent" to debate and pass legislation, sometimes with as few as fifty members present to vote. The rest were absent either to manage their own illnesses or to care for ailing relatives. This arrangement worked only if no one made a quorum call. A "gentlemen's agreement" to ignore the missing quorum allowed the House to conduct some business in spite of devastating absences (US House "Historical Highlights" n.d.; US House "Whereas" 2018).

When the COVID-19 pandemic forced the US to shut down in March 2020, the 1918 experience provided little relevant guidance to Pelosi and those determined to keep the House operational. For instance, any sort of collegial agreement to ignore parliamentary niceties, such as lacking a quorum, was not likely in a deeply divided House in which the Speaker was despised by the other party. Also, in part because President Trump downplayed the severity of the pandemic and its consequences and various conspiracy theorists claimed that the pandemic was a hoax, masking requirements became a political hot-button issue. Many Republicans in the House repeated these assertions as well. By December 2020, the first COVID-19 vaccine was given emergency-use authorization by the US Food and Drug Administration (Mayo Clinic 2022), a remarkable achievement for the Trump administration and the scientific community. However, COVID-19 vaccinations became another partisan cleavage, with many conservatives refusing to become vaccinated for various reasons. Counties that President Trump won in 2020 have lower vaccination rates than counties that President Biden won, by a margin of more than 10 percent (Kates, Tolbert and Rouw 2022).

Pelosi used the powers of the Speaker's office to adopt several COVID-19 protocols. One, holding committee meetings and hearing testimony via video conference, was not controversial. Two—allowing proxy voting and instituting a mask mandate in the Capitol—were. House Republicans objected to proxy voting, arguing that this accommodation was unconstitutional. They argued that the Constitution requires Congress to meet in person to vote. Moreover, Republicans have a history of objecting to proxy voting, banning the practice in subcommittees, where it was widely practiced, in 1995. Pelosi used other members of the organizational cartel, namely, Majority Leader Steny Hoyer and Rules Committee chair Jim McGovern (D-MA), to make the case for proxy voting on the House floor. After proxy voting was adopted in May 2020, Minority Leader Kevin McCarthy sued to end the practice. He charged that proxy voting was "a power grab" and a "raw abuse of power" on Pelosi's part. However, the case was dismissed by federal courts (Wang 2021).

The mask controversy played out similarly. Nationwide, many conservative and Republican Americans bristled at mask mandates in schools and public places, stating that the requirement to wear one violated their personal freedoms. Many House Republicans shared this disdain for masking. Under Pelsoi, the House instituted a mask requirement in July 2020. Violators were subject to a $500 fine for the first violation and $2,500 for subsequent violations. The controversy intensified when the Centers for Disease Control and Prevention temporarily dropped the indoor mask recommendation for vaccinated persons in May 2021. As a result, many state and local governments, schools, and businesses dropped their mask requirements immediately. However, Pelosi refused to lift the mandate for floor access. Pelosi's justification was that about 25 percent of House members were unvaccinated, thus putting themselves and others at risk (Elfrink 2021).

Republicans balked. Thirty-four signed a letter demanding that Pelosi end the mandate. Minority Whip Steve Scalise said the mandate was "all about control" (Elfrink 2021). Minority Leader Kevin McCarthy said, "That is not a speaker for America. That's a Speaker only concerned about her own wealth, her own direction, and our own control [sic]. . . . This is the people's House, not Pelosi's House." Representative Scott Perry (R-PA) called the mask rule "tyranny" (Finn 2021). Three members who were fined for failing to wear masks on the House floor, Marjorie Taylor Greene (R-GA), Thomas Massie (R-KY), and Ralph Norman (R-SC), filed a lawsuit against Pelosi, claiming that the mask mandate violated the First and

Twenty-seventh Amendments (Williams 2021). The case, *Massie vs. Pelosi*, was dismissed by a federal district judge in March 2022 (Allsup 2022). Representatives Greene and Andrew Clyde (R-GA) eventually accrued penalties of more than $90,000 and $60,000, respectively. The mask mandate was lifted in February 2022, shortly before the State of the Union address (Kaplan and MacFarlane 2022).

Another controversy arose after the January 6, 2021, attack on the Capitol. Driven by fears about continued violence and concerns that members of Congress might wish to bring guns to the floor, Pelosi installed metal detectors at the entrances to the House chamber and required members to walk through them.[10] Many Republicans responded with outrage, calling Pelosi "communist" and condemning the requirement as a waste of money, "bullshit," "crap," "stupid," and "unconstitutional." GOP leaders also condemned the Democratic leadership for taking this step without consulting the Republican minority. Ultimately, ten Republican members refused to walk through the metal detectors, and Representative Lauren Boebert (R-CO) refused to allow the Capitol police to inspect her handbag (Clark, Moe, and Talbot 2021). In early February, the House then instituted fines for members who refused to go through metal detectors. Members could be fined $5,000 for the first instance and $10,000 for the second (Marcos 2021). In both cases—the mask requirement and the metal detectors—Republican members accused Pelosi of hypocrisy when she was seen not wearing a mask at other public events and allegedly bypassing the security screening she installed (Nelson and Brufke 2021; Kaplan and MacFarlane 2022).

The gendered dynamics in these case studies are quite obvious. In seeking a bipartisan commission, Pelosi spoke in very feminine terms and downplayed her own power. However, when that approach failed, she assumed a more "masculine" strategy of creating an investigatory committee and vetoing some Republican members—all for the protection of democracy itself.[11] Similarly, Pelosi justified the House's COVID-19 mask rules and installation of metal detectors in terms of assuring the health and safety of House members. These threats were real. Many members of Congress developed COVID, and one, Representative-elect Luke Letlow

---

10. Interestingly, members of Congress are exempt from the rules banning firearms in the Capitol. Rather, members may keep guns in their offices or transport them elsewhere on the grounds, as long as they are "securely wrapped" and unloaded. However, firearms were always prohibited on the House and Senate floors (Marcos 2021).

11. For a discussion of how democracy itself is gendered feminine, see Kedrowski 2022.

(R-LA), died of COVID complications in December 2020, before he took the oath of office (Helsel 2020). The mob on January 6 badly damaged Pelosi's office and threatened her personally (Kedrowski 2022). Moreover, the Capitol's administration and security fall under the Speaker's purview. Therefore, the steps Pelosi took were legitimately within her responsibility as Speaker. However, with terms such as "power grab," "abuse of power," "control," and "tyranny," Pelosi's opponents' rhetoric implies that a woman who exercises power is somehow illegitimate even when she is *engaged in institutional care work*. Rhetorical excesses aside, some of her Republican opponents further seek to undermine Pelosi's institutional power through their lawsuits and blatant disregard for House rules—while paying fines in the process. In terms of repeatedly justifying her position of power, this woman's work was never done.

Stepping Down from the Speakership. The Democrats lost the House majority after the 2022 election, although by a much smaller margin than predicted. Republicans held the 435-member House by just seven votes. Pelosi announced her decision to step down as Democratic leader, on November 17, 2022, when the results of the 2022 election were finalized (Hulse 2023). Her announcement came about three weeks after her husband, Paul, was brutally attacked in their San Fransisco home by Paul DePape. DePape was looking for Nancy Pelosi herself, with the plan to kidnap her and break her kneecaps (Medina 2023). There was some spectulation that Pelosi would not have survived the leadership vote had she chosen to run for Democratic leader. However, no opponent emerged and Pelosi herself said that she would have had sufficient support to remain as leader (Hulse 2022).

Shortly after her announcement, Democratic Leader Steny Hoyer announced that he too would step away from the leadership. Jim Clyburn remains in the Democratic Leadership, serving again as Assistant Leader. Unlike her recent predecessors, Pelosi remains in Congress. However, she claims that she is not a shadow leader, characterizing her intention in typically gendered terms: "I have no intention of being the mother-in-law in the kitchen saying, 'My son doesn't like it this way'" (Hulse 2022).

Just as Pelosi faced a leadership challenge from within her party in 2018–2019, so did her successor, Kevin McCarthy. McCarthy lost the first ballot by fifteen votes, with nineteen members of the Republican Conference voting against him. Most of McCarthy's opponents were members of the Freedom Caucus (McPherson 2023). The fifteen-vote, four-day drama placed the differences between Pelosi and McCarthy into gross relief. On the one hand, the horse-trading the Pelosi used to secure her leadership position in 2019 was on public display, including creating a committee on "weaponizing" the federal government and future spending cuts (Caldwell and Meyer 2023). On the other hand, McCarthy was willing to make concessions that could seriously undermine the organizational cartel, especially the rule that would allow just one member to make a motion to "vacate the chair,"—essentially calling for a vote of no confidence in the Speaker (Watson 2023). With only a seven-vote majority, the Speaker McCarthy is at the mercy of a small cabal of members who might be unhappy with his decisions. In addition, the House Rules end two practices instituted by Pelosi as part of her institutional care work: fines for members who refuse to wear masks and proxy voting (Watson 2023).

Conclusion

Nancy Pelosi was the Democratic leader for two decades, demonstrating clearly, in Escobar-Lemmon and Taylor-Robinson's (2016) terms, that she is a "survivor." When examined alone, the 2018 challenge to Pelosi seems very puzzling, especially given the Democrats' decisive victory. However, when analyzed in the context of Pelosi's entire leadership history, it is less surprising. Intraparty challenges to Pelosi's leadership, whether direct or proxy, were almost normal business. Yet she also survived external challenges: the Republican Party's demonization of her in its ads for over a decade; the party's personal antipathy toward her, which has led to court cases and rule breaking; and President Trump's attempts to undermine her.

Pelosi has kept her balance on the gendered tightrope through a combination of feminine leadership traits: sharing credit, framing leadership in the language of care work and motherhood, appearing cisgender, and appealing to the common good. However, Pelosi also "knows her power," and as Speaker, Pelosi's power was considerable. Her political skills and understanding of the organizational cartel have enabled her to fend off leadership challenges and to secure major legislative victories like the ACA. However, when she does exercise her power, demonstrate loyalty to her friends, and maintain order and safety within the House, Pelosi is adopting agentic, masculine traits that either are framed as character flaws or lead to accusations of unconstitutional power grabs. In terms of the latter, the sheer magnitude of the protests—mask wearing is hardly tyrannical and walking through a metal detector does not equate to living under communism—demonstrates her opponents' discomfort with a woman who is comfortable with power.

Margaret Thatcher was known as the Iron Lady, and Theresa May was known for her kitten heels. Both walked a gendered tightrope in their leadership positions and arguably were deposed for being either too masculine (Thatcher) or insufficiently so (May). Pelosi managed to stay on the gendered tightrope, even in stilettos, until she stepped away under her own volition.

FIVE

Staying On or Falling Off the Tightrope
Lessons Learned

In the preceding chapters, we explored the careers of Theresa May and Nancy Pelosi, both leaders of their respective legislatures, as they faced repeated leadership challenges during their tenures. Both Pelosi and May faced challenges after they had achieved their principal goals: to win the House majority in Pelosi's case and to successfully negotiate a Brexit agreement framework with Europe but not her own party in May's case. Focusing on these achievements is not sufficient to understand the gender dynamics and contradictory expectations that both leaders faced throughout their careers. This chapter will explore these lessons in the context of what we know of the experiences and expectations of women leaders.

This discussion has benefited from the work of many feminist scholars, most prominently, Sarah Childs and Mona Lena Krook; Maria Escobar-Lemmon and Michelle Taylor-Robinson; Claire Annesley, Karen Beckwith, and Susan Franceschet; and Karen Celis and Joni Lovenduski. We have relied upon Childs and Krook's articles concerning the idea of critical actors rather than critical mass and the constraining or enabling features of the "old" US and UK first-past-the-post democracies with adversarial lower Houses. We have used Annesley, Beckwith, and Franceschet's work on the affiliational, experiential, and representational characteristics of female cabinet ministers to discuss the career trajectories of both May and Pelosi. Annesley, Beckwith, and Franceschet refer to Ostrom's typology of the institutional characteristics "prescribing, prohibiting or permitting," which map nicely onto Childs and Krook's 2009 typology of "constraining or enabling" legislative contexts (Annesley, Beckwith, and Franceschet 2019, 210; Childs and Krook 2009, 128). Annesley, Beckwith, and Franceschet refer to experiential and representational characteristics as prescriptive, while affiliational ones are permitted. Escobar-Lemmon and Taylor-Robinson (2016) help explain the resources both May and Pelosi brought to their positions.

We also agree with Celis and Lovenduski's notes regarding positional power in adversarial systems and how the zero-sum nature of first-past-the-post politics leads to males planning to remove female leaders once their "heavy lifting" has been accomplished. In May's case, this was with regard principally to negotiating the text of the Withdrawal Agreement Bills and WABs with the EU. Her successor, Boris Johnson, was able to win a large majority, something denied to both Cameron and May, in December 2019 by claiming he would "get Brexit done." As of 2023, it remains unfinished, given Johnson's crafting of the Northern Ireland Protocol to get around the allergies of the ERG members to May's UK-wide backstop until the UK and EU could agree on removing Northern Ireland from EU phytosanitary standards. Thus, checks down the Irish Sea and Northern Ireland's place in the EU single market continue, and Stormont has, after a brief interlude, crashed apart yet again after Sinn Fein won a historic first in the Northern Ireland elections in May 2022. For Nancy Pelosi, her heavy lifting on both the 2008 bailout and the 2010 ACA was "rewarded" with the Democrats losing their House majority from 2010 to 2018. However, her hard work, especially in building her caucus and its electoral strength, resulted in a historic House Democratic win in 2018. Nonetheless, some who wished to remain glued to the past, both male and female House Democrats, signaled they would not support her for Speaker again, and like Theresa May, she had to term-limit herself for the future so that she could win reelection. Of course, since Pelosi was always a pro at counting votes, she likely knew that holding onto the House in 2022 was going to be a difficult issue. After her reelection as Speaker, Pelosi went on to preside over several unprecedented events: overseeing both Trump impeachments, investigating an insurrection, and installing pandemic safety procedures.

Both women performed multiple roles as required by institutional history. PM May was simultaneously the legislative leader of the House of Commons, the head of the executive branch as prime minister, and the person on the hook for negotiating with the EU and Northern Ireland over Brexit. Speaker Pelosi was concurrently leader of the US House and of its majority party. While not the formal organizational chairs of their parties, both women played roles in shaping and translating party agendas into practice in their institutions.

Bringing Together Escobar-Lemmon and Taylor-Robinson and Annesley, Beckwith, and Franceschet

As also previously discussed, we found complementarities between the two sets of frameworks detailed in the 2015 and 2016 works by Escobar-Lemmon and Taylor-Robinson and in the 2019 study by Annesley, Beckwith, and Franceschet. The former identified three sets of criteria important to women getting into cabinets and surviving them as potential members of a group selected for leadership in the future. They include *political experience*, covering educational and work credentials (either inside or outside government), links to the president making the appointments, and the issue of whether the person was an *organizational partisan*, previously having held party office (Escobar-Lemmon and Taylor-Robinson 2016, 673–76). They also consider *policy expertise* and the question of linkages to clienteles of their ministry. The authors found that "cabinet survivors," such as Theresa May from 2010 to 2016, are equally represented between men and women (678–81). They also note that ministers with political experience could meet a "bad end" (i.e., be forced out before the end of the governmental mandate), although this did not happen in May's case (678). Escobar-Lemmon and Taylor-Robinson's 2015 study also concluded that policy expertise, prior office, or personal connections to the leader (president) are generally unrelated to staying on through the term or leaving early (678). The crucial piece of the 2015 study shows that organizational partisans, such as May and Pelosi, are 53 percent less likely to meet a "bad end" (retire early or get fired). In the 2015 study, based in Latin American presidential systems, clientele links were even more important, where a minister possessing such links has a 69 percent chance of staying in office (678). While their significant work as organizational partisans helped leaders to ascend the legislative and executive ladders (in May's case), it also put targets on their backs in later years. This was especially true for May when she became prime minister in 2016, as her lack of clientele links to bankers and corporate owners and those supported by the ERG in the Conservative Party made her extraordinarily vulnerable to the ERG tactics of denying her a Brexit victory in Parliament from 2018 onward. For Pelosi, her ongoing work as an organizational partisan both in House elections and in the US House made her a target of first the centrists after the Democratic majority was lost in the House in 2016 and then the Progressive Caucus—and some moderates—after it was regained in 2018.

As also discussed, the three-part framework of Annesley, Beckwith, and Franceschet (2019) shares some important characteristics of the Escobar-Lemmon and Taylor-Robinson framework. They include policy and educational experience and expertise in their first category of *experiential* criteria (111). Their second group, *affiliational* criteria, covers some of the "relationship to leadership" mentioned in Escobar-Lemmon and Taylor-Robinson's framework in terms of political party credentials and campaign experience but not leadership experience (132–37). Annesley, Beckwith, and Franceschet's third set of characteristics is *representational* criteria, covering what the party has decided are important features of prominent cabinet (and, in our work, potential leadership) candidates (156). Representational bases may include intraparty factions, as they have in our cases; territorial identities or social groups (race, ethnicity, class, sexual orientation, gender). Annesley, Beckwith, and Franceschet adopted Ostrom's framework of rules prescribing, prohibiting, or permitting various selection options for cabinet. As they note, "Rules require selectors to use experiential or representational criteria" when cabinet slating. Affiliational criteria are permitted but not prescribed or required (134).

Our conclusions are that both Pelosi and May performed large amounts of party service, which helped them in their leadership bids. Party service, however, is an expectation that is still unfortunately largely gendered, especially in zero-sum single-member systems. While both women played by the unwritten and written rules of their respective institutional systems, they became vulnerable to gendered judgments about their suitability for office even as they performed qualitatively better than their male counterparts. For May, the criteria applied to her long-term service as a cabinet survivor in the most difficult of portfolios, home secretary, did not last long once she became prime minister in July 2016. While she had been able to traverse the modernizer, Remainer, and Brexiteer factions through her presence in the national party and Parliament since 1997, that tightrope was frayed to ribbons when she was PM. First, the EU issued a series of red lines the day after the referendum in 2016. The Brexiteers and Remainers, each supported by powerful corporate interests and funds, were busily cutting off large swaths of the tightrope from each end, leaving her to fall from it in the middle in May 2019. The DUP, which did not represent Northern Ireland's Remain vote, also refused to play ball under the confidence and supply agreement from June 2017 onward since that would mean it had to take principled and firm stands to restore the Stormont Parliament. While May was reputed to have considered resigning after the June 2017 loss of the thin Conservative majority, since neither pro-Remain Labour nor the Liberal Democrats would partner with the Conservatives, she chose to continue with the ruinous policy of trying to get Brexit through with a minority government. While during her years as home secretary she had emphasized her right-wing Conservative credentials as being tough on immigration, that did not match up well with the issue definition of the ERG and other Brexiteers on Brexit, especially after 2018. At that point, the Brexiteers' dominant mantra was to "completely take back control" from the EU on all matters, including regulation, a goal still off in the future.

For Pelosi, her long-term presence as party workhorse since the 1980s and her understanding of the US House from her father's ten-year tenure in it became a two-sided coin. While she certainly used her fundraising and candidate-slating skills to climb the leadership ladder in the House after 1987, she fell prey to an intraparty divide, as May did once she became leader. While May's divide was between the right and further right wings and Pelosi's was between the left and centrist wings, the presence of member intransigence in systems where the legislative member, rather than the party, is on the ballot for reelection is an enormous obstacle. At that point, the members have more incentive not to cooperate than to "follow the leader," as it were. Annesley, Beckwith, and Franceschet's (2019) mention of the ability of a leader to use representational criteria to cover party factions and social criteria in cabinet or leadership slating is important. Theresa May paid a great deal of attention to equalizing Remain and Brexit factions in her cabinet, which predictably did not work in the end, as well as those from various social groups. Similarly, under Pelosi's speakerships, women gained historic prominence as important committee and caucus leaders, as did members of the CBC and the Progressive Caucus. Pelosi had also traversed the left and right divides within the Democratic Party during her House service, including being left-wing on AIDS funding, the Iraq War, and China's accession to the WTO, based on human rights violations. She was also seen by members of the Progressive Caucus as too accommodating to right-wing and centrist Democrats on issues such as the Troubled Asset Relief Program and the Stupak Amendment on the ACA. Since her name was not on the ACA but rather President Obama's, she was not held responsible for the entire package (unlike May with Brexit). However, Pelosi's ability to "duck and cover" on the ACA was lost in the 2010 House elections.

Fresh Face or Special Circumstances

As noted in chapter 1, women ascend to leadership positions when "special circumstances" arise and there is need for a "fresh face." May typifies the special circumstances that often bring women to power. The Brexit referendum had passed, unexpectedly, in spite of elite opposition. This led to a period of turmoil within the UK, as the country sought to understand what the UK without the EU would look like. When May was elected prime minister, she dutifully promised to negotiate a Brexit deal with the EU even though she disagreed with the referendum's results.

Nancy Pelosi typifies the fresh face scenario. She was briefly recruited to run against then-Speaker Tom Foley in 1994 as a fresh face when Democrats still expected to maintain control of the House indefinitely. While Pelosi demurred at that time, when she ran for Democratic leader in 2001, her argument included a case for increasing descriptive representation among the leaders.

Leading While Female

The literature intimates that women who come to power during a crisis or special circumstances are often seen as weak or illegitimate leaders. Arguably the same case could be made for women who eschew traditional paths to leadership, as Pelosi did. In highly masculine institutions, women leading men must walk a tightrope between overtly exercising power and behaving as a woman should. In both cases, we see that Pelosi and May faced leadership challenges from their earliest days in office, suggesting that their positions as leaders were never fully accepted.

In May's case, we see this as criticisms of her early decisions to replace a number of Conservative cabinet members and to call an election in 2017. Moreover, she faced revolts and dissention within her own party as she walked the tightrope between "hard" and "soft" Brexiteers while attempting to accommodate Northern Ireland and to stave off a challenge from Labour Party leader Corbin in 2017. Intraparty challenges to May's leadership became more frequent from 2017 into 2018 as positions hardened and bases for compromise disappeared. By 2018, May was promising to step down in exchange for support for the Brexit agreement—first in some months hence and later immediately. She ended up losing her position without a deal. In Escobar-Lemmon and Taylor-Robinson's terms, "May came to a 'bad end' as PM in summer 2019.

In Pelosi's case, we see this through the repeated leadership challenges she faced, starting just eight months after she was elected Democratic leader. Within the space of eight months, Pelosi had morphed from representing "new ideas" to being "a throwback." While many commentators today note Pelosi's skill, political acumen, and staying power, the repeated direct or proxy challenges to her position as Democratic leader—all by males—imply that her position as a woman leader has never been fully and completely embraced, even by members of her own party. What's even more remarkable is that the other two Democratic leaders, Steny Hoyer and James Clyburn, did not face any challenges to their leadership.

Pelosi's 2018 leadership challenge is particularly illustrative. Pelosi had just led the Democrats to victory in the midterm election, and she was poised to make history by being elected Speaker for the second time. She had raised prodigious sums of money for Democratic candidates and had successfully recruited candidates to run in swing districts. She had successfully stood up to President Trump during the government shutdown and the impasse over funding the border wall and, as Democratic leader, had successfully negotiated major concessions with the Republican majority when the Freedom Caucus balked. Yet, none of this mattered. One can only wonder if a group of thirty members would have dared to deprive a male leader of his institutional powers immediately after a resounding victory.

We cannot forget a larger political context that also has gendered overtones. The national Republican Party used Nancy Pelosi as a campaign target and flashpoint for over a decade. At the same time, partisan rancor on the Hill has also increased. Even so, the Republican members responded to instituting proxy voting during the pandemic, mandating masks on the House floor, and installing metal detectors after a violent incident with hysterical rhetoric completely out of proportion to stimuli and with frivolous lawsuits. These examples also imply that Pelosi's legitimacy as a leader was never widely accepted.

Sexism Isn't Dead

Sexism, both implicit and explicit, plays a role in both cases. In Pelosi's case, sexism is explicit in the Republican Party's repeated and relentless attack ads on her. These ads, as previously noted, depicted Pelosi in threatening and often sexist ways, and they worked to erode her popularity. The implicit sexism is that the solution to this problem was for Pelosi to step aside rather than for the Democrats to develop a strategy to counter this narrative. This solution also implies that similar Republican attacks on a (presumably male) successor wouldn't resonate as well as they did with Pelosi.

Similarly, in the repeated speculation that Pelosi might be defeated or retire, commentators always mentioned her age and status as a grandmother, intimating that she might retire to spend more time with her young progeny. However, both Hoyer and Clyburn are approximately the same age as Pelosi, and both are grandfathers (in Hoyer's case, a great-grandfather), yet there was no concomitant speculation of their impending retirements or supposed desire to spend time with family members.

Most dramatically, Pelosi herself was targeted personally by the insurrectionists who stormed the Capitol on January 6, 2021 While Vice President Pence's life was also threatened, it was Pelosi's office that was broken into and damaged and her laptop that was stolen. It was Pelosi's departure from the House chamber that was tweeted by a Republican member of Congress. It was Pelosi's staff who barricaded themselves in a conference room, and it was in the outer Speaker's office where an intruder, photographed with his feet on a desk, left a threatening message. Other members of Congress were traumatized and concerned for their safety, but only Pelosi suffered such personal targeting. History repeated itself in part in October 2022 when Paul Pelosi was attacked by an extremist who intended to kidnap and maim the Speaker.

Theresa May likewise faced continual challenges to her leadership, starting with the terror attacks during the 2017 election campaign, when one of Prime Minister Cameron's former advisers and Labour leader Jeremy Corbyn called on her to resign for not having been "tough enough" on terrorism while home secretary. The challenges continued, with the DUP mulling over whether to bring her government down in 2018 and Jacob Rees-Mogg and Boris Johnson of the ERG openly working against her. In 2019, the Remainers resigned from the party to join the newly formed Independent Group.

Using Gender as a Leadership Strategy

While women leaders have to walk a tightrope between gendered expectations of behavior and the masculine role of leader, Pelosi was able to walk this tightrope successfully in part because she used gender artfully in public and wielded masculine power outside of public view. For instance, her initial election called upon the Democrats to bring a woman into the highest ranks of the party. Pelosi sought to enter leadership because she wanted to take care of the party—and bring it to power again. Similarly, she famously asked children to join her at the Speaker's podium in 2007 and declared the work of Congress to be for future generations. She talked about how raising five children prepared her for leadership and called the Trump administration officials to task for talking over her. Pelosi wore feminine attire, including her signature high heels, while creating—inadvertently or on purpose— iconic moments for social media; deflected calls for impeachment for the sake of unity; and devised ways to protect vulnerable moderate Democrats. Even her responses to the pandemic and the insurrection were framed as institutional care work: protecting members, their families, and their staffs.

Pelosi's more masculine uses of power happened behind closed doors, such as in meetings with the Steering and Policy Committee in which she expressed her preference for committee placements and chairs. She also dispensed favors to win back defectors; negotiated deals with Republican leaders, the Senate, or the administration; discussed leadership strategy; chose impeachment managers; and otherwise engaged in the Speaker's powers outside the public eye. Only rarely did the public get a glimpse of this Pelosi—the skilled political operative— as it did during the now infamous meetings with President Trump. It is this balance of the publicly feminine and the privately masculine that allowed Pelosi to successfully walk the tightrope of power for more than two decades. Again, the responses to the pandemic and the insurrection are rare examples of the public exercise of power. While Pelosi framed these decisions in the language of care, she made the decisions as the leader of the organizational cartel and without consultation with the minority. Such public displays of authority probably fueled the acrimony.

May's history of walking the gendered tightrope came early in her parliamentary career, when she became the first woman chair of the Conservative Party from 2002 to 2003. Hers was a central face of the Conservatives' campaign to decontaminate the party after the huge Labour victory of 1997 and of enmity from local Conservative associations as well as high-up Brexiteers in the party who claimed she was "grabbing away power" from the local nominating committees. Even as May worked to include more women candidates in particular, she earned hostility from the traditional male selectorate.

Women Leaders Matter and May Not Get Credit for Their Work

Both May and Pelosi have done much to promote gender equality while in leadership. They both wrestled with sexual harassment scandals within their Houses and had to develop policies to deal aggressively with accusations and offenders. May also worked to promote LGBT rights as home secretary and worked with the Conservative Party leadership to develop a gender-balanced A-list of party nominees. Pelosi, for her part, promoted women to committee and subcommittee chairs, dramatically increasing the number of women in these key roles. Women were also among the House impeachment managers who presented the cases against Trump to the Senate and women held prominent positions on the January 6 House Select Committee.

In the most ironic twist, Boris Johnson eventually secured a Brexit compromise plan after encountering many of the same problems that May faced and was criticized for. Johnson handled them no better. Moreover, most of the provisions in Johnson's Brexit deal had been negotiated by May.

Similarly, the ACA is often touted as President Obama's signature piece of legislation. However, the legislation would have failed without Pelosi's skill and determination. She was responsible for ensuring a comprehensive benefits package and community rating. She negotiated the final deal with the pro-life members. She figured out how to get the House Democrats to support a deeply flawed Senate bill and determined how to make sure the most objectionable provisions were eventually eliminated. Pelosi's acumen was vital to the eventual success of the legislation, and her role is often overlooked or minimized.

What Comes Next?

Theresa May remained in the House of Commons after she stepped down as prime minister. There she has established herself as a critique and conscience of Johnson's Conservative government. In July 2021, Ungoed-Thomas and Farag of the *Daily Mail* noted that she had earned the second-highest amount of any MP due to speaking fees, which had amassed her about £760,000 between 2020 and 2021 (Ungoed-Thomas and Farag 2021; Forrest 2021). Ungoed-Thomas and Farag also quoted former president Donald Trump as saying he'd pay £100,000 not to hear her, showing the continued misogynistic cast of politics.

Pelosi's choice to remain in the House after leaving the leadership is a departure from her predecessors, who left the House. Pelosi decided to stay in Congress in part because of the attack on her husband, which some Republicans cruelly ridiculed (Bouie 2022). "I couldn't give them that satisfaction," she said (Hulse 2022). Notably, Pelosi's two decades in the leadership were unmarred by political scandal, unlike her predecessors Jim Wright (D-TX), Newt Gingrich (R-GA), and Dennis Hastert (R-IL). Rather than spending her post-leadership career in punditry, public speaking, and writing her memoirs, Pelosi described her future as a back bencher in typically feminine terms, as "meeting the needs of the people of San Francisco" (Hulse 2022).

Contributions of This Study to the Gender, Politics, and Leadership Literature

This work demonstrates that comparing the UK House of Commons and the US House of Representatives is possible, is appropriate for our study and yields interesting insights. We hope that other scholars will follow our lead. In addition, the stories of Theresa May and Nancy Pelosi uphold central points of studies concerning women's ascent through the institutional ladders that lead to legislative and executive leadership, with more commonalities than differences across the two single-member district systems we studied. This is largely due to the fact that only one person can occupy a seat at a time, and white men, with histories of longer social power, wish to occupy those seats. From the works of Escobar-Lemmon and Taylor-Robinson (2015, 2016) and Annesley, Beckwith, and Franceschet (2019), it is clear that while political experience, policy expertise, and educational credentials are "prescriptive" in Ostrom's (1986) framework, they serve merely to justify the selection of a candidate for cabinet or leadership, not insulate her forever. This is also true for the representational criteria identified by Annesley, Beckwith, and Franceschet. While, unfortunately, affiliational criteria are most important in the US and Westminster systems, they are also termed by Annesley, Beckwith, and Franceschet as permissive only. From these studies, the most useful issue for our purposes has been that of organizational partisans from Escobar-Lemmon and Taylor-Robinson's 2015 and 2016 works, which apply to both May and Pelosi, and the issue of cabinet survivorship, which applies to May. Again, while experiential credentials are necessary to get into cabinet (and leadership), they are not always sufficient to retain leadership. This has been shown both in May's case and in the challenges to Pelosi.

Table 1. Multilevel and Domestic Actions and Reactions on the UK-European Relationship, 1949–2019

Prime Minister	Pro-Europe Action	Anti-Europe Action	Intraparty Response
Winston Churchill • Conservative • 1940–45 • 1950–51	Helped with ECHR • linked to Council of Europe formed in London 1949 Convention adjudicated by Euro Ct. of Human Rights		Concerns raised since UK only member of ECHR with common law system (continual issue for Euroskeptics)
Harold Macmillan • Conservative • 1957–63	European Economic Community created 1957 (forerunner to EU Common Market) ECJ, European Parl. established 1952; Council of European Union, European Commission (exec.) created 1967 Requested membership from DeGaulle; was turned down		
Ted Heath • Conservative • 1970–74	Requested EEC membership again under Pompidou, 1973 Ratified in 1975 through domestic referendum		Domestic problems: Labor strikes, 3-day workweek, power shortages Put forth election in 1974, went into Opposition
Margaret Thatcher • Conservative • Leader 1975 • PM 1979–90 Beats Heath narrowly first ballot; brings right wing of party, monetarists to fore	Supported UK's entry into EEC and 1975 ref. Single European Act of 1985 removing nontariff barriers	Against "federalization" of EU (Delors's project—pres. of European Commission 1985–95)—expressed in Bruges speech 1988 Got UK amount of VAT paid to EU reduced in 1984 Against the ERM—long-term paving of way for Eurozone—"Madrid ambush" by Howe/Lawson June 1989 at European Council conference (similar to charges that May was "bullied by Europe")—Lawson resigned Oct. 89, Howe Now.—she agreed to join ERM Oct. 1990, was turfed on November 28, 1990. UK pound crashed out of ERM (too low for the narrow exchange rate band) on Sept. 16, 1992	

Prime Minister	Pro-Europe Action	Anti-Europe Action	Intraparty Response
John Major • Conservative • 1990–97	Joining of Maastricht Treaty 3 parts: (1) Free movement of capital 1990–93 (2) 1994–98-cooperation between central banks of member states and increased alignment of economic policies (3) 1999 on envisioned Euro by 2002 and single monetary policy 1991: Major got concessions from European Community including common currency (euro), social chapter on employment law and deletion of "federal" from Maastricht Major tabled the Maastricht ratification immediately after the April 1992 election; had to promise a parliamentary vote on rejoining the ERM and joining euro if Conservs won the next election (Labour won huge victory in 1997) Major needed more than a year to get the proposal to join Maastricht through, into 1993—he faced 62 rebellions, including 50 MPs who cast 1,100 dissenting votes (Cowley and Stuart 2012, 403). In July 1993 he lost the vote on the bill and threatened to dissolve the Commons for an election (an option removed by the Fixed Term Parliaments Act (2011)—neither side felt ready for an election after one in 1992 (Labour or Conservs)	Fresh Start anti-EU actions (discussed in chap. 2):W (1) Feb. 2012 100+ signatures sent to *Telegraph* to get out of EU's policing/criminal justice framework (2) "Options for Change Green Paper" 2012—Common Market OK; by Feb. 2016 FS decided not OK (3) Backbench rebellion on proposal for EU referendum (in next Conserv govt) was 41	Fontana and Parsons (2015) note 63 new member intake in 1992 • "Thatcher's children" included 10 hard Euroskeptics, such as Alan Duncan, Bernard Jenkin, Iain Duncan Smith, John Whittindale, Liam Fox • joined previously elected euro skeptics including Bill Cash, David Davis, Michael Portillo, John Redwood • 63 replaced 50 pro-Europe conservs. who didn't run in 92—Major called the Euroskeptics "bastards" Euroskeptic wrath after Maastricht vote was taken out on Chancellor Ken Clarke's 1994 budget (increased fuel taxes and payments to EU) —8 Conserv. MPs abstained. In June 1995, Major called a leadership contest in the Conservative Party, with Euroskeptic John Redwood running against him—Major won by 218 to Redwood's 89. By December 1996, the Conservatives had lost their majority in the Commons, due to election defeats and defections (including Peter Thurnham, Dec. 1996).

July 23: two days after previous vote, Major won 399–299

3 pillars of EU, 1993–2009:
(1) European Communities pillar—covered economic, social, and enviro policies (mechanisms: European Community, European Coal and Steel Community through 2002 expiry, and European Atomic Energy Committee)
(2) Common Foreign and Security Policy
(3) Police and Judicial Co-operation in Security Matters (originally titled Justice and Home Affairs)

Member and research groups formed in the 1990s in response to Maastricht:
(1) Fresh Starr, formed by MP Michael Spicer in 1992—first issue was to delay Major's vote on Maastricht after Denmark voted to reject the euro
(2) ERG—KEEP again formed by Spicer in 1994

Key players:
Steve Baker (first elected in 2010—ERG); Daniel Hannan—anti European MEP (!); Bill Cash, IDS, IDS, Bernard Jenkin, John Redwood; 1997 onward intakes—Priti Patel, Penny Mordaunt, Jacob Rees-Mogg, Christopher Heaton—Harris FS—1997 intakes onward—Graham Brady, Sarah Wollaston Andrea Leadsom, Chris Grayling, Dominic Raab, Martin Vickers, Karen Brady—some favored continued presence in EU single market (EU would not allow)

80% of UK's economic output is in services, including financial

Tony Blair
• Labour
• 1997–2007

Switch to PR elections for Euro Parl; allowed UKIP (originally Anti-Federalist League, 1993) to gain seats in first R elections, 1999

Blair's decision (along with Sweden, Ireland) to open UK labor market to "accession state" (A8) migrants immediately—with no brakes as most other EU countries did

First talks on European Constitution 2004—included in Lisbon Treaty, shepherded through Parl. by Labour MP Gordon Brown in 2007

Prime Minister	Pro-Europe Action	Anti-Europe Action	Intraparty Response
Gordon Brown • Labour • 2007–10	Lisbon Treaty—Brown defeated Conserv proposals for referendum 311–248 in March 2008 (29 Labour backbenchers rebelled)—violated its 2005 electoral pledge—Conservs, Lib Dems had also pledged one Lisbon Treaty gave more powers to European Parl, including a permanent president of the EU Council, a new high representative for foreign affairs and a new EU diplomatic service. EU was given a "full legal personality" and ability to sign treaties in the areas of its attributed powers. Included withdrawal mechanism in Article 50, first used by the UK in March 2017. European "Constitution" was in the appendix, not main body. Lisbon Treaty abolished the previous 3-pillar structure since 1993—European Court decisions applicable to the areas of justice/home affairs; the latter two pillars became part of the "supranational" European community		Increasing numbers of Euroskeptics elected from Conservs. 2005–15 (and socially conserv.) Membership of Conserv. Party since 2001—Cowley and Stuart 2012. Heppell et al. (2017) between 2010–2015 81 Conserv. MPs were "hard" Euroskeptics, 154 "softer" By 2016, "harder" Brexiteers had doubled to 144. Of the 306 Conservs. in the 2010 Parl., 50 were socially conserv, up to 82 of 330 after 2015 (Heppell et al. 2017)
David Cameron • Conservative • 2010–15 • Deputy PM: Nick Clegg	Difference of opinion within coalition; Lib Dems pro-EU Conservs anti	After eurozone and global crash of 2008, "wiggle room" on portraying EU as positive for UK, especially given London as financial/banking center, difficult (1) Cameron tried to keep UK out of eurozone payments; was outvoted under qualified majority voting system of EU (2) Wanted to introduce "emergency" brake on immigration (after Blair hadn't negotiated this previously)—Merkel said no	2011: Backbench Business Committee (BBC) of Euroskeptics drove an e-petition to force a referendum vote on EU membership—stay or leave or "renegotiate" EU membership (which Cameron kept trying to do, unsuccessfully—akin to Blair strategy—Cameron's problems regarding Chancellor Merkel and European Commission President Juncker starting in 2014 (pres until 2019) The BBC Committee got matter brought to a vote in Commons but govt. defeated it October 2011 by a 483–111 vote

(3) Also wanted to cut benefits eligibility for immigrants

Fiscal Stability Pact of 2011 proposed, setting off Euroskeptics—by which EU members would have to submit national budgets to the scrutiny of the European Commission and possibly be required to change. By 2012 all EU members had signed except Hungary, UK.

January 2013 Cameron delivers Bloomberg speech in London, promising in and out referendum by Dec. 2017 if Conservs. won next election (thus ruling out coalition with pro-EU Liberal Democrats). 5 themes of speech:

(1) Single market good but need to deal with services, energy, digital

(2) Flexibility needed so that those not wanting more political or econ. integration (UK) could stay in EU—UK did not join Schengen immigration framework but availed itself of its benefits; euro issue and "greater centralization happening with ECJ"

(3) Power must flow back to member states

(4) National parliaments are the source of democratic legitimacy/accountability (not Euro. Parl.)

(5) Fairness for those outside eurozone too

Overall: need to have divergence (May repeats [1] at Mansion House 2018)—that EU currently has "2 speed" members—17 EU members in Eurozone, 10 not—26 EU countries are in Schengen, including 4 outside EU—Switzerland, Norway, Liechtenstein, and Iceland; 2 EU countries (UK, Irish Republic) retained own border controls

—after that loss nearly 100 MPs delivered petition to PM Cameron that a commitment to hold vote no. 2 before the next general election

Helen Thompson (2017)—argues successive leaders in all parties tried to "extol" the virtues of European membership while "kicking the can down the road" on UK sovereignty-monetary union contradiction

• Irony she points up: that successive negotiation losses by Cameron showed that the UK did not have the necessary voting strength within the EU

Fresh Start group issues manifesto same month of Bloomberg speech claiming:

(1) Cameron must negotiate emergency brake future on financial services legislation for Lisbon Treaty

(2) "repatriate competence in the area of social and employment law to member states"

(3) Opt out of "all existing criminal justice and policing procedures not already covered by the Lisbon Treaty" block opt-out (sets up conflict with then-Home Sec. May regarding ECHR)—oddly at the time FS supported staying in single market; position shifted by 2017

Prime Minister	Pro-Europe Action	Anti-Europe Action	Intraparty Response
David Cameron • Conservative • 2015–16		(a) Comparison—"Switzerland in single market but outside EU; Norway has Europe's biggest energy reserves, pays to be in single market, but 'no say over its rules'" (Mansion House speech) Economic argument: EU increasingly uncompetitive, "Europe's share of world output is projected to fall by almost a third in the next two decades" (Thompson, 2017) Basis for EU counterattack that UK is "cherrypicking" favored parts of EU; repeated ad nauseum against May In February 2016, Cameron negotiates some pieces with European Council president Donald Tusk (to answer some of Fresh Start critiques from 2013): (1) If 55% of national parliaments agree, they can block or veto a European Commission proposal; (2) Four-year "brake" (waiting period, based on residency) on the ability of EU migrants to claim tax credits, child benefits or publicly-financed housing (to take effect for 7 years, Cameron asked for 13) (3) Cameron won on non-eurozone countries not being required to contribute to eurozone bailouts (4) Cameron lost on being able to opt out from "level playing field" requirements with EU on London banking/financial services (what eventually drove the ERG support of Brexit). Date of June 23, 2016 referendum announced in House a. Odd two options within one question framing (Steve Baker of ERG claimed credit)	

Referendum loses by narrow margin on June 23, 2016 (52–48%). N.I./Scotland vote to remain. Cameron announces he will resign on June 24; Conserv. party begins leadership contest with ultimately two-person choice selected by MPs to be presented to the national party members.

Two-person contest whittled down to May vs. Andrea Leadsom (Fresh Start/ERG member); Leadsom drops out July 11, 2016, after unfortunate comments about motherhood

Theresa May
- Conservative
- 2016–19

June 24, 2016: EU lays out red lines for negotiations—while successive anti-May (like anti-Thatcher) MPs claimed she was "bullied by Europe"

(a) i.e., "settle the divorce first and any future trading relationship" second. Divorce issues included financial settlements from UK to EU, status of immigration between EU and UK and the Good Friday Agreement of 1998, with no hard borders between Ireland and N.I. (UK).

PM May announces future invocation of "exit clause" Article 50 of Lisbon Treaty in October 2016; formally invoked on March 29, 2017, through notice to European Council—the original timeframe for exiting the EU was 2 years from that date (March 29, 2019).

(a) Court challenges were brought up by British lawyer Gina Miller to May's assertion of "executive-only" agreement to start Article 50.

(b) January 24, 2017, Supreme Court ruled that Parliament had to be involved. Parliament passed the "European Union (Notification of Withdrawal Act)" March 16, 2017.

July 9, 2018: In response to Chequers, Secretary for Exiting the EU David Davis (who had been dumped as party chair in favor of Theresa May in 2002) and his department minister (and ERG chair, 2016–17 and 2019–20) Steve Baker, in a coordinated move reminiscent of the Lawson-Howe resignations in 1990 against Thatcher, resigned, and Foreign Secretary Boris Johnson resigned on July 10—he had been part of Brexit campaign.

- Ostensibly the issue was "interference" with Davis's white paper forthcoming in July 2018, but presenting issue by the three was also "UK could be stuck indefinitely under EU rule, subject to a decision of the EU" regarding backstop—ignoring the role of the necessity of restarting power sharing in N.I. in this. Wooing effort between ERG and DUP (in confidence and supply agreement with Conservs. after June 2017 election) to ensure neither "broke ranks" and supported May's proposal—gave DUP more time to prolong stalemate in N.I. as well

Prime Minister	Pro-Europe Action	Anti-Europe Action	Intraparty Response
		May's "Lancaster House" speech January 2017—response to EU red lines (a) Declaration that UK would leave single market (b) Says "any attempt to inflict a punitive outcome on the UK would be an act of "self harm" as the UK would then slash taxes and become even more of low-tax haven for global business (c) Other pieces—"new customs agreement, associate membership of customs union–like Switzerland and some Scandinavian countries had—or "remain a signatory to some elements of customs union" were all possible—broadest possible interpretation (d) She noted that "since joining the EU, trade as a percentage of GDP has broadly stagnated in the UK" and that "we want to get out into the wider world and do trade deals all around the globe" (to placate anti-EU Brexiteers who wanted to trade with US, other areas) —Johnson refers to her speech as "fantastic" (e) She also reiterated the historic importance of the Common Travel Area between the UK and I.R. since "nobody wants to return to the borders of the past" (f) "Not contribute huge sums to EU budget but pay towards specific programs"	ERG plotted an overthrow in fall 2018, along the lines of Thatcher's overthrow in November 1990—Guto Bebb, cited in Geoghegan 2020: "There was never any intention to support May's deal." Johnson holds an alternative "Chuck Chequers" event at the party conference October 1–2, 2018. Atlas Newtork associated groups began assault on May's proposals after Chequers (included London-based Institute of Economic Affairs and the Free Trade Initiative/Institute presented "alternative" frameworks, publicly supported by former secretary David Davis]—document released Sept. 8, 2018—contained extreme proposals to "remove all tariffs," zero competition for government procurement, prohibition on governments' use of anti-dumping trade measures (a) Second set of proposals later in Sept (Sept. 18): "Plan A+ for Brexit," proposing a "clean break with Europe"—Davis and Johnson broke the rules in arranging free use of Westminster facilities to launch the plan By December 2018, in response to May's successes in getting the first Withdrawal Act through Parliament in June, and the trade bill finished by September 2018, a three-pronged attack on her forward progress included:

(g) "Build new trading relationships outside EU"— 'Global Britain' strategy

(h) No longer be under ECJ jurisdiction (to appeal to Brexiteers)

Joint agreement between the UK and EU, 2017—acknowledged the need for a "legally watertight solution" to the border question

Munich speech to security conference Feb. 17, 2018—emphasized importance of security, anti-terrorism cooperation between EU and UK (EU would get to use the huge UK security apparatus)

(a) "Climbdown" from Lancaster House speech some say—"when cooperating with European agencies, Britain would respect the jurisdiction of the ECJ" (already obvious to many but not Brexiteers)—also by then she had "committed to divorce settlement of 39 billion pounds and to a transition period to adhere to EU rules" (Bennhold and Erlinger, NYT.com, Feb. 17, 2018)—criticism by opponents that her "red lines were turning pink"

Mansion House speech, March 2, 2018—

(1) the DUP, which did not want Brexit concluded before Stormont was restored

(2) the ERG, which did not want to remain (theoretically) in a UK-wide customs backstop with the EU so that Brexiteers would not be free to conduct new trade agreements outside the EU—also that EU-UK consent was required to end the backstop

(3) Remainers, within the Conserv. Party who wanted a second referendum and within Labour who refused to back anything if a full customs union weren't retained

November 2018: In response to the fact that May had a proposed agreement with the EU to present before Parliament, ERG members Suella Braverman, Dominic Raab, and Esther McVey resigned from cabinet—based on "lack of trust that the EU would agree to a temporary backstop," despite lack of evidence

By December 2018, enough ERG members got the required signatures sent to Sir Graham Brady, chair of the 1922 backbench committee, to force a leadership vote.

- May went to the committee before the vote and said she would not contest another election as PM if they supported her

Prime Minister	Pro-Europe Action	Anti-Europe Action	Intraparty Response
		(1) Recognized level playing field (so that UK did not go to "hard Brexit" and undercut EU tax regime)	• former party chair Michael Ashcroft weighed in on his blog's home page, ConservativeHome, urging party to drop her (December 12, 2018). May survived the vote 200–117.
		(2) Reiterated need for an independent arbitration mechanism (as stated in August 2018)—however, "makes clear that any suggestion the ECJ is the future sole arbiter is ruled out"	Vote on January 15, 2019, was 432 against (including 118 Remainers and Leavers, including Remainers hoping for a second Brexit referendum—(Aidt, Gray and Savu 2019, 587). 202 voted in favor of the bill.
		(3) Called for a robust deal on data services—"going beyond the typical 'adequacy' decision offered by the EU to third countries"—adequacy is a unilateral decision by the European Commission that could be revoked	(a) January 2019, a Remain group formed, calling itself "Right to Vote," in favor of a second referendum.
		(a) Also called for allowing the info. commissioner to attend the regulator's forum	(b) February 2019, along the lines of the then Europhiles who exited Thatcher's cabinet in 1990 (Lawson/Howe), Conservative MPs Heidi Allen, Sarah Wollaston, and Anna Soubry left the party, denying May a working majority (as 3 rightist Euroskeptics had threatened Major with in 1993—Lilley, Howard, and Portillo); one MP crossed the floor in 1996, denying Major a working majority).
		(4) Migration—as the Institute for Government, March 2, 2018, said, "This speech was the first mention that migration could be a topic for negotiation"	(c) On January 16, 2019, Labour leader Corbyn called a no-confidence vote on May to precipitate an election; as under Major, not enough MPs wanted a new election so she won (325–306), with the DUP supporting her so as not to face an election

(5) Goods trade—"We must ensure that as now products only need to undergo one series of approvals in one country . . . we will need a comprehensive system of mutual recognition . . . UK and EU regulatory standards will remain substantially similar in the future."

(a) "Our default is that UK law may not necessarily be identical to EU law but it should achieve the same outcomes."

(b) "There will need to be an independent mechanism to oversee these arrangements."

(c) The UK will want to align its regulations in some areas, but in others it wants the freedom to meet the same standards but by different means and to diverge in the future, even though that may bring "market access consequences."

(d) As the Institute for Government IFG *Explainer* noted, the only other example of "comprehensive frictionless mutual recognition" (which EU was rejecting at the time) was the Trans–Tasman Mutual Recognition Agreement, but without having the "highly regulated areas important to the UK."

IFG noted that was consistent with her September 2017 Florence speech and David Davis (ex-EU secretary) Vienna speech (Feb. 20, 2018)

By May 23, 2019. the PM's position was untenable;

(1) UKIP's new variant, the "Brexit Party", got its highest percentage of UK votes and seats on May 23, 2019 EP elections; also

(2) More than 1,300 Conserv. seats lost in local elections spring 2019

Prime Minister	Pro-Europe Action	Anti-Europe Action	Intraparty Response
		(6) On future agency relationships, the IFG noted the speech went beyond the Munich one in stating that the UK "could abide by rules of the agencies and making appropriate financial contributions" (Munich speech only committed to security relationships)—this called for potential "high alignment" in the single market	
		(7) Customs—nothing new since 2017 but reiterated two options:	
		(a) customs partnership between EU and UK (untried, and govt. admitted it would take at least 5 years to work out)	
		(b) "highly streamlined" customs arrangement—"We would jointly agree to implement a range of measures to minimise frictions to trade, including specific provisions for Northern Ireland"—as IFG piece noted, this would result in friction between standards	
		(c) Agriculture—leave CAP—but future environmental and food safety standards "less clear"	
		(d) leave Common Fisheries Policy	
		(8) Services—PM wanted to go beyond agreed precedents and setting out "forms of further liberalisation that could be agreed"—important as services are 80% of UK GDP	
		(a) "Agree an appropriate labour mobility framework"—based on "mode 4," ability of people to travel and provide cross-border services to clients—included in the Canada-EU FTA (CETA)	

(b) Reiteration of "mutual recognition of qualifications" (such as accountants or architects)—this was tried in round 1 of negotiations with Europe but EU kicked the can down into phase 2 of negotiations

(c) "Two areas never covered in a meaningful way before in an FTA are broadcasting and financial services"—UK wanted both

(d) Trying to keep the single electricity market in N.I./Rep. of Ireland

(e) Digital services—"UK will diverge, provide leadership"

(9) Civil-judicial cooperation—"We want our agreement to cover this, following the Lugano Convention with non-member states," while desiring a broader agreement"—UK wished to expand on the convention allowing the signatories' judgments in civil and commercial courts to be recognized and enforced in different jurisdictions" (Institute for Government, *Explainer*, March 2, 2018).

(10) Withdrawal Agreement Bill (WAB 1) June 2018—responding to EU red lines, ERG and Fresh Start and Remainers:

(a) Government-proposed "amendments in lieu" to ensure UK Parliament would have a vote in the cases of:

a. if either House rejected Withdrawal Agreement or no agreement reached with EU by November 30, 2018

b. if Parl. did not approve Withdrawal Agreement, a minister would set out the framework for how the govt. would propose to proceed within 28 days—

Prime Minister	Pro-Europe Action	Anti-Europe Action	Intraparty Response
		(c) that the Commons could vote on a "neutrally framed" motion to consider the min. statement and	
		(d) again if no deal had been reached with the EU by Jan. 21, 2019.	
		(e) Third amendment in lieu was that any new border arrangements would have to be negotiated between the EU and the UK and could only pertain to "physical infrastructure including border posts or checks and controls"	
		(f) First *Withdrawal Act* of June 2018 ensured relevant EU law would be transposed into UK law	
		(11) Chequers Conference at PM's retreat July 6–7, 2018.	
		(a) Contained 12 points, like Lancaster House speech of January 2017, most of which had either already been passed the previous month in the Withdrawal Act or been agreed in negotiations with the EU.	
		(b) Chequers language included that:	
		(c) "commitment of the UK to continued harmonization with the EU on all goods, including agriculture, but not services, after Brexit	
		(d) right of Parliament to oversee trade policy and to choose to diverge from EU rules	
		(e) restoring the supremacy of British courts by ending the jurisdiction of the ECJ in the UK" (fudging since trade with EU trade still occurs under ECJ oversight)	

(f) "Borders between the EU/UK would be treated as a combined customs territory (for goods trade, including agriculture)—UK-wide customs union would be temporary" (could be negotiated once power-sharing govt. returned to N.I.)

(g) Argument in Chequers that this UK-wide customs territory would obviate the EU's proposal for the default backstop (where EU-UK would negotiate when to end)—that Ch. Would keep N.I. within the EU customs territory and common regulatory area covering goods and sanitary/phytosanitary regs.—regarding plants/animals—this would include N.I. in framework so as not to separate it out from the rest of the UK

(h) UK would apply domestic tariffs and trade policies for goods intended for the UK but charge EU tariffs and their equivalents for goods going to the EU

(12) In amendments to the customs legislation to be voted on by Parliament in Fall 2018, to appeal to the ERG (as May had compromised with Remainers to get the Withdrawal Act through in June 2018). Chequers language on various items was removed, including:

(a) UK collecting taxes on behalf of EU and vice versa (unless all member states agreed)

(b) ERG amendment on removing the UK from EU's VAT

Prime Minister	Pro-Europe Action	Anti-Europe Action	Intraparty Response
		(c) Important for future (Boris Johnson), amendment was included at behest of ERG, Kate Hoey (Labour) and DUP that Brexit would not bring about a customs border in the Irish Sea ("Clause 37")	
		Customs legislation passed July 16, 2018	
		(13) Second element, the trade bill to "include some 40 trade agreements signed by the EU with third countries and place them in UK law" passed	
		The Taxation (Cross-border Trade) Act of 2018 was given royal assent on Sept. 13, 2018	
		In October 2018, May was sandwiched between EU (and Dutch who previously supported her) where they said N.I.—only backstop was preferred and Arlene Foster, head of DUP (which was theoretically in a confidence and supply relationship with the Conservs. after June 2017 election but rarely supported them) said only an N.I. backstop would not be acceptable (which is post-2021 and Brexit still in place under the Northern Ireland Protocol, with the tariff border down the Irish Sea between N.I. and the rest of the UK)—Foster had every incentive to delay the Brexit legislation, along with the ERG, since Stormont had not been functional since January 2017	
		November 2018: the EU and PM May had a 585-page agreed Withdrawal Agreement to be voted on by Parl. (the result of negotiations since 2017); EU had moved to agree a temporary all UK backstop, not just a N.I.-based one	

(14) First vote on Withdrawal Agreement Bill with 26-page Political Declaration Jan. 15, 2019 (pulled after planned December vote after lack of support in Conservative caucus)
   (a) contained the UK-wide backstop and requirement for UK to stay in transition period for at least a year after conclusion of the Withdrawal agreement (originally thought to be January 2020)
   (b) January–March 2019, May negotiated with the EU to establish a "joint interpretative instrument" so that the UK could unilaterally enter arbitration on the backstop post-Brexit if the EU refused to negotiate
   (c) EU also approved the potential for UK to unilaterally leave the backstop if negotiations broke down
   (d) Also added to the Political Declaration that both sides were committed to seeking alternative arrangements for the Irish border so as to end the backstop by December 2020
(15) Second vote on Withdrawal Agreement and Political Declaration March 12, 2019—anti-majority somewhat smaller than in January (149 nays vs. 230 in January) the overall vote was still 391 vs. 242 in favor

Prime Minister	Pro-Europe Action	Anti-Europe Action	Intraparty Response
		March 19, 2019: May was allowed to bring the vote up again (Speaker, given the power in the 2018 agreement to decide if there was a substantially different question) allowed a vote on the Political Declaration only (which would not have affected Brexit). Government lost that vote, getting the most votes in favor, 277, but still losing. May offered to Conservative MPs that she would resign if they supported this bill.	
		(a) Emergency summit with EU on April 10 to extend the Brexit withdrawal date until October 31 at the latest. EU commits to a summit June 20–21 to review UK progress toward Brexit.	
		(b) EU leaders fought over the timeframe; Chancellor Merkel wanted to give May a longer extension to try to force a Conservative vote for the package; PM Macron of France argues for shorter timeframe to "prevent the UK from interfering in the EU political cycle" (A. Sloat, www.brookings.edu, May 30, 2019).	
		(c) May tries on May 21 for a fourth parliamentary vote on Brexit, promising, among other things, a second (binding) referendum, since the first was not; language to ensure that UK labor and environmental standards do not fall below those of the EU after Brexit. This is aimed at trying to get Remain Conservative and Labour votes. Cabinet says no to her offer.	
		(D) After poor results in the May 23, 2019, European Parliament elections, May resigns as party leader on May 24; says she will stay on as interim PM until new leadership contest is finished	
		(a) July 23, 2019: Johnson wins leadership contest	

References

Abrams, Jim, Laurie Kellman, Julie Hirshfeld Davis, and Donna Cassata. 2010. "US House Democrats Elect Nancy Pelosi to Remain as Their Leader Despite Big Election Losses." *Canadian Press*, November 17, 2010.

Acheson, Ian. 2019. "How Theresa May's War on the Police Backfired." *The Spectator*, July 10, 2019. https://www.spectator.co.uk/article/how-theresa-may-s-war-on-the-police-backfired.

Adam, Karla. 2011. "Cameron Defends Veto of European Treaty." *Washington Post*, December 12, 2011. https://www.washingtonpost.com/world/europe/cameron-defends-veto-of-european-treaty/2011/12/12/gIQAmGiJqO_story.html.

Adam, Rudolf G. 2020. *Brexit: Causes and Consequences*. Basel, Switzerland: Springer.

Addley, Esther. 2017. "Osborne's *Evening Standard* Savages Theresa May's Election Campaign." *The Guardian*, May 30, 2017. https://www.theguardian.com/media/2017/may/30/osbornes-evening-standard-savages-theresa-mays-election-campaign.

Adragna, Anthony, and Zack Coleman. 2018. "Ocasio-Cortez, Youth Protesters Storm Pelosi's Office to Push for Climate Plan." *Politico*, November 13, 2018. https://www.politico.com/story/2018/11/13/ocasio-cortez-climate-protestors-push-pelosi-962915.

Ahmed, Kamal. 2018. "The Hidden Message in Hammond's EU Speech." *BBC*, March 6, 2018. https://www.bbc.com/news/business-43309882.

Aidt, Toke, Felix Gray, and Alexandru Savu. 2021. "The Meaningful Votes: Voting on Brexit in the British House of Commons." *Public Choice* 186, no. 3–4 (March): 587–617. https://doi.org/10.1007/s11127-019-00762-9.

Alderman, Keith. 1999. "Revision of Leadership Election Procedures in the Conservative Party." *Parliamentary Affairs* 52, no. 2 (April): 260–74. https://doi.org/10.1093/pa/52.2.260.

Alderman, R. K., and Martin J. Smith. 1990. "Can British Prime Ministers Be Given the Push by Their Parties?" *Parliamentary Affairs* 43, no. 3 (July): 260–76. https://doi.org/10.1093/oxfordjournals.pa.a052252.

Aldrich, John H., and David W. Rohde. 2011. "The Logic of Conditional Party Government: Revisiting the Electoral Connection." *The Monkey Cage*, July 2011. https://themonkeycage.org/wp-content/uploads/2011/07/aldrich-and-rohde.pdf.

Alexandre-Collier, Agnès. 2019. "'Less Stale, Only Slightly Less Male, but Overwhelmingly Less Pale': The 2015 New Conservative Brexiters in the House of Commons." *Parliamentary Affairs* 72, no. 3 (November): 588–615. https://doi.org/10.1093/pa/gsy023.

Allen, Jonathan. 2010. "'Assistant Leader' for Clyburn." *Politico*, November 13, 2010. https://www.politico.com/story/2010/11/assistant-leader-for-clyburn-045077.

Allen, Nicholas. 2019. "Theresa May the Worst Prime Minister Ever? David Cameron Got Britain into This Mess." *The Conversation*, January 16, 2019. https://theconversation.com/theresa-may-the-worst-prime-minister-ever-david-cameron-got-britain-into-this-mess-109988.

Allsup, Maeve. 2022. "GOP Members' Suit against Pelosi over House Mask Mandate Tossed." *Bloomberg Law*, March 9, 2022. https://news.bloomberglaw.com/us-law-week/gop-members-suit-against-pelosi-over-house-mask-mandate-tossed.

Alter, Karen, and David Steinberg. 2007. "The Theory and Reality of the European Coal and Steel Community." In *Making History: European Integration and Institutional Change at the 50th Anniversary of the Treaty of Rome*, edited by Sophie Meunier and Karen McNamara, 89–104. Oxford: Oxford University Press.

Amaro, Silvia. 2018. "Theresa May's Brexit Deal Is 'Good for Both Sides,' Analysts Say." *CNBC*, December 5, 2018. https://www.cnbc.com/2018/12/05/brexit-witdrawal-deal-benefits-uk-and-eu.html.

Andrews, Mark. 2019. "How Midland MP's Rocked Major Government." *Express and Star*, November 28, 2019. https://www.expressandstar.com/news/politics/general-election-2019/2019/11/28/how-midland-mps-rocked-major-government.

Annesley, Claire. 2015. "Rules of Ministerial Recruitment." *Politics & Gender* 11, no. 4 (December): 618–42. https://doi.org/10.1017/S1743923X15000434.

Annesley, Claire, Karen Beckwith, and Susan Franceschet. 2014. "Informal Institutions and the Recruitment of Political Executives." Paper presented at the American Political Science Association, August 2014.

Annesley, Claire, Karen Beckwith, and Susan Franceschet. 2019. *Cabinets, Ministers and Gender*. Oxford: Oxford University Press.

Annesley, Claire, and Francesca Gains. 2010. "The Core Executive: Gender, Power and Change." *Political Studies* 58, no. 5 (December): 909–29. https://doi.org/10.1111%2Fj.1467-9248.2010.00824.x.

Annesley, Claire, and Francesca Gains. 2014. "Can Cameron Capture Women's Votes? The Gendered Impediments to a Conservative Majority in 2015." *Parliamentary Affairs* 67, no. 4 (October): 767–82. https://doi.org/10.1093/pa/gsu001.

AP. 2017. "UK Conservative Candidate Charged in Expenses Inquiry." *AP News*, June 2, 2017. https://apnews.com/article/cfc9b888b787417aac4d6f8ec15932df.

Ashe, Jeannette, Rosie Campbell, Sarah Childs, and Elizabeth Evans. 2010. "'Stand by Your Man': Women's Political Recruitment at the 2010 UK General Election." *British Politics* 5, no. 4 (December): 455–80. https://doi.org/10.1057/bp.2010.17.

Asthana, Anushka, and Heather Stewart. 2017. "'Come Off It, Sunshine': Boris Johnson Hits Back at John Major." *The Guardian*, February 28, 2017. https://www.theguardian.com/politics/2017/feb/28/come-off-it-sunshine-boris-johnson-hits-back-at-john-major.

Asthana, Anushka, Heather Stewart, and Jessica Elgot. 2017. "Brexit: May's Threat to Europe: 'No Deal for Britain Is Better than a Bad Deal.'" *The Guardian*, January 17, 2017. https://www.theguardian.com/politics/2017/jan/17/prime-minister-vows-to-put-final-brexit-deal-before-parliament.

Aupperlee, Aaron. 2019. "Conor Lamb Upholds Promise Not to Vote Nancy Pelosi as Speaker." *Trib Live*, January 3, 2019.

Ayman, Roya, Karen Korabik, and Scott Morris. 2009. "Is Transformational Leadership Always Perceived as Effective? Male Subordinates' Devaluation of Female Transformational Leaders." *Journal of Applied Social Psychology* 39, no. 4 (April): 852–79.

Bade, Rachael, and Mike DeBonis. 2019. "'Outright Disrepectful': Four House Women Struggle as Pelosi Isolates Them." *Washington Post*, July 10, 2019. https://www.washingtonpost.com/politics/outright-disrespectful-four-house-women-struggle-as-pelosi-isolates-them/2019/07/10/a33c63a8-a33f-11e9-b7b4-95e30869bd15_story.html.

Bainbridge, Laura. 2020. "Police and Crime Commissioners: New Agents of Crime and Justice Policy Transfer?" *Policing and Society* 31, no.6 (May): 721–34. https://doi.org/10.1080/10439463.2020.1766461.

Baker, David, Andrew Gamble, Steve Ludlam, and David Seawright. 1999. "Backbenchers with Attitude: A Seismic Study of the Conservative Party and Dissent on Europe." In *Party Discipline and Parliamentary Government*, edited by Shaun Bowler, David M. Farrell, and Richard S. Katz, 72–98. Columbus: Ohio State University Press. https://doi.org/10.2307/j.ctv177tghd.

Baker, Ross K. 2002. "Liberal Leader of a Liberal Party." *Los Angeles Times*, November 12, 2002. https://www.latimes.com/archives/la-xpm-2002-nov-12-oe-baker12-story.html.

Baker, Steve. 2013. "Mark Carney's Grand Experiment Began Today." Cobden Centre, August 7, 2013. https://www.cobdencentre.org/2013/08/mark-carneys-grand-experiment-began-today/.

Baldez, Lisa. 2010. "The Gender Lacuna in Comparative Politics." *Perspectives on Politics* 8, no. 1 (March): 199–205. https://doi.org/10.1017/S1537592709992775.

Bale, Tim. 2011. "Face Down the Eurosceptics in Your Party, David Cameron." *The Guardian*, October 21, 2011. https://www.theguardian.com/commentisfree/2011/oct/21/david-cameron-eurosceptics.

Bale, Tim. 2016. *The Conservative Party: From Thatcher to Cameron*. 2nd ed. Cambridge, UK, and Malden, MA: Polity Press.

Bale, Tim, and Paul Webb. 2018. "'We Didn't See It Coming': The Conservatives." In *Britain Votes 2017*, edited by Jonathan Tonge, Cristina Leston-Bandeira, and Stuart Wilkes-Heeg, 46–58. Oxford: Oxford University Press.

Bale, Tim, Paul Webb, and Monica Poletti. 2020. *Footsoldiers: Political Party Membership in the 21st Century*. London: Routledge.

Ball, Molly. 2020. *Pelosi*. New York: Henry Holt.

Barrett, David. 2014. "Theresa May Introduces New Restrictions on Stop and Search Powers." *The Telegraph*, August 26, 2014. https://www.telegraph.co.uk/news/uknews/crime/11054788/Theresa-May-introduces-new-restrictions-on-stop-and-search-powers.html.

Barry, Ellen, and Stephen Castle. 2019. "Amid Parliament's Brexit Rebellion, a Tectonic Shift in How Britain Is Governed." *New York Times*, January 15, 2019. https://www.nytimes.com/2019/01/15/world/europe/brexit-britain-parliament-theresa-may.html.

Bashevkin, Sylvia. 1993. *Toeing the Lines: Women and Party Politics in English Canada*. 2nd ed. Oxford: Oxford University Press.

Baynes, Chris. 2019. "All the MPs Who Voted against Lifting Abortion Ban and Same-Sex Marriage in Northern Ireland." *The Independent*, July 10, 2019. https://www.independent.co.uk/news/uk/politics/same-sex-marriage-northern-ireland-list-every-mp-voted-against-lifting-abortion-ban-a8998456.html.

BBC. 2011a. "David Cameron Blocks EU-Wide Deal to Tackle Euro Crisis." *BBC*, December 9, 2011. https://www.bbc.com/news/uk-16104275

BBC. 2011b. "EU Referendum: Cameron Says No Bad Blood Towards Rebels." *BBC*, October 25, 2011. https://www.bbc.com/news/av/uk-politics-15446312.

BBC. 2012a. "London Mayor Gains Powers over the Metropolitan Police." *BBC*, January 16, 2012. https://www.bbc.com/news/uk-england-london-16567959.

BBC. 2012b. "Theresa May to Split up UK Border Agency." *BBC*, February 20, 2012. https://www.bbc.com/news/uk-politics-17099143.

BBC. 2013. "Thatcher and Her Tussles with Europe." *BBC*, April 8, 2013. https://www.bbc.com/news/uk-politics-11598879.

BBC. 2015a. "Grant Shapps Quits amid Tory Bullying Claims." *BBC*, November 28. https://www.bbc.com/news/uk-politics-34952981.

BBC. 2015b. "Timeline: Campaigns for a European Union Referendum." *BBC*, May 21, 2015. https://www.bbc.com/news/uk-politics-15390884.

BBC. 2016a. "Brexit: Stop Blaming Theresa May, Says Iain Duncan Smith." *BBC*, September 25, 2016. https://www.bbc.com/news/uk-politics-37467502.

BBC. 2016b. "EU Deal Gives UK Special Status, Says Cameron." *BBC*, February 20, 2016. https://www.bbc.com/news/uk-politics-35616768.
BBC. 2016c. "Q & A: Police and Crime Commissioners." *BBC*, April 21, 2016. https://www.bbc.com/news/uk-politics-19504639.
BBC. 2016d. "Who's Who in Team Theresa May." *BBC*, July 14, 2016. https://www.bbc.com/news/uk-politics-36783185.
BBC. 2017a. "Reality Check: Migration to the UK." *BBC*, May 25, 2017. https://www.bbc.com/news/election-2017-40015269.
BBC. 2017b. "Security Services 'Prevented 13 Terror Attacks on the UK since 2013.'" *BBC*, March 6, 2017. https://www.bbc.com/news/uk-39176110.
BBC. 2018a. "At-a-Glance: The New UK Brexit Plan Agreed at Chequers." *BBC*, July 7, 2018. https://www.bbc.com/news/uk-politics-44749993.
BBC. 2018b. "Brexit: Theresa May Accused of 'Cowardice.'" *BBC*, July 17, 2018. https://www.bbc.com/news/uk-northern-ireland-44850571.
BBC. 2019a. "Brexit: Theresa May's Deal Is Voted Down in Historic Commons Defeat." *BBC*, January 15, 2019. https://www.bbc.com/news/uk-politics-46885828.
BBC. 2019b. "Brexit: What Is in Boris Johnson's New Deal with the EU?" *BBC*, October 21, 2019. https://www.bbc.com/news/uk-50083026.
BBC. 2019c. "Theresa May Says Domestic Abuse Bill 'Once-in-a-Generation Opportunity.'" *BBC*, October 2, 2019. https://www.bbc.com/news/uk-politics-49910926.
BBC. 2020a. "George Osborne to Step Down as *Evening Standard* Editor." *BBC*, June 12, 2020. https://www.bbc.com/news/entertainment-arts-53025480.
BBC. 2020b. "Reshuffle 2020: Who Is in Boris Johnson's New Cabinet?" *BBC*, February 14, 2020. https://www.bbc.com/news/uk-politics-49043973.
Becker, Lawrence A., and Vincent G. Moscardelli. 2008. "Congressional Leadership on the Front Lines: Committee Chairs, Electoral Security, and Ideology." *PS: Political Science and Politics* 41, no. 1 (April): 77–82. https://doi.org/10.1017/S1049096508080116.
Beckwith, Karen. 2010. "Introduction: Comparative Politics and the Logics of a Comparative Politics of Gender." *Perspectives on Politics* 8, no. 1 (March): 159–68. https://doi.org/10.1017/S1537592709992726.
Beckwith, Karen. 2015. "Before Prime Minister: Margaret Thatcher, Angela Merkel, and Gendered Party Leadership Contests." *Politics & Gender* 11, no. 4 (December): 718–45. https://doi.org/10.1017/S1743923X15000409.
Behr, Rafael. 2017. "The EU Withdrawal Bill Is Nothing Less Than an Executive Coup." *The Guardian*, September 5, 2017. https://www.theguardian.com/commentisfree/2017/sep/05/eu-withdrawal-bill-executive-coup-brexit.
Beinart, Peter. 2018. "The Nancy Pelosi Problem." *The Atlantic*, April 2018. https://www.theatlantic.com/magazine/archive/2018/04/the-nancy-pelosi-problem/554048/.
Belfast Telegraph. 2018. "Bid to Introduce Same-Sex Marriage in Northern Ireland Blocked." May 11, 2018. https://www.belfasttelegraph.co.uk/news/northern-ir

eland/bid-to-introduce-same-sex-marriage-in-northern-ireland-blocked-3689 7894.html.

Belfast Telegraph. 2019. "The European Research Group: Who Are They?" February 15, 2019. https://www.belfasttelegraph.co.uk/news/uk/the-european-research-group-who-are-they-37819915.html.

Bendavid, Naftali. 2009. "U.S. News: Pelosi Key to GOP 2010 Playbook—Republicans Hope Linking House Speaker to Democrats Can Turn Centrist Districts." *Wall Street Journal*, October 12, 2009. A. 4. https://www.wsj.com/articles/SB125530046902979049.

Bennhold, Katrin, and Steven Erlanger. 2018. "Theresa May, in Munich, Calls for Swift Security Pact and Offers Concession." *New York Times*, February 17, 2018. https://www.nytimes.com/2018/02/17/world/europe/uk-theresa-may-munich.html.

Bennister, Mark, and Richard Heffernan. 2012. "Cameron as Prime Minister: The Intra-Executive Politics of Britain's Coalition Government." *Parliamentary Affairs* 65, no. 4 (October): 778–801. https://doi.org/10.1093/pa/gsr061.

Berg, Sanchia. 2018. "How a Conservative PM Faced a Rees-Mogg . . . in 1993." *BBC*, July 24, 2018. https://www.bbc.com/news/uk-politics-44924844.

Berman, Russell. 2016. "Can Nancy Pelosi Survive the Trump Aftershock?" *The Atlantic*, November 24, 2016. https://www.theatlantic.com/politics/archive/2016/11/can-nancy-pelosi-survive-the-trump-aftershock/508649/.

Berthezene, Clarisse, and Julie Gottleib, eds. 2018. *Re-thinking Right Wing Women: Gender and the Conservative Party, 1880s to the Present.* Manchester: University of Manchester Press.

"Biography of Steny Hoyer." 2020. https://hoyer.house.gov/about.

Bird, Mike. 2014. "Sorry New York, but London Is the World's Real Capital City." *Business Insider*, November 7, 2014. https://www.businessinsider.com/sorry-new-york-london-is-the-world-capital-city-2014-10.

Birrell, Ian, Katy Balls, and Andrew Gimson. 2018. "What Does This Vote of No Confidence Mean?" *The Guardian*, December 12, 2018. https://www.theguardian.com/commentisfree/2018/dec/12/no-confidence-vote-theresa-may-panel.

Blanchard, Jack. 2018. "Night at the Museum–War Cabinet Part 2—Harassment in the Commons." *Politico EU*, February 8, 2018. https://www.politico.eu/newsletter/london-playbook/politico-london-playbook-night-at-the-museum-war-cabinet-part-2-harassment-in-the-commons/.

Boffey, Daniel. 2015. "Theresa May's New FGM Reporting Rules 'Will Stop Families Seeking Help.'" *The Guardian*, January 17, 2015. https://www.theguardian.com/society/2015/jan/17/theresa-may-fgm-rules-doctors-stop-victims-seeking-help.

Boffey, Daniel, and Jennifer Rankin. 2018. "UK Will Stay in Customs Union without Fishing Deal, Says Macron." *The Guardian*, November 25, 2018. https://uk.trem.media/politics/2018/nov/25/eu-leaders-back-theresa-mays-brexit-deal-in-brussels.

Bolzendahl, Catherine. 2014. "Opportunities and Expectations: The Gendered Organization of Legislative Committees in Germany, Sweden, and the United States." *Gender & Society* 28, no. 6 (August): 847–76. https://doi.org/10.1177/0891243214542429.

Bond, Jon R., and Richard Fleisher, eds. 2000. *Polarized Politics: Congress and the President in a Partisan Era*. Washington, DC: CQ Press.

Booth, Robert. 2016. "How It All Went Wrong for Andrea Leadsom's Leadership Bid." *The Guardian*, July 11, 2016. https://www.theguardian.com/politics/2016/jul/11/how-it-all-went-wrong-for-andrea-leadsoms-leadership-bid.

Boscia, Stefan. 2020. "Theresa May Slams Brexit Trade Deal for Not Including Financial Services." *City A.M.*, December 30, 2020. https://www.cityam.com/theresa-may-slams-brexit-trade-deal-for-not-including-financial-services/.

Bouie, Jamelle. 2022. "This is What Happens When Republicans Tear Off Their Masks." *New York Times*, November 4, 2022. https://www.nytimes.com/2022/11/04/opinion/paul-pelosi-youngkin-lake.html.

Bremmer, Ian. 2019. "What Boris Johnson's Premiership Means for Brexit and the UK." *Time*, July 26, 2019. https://time.com/5636590/what-boris-johnsons-premiership-means-for-brexit-and-the-u-k/.

Bresnahan, John. 2010. "The Rise and Fall of Nancy Pelosi." *Politico*, November 3, 2010. https://www.politico.com/story/2010/11/the-rise-and-fall-of-nancy-pelosi-044598.

Bresnahan, John, and Alex Isenstadt. 2011. "Pelosi, Reid Raise Super PAC Cash." *Politico*, June 27, 2011. https://www.politico.com/story/2011/06/pelosi-reid-raise-super-pac-cash-057884.

Brill, Stephen. 2015. *America's Bitter Pill: Money, Politics Backroom Deals, and the Fight to Fix Our Broken Healthcare System*. New York: Random House.

Broder, John M., and Carl Hulse. 2008. "Behind House Struggle, Long and Tangled Roots." *New York Times*, November 22, 2008. https://www.nytimes.com/2008/11/23/us/politics/23waxman.html.

Brodie, Mollyann, Elizabeth C. Hamel, Ashley Kirzinger, and Bianca DiJulio. 2019. "Partisanship, Polling and the Affordable Care Act." *Public Opinion Quarterly* 83, no. 2 (Summer): 423–49. https://doi.org/10.1093/poq/nfz016.

Brown, Derek. 1984. "Thatcher Settles for 66pc Rebate." *The Guardian*, June 27, 1984. https://www.theguardian.com/politics/1984/jun/27/past.eu.

Bryson, Valerie, and Timothy Heppell. 2010. "Conservatism and Feminism: The Case of the British Conservative Party." *Journal of Political Ideologies* 15, no. 1 (February): 31–50. https://doi.org/10.1080/13569310903512209.

Buchler, Justin. 2010. "Going Off the Rails on a Crazy Train: Internet Infamy and Congressional Extremism." Paper presented at the Annual Meeting of the American Political Science Association.

Burton-Cartledge, Phil. 2019. "How Did the ERG Go from Hating Any Brexit Deal to Loving Boris Johnson's?" *The Guardian*, October 23, 2019. https://www.theguardian.com/commentisfree/2019/oct/23/erg-brexit-deal-boris-johnson-financial-interests.

Bzdek, Vincent. 2008. *Woman of the House: The Rise of Nancy Pelosi*. New York: Palgrave MacMillan.

Caldwell, Leigh Ann, and Theordoric Meyer with Tobi Raji. 2023. "Kevin McCarthy Will Learn His Fate Today." *Washington Post*, January 3, 2023. https://www.washingtonpost.com/politics/2023/01/03/kevin-mccarthy-will-learn-his-fate-today/.

Cameron, Chris. 2022. "These Are the People Who Died in Connection with the Capitol Riot." *New York Times*, January 5, 2022. https://www.nytimes.com/2022/01/05/us/politics/jan-6-capitol-deaths.html.

Campbell, John. 2020. "Brexit: Why a Trade Deal Is Different for Northern Ireland." *BBC*, December 24, 2020. https://www.bbc.com/news/uk-northern-ireland-55427004.

Campbell, Rosie. 2016. "Representing Women Voters: The Role of the Gender Gap and the Response of Political Parties." *Party Politics* 22, no. 5 (July): 587–97. https://doi.org/10.1177/1354068816655565.

Campbell, Rosie, and Sarah Childs, eds. 2014. *Deeds and Words: Gendering Politics after Joni Lovenduski*. Colchester, UK: ECPR Press.

Campbell, Rosie, and Sarah Childs. 2018. "The (Feminised) Contemporary Conservative Party." In *Rethinking Right-Wing Women: Gender and the Conservative Party, 1880s to the Present*, edited by Clarisse Berthezene and Julie V. Gottleib, 196–229. Manchester: University of Manchester Press.

Campbell, Rosie, Sarah Childs, and Joni Lovenduski. 2006. "Women's Equality Guarantees and the Conservative Party." *Political Quarterly* 77, no. 1 (January–March): 18–27. https://doi.org/10.1111/j.1467-923X.2006.00726.x.

Carrington, Damian. 2019. "The UK Has Biggest Fossil Fuel Subsidies in the EU, Finds Commission." *The Guardian*, January 23, 2019. https://www.theguardian.com/environment/2019/jan/23/uk-has-biggest-fossil-fuel-subsidies-in-the-eu-finds-commission.

Carroll, Rory. 2019. "DUP and Sinn Fein under Pressure to Restore Power-Sharing." *The Guardian*, December 23, 2019. https://www.theguardian.com/uk-news/2019/dec/13/dup-and-sinn-fein-under-pressure-to-restore-power-sharing.

Carswell, Simon. 2018. "Brexit Explained: Why Does the Border Matter and What Is the Backstop?" *Irish Times*, October 12, 2018. https://www.irishtimes.com/news/politics/brexit-explained-why-does-the-border-matter-and-what-is-the-backstop-1.3661518.

Castle, Stephen. 2018. "Theresa May Secures Cabinet Agreement over Brexit Plan." *New York Times*, July 6, 2018. https://www.nytimes.com/2018/07/06/world/europe/theresa-may-brexit.html.

Castle, Stephen, and Ellen Barry. 2019. "May and Brexit Face Uncertain Future after Crushing Vote in Parliament." *New York Times*, January 15, 2019. https://www.nytimes.com/2019/01/15/world/europe/brexit-vote-theresa-may.html?module=inline.

Castle, Stephen, and Richard Pérez-Peña. 2019. "May Survives No-Confidence Vote in British Parliament." *New York Times*, January 16, 2019. https://www.nytimes.com/2019/01/16/world/europe/brexit-theresa-may-no-confidence-vote.html.

Caygle, Heather. 2019. "Frank Pallone and Nancy Pelosi Reign in the Left." *Politico*, July 9, 2019. https://www.politico.com/story/2019/07/09/pallone-pelosi-progressives-1395931.

Caygle, Heather, John Bresnahan, and Sarah Ferris. 2019. "Pelosi Clashes with Fellow Dems in Closed Door Debate on Impeachment." *Politico*, May 20, 2019. https://www.politico.com/story/2019/05/20/nancy-pelosi-impeachment-1336587.

Caygle, Heather, and Sarah Ferris. 2021. "Democrats Start to Eye a Post-Pelosi Era." *Politico*, January 4, 2021. https://www.politico.com/news/2021/01/04/house-lookahead-pelosi-leaders-454902.

Celis, Karen, and Joni Lovenduski. 2018. "Power Struggles: Gender Equality in Political Representation." *European Journal of Politics and Gender* 1, no. 1–2 (July): 149–66. https://doi.org/10.1332/251510818X15272520831085.

Center for American Women and Politics. 2018. "Results: Women Candidates in the 2018 Elections." Eagleton Institute of Politics, Rutgers. November 29, 2018. https://cawp.rutgers.edu/sites/default/files/resources/results_release_5bletterhead5d_1.pdf.

Center for American Women and Politics. 2020. "History of Women in the US Congress." Eagleton Institute of Politics, Rutgers University. https://cawp.rutgers.edu/history-women-us-congress.

Center for American Women and Politics. 2021. "Women in Congress: Leadership Roles and Committee Chairs. 117th Congress 2021–2023." Eagleton Institute of Politics, Rutgers University, February 11, 2021. https://cawp.rutgers.edu/sites/default/files/resources/conglead-hist.pdf.

Chaddock, Gail Russell. 2010. "Why Nancy Pelosi Remains Leader of House Democrats Despite Huge Loss." *Christian Science Monitor*, November 17, 2010. https://www.csmonitor.com/USA/Politics/2010/1117/Why-Nancy-Pelosi-remains-leader-of-House-Democrats-despite-huge-loss.

Chakelian, Anoosh. 2014. "Police Adopt New Stop and Search Code of Conduct: Analysing Theresa May's Role." *New Statesman*, August 26, 2014. https://www.newstatesman.com/politics/uk-politics/2014/08/police-adopt-new-stop-and-search-code-conduct-analysing-theresa-mays-role.

Chakelian, Anoosh. 2021. "Tories Fail to Block Police Probe into Election Fraud Allegations in Thanet South." *New Statesman*, July 27, 2021. https://www.newstatesman.com/politics/2016/06/tories-fail-block-police-probe-election-fraud-allegations-thanet-south.

Channel 4 News. 2017. "Election Expenses: New Emails Reveal PM's Top Aide in Central Role in Local Campaign." *Channel 4*, February 28, 2017. https://www.channel4.com/news/election-expenses-new-emails-reveal-pms-top-aide-in-central-role-in-local-campaign.

Chappell, Bill. 2021. "Architect of the Capitol Outlines $30 Million in Damages from Pro-Trump Riot." *NPR*, February 24, 2021. https://www.npr.org/sections/insurrection-at-the-capitol/2021/02/24/970977612/architect-of-the-capitol-outlines-30-million-in-damages-from-pro-trump-riot.

Chappell, Louise, and Georgina Waylen. 2013. "Gender and the Hidden Life of Institutions." *Public Administration* 91, no. 3 (September): 599–615. https://doi.org/10.1111/j.1467-9299.2012.02104.x.

Childs, Sarah, and Miki Caul Kittilson. 2016. "Feminizing Political Parties: Women's Party Member Organizations within European Parliamentary Parties." *Party Politics* 22, no. 5 (July): 598–608. https://doi.org/10.1177/1354068816654320.

Childs, Sarah, and Mona Lena Krook. 2009. "Analysing Women's Substantive Representation: From Critical Mass to Critical Actors." *Government and Opposition* 44 (2): 125–45. https://doi.org/10.1111/j.1477-7053.2009.01279.x.

Childs, Sarah, and Paul Webb. 2012. *Sex, Gender and the Conservative Party: From Iron Lady to Kitten Heels*. Basingstoke, UK: Palgrave.

Childs, Sarah, Paul Webb, and Sally Marthaler. 2009. "The Feminisation of the Conservative Parliamentary Party: Party Members' Attitudes." *The Political Quarterly* 80, no. 2 (April): 204–13. https://doi.org/10.1111/j.1467-923X.2009.01979.x.

Childs, Sarah, and Julie Withey. 2004. "Women Representatives Acting for Women: Sex and the Signing of Early Day Motions in the 1997 British Parliament." *Political Studies* 52, no. 3 (October): 552–64. https://doi.org/10.1111/j.1467-9248.2004.00495.x.

Cillizza, Chris. 2014. "The Fix: Nancy Pelosi Lost a Major Proxy Battle Today." *Washington Post*, November 19, 2014. https://www.washingtonpost.com/news/the-fix/wp/2014/11/19/nancy-pelosi-lost-a-major-proxy-battle-today/.

Cisneros, Gil, Jason Crow, Chrissy Houlahan, Elaine Luria, Mikie Sherrill, Elissa Slotkin, and Abigail Spanberger. 2019. "Seven Freshmen Democrats: These Allegations Are a Threat to All We've Sworn to Protect." *Washington Post*, September 23, 2019. https://www.washingtonpost.com/opinions/2019/09/24/seven-freshman-democrats-these-allegations-are-threat-all-we-have-sworn-protect/.

Clark, Daniel. 2022. "Number of Homicides Involving a Knife in England and Wales from 2010/11 to 2020/21." *Statista.com*, February 10, 2022. https://www.statista.com/statistics/978830/knife-homicides-in-england-and-wales.

Clark, Dartunorro, Alex Moe, and Haley Talbot. 2021. "Republicans Protest, Circumvent New Metal Detectors Inside Capitol after Riot." *NBC News*, January 12, 2021. https://www.nbcnews.com/politics/congress/republicans-protest-circumvent-new-metal-detectors-inside-capitol-after-riot-n1254011.

Clarke, Andrew J. n.d. "The House Freedom Caucus: Extreme Faction Influence in the U.S. Congress." Unpublished manuscript.

Clarke, Harold, David Sanders, Marianne Stewart, and Paul Whiteley. 2004. *Political Choice in Britain*. Oxford: Oxford University Press.

Clarke, Kenneth Rt. Hon. 2017. *Kind of Blue: A Political Memoir*. London: Macmillan.

Clymer, Adam. 1994. "Democrats Pick Gephardt as House Majority Leader." *New York Times*, December 1, 1994, A28. https://www.nytimes.com/1994/12/01/us/democrats-pick-gephardt-as-house-majority-leader.html.

CNN. "Best 'Oddball' Political Ads." *CNN*, September 14, 2010. https://www.youtube.com/watch?v=4wEtTX9Hj2s.

Cohen, Robin A., and Michael E. Martinez. 2009. "Health Insurance Coverage: Early Release of Estimates from the National Health Interview Survey, 2008." Centers for Disease Control and Prevention. https://www.cdc.gov/nchs/data/nhis/earlyrelease/insur200906.htm.

Cohn, Jonathan. 2010. "How They Did It: The Inside Account of Health Care Reform's Triumph." *New Republic*, June 10, 2010, 14–25. https://newrepublic.com/article/75077/how-they-did-it.

Cohn, Jonathan. 2021. *The Ten Year War: Obamacare and the Unfinished Crusade for Universal Coverage*. New York: St. Martin's.

Colson, Thomas. 2017. "George Osborne's First *Evening Standard* Calls Brexit a 'Historic Mistake' and Carries an Unflattering Cartoon of Theresa May." *Business Insider*, May 22, 2017. https://www.businessinsider.com/evening-standard-george-osborne-editor.

Colson, Thomas. 2019. "Conservative Donors Abandon Theresa May's Party to Back New Brexit Referendum Campaign." *Business Insider*, May 1, 2019. https://www.businessinsider.com/disgruntled-tory-donors-divert-100000s-to-second-brexit-referendum-campaign-2019-4.

Colson, Thomas, and Adam Bienkov. 2019. "Bankers, Climate Change Sceptics, and Brexiteers: The Donors Funding Boris Johnson's Campaign for Prime Minister." *Business Insider*, July 1, 2019. https://www.businessinsider.com/who-is-funding-boris-johnson-conservative-leadership-prime-minister-campaign-2019-6.

Comer, Lucette B., and Tanya Drollinger. 1997. "Looking Inside the 'Glass Walls:': The Case of Women on the Industrial Sales Force." *Equal Opportunities International* 16, no. 4 (April): 1–18.

Congressional Progressive Caucus. nd. "About the CPC." https://progressives.house.gov/about-the-cpc.

Connelly, William F., Jr., and John J. Pitney. 1994. *Congress' Permanent Minority?* Lanham, MD: Rowman and Littlefield.

Conservative Party. 2021. "Party Structure and Organisation." https://www.conservatives.com/organisation/party-structure-and-organisation.

Consterdine, Erica. 2016. "The Huge Political Cost of Blair's Decision to Allow Eastern European Migrants Unfettered Access to Britain." *The Conversation*, November 16, 2016. https://theconversation.com/the-huge-political-cost-of-blairs-decision-to-allow-eastern-european-migrants-unfettered-access-to-britain-66077.

Cook, Chris. 2017. "Election 2017: How the Tory Campaign Went So Wrong." *BBC*, June 9, 2017. https://www.bbc.com/news/uk-politics-40222733.

Cottle, Michelle. 2016. "Pelosi Remains as Leader, but the Democrats Are Restless." *The Atlantic*, December 1, 2016. https://www.theatlantic.com/politics/archive/2016/12/pelosi-remains-leader-but-the-democrats-are-restless/509279/.

Cowley, Philip, and Mark Stuart. 2012. "The Cambusters: The Conservative European Union Referendum Rebellion of October 2011." *Political Quarterly* 83, no. 2 (March): 402–6. https://doi.org/10.1111/j.1467-923X.2012.02291.x.

Cowley, Philip, and Mark Stuart. 2013. "Cambo Chained: Coalition's Backbench MP's Set for Rebellion Record." University of Nottingham, May 24, 2013. https://www.nottingham.ac.uk/news/pressreleases/2013/may/cambo-chained-coalitions-backbench-mps-set-for-rebellion-record-.aspx.

Cox, Gary W., and Matthew D. McCubbins. 2005. *Setting the Agenda: Responsible Party Government in the U.S. House of Representatives*. New York. Cambridge University Press.

Cox, Gary, and Matthew D. McCubbins. 2007. *Legislative Leviathan: Party Government in the House*. 2nd ed. New York: Cambridge University Press.

Crace, John. 2018. "Hard Brexiters' New Plan Gets A+ for Idiocy." *The Guardian*, September 24, 2018. https://www.theguardian.com/politics/2018/sep/24/hard-brexiters-new-plan-gets-a-for-idiocy.

Craig, Paul. 2013. "The United Kingdom and the European Union, and Sovereignty." In *Sovereignty and the Law: Domestic, European, and International Perspectives*, edited by Richard Rawlings, Peter Leyland, and Allison Young, chapter 10. Oxford: Oxford University Press.

Craig, Philip P., and Gráinne de Búrca. 2003. *EU Law, Text, Cases and Materials*. 3rd ed. Oxford: Oxford University Press.

Crerar, Pippa. 2018a. "May Sees Off Rebellion on Customs Union as Amendment Is Defeated." *The Guardian*, July 17, 2018. https://www.theguardian.com/politics/2018/jul/17/theresa-may-sees-off-rebellion-customs-union-amendment-defeated.

Crerar, Pippa. 2018b. "Where Do Theresa May's Ministers Stand on Brexit?" *The Guardian*, November 12, 2018. https://www.theguardian.com/politics/2018/nov/12/where-do-theresa-mays-ministers-stand-on-brexit.

Crerar, Pippa, and Matthew Weaver. 2018. "McVey and Raab Quit as May Addresses MP's over Brexit Deal." *The Guardian*, November 15, 2018. https://www.theguardian.com/politics/2018/nov/15/dominic-raab-quits-as-brexit-secretary-over-eu-withdrawal-deal.

Crisp, James, and Daniel Capurro. 2021. "Farewell, Michel Barnier: What Lessons and Legacy Will He Leave Behind?" *The Telegraph*, April 1, 2021.

Cross, William, and André Blais. 2012a. *Politics at the Centre: The Selection and Removal of Party Leaders in the Anglo Parliamentary Democracies*. Oxford: Oxford University Press.

Cross, William, and André Blais. 2012b. "Who Selects the Party Leader?" *Party Politics* 18, no. 2 (March): 127–50. https://doi.org/10.1177/1354068810382935.

Cross, William, and Jean-Benoit Pilet, eds. 2015. *The Selection of Political Party Leaders in Comparative Perspective*. Oxfordshire, UK, and New York: Routledge.

Cruz Lera, Estefania. 2020. "Women from the Establishment Versus the 'Squad': Feminine Political Representation in the US Congress."*Norteamérica*, 15, no. 1 (January-June). https://doi.org/10.22201/cisan.24487228e.2019.2.389.

Culhane, Leah. 2019. *Sexual Harassment in Parliament: Protecting MPs, Peers, Volunteers and Staff*. London: Fawcett Society.

Cunningham, Sheryl L. 2012. "'Taking Care of the Children and the Country': Nancy Pelosi and the Trope of Motherhood in Partisan and Mainstream Media." In *Media Depictions of Brides, Wives and Mothers*, edited by Alena Amato Ruggerio, 155–67. Lanham, MD: Lexington Books.

Currinder, Marian. n.d. "Follow the Leader (and the Money!)." Georgetown University Government Affairs Institute. https://gai.georgetown.edu/follow-the-leader-and-the-money/.

Curry, Chris. 2017. "Everything You Always Wanted to Know about the Triple Lock but Were Afraid to Ask." Pensions Policy Institute, *Policy Briefing Note Number 96*, May 2017. https://www.pensionspolicyinstitute.org.uk/media/1364/201705-bn96-everything-you-always-wanted-to-know-about-the-triple-lock-but-were-afraid-to-ask.pdf.

Curtice, John. 2010. "So What Went Wrong with the Electoral System? The 2010 Election Result and the Debate about Electoral Reform." *Parliamentary Affairs* 63, no. 4 (October): 623–38. https://doi.org/10.1093/pa/gsq018.

Cutts, David, Sarah Childs, and Edward Fieldhouse. 2008. "This Is What Happens When You Don't Listen: All-Women Shortlists at the 2005 General Election." *Party Politics* 14, no. 5 (September): 575–95. https://doi.org/10.1177/1354068808093391.

Dabbous, Yasmine, and Amy Ladley. 2010. "A Spine of Steel and a Heart of Gold: Newspaper Coverage of the First Female Speaker of the House." *Journal of Gender Studies* 19, no. 2 (June): 181–94. https://doi.org/10.1080/09589231003695971.

Dahlerup, Drude. 1988. "From a Small to a Large Minority: Women in Scandinavian Politics." *Scandinavian Political Studies* 11, no. 4 (December): 275–98. https://doi.org/10.1111/j.1467-9477.1988.tb00372.x.

Dahlerup, Drude. 2013. "Introduction." In *Breaking Male Dominance in Old Democracies*, edited by Drude Dahlerup and Monique Leyenaar, 1–22. Oxford: Oxford University Press.

Dahlerup, Drude. 2014. "Representing Women: Defining Substantive Representation of Women." In *Representation: The Case of Women*, edited by Maria Escobar-Lemmon and Michelle Taylor-Robinson, 58–78. Oxford: Oxford University Press.

Dahlerup, Drude, and Monique Leyenaar, eds. 2013. *Breaking Male Dominance in Old Democracies*. Oxford: Oxford University Press.

(The) Daily Beast. 2017. "House Dems Weigh Further Punishment for Conyers if He Refuses to Resign." November 30, 2017, https://www.thedailybeast.com/house-dems-weigh-further-punishment-for-conyers-if-he-refuses-to-resign.

Dalby, Douglas. 2015. "Northern Ireland Faces Crisis as Unionist First Minister Resigns." *New York Times*, September 10, 2015. https://www.nytimes.com/2015/09/11/world/europe/northern-ireland-peter-robinson-resigns-from-parliament.html.

D'Ancona, Matthew. 2014. "Tories on Top: What Now for the Modernisers?" In *The Modernisers' Manifesto*, edited by Ryan Shorthouse, Kate Maltby, and James Brenton, 20–29. London: Bright Blue Campaign. www.brightblue.org.uk.

D'Arcy, Mark. 2016. "How Rebel MP's Outfoxed Cameron to Get an EU Referendum." *BBC*, December 29, 2016. https://www.bbc.com/news/uk-politics-parliaments-38402140.

Davies, Anjuli, Huw Jones, and Andrew MacAskill. 2017. "How Brexit Is Set to Hurt Europe's Financial Systems." *Reuters*, July 12, 2017. https://www.reuters.com/investigates/special-report/britain-europe-cost/.

Davis, David Rt. Hon. 1988. *How to Turn Round a Company*. London: Director Books.

Davis, Julie Hirschfeld. 2018. "Pelosi and Dissident Democrats Reach Deal to Limit Her Speakership to 4 Years." *New York Times*, December 12, 2018, A1. https://www.nytimes.com/2018/12/12/us/politics/nancy-pelosi-democrat-leadership.html.

Davis, Rebecca. 1997. *Women and Power in Parliamentary Democracies: Cabinet Appointments in Western Europe*. Lincoln: University of Nebraska Press.

Davis, Susan. 2010. "Dems Want Extreme Makeover for Pelosi." *National Journal*, November 11, 2010. https://link.gale.com/apps/doc/A403311897/AONE?u=iastu_main&sid=AONE&xid=af346ae8.

Dayen, David. 2021a. "Pelosi Tries to Bulldoze Progressives on the Infrastructure Bill." *American Prospect*, September 28, 2021. https://prospect.org/infrastructure/building-back-america/pelosi-tries-to-bulldoze-progressives-on-infrastructure-bill/

Dayen, David. 2021b. "The Progressive Caucus Wields Power." *American Prospect*, October 1, 2021. https://prospect.org/infrastructure/building-back-america/progressive-caucus-wields-power/.

DeBonis, Mike. 2018a. "Nine Democrats Want Promises From Pelosi in Exchange for Speaker Votes." *Washington Post*, November 13, 2018. https://www.washingtonpost.com/politics/2018/11/14/nine-democrats-want-reforms-pelosi-exchange-speaker-votes/.

DeBonis, Mike. 2018b. "Pelosi Is Star of GOP Attack Ads, Worrying Democrats Upbeat about Midterms." *Washington Post*, August 9, 2018. https://www.washingtonpost.com/powerpost/pelosi-is-the-star-of-gop-attack-ads-worrying-democrats-upbeat-about-midterms/2018/08/09/f85a2474-9b43-11e8-8d5e-c6c594024954_story.html.

Deering, Christopher, and Steven S. Smith. 1997. *Committees in Congress*. New York: Sage.

Deloitte. 2016. "Leaving the EU: What Will It Mean for Banking and the Financial Services Industry?" https://www2.deloitte.com/content/dam/Deloitte/cy/Documents/financial-services/CY_FinancialServices_Brexit_Noexp.pdf.

De Mars, Sylvia, Colin Murray, Aoife O'Donoghue, and Ben Warwick. 2018. *Bordering Two Unions: Northern Ireland and Brexit*. Bristol: Bristol University Press.

Demirjian, Karoun. 2021. "House Votes to Create a Select Committee for Investigating Jan. 6 Attack on the Capitol." *Washington Post*, June 30, 2021. https://www.washingtonpost.com/national-security/house-select-committee-january-6/2021/06/30/a52179ba-d998-11eb-bb9e-70fda8c37057_story.html.

Democratic Congressional Campaign Committee (DCCC). nd. Fundraising Letter.

Dempsey, Noel, Pat Strickland, and Anna Moses. 2016. *Police and Crime Commissioner Elections: 2016*. House of Commons Briefing Paper, CBP 07595. May 19, 2016. London: House of Commons.

Denham, Andrew, and Kieron O'Hara. 2008. *Democratising Conservative Leadership Selection: From Grey Suits to Grassroots*. Manchester: Manchester University Press.

Denver, David. 2018. "The Results: How Britain Voted." In *Britain Votes 2017*, edited by Jonathan Tonge, Christina Leston-Bandeira, and Stuart Wilks-Heeg, 8–28. Oxford: Oxford University Press.

Detroit News. 2007. "Dingell, Pelosi Reach Climate Panel Détente." February 7, 2007, 2C.

Deutsch, Francine, Carla M. Zalenski, and Mary E. Clark. 1986. "Is There a Double Standard in Aging?" *Journal of Applied Social Psychology* 16, no. 9 (December): 771–85. https://doi.org/10.1111/j.1559-1816.1986.tb01167.x.

Dickson, Annabelle. 2018. "What the 8 Tory Brexit Tribes Want." *Politico EU*, August 28, 2018. https://www.politico.eu/article/brexit-8-tory-tribes-conservative-party/.

Dittmar, Kelly, Kira Sanbonmatsu, and Susan Carroll. 2018. *A Seat at the Table: Congresswomen's Perspectives on Why Their Presence Matters*. New York: Oxford University Press.

Diver, Tony. 2021. "The Brexit Deal Gutted: What Are the Good and Bad Bits for Britain?" *The Telegraph*, January 2, 2021. https://www.telegraph.co.uk/politics/0/brexit-deal-positives-negatives-uk/.

Doherty, Denis. 2018. "Brexit: The History of the Tories' Influential European Research Group." *BBC*, January 19, 2018. https://www.bbc.com/news/uk-politics-42719026.

Dolan, Kathleen. 2014. *When Does Gender Matter? Women Candidates and Gender Stereotypes in American Elections*. New York: Oxford University Press.

Draper, Robert. 2018. "Nancy Pelosi's Last Battle." *New York Times Magazine*, November 25, 2018. https://www.nytimes.com/2018/11/19/magazine/nancy-pelosi-house-democrats.html?searchResultPosition=1.

Dsouza, Deborah. 2019. "How London Became the World's Financial Hub." *Investopedia*, June 25, 2019. https://www.investopedia.com/how-london-became-the-world-s-financial-hub-4589324.

Duerst-Lahti, Georgia. 2002. "Knowing Congress as a Gendered Institution: Manliness and the Implications of Women in Congress." In *Women Transforming Congress*, edited by Cindy Simon Rosenthal, 20–49. Norman: University of Oklahoma Press.

Duerst-Lahti, Georgia, and Rita Mae Kelly, eds. 1995. *Gender Power, Leadership, and Governance*. Ann Arbor: University of Michigan Press. https://doi.org/10.3998/mpub.10371.

Duffy, Patrick. 2018. "Northern Ireland Equal Marriage Measure Passed by MPs in Symbolic Vote." *Pink News*, October 24, 2018. https://www.pinknews.co.uk/2018/10/24/parliament-northern-ireland-equal-marriage/.

Dumain, Emma. 2014a. "Eshoo, Pallone Collect Endorsements in Race for Ranking Member." *Roll Call*, March 6, 2014. https://eshoo.house.gov/media/in-the-news/roll-call-eshoo-pallone-collect-endorsements-race-ranking-member.

Dumain, Emma. 2014b. "Eshoo Wins Backing of Steering and Policy Committee over Pallone." *Roll Call*, November 18, 2014. https://www.rollcall.com/2014/11/18/eshoo-wins-backing-of-steering-and-policy-committee-over-pallone/.

Dumain, Emma. 2014c. "Pallone Defeats Eshoo for Energy and Commerce Slot (Updated)." *Roll Call*, November 19, 2014. https://www.rollcall.com/2014/11/19/pallone-defeats-eshoo-for-energy-and-commerce-slot-updated-2/.

Dumain, Emma. 2014d. "Pelosi Downplays Seniority System in Endorsing Anna Eshoo for Committee Assignment." *Roll Call*, November 10, 2014.

Duncan, Alan. 2021. *In the Thick of It: The Private Diaries of a Minister*. Glasgow, Scotland: William Collins.

Dunin-Wasowicz, Roch. 2017. "The Brexit Referendum Question Was Flawed in Its Design." *LSE Brexit*, May 17, 2017. https://blogs.lse.ac.uk/brexit/2017/05/17/the-brexit-referendum-question-was-flawed-in-its-design/.

Dunn, Tom Newton. 2017. "May's Tax Lock Axe: Theresa May Vows to End the Triple Lock on Pensions and Scrap Tories' Tax Lock in Conservative Election Manifesto." *The Sun*, May 17, 2017. https://www.thesun.co.uk/news/3588313/theresa-may-pension-triple-lock-taxes-conservative-manifesto/.

Durrant, Tim, Lewis Lloyd, and Maddy Thimont Jack. 2018. "Negotiating Brexit: Policing and Criminal Justice." Institute for Government, September 2018. www.instituteforgovernment.org.uk/brexit.

Eagly, Alice H., and Linda Carli. 2007. "Women and the Labyrinth of Leadership." *Harvard Business Review*, September 2007. https://hbr.org/2007/09/women-and-the-labyrinth-of-leadership.

Eagly, Alice H., and Steven J. Karau. 2002. "Role Congruity Theory of Prejudice Toward Female Leaders." *Psychological Review* 109, no. 3: 573–98.

Eaton, George. 2017. "How to Remove a Conservative Leader." *New Statesman*, October 6, 2017. https://www.newstatesman.com/politics/uk-politics/2017/10/how-remove-conservative-leader.

The Economist. 2010. "Open Europe: The Euroskeptic Group That Controls British Coverage of the EU." March 31, 2010. https://www.economist.com/charlemagne/2010/03/31/open-europe-the-eurosceptic-group-that-controls-british-coverage-of-the-eu.

The Economist. 2018a. "Boris Johnson's Bid for the Tory leadership." September 13, 2018. https://www.economist.com/britain/2018/09/13/boris-johnsons-bid-for-the-tory-leadership.

The Economist. 2018b. "Facing Heavy Defeat on Her Brexit Deal, May Delays the Vote." December 10, 2018. https://www.economist.com/britain/2018/12/10/facing-heavy-defeat-on-her-brexit-deal-theresa-may-delays-the-vote.

The Economist. 2018c. "How Brexit Weakens and Strengthens Britain's Conservatives." September 27, 2018. https://www.economist.com/briefing/2018/09/27/how-brexit-weakens-and-strengthens-britains-conservatives.

Elfink, Tim. 2021. "Pelosi Keeps Mask Mandate on House Floor Despite CDC Change, Sparking GOP Backlash: It's All about Control." *Washington Post*, May 14, 2021. https://www.washingtonpost.com/nation/2021/05/14/pelosi-mask-mandate-house-scalise/.

Elgot, Jessica. 2017. "Osborne Says Theresa May Is a 'Dead Woman Walking.'" *The Guardian*, June 11, 2017. https://www.theguardian.com/politics/2017/jun/11/george-osborne-says-theresa-may-is-a-dead-woman-walking.

Elgot, Jessica. 2018a. "Commons Bullying Inquiry Suggests John Bercow Should Consider His Position." *The Guardian*, October 15, 2018. https://www.theguardian.com/politics/2018/oct/15/house-of-commons-culture-enabled-bullying-and-sexual-harassment-inquiry.

Elgot, Jessica. 2018b. "Pro-Remain Tory MPs Will Form Group to Vote Down May's Brexit Deal." *The Guardian*, October 10, 2018. https://www.theguardian.com/politics/2018/oct/10/pro-remain-tory-mps-will-form-group-vote-down-may-brexit-deal.

Elgot, Jessica. 2020. "Harassment Claims: Did Westminster's Culture of Impunity Ever Go Away?" *The Guardian*, August 3, 2020. https://www.theguardian.com/politics/2020/aug/03/did-westminsters-culture-of-impunity-ever-go-away.

Elgot, Jessica, and Rowena Mason. 2017. "Conservatives Fined Record 70,000 Pounds for Campaign Spending Failures." *The Guardian*, March 16, 2017. https://www.theguardian.com/politics/2017/mar/16/conservatives-fined-70000-for-campaign-spending-failures.

Emerson, Newton. 2018. "DUP Faces Heavy Responsibility for Brexit Position Taken Lightly." *Irish Times*, May 10, 2018. https://www.irishtimes.com/opinion/dup-faces-heavy-responsibility-for-brexit-position-taken-lightly-1.3489256.

Emmanuel, Ezekiel. 2014. *Reinventing American Health Care: How the Affordable Care Act Will Improve Our Terribly Complex, Blatantly Unjust, Outrageously Expensive, Grossly Inefficient, Error Prone System*. New York: Public Affairs Books.

Emmerson, Carl. 2017. "Would You Rather? Further Increases in the State Pension Age Are Abandoning the Triple Lock." Institute for Fiscal Studies, February 27, 2017. www.ifs.org.uk.

Escobar-Lemmon, Maria, and Michelle Taylor-Robinson, eds. 2014. *Representation: The Case of Women*. Oxford: Oxford University Press.

Escobar-Lemmon, Maria, and Michelle Taylor-Robinson. 2015. "Sex, Survival, and Scandal: A Comparison of How Men and Women Exit Presidential Candidates." *Politics & Gender* 11, no. 4 (December): 665–88. https://doi.org/10.1017/S1743923X15000422.

Escobar-Lemmon, Maria, and Michelle Taylor-Robinson. 2016. *Women in Presidential Cabinets: Power Players or Abundant Tokens?* Oxford: Oxford University Press.

European Central Bank. 2020. "Five Things You Need to Know about the Maastricht Treaty." February 5, 2020. https://www.ecb.europa.eu/ecb/educational/explainers/tell-me-more/html/25_years_maastricht.en.html.

European Parliament. 2020. "Fact Sheets on the European Union." https://www.europarl.europa.eu/factsheets/en/home.

Evans, Geoffrey, and Anand Menon. 2017. *Brexit and British Politics*. Cambridge: Polity Press.

Evans, Martin. 2019. "Theresa May Was the 'Most Disastrous' Home Secretary and Prime Minister for Policing, Says Former Met Chief." *The Telegraph*, July 5, 2019. https://www.telegraph.co.uk/news/2019/07/05/theresa-may-disastrous-home-secretary-prime-minister-policing/.

Evans, Rob, and David Pegg. 2019. "Peers and MPs Receiving Millions in EU Farm Subsidies." *The Guardian*, January 27, 2019. https://www.theguardian.com/environment/2019/jan/27/revealed-the-mps-and-peers-receiving-millions-in-eu-farm-subsidies-cap.

Evening Standard. 2012. "David Cameron Warns 'Turnip Taliban' They Could Damage Whole Party." April 13, 2012. https://www.standard.co.uk/hp/front/david-cameron-warns-turnip-taliban-they-could-damage-whole-party-6747513.html.

Faiola, Anthony. 2011. "Talks on E.U.-Wide Debt Deal Collapse." *Washington Post*, December 9, 2011. www.washingtonpost.com.

Fairbanks, Eve. 2007. "Nancy Pelosi: The Extreme Moderate." *Los Angeles Times*, April 15, 2007. https://www.latimes.com/la-op-fairbanks15apr15-story.html.

Fandos, Nicholas. 2021a. "Trump, After Inciting Rampage in Capitol, Is First President to Face 2nd Senate Trial." *New York Times*, January 14, 2021. https://www.nytimes.com/2021/01/13/us/politics/trump-impeached.html?searchResultPosition=1.

Fandos, Nicholas. 2021b. "Why Jim Banks and Jim Jordan Were Blocked from the Capitol Riot Panel." *New York Times*, July 21, 2021. https://www.nytimes.com/2021/07/21/us/politics/jim-banks-jim-jordan.html.

Featherstone, Lynne. 2016. *Equal Ever After: The Fight for Same-Sex Marriage—and How I Made It Happen*. London: Biteback.

Financial Post. 2020. "British PM Sold Out Fish in Brexit Trade Deal, Fishermen Say." December 6, 2020. https://financialpost.com/pmn/business-pmn/british-pm-sold-out-fish-in-brexit-trade-deal-fishermen-say.

Financial Times. 2018. "Theresa May's Brexit Speech at Mansion House-Annotated." March 2, 2018. https://ig.ft.com/may-brexit-speech-annotated/.

Finegold, Kenneth, Ann Conmy, Rose C. Chu, Arielle Bosworth, and Benjamin D. Sommers. 2021. "Trends in the U.S. Uninsured Population, 2010–2020." Department of Health and Human Services Office of Health Policy Issue Brief, February 2021.

Finn, Teaganne. 2021. "House Republicans Spar with Pelosi Over Return of Mask Requirements." *NBC News*, July 29, 2021. https://www.nbcnews.com/politics/congress/house-republicans-spar-pelosi-over-return-mask-requirements-n1275440.

Fish, Steven, and Matthew Kroenig. 2009. *The Handbook of National Legislatures*. Cambridge: Cambridge University Press. https://doi.org/10.1017/CBO9780511575655.

Fisher, Justin. 2018. "Party Finance." *Parliamentary Affairs* 71, no. suppl. 1 (March): 171–88. https://doi.org/10.1093/pa/gsx055.

Flinders, Matthew. 2018. "The (Anti-) Politics of the General Election: Funnelling Frustration in a Divided Democracy." In *Britain Votes 2017*, edited by Jonathan Tonge, Cristina Leston-Bandeira, and Stuart Wilkes-Heeg, 46–58. Oxford: Oxford University Press.

Fontana, Cary, and Craig Parsons. 2015. "'One Woman's Prejudice': Did Margaret Thatcher Cause Britain's Anti-Europeanism?" *Journal of Common Market Studies* 53, no. 1 (January): 89–105. https://doi.org/10.1111/jcms.12205.

Freeman, Jo. 1986. "The Political Culture of the Democratic and Republican Parties." *Political Science Quarterly* 10, no. 3: 327–60. https://doi.org/10.2307/2151619.

French, Lauren. 2014. "Energy Fight Turns into Money War." *Politico*, August 4, 2014. https://www.politico.com/story/2014/08/frank-pallone-anna-eshoo-energy-panel-109690.

French, Lauren, and John Bresnahan. 2014. "N.J.'s Pallone Fighting for Top Dem Spot on Committee." *Politico*, November 18, 2014. https://www.politico.com/story/2014/11/frank-pallone-anna-eshoo-energy-commerce-committee-112994.

Fresh Start Project. 2012. "Options for Change Green Paper: Renegotiating the UK's Relationship with the EU." European Parliament, July 2012. www.europarl.europa.eu; www.eufreshstart.org.

Full Fact. 2019. "Did Crime Fall While Boris Johnson Was Mayor of London?" June 18, 2019. https://fullfact.org/crime/boris-johnson-mayor-crime/.

Galligan, Yvonne. 2020. "Women MPs from Northern Ireland: Challenges and Contributions, 1953–2020." *Open Library of Humanities* 6, no. 2: 1–45. https://doi.org/10.16995/olh.591.

Gallup Poll. n.d. "Favorability: People in the News." https://news.gallup.com/poll/1618/favorability-people-news.aspx.

Garber, Megan. 2017. "It Took Pelosi Three Tries to Get Her Harassment Statement Right." *The Atlantic*, November 28, 2017. https://www.theatlantic.com

/entertainment/archive/2017/11/it-took-nancy-pelosi-three-tries-to-get-her-harassment-statement-right/546824/.

Garside, Juliette, Hilary Osborne, and Ewen MacAskill. 2017. "The Brexiters Who Put Their Money Offshore." *The Guardian*, November 9, 2017. https://www.theguardian.com/news/2017/nov/09/brexiters-put-money-offshore-tax-haven.

Gartside, Ben, and Thomas Colson. 2018. "Here Is the Hard Brexiteers' Plan to Scrap Theresa May's Chequers Deal." *Business Insider*, September 24, 2018. https://www.businessinsider.com/here-is-the-hard-brexiteers-plan-to-scrap-theresa-mays-chequers-deal-2018-9.

Geoghegan, Peter. 2020. *Democracy for Sale: Dark Money and Dirty Politics*. London: Apollo.

Gertzog, Irwin N. 2002. "Women's Changing Pathways to the U.S. House of Representatives: Widows, Elites, and Strategic Politicians." In *Women Transforming Congress*, edited by Cindy Simon Rosenthal, 95–118. Norman: University of Oklahoma Press.

Gimson, Andrew. 2013. "Lord Ashcroft: 'The Prime Minister's Most Damaging Critic.'" *New Statesman*, February 14, 2014. https://www.newstatesman.com/politics/2013/02/lord-ashcroft-full-interview.

Gimson, Andrew. 2019. "Philip May: The Prime Minister's Closest Political Adviser." *New Statesman*, January 23, 2019. https://www.newstatesman.com/politics/uk-politics/2019/01/philip-may-prime-minister-s-closest-political-adviser.

Glass Ceiling Commission. 1995. *Glass Ceiling Commission—Good for Business: Making Full Use of the Nation's Human Capital*. Washington, DC: US Department of Labor. https: hdl.handle.net/1813/79348.

Goes, Eunice. 2018. "'Jez, We Can!' Labour's Campaign: Defeat with a Taste of Victory." In *Britain Votes 2017*, edited by Jonathan Tonge, Christina Leston-Bandeira, and Stuart Wilks-Heeg, 59–71. London: Oxford University Press.

Goodhart, Philip. 1973. *The 1922*. London: Macmillan London.

Goodman, Paul. 2018. "May's Policy Leads Inexorably to No Brexit or No Deal. If Tory MP's Fear Either, They Should Take a Chance on Change Today." *ConservativeHome*, December 12, 2018. https://conservativehome.com/2018/12/12/mays-policy-leads-inexorably-to-no-brexit-or-no-deal-if-tory-mps-reject-either-they-should-take-a-chance-on-change/.

Goodman, Paul. 2019. "If May Isn't on Her Way Out by the End of Today, Don't Back Her in Tomorrow's European Elections." *ConservativeHome*, May 22, 2019. https://conservativehome.com/2019/05/22/if-may-isnt-on-her-way-out-by-the-end-of-today-dont-back-her-in-tomorrows-european-elections/.

Gotev, Georgi. 2016. "UK Reimbursed in Excess of 111 Billion Euros since 1985." *Euractiv*, May 23, 2016. https://www.euractiv.com/section/uk-europe/news/the-thatcher-rebate-uk-reimbursed-in-excess-of-e111-billion-by-eu-since-1985/.

Graham, Garry. 2019. "MP's Staff Are Still Being Failed a Year after the Cox

Report." *The Times*, October 15, 2019. https://www.thetimes.co.uk/article/mps-staff-are-still-being-failed-a-year-after-the-cox-report-f393l97d8.

Green, Matthew N. 2008. "The Race for Democratic Majority Leader: Money, Policy, and Personal Loyalty," *PS: Political Science and Politics* 41, no. 1 (January): 63–67. https://doi.org/10.1017/S1049096508080098.

Green, Matthew N. 2010. *Speaker of the House: A Study of Leadership*. New Haven: Yale University Press.

Green, Matthew N. 2015. *Underdog Politics: The Minority Party in the U.S. House of Representatives*. New Haven: Yale University Press.

Green, Matthew N. 2019. *Legislative Hardball: The House Freedom Caucus and the Power of Threat-Making in Congress*. New York: Cambridge University Press.

Green, Mathhew N., and Briana Bee. 2016. "Keeping the Team Together: Explaining Party Discipline and Dissent in the US Congress." In *Party and Procedure in the United States Congress*, 2nd edition, edited by Jacob R. Strauss and Mathhew Glassman, 41–62. Lanham, MD: Rowman & Littlefield.

Green, Matthew N., and Douglas B. Harris. 2019. *Choosing the Leader: Leadership Elections in the U.S. House of Representatives*. New Haven: Yale University Press.

Green, Matthew N., and Douglas B. Harris. 2020. "Maintaining the Organizational Cartel: How Nancy Pelosi Won Election as Speaker of the House." *SSRN*, February 24, 2020. https://ssrn.com/abstract=3638134.

Grey, Sandra. 2006. "Numbers and Beyond: The Relevance of Critical Mass in Gender Research." *Politics & Gender* 2, no. 4 (November): 492–502. https://doi.org/10.1017/S1743923X06221147.

Grierson, Jamie. 2017. "Grant Shapps: From Rising Tory Star to Plotter against the PM." *The Guardian*, October 6, 2017. https://www.theguardian.com/politics/2017/oct/06/grant-shapps-from-rising-tory-star-to-plotter-of-may-ouster.

The Guardian. 2018. "John Bercow Bullying Inquiry Blocked by MPs' Committee." May 16, 2018. https://www.theguardian.com/politics/2018/may/16/john-bercow-no-investigation-bullying-claims.

The Guardian. 2019. "Response to Westminster Bullying Report a Disgrace, Says Ex-Minister." January 1, 2019. https://www.theguardian.com/world/2019/jan/01/ex-minister-condemns-disgraceful-handling-of-westminster-harassment-report-maria-miller.

Guiney, Thomas. 2019. "Boris Johnson's 'Crime Week' and the Conservative Politics of Law and Order." *LSE*, August 27, 2019. https://blogs.lse.ac.uk/politicsandpolicy/boris-johnsons-crime-week/.

Haberkorn, Jennifer, and Darren Goode. 2014. "Democrats Anna Eshoo and Frank Pallone Vie for Top Slot on Energy and Commerce Committee." *Politico*, February 6, 2014. https://eshoo.house.gov/media/in-the-news/politico-democrats-anna-eshoo-and-frank-pallone-vie-top-slot-energy-and-commerce.

Haddon, Catherine. 2015. "The (Not So) Fixed-Term Parliaments Act." Institute for Government, April 14, 2015. https://www.instituteforgovernment.org.uk/blog/not-so-fixed-term-parliaments-act.

Halloran, Liz. 2010. "Obama Humbled by Election 'Shellacking.'" *NPR*, November 3, 2010. https://www.npr.org/templates/story/story.php?storyId=131046118.

Harris, Douglas B., and Matthew Green. 2018. "Why So Little Dissent? Explaining the Stability in This Week's House GOP Leadership Contests." *Legbranch.org*, November 16, 2018. https://www.legbranch.org/why-so-little-dissent-explaining-the-stability-in-this-weeks-house-gop-leadership-contests/.

Harris, Douglas B., and Garrison Nelson. 2008. "Middlemen No More? Emergent Patterns in Congressional Leadership Selection." *PS: Political Science and Politics* 41, no. 1 (January): 49–55. https://doi.org/10.1017/S1049096508080074.

Harrison, Sarah. 2018. "Young Voters." In *Britain Votes 2017*, edited by Jonathan Tonge, Christina Leston-Bandeira, and Stuart Wilks-Heeg, 255–66. London: Oxford University Press.

Hattersley, Roy. 2009. "The Party's Over." *The Guardian*, March 22, 2009. https://www.theguardian.com/politics/2009/mar/22/james-callaghan-labour-1979-thatcher.

Hayes, Bernadette C., and John Nagel. 2019. "Ethnonationalism and Attitudes towards Same-Sex Marriage and Abortion in Northern Ireland." *International Political Science Review* 40, no. 4 (September): 455–69.

Hayes, Christal. 2019. "'It Wasn't Sarcastic:' Pelosi Takes on Viral Clapping During Trump's State of the Union." *USA Today*, February 7, 2019. https://www.usatoday.com/story/news/politics/2019/02/07/nancy-pelosi-says-clapping-trump-state-union-wasnt-sarcastic/2806817002/.

Heer, Jeet. 2019. "Pelosi Proves Triangulation Is Really Self-Strangulation." *The Nation*, July 19, 2019. https://www.thenation.com/article/archive/pelosi-trump-squad-moderate/.

Helm, Toby, Jamie Doward, and Rajeev Syal. 2010. "Lord Ashcroft Goes from Tory Saviour to Liability in Marginal Seats." *The Guardian*, March 7, 2010. https://www.theguardian.com/politics/2010/mar/07/lord-ashcroft-donations-marginal-seats.

Helmke, Gretchen, and Steven Levitsky. 2004. "Informal Institutions and Comparative Politics: A Research Agenda." *Perspectives on Politics* 2, no. 4 (December): 725–40. https://doi.org/10.1017/S1537592704040472.

Helsel, Phil. 2020. "Rep.-Elect Luke Letlow Dies from COVID Complications Days before Being Sworn In." *NBC News*, December 29, 2020. https://www.nbcnews.com/politics/congress/congressman-elect-luke-letlow-dies-after-covid-diagnosis-n1252520.

Henley, Jon. 2018. "Theresa May's Brexit Deal: Everything You Need to Know." *The Guardian*, November 15, 2018. https://www.theguardian.com/politics/2018/nov/14/theresa-mays-brexit-deal-everything-you-need-to-know.

Heppell, Timothy. 2015. "The Cameron-Clegg Coalition: Lessons Learned?" *Political Insight* 6, no. 1 (March): 4–7. https://doi.org/10.1111/2041-9066.12079.

Heppell, Timothy, Andrew Crines, and David Jeffery. 2017. "The United Kingdom Referendum on European Union Membership: The Voting of Conservative Parliamentarians." *Journal of Common Market Studies* 55, no. 4 (January): 762–78. https://doi.org/10.1111/jcms.12529.

Herszenhorn, David M., and Jacopo Barigazzi. 2018. "Michel Barnier: EU Ready to 'Improve' Irish Border Proposal." *Politico EU*, September 18, 2018. https://www.politico.eu/article/michel-barnier-eu-irish-border-proposal-improved-brexit-red-lines/.

Hertel-Fernandez, Alexander, and Theda Skocpol. 2016. "Democrats Are Losing to Republicans at the State Level, and Badly. Here's Why." *Vox*, July 3, 2016. https://www.vox.com/2016/8/3/12368070/democrats-losing-state-level.

Hickey, Walt, Mariana Alfarao, Grace Panetta, and Taylor Ardrey. 2021. "How Nancy Pelosi Went from San Francisco Housewife to the Most Powerful Woman in US Politics." *Business Insider*, January 3, 2021. https://www.businessinsider.com/nancy-pelosi-2013-3.

Hogarth, Raphael, and Lewis Lloyd. 2017. "Who's Afraid of the ECJ? Charting the UK's Relationship with the European Court." Institute for Government, December 2017. www.instituteforgovernment.org.uk.

Hohmann, James, with Breanne Deppish. 2016. "The Daily 202: How Tim Ryan Decided to Challenge His Mentor, Nancy Pelosi, for Democratic Leader." *Washington Post*, November 21, 2016. https://www.washingtonpost.com/news/powerpost/paloma/daily-202/2016/11/21/daily-202-how-tim-ryan-decided-to-challenge-his-mentor-nancy-pelosi-for-democratic-leader/58324a8be9b69b7e58e45f18/.

Holder, Daniel. 2017. "Brexit and the Risks of a 'Racist' Land Border in Ireland." *UK in a Changing Europe*, September 20, 2017. https://ukandeu.ac.uk/brexit-and-the-risks-of-a-racist-land-border-in-ireland/.

Holder, Josh, Caelainn Barr, and Niko Kommenda. 2017. "Datablog: Young Voters, Class and Turnout: How Britain Voted in 2017." *The Guardian*, June 20, 2017. https://www.theguardian.com/politics/datablog/ng-interactive/2017/jun/20/young-voters-class-and-turnout-how-britain-voted-in-2017.

Home Office, Government of the UK. 2011. "Police Reform: Home Secretary's Speech of 16 August 2011." https://www.gov.uk/government/speeches/police-reform-home-secretarys-speech-of-16-august-2011.

Home Office, Government of the UK. 2014a. "Clare's Law Rolled Out Nationally on International Women's Day." March 8, 2014. https://www.gov.uk/government/news/clares-law-rolled-out-nationally-on-international-womens-day.

Home Office, Government of the UK. 2014b. "Home Secretary Speech at Girl Summit." July 22, 2014. https://www.gov.uk/government/speeches/home-secretary-speech-at-girl-summit-2014.

Hope, Christopher. 2012. "Repatriate Powers on Crime and Policing, Say Conservative MP's." *The Telegraph*, February 6, 2012. https://www.telegraph.co.uk/co

mment/letters/9062615/Repatriate-powers-on-crime-and-policing-say-Conservative-MPs.html.

House, Billy. 2011. "Pelosi: The Golden Handcuffs." *National Journal*, June 2, 2011.

House, Billy. 2014. "Pelosi's Power on the Line in Committee Leadership Race." *National Journal*, September 18, 2014.

House of Commons Library. 2018. "Leadership Elections: Conservative Party." UK Parliament, December 13, 2018. https://researchbriefings.parliament.uk.

House of Commons Library. 2022. "Economic Indicators." UK Parliament, March 24, 2022. Research Briefing 9040. https://commonslibrary.parliament.uk/research-briefings/cbp-9040/.

Howker, Ed, and Guy Basnett. 2017. "The Inside Story of the Tory Election Scandal." *The Guardian*, March 23, 2017. https://www.theguardian.com/news/2017/mar/23/conservative-election-scandal-victory-2015-expenses.

Hudiburg, Jane A. 2019. *House Rules Changes Affecting Committee Procedure in the 116th Congress (2019–2020)*. CRS Report to Congress, May 21, 2019. https://crsreports.congress.gov/product/pdf/R/R45731.

Hughes, Laura. 2018a. "Abuse of Power: The Truth about Sexual Harassment in Westminster." *Financial Times*, June 13, 2018. https://www.ft.com/content/5e6a296c-6e9e-11e8-92d3-6c13e5c92914.

Hughes, Laura. 2018b. "John Bercow Faces Mounting Calls to Resign over Inquiry." *Financial Times*, October 16, 2018. https://www.ft.com/content/c276c8a2-d159-11e8-a9f2-7574db66bcd5.

Hughes, Laura, and Barney Henderson. 2016. "Theresa May Wields the Axe on Cameron's Notting Hill Set in 'Most Ruthless Cull in Modern British History' with Michael Gove among Nine Ministerial Sackings or Resignations." *The Telegraph*, July 14, 2016. https://www.telegraph.co.uk/news/2016/07/14/theresa-mays-cabinet-reshuffle-who-will-join-boris-johnson-and/.

Hughes, Melanie M., and Pamela Paxton. 2008. "Continuous Change, Episodes, and Critical Periods: A Framework for Understanding Women's Political Representation over Time." *Politics & Gender* 4, no. 2 (May): 233–64. https://doi.org/10.1017/S1743923X08000329.

Hulse, Carl. 2002. "Pelosi Likely to Lead House Democrats." *New York Times*, November 8, 2002.

Hulse, Carl. 2022. "Pelsoi Steps Aside, Signaling End to Historic Run as Top House Democrat." *New York Times*, November 17, 2022. https://www.nytimes.com/2022/11/17/us/elections/nancy-pelosi-congress-house-leadership.html.

Hymas, Charles, and Steven Swinford. 2019. "Sajiv Javid Clashes with Theresa May on Demand for Extra Millions to Combat Knife Crime Crisis." *The Telegraph*, March 5, 2019. https://www.telegraph.co.uk/politics/2019/03/05/sajid-javid-clashes-theresa-may-demand-extra-millions-combat/.

Ibarra, Herminia, Robin J. Ely, and Deborah M. Kolb. 2013. "Women Rising: The Unseen Barriers." *Harvard Business Review*, September 2013. https://hbr.org/2013/09/women-rising-the-unseen-barriers.

Ikenson, Daniel, Simon Lester, and Daniel Hannan. 2018. "The Ideal US-UK Free Trade Agreement." Initiative for Free Trade, September 2018. https://papers.ssrn.com/sol3/papers.cfm?abstract_id=3853574.

The Independent. 2019. "Theresa May's Brexit Defeat Makes History as Biggest-Ever Government Loss in the Commons." January 16, 2019. https://www.independent.co.uk/news/uk/politics/brexit-vote-theresa-may-defeat-mps-history-biggest-ever-loss-commons-a8729791.html.

Inman, Phillip. 2017. "'Dementia Tax' and Social Care Funding: The Conservative Plans Explained." *The Guardian*, May 18, 2017. https://www.theguardian.com/society/2017/may/18/social-care-funding-what-are-the-conservatives-proposing.

Institute for Government. 2018. "Theresa May's Brexit Speech: Mansion House." March 2, 2018. https://www.instituteforgovernment.org.uk/explainers/theresa-may-brexit-speech-mansion-house.

Institute for Government. 2020a. "EU Withdrawal Bill: Amendments and Debates." February 25, 2020. https://www.instituteforgovernment.org.uk/explainers/eu-withdrawal-bill-amendments-and-debates.

Institute for Government. 2020b. "Irish Backstop." February 24, 2020. https://www.instituteforgovernment.org.uk/explainers/irish-backstop.

Institute for Government. 2021. "Ministerial Code." https://www.instituteforgovernment.org.uk/explainers/ministerial-code.

Institute of Economic Affairs (IEA). 2012. "Free Enterprise Group & Institute of Economic Affairs Growth Forum Proposals Launched." *Institute of Economic Affairs*, February 27, 2012. https://iea.org.uk/in-the-media/press-release/free-enterprise-group-institute-of-economic-affairs-growth-forum-proposal.

Irish Times. 2018. "EU Rejects Proposed Plan for Banks Put Forth by UK financial Industry." *Irish Times*, January 31, 2018. https://www.irishtimes.com/business/financial-services/eu-rejects-brexit-plan-for-banks-proposed-by-uk-financial-industry-1.3375183.

Isenstadt, Alex. 2011. "GOP Has a New Favorite Villain." *Politico*, November 17, 2011. https://www.politico.com/story/2011/11/gop-has-a-new-favorite-villain-068633.

Itkowitz, Colby. 2018. "Who Are the 'Problem Solvers' Trying to Hold Nancy Pelosi's Speakership Hostage?" *Washington Post*, November 27, 2018. https://www.washingtonpost.com/politics/2018/11/27/who-are-problem-solvers-trying-hold-nancy-pelosis-speakership-hostage/.

Itkowitz, Colby. 2021. "'Normal Tourist Visit:' Republicans Recast Deadly Jan. 6 Attack by Pro-Trump Mob." *Washington Post*, May 21, 2021. https://www.washingtonpost.com/politics/trump-riot-capitol-republicans/2021/05/12/dcc03342-b351-11eb-a980-a60af976ed44_story.html.

Jackman, Tom. 2021. "Police Union Says 140 Officers Injured in Capitol Riot." *Washington Post*, January 27, 2021. https://www.washingtonpost.com/local/public-safety/police-union-says-140-officers-injured-in-capitol-riot/2021/01/27/60743642-60e2-11eb-9430-e7c77b5b0297_story.html.

Jackson, Ben. 2012. "The Think-Tank Archipelago: Thatcherism and Neo-Liberalism." In *Making Thatcher's Britain*, edited by Ben Jackson and Robert Saunders, 43–62. Cambridge: Cambridge University Press.

Jackson, Ben, and Robert Saunders. 2012a. "Introduction." In *Making Thatcher's Britain*, edited by Ben Jackson and Robert Saunders, 1–21. Cambridge: Cambridge University Press.

Jackson, Ben, and Robert Saunders, eds. 2012b. *Making Thatcher's Britain*. Cambridge: Cambridge University Press.

Jacobs, Emily. 2020. "'Forget Him': Pelosi Defends Not Speaking to Trump for Almost a Year." *New York Post*, September 15, 2020. https://nypost.com/2020/09/15/forget-him-pelosi-defends-not-speaking-to-trump-for-a-year/.

Jalalzai, Farida. 2008. "Women Rule: Shattering the Executive Glass Ceiling." *Politics & Gender* 4, no. 2 (May): 205–31. https://doi.org/10.1017/S1743923X0800 0317.

Jalalzai, Farida. 2016. *Shattered, Cracked, or Firmly Intact?* Oxford: Oxford University Press. https://doi.org/10.1093/acprof:oso/9780199943531.001.0001.

Jarrett, Tim. 2015. "Social Care: How the Postponed Changes to Paying for Care, Including the Cap, Would Have Worked (England)." July 24, 2015. House of Commons Briefing Paper 07106. https://researchbriefings.files.parliament.uk/documents/SN07106/SN07106.pdf.

Jenkins, Jeffery A., and Charles Stewart III. 2013. *Fighting for the Speakership: The House and the Rise of Party Government*. Princeton: Princeton University Press.

Jenkins, Simon. 2017. "Why Are 40 Hardline MP's Setting the Tone of the Brexit Debate?" *The Guardian*, September 8, 2017. https://www.theguardian.com/commentisfree/2017/sep/08/brexit-40-mps-hardline-soft-hard-legislation.

Johnson, Boris. 2016. "I Cannot Stress too Much That Britain Is Part of Europe—and Always Will Be." *The Telegraph*, June 16, 2016. https://www.telegraph.co.uk/politics/2016/06/26/i-cannot-stress-too-much-that-britain-is-part-of-europe and-alw/.

Johnson, Steve. 2011. "Tobin Tax Costs 'Would Fall on Investors." *Financial Times*, December 17, 2011. https://www.ft.com/content/54e1aab8-25a9-11e1-856e-00144feabdc0.

Jones, David R., and Monika L. McDermott. 2011. "The Salience of the Democratic Congress and the 2010 Elections." *PS: Political Science and Politics* 44, no. 2 (April): 297–301. https://doi.org/10.1017/S1049096511000126.

Jones, Jeffrey M. 2021. "U.S. Political Party Preferences Shifted Greatly during 2021." Gallup Poll. https://news.gallup.com/poll/388781/political-party-preferences-shifted-greatly-during-2021.aspx.

Jones, Simon. 2020. "Northern Ireland's Government Reopens." *Le Monde Diplomatique*, February 2020. https://mondediplo.com/2020/02/05northern-ireland.

The Journal. 2019. "Timeline: How the DUP Went from 'Blood Red Lines' to a Brexit Compromise." October 13, 2019. https://www.thejournal.ie/dup-brexit-backstop-blood-red-line-arlene-foster-4846928-Oct2019/.

Kanath, Sanjana. 2019. "Pelosi Stands by Her Dismissal of Freshman Democrats: 'Regrets Is Not What I Do.'" *Huffington Post*, July 11, 2019. https://www.huffpost.com/entry/nancy-pelosi-defends-dismissal-freshmen-house-democrats_n_5d26a52de4b0cfb596007094.

Kanthak, Kristin. 2007. "Crystal Elephants and Committee Chairs: Campaign Contributions and Leadership Races in the U.S. House of Representatives." *American Politics Research* 35, no. 3 (May): 389–406. https://doi.org/10.1177/1532673X06298079.

Kaplan, Rebecca, and Scott MacFarlane. 2022. "Congress Drops Mask Mandate in Time for State of the Union." *CBS News*, February 28, 2022. https://www.cbsnews.com/news/congress-mask-mandate-state-of-the-union/.

Karasz, Palko, and Stephen Castle. 2018. "What Is a No-Confidence Vote, and What Did It Mean for Theresa May?" *New York Times*, December 12, 2018. https://www.nytimes.com/2018/12/12/world/europe/no-confidence-vote-brexit.html.

Kates, Jennifer, Jennifer Tolbert, and Anna Rouw. 2022. "The Red/Blue Divide in COVID-19 Vaccination Rates Continues: An Update." Report by the Kaiser Family Foundation. January 19, 2022. https://www.kff.org/policy-watch/the-red-blue-divide-in-covid-19-vaccination-rates-continues-an-update/.

Kathlene, Lyn. 1995. "Position Power versus Gender Power: Who Holds the Floor?" In *Gender Power, Leadership, and Governance*, edited by Georgia Duerst-Lahti and Rita Mae Kelly, 167–94. Ann Arbor: University of Michigan Press.

Kedrowski, Karen M. 2022. "Performing Toxic Masculinity during the January 6 Insurrection." *eJournal of Public Affairs* 11, no. 1 (March). https://bearworks.missouristate.edu/ejopa/.

Kedrowski, Karen M., and Rachel Gower 2009. "Gender and the Public Speakership: News Media Coverage of Speaker Nancy Pelosi." Paper presented at the 2009 Southern Political Science Association meeting, New Orleans.

Kellner, Peter. 2015. "General Election 2015: How Britain Really Voted." *YouGov.uk*, June 8, 2015. https://yougov.co.uk/topics/politics/articles-reports/2015/06/08/general-election-2015-how-britain-really-voted.

Kelly, Richard. 2019. "Confidence Motions." House of Commons Library, Briefing Paper 02873, March 14, 2019. https://commonslibrary.parliament.uk/research-briefings/sn02873/.

Kelly, Richard. 2021. "Independent Complaints and Grievance Scheme." House of Commons Library, Research Briefing 8369, April 27, 2021. https://commonslibrary.parliament.uk/research-briefings/cbp-8369/.

Kenny, Meryl. 2013. *Gender and Political Recruitment: Theorizing Institutional Change*. New York: Palgrave. https://doi.org/10.1017/S1537592715000924.

Kenny, Meryl. 2014. "A Feminist Institutionalist Approach." *Politics & Gender* 10, no. 4 (December): 679–83. https://doi.org/10.1017/S1743923X14000488.

Kenny, Meryl. 2015. "Why Aren't There More Women in British Politics?" *Political Insight* 6, no. 2 (August): 12–15. https://doi.org/10.1111/2041-9066.12094.

Kentish, Benjamin. 2018. "DUP Abstains on Crucial Votes in Warning over May's

Brexit Agreement." *The Independent*, November 19, 2018. https://www.indepen
dent.co.uk/news/uk/politics/dup-brexit-budget-vote-theresa-may-government
-confidence-and-supply-agreement-terms-a8642131.html.

Kirsch, Richard. 2011. *Fighting for Our Health: The Epic Battle to Make Health Care a Right in the United States*. Albany, NY: Rockefeller Center Press.

Kite, Melissa. 2010. "Are the Tories Only Looking for 'Cutie' Candidates?" *The Telegraph*, February 4, 2010. https://www.telegraph.co.uk/comment/7231474/Are-the-Tories-only-looking-for-cutie-candidates.html.

Kittilson, Miki Caul. 2006. *Challenging Parties, Changing Parliaments: Women and Elected Office in Contemporary Western Europe*. Columbus: Ohio State University Press.

Knight, Sam. 2016. "The Man Who Brought You Brexit." *The Guardian*, September 9, 2016. https://www.theguardian.com/politics/2016/sep/29/daniel-hannan-the-man-who-brought-you-brexit.

Knight, Sam. 2018. "Theresa May's Impossible Choice." *New Yorker*, July 23, 2018. https://www.newyorker.com/magazine/2018/07/30/theresa-mays-impossible-choice.

Krook, Mona Lena. 2010. "Studying Political Representation: A Comparative-Gendered Approach." *Perspectives on Politics* 8, no. 1 (March): 233–40. https://doi.org/10.1017/S1537592709992817.

Krook, Mona Lena, and Fiona Mackay, eds. 2011. *Gender, Politics and Institutions: Toward a Feminist Institutionalism*. Basingstoke, UK: Palgrave.

Kuenssberg, Laura. 2016. "Boris Johnson Made Foreign Secretary by Theresa May." *BBC*, July 13, 2016. https://www.bbc.com/news/uk-politics-36789972.

Kuenssberg, Laura. 2017. "Lessons from the Government's Abortion Climbdown." *BBC*, July 29, 2017. https://www.bbc.com/news/uk-politics-40446923.

Kuenssberg, Laura. 2018. "What Just Happened in the Commons?" *BBC*, July 16, 2018. https://www.bbc.com/news/uk-politics-44855123.

Kwarteng, Kwasi, Priti Patel, Dominic Raab, Chris Skidmore, and Elizabeth Truss. 2012. *Britannia Unchained: Global Lessons for Growth and Prosperity*. London: Palgrave Macmillan.

Lakoff, Robin Tomach. 2005. "The Politics of Nice." *Journal of Politeness Research* 1, no. 2 (July): 173–91. https://doi.org/10.1515/jplr.2005.1.2.173.

Landers, Elizabeth, and Manu Raju. 2018. "Nine Democrats Vow to Oppose Pelosi for Speaker Unless House Rule Changes Are Adopted." *CNN*, November 23, 2018. https://www.cnn.com/2018/11/23/politics/pelosi-democrats-letter-problem-solvers-caucus.

Laurent, Lionel. 2020. "The EU's Tobin Tax Is Being Resurrected." *Bloomberg News*, July 27, 2020.

Lawless, Jennifer L. 2012. *Becoming a Candidate: Political Ambition and the Decision to Run for Office*. New York: Cambridge University Press.

Lawless, Jennifer L., and Richard L. Fox. 2005. *It Takes a Candidate: Why Women Don't Run for Office*. New York: Cambridge University Press.

Lawless, Jennifer L., and Richard L. Fox. 2010. *It Still Takes a Candidate: Why Women Don't Run for Office*. New York: Cambridge University Press.

Lawless, Jennifer L., and Kathryn Pearson. 2008. "The Primary Reason for Women's Underrepresentation? Reevaluating the Conventional Wisdom." *Journal of Politics* 70 no. 1 (January): 67–82. https://doi.org/10.1017/S002238160708005X.

Lawrence, Felicity. 2017. "Brexit Could Destroy the UK's Food and Farming Industry—Or Be the Making of It." *The Guardian*, June 26, 2017. https://www.theguardian.com/commentisfree/2017/jun/26/brexit-watershed-farming-food-industry-michael-gove.

Lawrence, Felicity, Rob Evans, David Pegg, Caelainn Barr, and Pamela Duncan. 2019. "How the Right's Radical Thinktanks Reshaped the Conservative Party." *The Guardian*, November 29, 2019. https://www.theguardian.com/politics/2019/nov/29/rightwing-thinktank-conservative-boris-johnson-brexit-atlas-network.

Lawrence, John A. 2018. "How the 'Watergate Babies' Broke American Politics." *Politico*, May 26, 2018.

Lawrence, John A. 2023. *Arc of Power: Inside Nancy Pelosi's Speakership, 2005–2010*. Lawrence: University Press of Kansas.

Lazarus, Jeffrey, and Amy Steigerwalt. 2018. *Gendered Vulnerability: How Women Work Harder to Stay in Office*. Ann Arbor: University of Michigan Press. https://doi.org/10.3998/mpub.9718595.

Leading Britain's Conversation. 2018. "What Is the Chequers Deal? Theresa May's Brexit Plan Explained." October 8, 2018. https://www.lbc.co.uk/politics/the-news-explained/theresa-mays-chequers-deal-explained/.

Leadsom, Andrea. 2016. "Andrea Leadsom: Introducing the Fresh Start Alternative to EU Membership." *ConservativeHome*, May 24, 2016. https://archive.ph/sxMEz.

LeDuc, Larry, Richard Niemi, and Pippa Norris, eds., *Comparing Democracies*. 3rd ed. Thousand Oaks, CA: Sage.

Letwin, Oliver. 2017. *Hearts and Minds: The Battle for the Conservative Party from Thatcher to the Present*. London: Biteback.

Lewis, Helen. 2015. "Since 1967, Gay Activists Have Piled Up Victories—But Abortion Rights Are Fragile and Constantly Attacked." *New Statesman*, June 25, 2015. https://www.newstatesman.com/politics/2015/06/1967-gay-activists-have-piled-victories-abortion-rights-are-fragile-and-constantly.

Lewis, Jeff. 2019a. "Why Are Ocasio-Cortez, Omar, Pressley, and Talib Estimated to Be Moderates by NOMINATE?" *Voteview.com*, August 5, 2019.

Lewis, Jeff. 2019b. "Why Is Alexandria Ocasio-Cortez Estimated to Be a Moderate by NOMINATE?" *Voteview.com*, August 5, 2019.

Lewis, Jeffrey B., Keith Poole, Howard Rosenthal, Adam Boche, Aaron Rudkin, and Luke Sonnet. 2021. *Voteview: Congressional Roll Call Votes Database*. https://voteview.com/.

Library of Parliament. 2017. "Legislating for Brexit: The Great Repeal Bill." Research Briefing, May 2, 2017. https://commonslibrary.parliament.uk/research-briefings/cbp-7793/.

Lijphart, Arend. 1999. *Patterns of Democracy*. 2nd ed. New Haven: Yale University Press.

Lillis, Mike. 2016. "Tim Ryan Ponders Pelosi Challenge." *The Hill*, November 14, 2016. .

Linderman, Juliet. 2018. "$300K in Taxpayer Funds Has Been Spent Settling Sexual Harassment Claims Against Congress, Report Says." *PBS*, January 12, 2018. https://www.pbs.org/newshour/politics/300k-in-taxpayer-funds-has-been-spent-settling-sexual-harassment-claims-against-congress-report-says.

Lipinski, Daniel. 2021. "How Representation and Policymaking Fail in a Party-Dominated House." In *Under the Iron Dome*, edited by Paul Herrnson, Colton Campbell, and David Dulio, chap. 11. London: Routledge.

Lipton, Eric. 2014. "Proposal Would Require Think Tanks to Disclose Funding by Foreign Governments." *New York Times*, September 17, 2014. https://www.nytimes.com/2014/09/18/us/politics/house-proposal-would-require-think-tanks-to-disclose-foreign-funding.html.

Llanera, Alex Anthony C. 2013. "The Influence of Religion on the Congressional Vote on the Stupak-Pitts and Nelson Amendments." Master's thesis, St. Louis University.

London Review of Books. 2017. "Do Your Homework David Runciman." 39, no. 6 (March 2017). https://www.lrb.co.uk/the-paper/v39/n06/david-runciman/do-your-homework.

Lovenduski, Joni. 1996. "Sex, Gender and British Politics." *Parliamentary Affairs* 49, no. 1 (January): 1–12. https://doi.org/10.1093/oxfordjournals.pa.a028660.

Lovenduski, Joni. 2001. "Women and Politics: Minority Representation or Critical Mass?" *Parliamentary Affairs* 54, no. 4 (October): 743–58. https://doi.org/10.1093/parlij/54.4.743.

Lovenduski, Joni. 2005. *Feminizing Politics*. Cambridge: Polity Press.

Lovenduski, Joni, and Pippa Norris. 2003. "Westminster Women: The Politics of Presence." *Political Studies* 51, no.1 (March): 84–102. https://doi.org/10.1111/1467-9248.00414.

Lowndes, Vivien. 2014. "How Are Things Done Around Here? Uncovering Institutional Rules and Their Gendered Effects." *Politics & Gender* 10, no. 4 (December): 685–91. https://doi.org/10.1017/S1743923X1400049X.

Lowndes, Vivien, and Mark Roberts. 2013. *Why Institutions Matter: The New Institutionalism in Political Science*. New York: Palgrave Macmillan.

Lupo, Lisa. 2017. "From the Concrete Wall to the Glass Ceiling to the Labyrinth: Gendering Leadership for Transformative Change." United Nations Research Institute for Social Development (UNRISD), March 28, 2017. https://www.researchgate.net/publication/330652323_From_the_Concrete_Wall_to_the_Glass_Ceiling_to_the_Labyrinth_Gendering_Leadership_for_Transformative_Change_UNRISD_BlogThink_Pieces_Series/citation/download.

Lynch, Philip, and Richard Whitaker. 2018. "All Brexiteers Now? Brexit, the Conservatives and Party Change." *British Politics* 13, no. 1 (April): 31–47. https://doi.org/10:1057/s41293-017-0064-6.

MacAskill, Ewen. 2016. "'Extreme Surveillance' Becomes UK Law with Barely a Whimper." *The Guardian*, November 19, 2016. https://www.theguardian.com/world/2016/nov/19/extreme-surveillance-becomes-uk-law-with-barely-a-whimper.

MacIntyre, Donald. 1994. "PM Rakes Revenge on Tory Renegades." *The Independent*, November 29, 1994. https://www.independent.co.uk/news/pm-takes-revenge-on-tory-renegades-1440013.html.

Mackay, Fiona. 2008. "'Thick' Conceptions of Substantive Representation: Women, Gender and Political Institutions." *Representation* 44, no. 2 (June): 125–39. https://doi.org/10.1080/00344890802079607.

Mackay, Fiona. 2014. "Nested Newness, Institutional Innovation, and the Limits of Gendered Change." *Politics & Gender* 10, no. 4 (December): 549–71. https://doi.org/10.1017/S1743923X14000415.

Mance, Henry. 2017. "Former Obama Adviser Jim Messina under Scrutiny after UK Election." *Financial Times*, June 12, 2017. https://www.ft.com/content/479aedd0-4f5e-11e7-a1f2-db19572361bb.

Mann, Thomas, and Norman Ornstein. 2008. *The Broken Branch: How Congress Is Failing America and How to Get It Back on Track*. New York: Oxford University Press.

Mann, Thomas, and Norman Ornstein. 2013. *It's Even Worse than It Looks: How the American Constitutional System Collided with the New Politics of Extremism*. New York: Basic Books.

Marcos, Christina. 2020. "Pelosi Defends Not Speaking to Trump for Almost a Year." *The Hill*, September 14, 2020. https://thehill.com/homenews/house/516320-pelosi-defends-not-speaking-to-trump-for-almost-a-year/.

Marcos, Christina. 2021. "Fourth House GOP Lawmaker Issued $5,000 Metal Detector Fine." *The Hill*, May 18, 2021. https://thehill.com/homenews/house/554182-fourth-house-gop-lawmaker-issued-5000-metal-detector-fine/.

Martin, Sara. 2007. "Women Leaders: The Labyrinth to Leadership." *American Psychological Association Monitor* 38, no. 7 (July/August): 90.

Masciulli, Joseph, Mikhail A. Molchanov, and W. Andy Knight, eds. 2009. *The Ashgate Research Companion to Political Leadership*. Surrey, UK, and Burlington, VT: Ashgate.

Mason, Rowena. 2014. "Nicky Morgan's Gay-Marriage Stance Causes Equalities Role Confusion . . . Again." *The Guardian*, July 25, 2014. https://www.theguardian.com/society/2014/jul/15/equalities-minister-voted-against-gay-marriage-nicky-morgan.

Mason, Rowena. 2016. "Lib Dems Fined 20,000 Pounds for Undeclared Election Spending." *The Guardian*, December 7, 2016. https://www.theguardian.com/politics/2016/dec/07/lib-dems-fined-20000-for-undeclared-election-spending.

Mason, Rowena. 2017a. "Davis Dismissive of Johnson's Influence on Florence Speech." *The Guardian*, September 24, 2017. https://www.theguardian.com/politics/2017/sep/24/theresa-may-has-faced-series-of-cabinet-plots-to-oust-her-book-says.

Mason, Rowena. 2017b. "Tory Election Spending Claims: 12 Police Forces Pass Files to CPS." *The Guardian*, March 15, 2017. https://www.theguardian.com/global/2017/mar/15/second-tory-reveals-police-investigated-him-over-spending-allegations.

May, Theresa. 2014a. "Theresa May: Fight Europe by All Means, but Not Over This Arrest Warrant." *The Telegraph*, November 9, 2014. https://www.telegraph.co.uk/news/politics/conservative/11216589/Theresa-May-Fight-Europe-by-all-means-but-not-over-this-Arrest-Warrant.html.

May, Theresa. 2014b. "Vignette—Gender and Party Politics: The 'Feminisation' of the Conservative Party." In *Deeds and Words: Gendering Politics after Joni Lovenduski*, edited by Rosie Campbell and Sarah Childs, 91–93. Colchester, UK: ECPR Press.

May, Theresa. 2016. "Speech to the International Crime and Policing Conference." *UK.gov*, March 23, 2016. https://www.gov.uk/government/collections/international-crime-and-policing-conference-2016.

May, Theresa. 2017. "The Government's Negotiating Objectives for Exiting the EU: PM Speech." *UK.gov*, January 17, 2017, updated February 3, 2017. www.gov.uk/government/speeches/.

Mayhew, David. 1974. *Congress: The Electoral Connection*. New Haven: Yale University Press.

Mayhew, Les. 2017. "Means Testing Adult Social Care in England." *Geneva Papers on Risk and Insurance—Issues and Practice* 42 (April): 500–529. https://dx.doi.org/10.1057/s41288-016-0041-0.

Mayo Clinic. 2022. "COVID-19 and Related Vaccine Development Research." https://www.mayoclinic.org/coronavirus-covid-19/history-disease-outbreaks-vaccine-timeline/covid-19.

McCarty, Nolan, Keith T. Poole, and Howard Rosenthal. 2009. "Does Gerrymandering Cause Polarization?" *American Journal of Political Science* 53, no. 3 (July): 666–80. https://doi.org/10.1111/j.1540-5907.2009.00393.x.

McCormack, Jayne. 2019. "Brexit Talks: What Does the DUP Want?" *BBC*, January 17, 2019. https://www.bbc.com/news/uk-northern-ireland-46903876.

McDonald, Henry. 2015. "Northern Ireland Assembly Votes to Legalise Same-Sex Marriage." *The Guardian*, May 2, 2015. https://www.theguardian.com/uk-news/2015/nov/02/northern-ireland-assembly-votes-to-legalise-same-sex-marriage.

McDonald, Henry. 2017. "Martin McGuinness Resigns as Deputy First Minister of Northern Ireland." *The Guardian*, January 10, 2017. https://www.theguardian.com/politics/2017/jan/09/martin-mcguinness-to-resign-as-northern-ireland-deputy-first-minister.

McEnhill, Libby. 2015. "Unity and Distinctiveness in UK Coalition Government:

Lessons for Junior Partners." *Political Quarterly* 86, no. 1 (January–March): 101–9. https://doi.org/10.1111/1467-923X.12147.

McGleenon, Brian. 2020. "Brexit Document LEAK: No Need for British Farmers—Explosive Whitehall Claim." *The Express*, March 1, 2020. https://www.express.co.uk/news/uk/1249341/Brexit-news-UK-farmers-not-needed-eu-subsidies-dominic-cummings-import-all-food-singapore.

McKay, David. 2019. "What Really Motivates the European Research Group?" *Prospect Magazine*, January 11, 2019. https://www.prospectmagazine.co.uk/politics/motivates-tories-erg-jacob-rees-mogg-european-research-group-brexit.

McKee, Seth C. 2010. *Republican Ascendancy in Southern US House Elections*. Boulder, CO: Westview.

McKeever, Anna. 2020. *Immigration Policy and Right-Wing Populism in Western Europe*. London: Palgrave.

McKoen, Nancy. 2011. "Women in the House Get a Restroom." *Washington Post*, July 28, 2011. https://www.washingtonpost.com/lifestyle/style/women-in-the-house-get-a-restroom/2011/07/28/gIQAFgdwfI_story.html.

McPherson, Lindsey. 2018a. "Pelosi Agrees to Deal Limiting Her Speakership to 4 Years." *Roll Call*, December 12, 2018. https://rollcall.com/2018/12/12/pelosi-agrees-to-deal-limiting-her-speakership-to-4-years/.

McPherson, Lindsey. 2018b. "Problem Solvers to Back Pelosi for Speaker after Reaching Agreement on Rules Changes." *Roll Call*, November 28, 2018. https://rollcall.com/2018/11/28/problem-solvers-to-back-pelosi-for-speaker-after-reaching-agreement-on-rules-changes/.

McPherson, Lindsey. 2018c. "16 Pelosi Opponents Sign Letter Saying They Won't Vote for Her for Speaker." *Roll Call*, November 18, 2018. https://rollcall.com/2018/11/19/16-pelosi-opponents-sign-letter-saying-they-wont-vote-for-her-for-speaker/.

McPherson, Lindsey. 2018d. "House Democrats to Discuss Term Limits on Committee Chairs, Pelosi Says." *Roll Call*, December 6, 2018. https://rollcall.com/2018/12/06/house-democrats-to-discuss-term-limits-on-committee-chairs-pelosi-says/.

McPherson, Lindsey. 2020. "Pelosi Reaffirms That Next Term as Speaker Will Be Her Last." *Roll Call*, November 18, 2020. https://rollcall.com/2020/11/18/pelosi-affirms-promise-that-next-term-as-speaker-will-be-her-last/.

McPherson, Lindsey. 2023. "Opponents Deny McCarthy Speaker's Gavel on First Vote." *Roll Call*, January 3, 2023. https://rollcall.com/2023/01/03/opponents-deny-mccarthy-speakers-gavel-on-first-vote/.

McTague, Tom. 2019. "How the UK Lost the Brexit Battle." *Politico EU*, March 27, 2019. https://www.politico.eu/article/how-uk-lost-brexit-eu-negotiation/.

McTague, Tom, Charlie Cooper, and Annabelle Dickson. 2017. "Northern Ireland's DUP Derails Theresa May's Trip to Brussels." *Politico EU*, December 4, 2017. https://www.politico.eu/article/arlene-foster-theresa-may-brexit-northern-irelands-dup-derail-theresa-mays-trip-to-brussels/.

Medina, Eduardo. 2023. "Paul Pelosi Attack Suspect Tells TV Station He Has No Remorse." *New York Times*, January 28, 2023. https://www.nytimes.com/2023/01/28/us/politics/pelosi-attacker-interview.html.

"Members Only." 2017. *Whereas: Stories From the People's House*. March 20, 2017. https://history.house.gov/Blog/2017/March/3-20-Members-Only/.

Merrick, Rob. 2017a. "Tories to Cut Winter Fuel Payments for Wealthiest Pensioners as They Launch Manifesto." *The Independent*, May 17, 2017. https://www.independent.co.uk/news/uk/politics/tories-manifesto-winter-fuel-payments-conservatives-election-2017-a7741761.html.

Merrick, Rob. 2017b. "UKIP: A Timeline of the Party's Turbulent History." *The Independent*, September 29, 2017. https://www.independent.co.uk/news/uk/politics/ukip-timeline-party-westminster-alan-sked-nigel-farage-conference-key-events-brexit-leadership-a7974606.html.

Metro. 2019. "Brexit Vote Results since 2015." March 14, 2019. https://metro.co.uk/2019/03/14/brexit-vote-results-since-2015-including-eu-referendum-8900771/.

Meyerson, Harold. 2004. "How Nancy Pelosi Took Control." *American Prospect*, May 12, 2004. https://prospect.org/features/nancy-pelosi-took-control/.

Millington, Alison. 2017. "The Life and Career of British Prime Minister Theresa May." *Business Insider*, June 9, 2017. https://www.businessinsider.com/life-and-career-of-british-prime-minister-theresa-may-2017-6.

Mississippi Center for Public Policy. n.d. "Our Story." https://mspolicy.org/our-story/.

Montenaro, Domenico. 2020. "Poll: Just a Quarter of Republicans Accept Election Outcome." *NPR*, December 9, 2020. https://www.npr.org/2020/12/09/944385798/poll-just-a-quarter-of-republicans-accept-election-outcome.

Montgomerie, Tim. 2012. "Ten Things You Need to Know about the Group of Four That Runs the Coalition." *ConservativeHome*, February 16, 2012. https://conservativehome.com/2012/02/16/ten-things-you-need-to-know-about-the-group-of-four-that-runs-the-coalition/.

Mooney, Attracta, Chris Newlands, and Aime Williams. 2016. "Philip May Assumes Supporting Role." *Financial Times*, July 13, 2016. https://www.ft.com/content/111f28c6-4914-11e6-b387-64ab0a67014c.

Moore, Luke. 2018. "Policy, Office and Votes: Conservative MPs and the Brexit Referendum." *Parliamentary Affairs* 71, no. 1 (January): 1–27. https://doi.org/10.1093/pa/gsx010.

Moravcsik, Andrew. 1991. "Negotiating the Single European Act: National Interests and Conventional Statecraft in the European Community." *International Organization* 45, no. 1 (Winter): 19–56.

Morris, Nigel. 2012. "Tories Quietly Drop David Cameron's 'A-list' for Minority Candidates." *The Independent*, October 5, 2012. https://www.independent.co.uk/news/uk/politics/tories-quietly-drop-david-cameron-s-alist-for-minority-candidates-8199985.html.

Mortimer, Caroline. 2017. "All the Anti-Gay and Lesbian Stances Theresa May

Has Taken in Her Career." *The Independent*, April 26, 2017. https://www.independent.co.uk/news/uk/politics/theresa-may-lgbt-rights-gay-commons-vote-same-sex-marriage-gay-adoption-tim-farron-a7702326.html.

Mullins, Brody. 2004. "Pelosi PAC Hit with $21K Fine." *Roll Call*, February 6, 2004. https://rollcall.com/2004/02/06/pelosi-pac-hit-with-21k-fine/.

Murray, Jenni. 2013. "What Did Margaret Thatcher Do for Women?" *The Guardian*, April 9, 2013. https://www.theguardian.com/politics/2013/apr/09/margaret-thatcher-women.

Murray, Rainbow, ed. 2010. *Cracking the Highest Glass Ceiling*. Westport, CT: Praeger.

Nather, David. 2014. "Dingell in '93: Clinton Health Bill 'in Disarray.'" *Politico*, February 28, 2014. https://www.politico.com/story/2014/02/john-dingell-hillary-clinton-health-care-bill-104091.

National Health Service. n.d. "Paying for Your Own Care (Self-Funding)." www.nhs.uk.

Naylor, Brian. 2021a. "Read Trump's Jan. 6 Speech, a Key Part of Impeachment Trial." *NPR*, February 10, 2021. https://www.npr.org/2021/02/10/966396848/read-trumps-jan-6-speech-a-key-part-of-impeachment-trial.

Naylor, Brian. 2021b. "Senate Republicans Block a Plan for an Independent Commission on Jan. 6 Capitol Riot." *NPR*, May 28, 2021. https://www.npr.org/2021/05/28/1000524897/senate-republicans-block-plan-for-independent-commission-on-jan-6-capitol-riot.

Neilan, Catherine. 2022. "Conservative MP's Call for Party to Oust Ben Elliot as Co-Chairman over 'Contaminating' Russian Links." *Business Insider*, March 9, 2022. https://www.businessinsider.com/tories-call-oust-co-chairman-ben-elliot-russia-links-2022-3.

Nelson, Garrison. 1977. "Partisan Patterns of House Leadership Change, 1789–1977." *American Political Science Review* 71, no. 3 (September): 918–39. https://doi.org/10.2307/1960098.

Nelson, Steven, and Juliegrace Brufke. 2021. "McCarthy Slams Pelosi 'Hypocrisy' on Mask Mandates after She Calls Him a 'Moron.'" *New York Post*, July 28, 2021. https://nypost.com/2021/07/28/nancy-pelosi-calls-kevin-mccarthy-a-moron-over-mask-mandate/.

Netchaeva, Ekaterina, Maryam Kouchaki, and Leah D. Sheppard. 2015. "A Man's (Precarious) Place: Men's Experienced Threat and Self-Assertive Reactions to Female Superiors." *Personality and Social Psychology Bulletin* 41, no. 9 (September): 1247–59. https://doi.org/10.1177/0146167215593491.

News Letter. 2018. "Sinn Fein Criticised by LGBT Group over Same-Sex Marriage Plans." February 23, 2018. https://www.newsletter.co.uk/news/sinn-fein-criticised-lgbt-group-over-same-sex-marriage-plans-345516.

Nilsen, Ella. 2018. "Here Are the House Democrats Who Oppose Nancy Pelosi for Speaker." *Vox*, November 28, 2018. https://www.vox.com/policy-and-politics/2018/11/15/18095869/nancy-pelosi-speaker-votes-democrats-letter.

Nolan, Martin F. 2011. "House Speaker Nancy Pelosi Is One for the Ages." *Cali-*

fornia Journal of Politics and Policy 3, no. 1 (January): 1–2. https://doi.org/10.50 70/P24K51.

Norris, Pippa. 1996. "Women Politicians: Transforming Westminster?" *Parliamentary Affairs* 49, no. 1 (January): 89–102. https://doi.org/10.1093/oxfordjournals.pa.a028675.

Norris, Pippa, ed. 1997. *Passages to Power: Legislative Recruitment in Advanced Democracies*. Cambridge: Cambridge University.

Norris, Pippa. 2004. *Electoral Engineering: Voting Rules and Political Behaviour*. Cambridge: Cambridge University Press. https://doi.org/10.1017/CBO9780511790980.

Norris, Pippa, and Joni Lovenduski. 1995. *Political Recruitment: Gender, Race and Class in the British Parliament*. Cambridge: Cambridge University Press.

Norris, Pippa, and Joni Lovenduski. 2001. "Blair's Babes: Critical Mass Theory, Gender, and Legislative Life." John F. Kennedy School of Government, Faculty Research Working Papers Series, RWP 01-039, September 2001. https://papers.ssrn.com/sol3/papers.cfm?abstract_id=288548.

Norton, Philip. 2016. "Fixed-Term Parliaments Act and Votes of Confidence." *Parliamentary Affairs* 69, no. 1 (January): 3–18. https://doi.org/10.1093/pa/gsv003.

O'Brien, Diana. 2015. "Rising to the Top: Gender, Political Performance, and Party Leadership in Parliamentary Democracies." *American Journal of Political Science* 59, no. 4 (October): 1022–39. https://doi.org/10.1111/ajps.12173.

O'Brien, Diana, Matthew Mendez, Jordan Carr Peterson, and Jihyun Shin. 2015. "Letting Down the Ladder or Shutting the Door: Female Prime Ministers, Party Leaders, and Cabinet Ministers." *Politics & Gender* 11, no. 4 (December): 689–717. https://doi.org/10.1017/S1743923X15000410.

O'Carroll, Lisa. 2019. "How Is Boris Johnson's Brexit Deal Different from Theresa May's?" *The Guardian*, October 27, 2019. https://www.theguardian.com/politics/2019/oct/17/how-is-boris-johnson-brexit-deal-different-from-theresa-may.

O'Connor, John. 2018. "Long Island Democrat Leading the Revolt against Nancy Pelosi." *WNYC News*, November 27, 2018. https://www.wnyc.org/story/long-island-democrat-leading-revolt-against-speaker-pelosi/.

O'Connor, Patrick. 2008. "Waxman Dethrones Dingell as Chairman." *Politico*, November 20, 2008. https://www.politico.com/story/2008/11/waxman-dethrones-dingell-as-chairman-015822.

O'Connor, Patrick. 2010. "Why Shuler Is Running against Pelosi." *Wall Street Journal*, November 17, 2010. https://blogs.wsj.com/washwire/2010/11/17/why-shuler-is-running-against-pelosi/.

Office for National Statistics. Government of the UK. 2020. "Crime in England and Wales: Year Ending December 2019." April 23, 2020. https://www.ons.gov.uk/peoplepopulationandcommunity/crimeandjustice/bulletins/crimeinenglandandwales/previousReleases.

Office of the Speaker. 2021a. "Pelosi Statement on Congressman John Conyers,

Jr." News Release. November 21, 2017. https://speaker.gov/newsroom/1121 17-2.

Office of the Speaker. 2017b. "Pelosi Statement on Former Staffer's Account of Congressman Conyers' Conduct." News Release. November 27, 2017.

Office of the Speaker. 2017c. "Pelosi Statement on Immediate Retirement of Congressman John Conyers, Jr." News Release. December 5, 2017. https://www.speaker.gov/newsroom/12517-6.

Office of the Speaker. 2021a. "Floor Speech on H.R. 3233, the National Commission to Investigate the January 6 Attack on the United States Capitol Complex Act." News Release. May 19, 2021. https://www.speaker.gov/newsroom/519 21-4.

Office of the Speaker. 2021b. "Pelosi Announces House Will Deliver Article of Impeachment to Senate on January 25." News Release. January 22, 2021. https://www.speaker.gov/newsroom/12221.

Office of the Speaker. 2021c. "Pelosi Statement on Republican Recommendations to Serve on the Select Committee to Investigate the January 6th Attack on the Capitol." News Release. July 21, 2021. https://www.speaker.gov/newsroom/72 121-2.

Oliver, Craig. 2017. *Unleashing Demons*. London: Hodder.

O'Neill, Brenda, and David Stewart. 2009. "Gender and Political Party Leadership in Canada." *Party Politics* 15, no. 6 (November): 737–57. https://doi.org/10.11 77/1354068809342526.

Open Secrets. 2020. "Home." https://www.opensecrets.org/.

Oppenheim, Maya. 2019. "Theresa May Rolled Back Women's Rights as Prime Minister, Say Campaigners." *The Independent*, May 24, 2019. https://www.independent.co.uk/news/uk/home-news/theresa-may-resign-womens-rights-austerity-benefits-conservative-leader-a8929141.html.

Ostrom, Elinor. 1986. "An Agenda for the Study of Institutions." *Public Choice* 48, no. 1 (January): 3–25. https://doi.org/10.1007/BF00239556.

Page, Susan. 2021. *Madam Speaker: Nancy Pelosi and the Lessons of Power*. New York: Twelve Publishers.

Palazzolo, Daniel J. 1992. *The Speaker and the Budget: Leadership in the Post-Reform House of Representatives*. Pittsburgh: University of Pittsburgh Press.

Parker, Ashley. 2017. "Trump and Democrats Strike DACA Deal. Yes? No? Sort Of? Trump's World Can Be Confusing." *Washington Post*, September 14, 2017. https://www.washingtonpost.com/politics/trump-and-democrats-strike-daca-deal-yes-no-sort-of-trumps-world-can-be-confusing/2017/09/14/ab6a40d4-9970-11e7-82e4-f1076f6d6152_story.html?utm_term=.e7a442cb78ee.

Parker, George. 2013. "Cameron Guarantees EU's Issue Dominance." *Financial Times*, January 22, 2013. https://www.ft.com/content/c8bc27ce-64be-11e2-ac53-00144feab49a.

Parker, George. 2016. "Gang of Six Free to Spread Eurosceptic Message after Brexit Deal." *Financial Times*, February 21, 2016. https://www.ft.com/content/df883c9a-d89c-11e5-98fd-06d75973fe09.

Parker, George, and James Pickford. 2017. "Theresa May's 'Dementia Tax' Triggers Conservative Backlash." *Financial Times*, May 19, 2017. https://www.ft.com/content/82ff3a76-3c98-11e7-ac89-b01cc67cfeec.

Paun, Akash, and Aron Cheung. 2017. "The 2017 Northern Ireland Assembly Election." Institute for Government, February 2017. https://www.instituteforgovernment.org.uk/publications/2017-northern-ireland-assembly-election.

Payne, Adam. 2018. "Theresa May's Government Edges Closer to Collapse as DUP Threatens to Pull the Plug." *Business Insider*, October 11, 2018. https://www.businessinsider.com/dup-threatening-to-collapse-theresa-mays-government-over-brexit-2018-10.

Peabody, Robert L. 1967. "Party Leadership Change in the US House of Representatives." *American Political Science Review* 61, no. 3 (September): 675–93. https://doi.org/10.2307/1976087.

Peabody, Robert L. 1976. *Leadership in Congress: Stability, Succession, and Change*. Boston: Little Brown.

Peake, Lucy. 1997. "Women in the Campaign and in the Commons." In *Labour's Landslide: The British General Election 1997*, edited by Jonathan Tonge and Andrew Geddes, 165–78. Manchester: University of Manchester Press.

Pearson, Kathryn. 2015. *Party Discipline in the U.S. House of Representatives*. Ann Arbor: University of Michigan Press. https://doi.org/10.3998/mpub.4402299.

Pearson, Kathryn. 2019. "Nancy Pelosi Victorious—Why the California Democrat Was Reelected Speaker of the House." *The Conversation*, January 3, 2019. https://theconversation.com/nancy-pelosi-victorious-why-the-california-democrat-was-reelected-speaker-of-the-house-107333.

Pearson, Kathryn, and Eric Schickler. 2009. "The Transition to Democratic Leadership in a Polarized House." In *Congress Reconsidered*, 9th ed., edited by Lawrence C. Dodd and Bruce I. Oppenheimer. Washington, DC: CQ Press.

Pegg, David, Felicity Lawrence, and Rob Evans. 2018. "Steve Baker, the Ex-Brexit Minister Hell-Bent on Torpedoing May's Chequers Plan." *The Guardian*, September 30, 2018. https://www.theguardian.com/politics/2018/sep/30/steve-baker-the-ex-brexit-minister-hell-bent-on-torpedoing-mays-chequers-plan.

Pelosi, Christine. 2019. *The Nancy Pelosi Way: Advice on Success, Leadership, and Politics from America's Most Powerful Woman*. New York: Skyhorse.

Pelosi, Nancy. 2008. *Know Your Power: A Message to America's Daughters*. With Amy Hill Hearth. New York: Doubleday.

Perkins, Anne, and Jessica Elgot. 2018. "Brexit 'Meaningful Vote': May Wins after Rebels Accept Compromise." *The Guardian*, June 20, 2018. https://www.theguardian.com/politics/2018/jun/20/lead-tory-rebel-dominic-grieve-accepts-brexit-meaningful-vote-compromise.

Peters, Ronald M. 1990. *The American Speakership: The Office in Perspective*. Baltimore: Johns Hopkins University Press.

Peters, Ronald M. 1995. *The Speaker: Leadership in the US House of Representatives*. Washington DC: CQ Press.

Peters, Ronald M., and Cindy Simon Rosenthal. 2010. *Speaker Nancy Pelosi and the New American Politics*. New York: Oxford University Press.

Petroff, Alanna, and Mark Thompson. 2013. "U.K. Moves to Block Europe's Tobin Tax." *CNN*, April 22, 2013. https://money.cnn.com/2013/04/22/news/economy/trading-tax-uk/index.html.

Philips, Anne. 1994. "Dealing with Difference: A Politics of Ideas or a Politics of Presence?" *Constellations* 1, no. 1 (December): 88–91. https://doi.org/10.1111/j.1467-8675.1994.tb00005.x.

Phillips, Anne. 1995. *The Politics of Presence*. Oxford: Oxford University Press. https://doi.org/10.1093/0198294158.001.0001.

Pilet, Jean-Benoit, and William Cross. 2015a. "Introduction." In *The Selection of Political Party Leaders in Comparative Perspective*, edited by Jean-Benoit Pilet and William Cross, 1–12. Oxfordshire, UK: Routledge.

Pilet, Jean-Benoit, and William Cross, eds. 2015b. *The Selection of Political Party Leaders in Comparative Perspective*. Oxfordshire, UK, and New York: Routledge.

Plank, Liz. 2020. "Nancy Pelosi Tears Up Trump's State of the Union Speech in Possible 2020 Tipping Point." *NBC News*, February 5, 2020. https://www.nbcnews.com/think/opinion/nancy-pelosi-tears-trump-s-state-union-speech-possible-2020-ncna1130776.

Politico EU. 2001. "Profile: Iain Duncan Smith." October 3, 2001.

Politics.co.uk. 2022. "Liz Truss." May 2022.

Polsby, Nelson W. 2004. *How Congress Evolves: Social Bases of Institutional Change*. New York: Oxford University Press.

Prince, Rosa. 2017. *Theresa May: The Enigmatic Prime Minister*. London: Biteback.

Problem Solvers Caucus. n.d. "About the Caucus." https://problemsolverscaucus-gottheimer.house.gov/about.

Quinn, Ben. 2020. "Ex-MP Charlie Elphicke Convicted of Sexual Assault." *The Guardian*, July 30, 2020. https://www.theguardian.com/uk-news/2020/jul/30/ex-mp-charlie-elphicke-convicted-of-sexual-assault.

Quinn, Thomas. 2005. "Leasehold or Freehold? Leader-Eviction Rules in the British Conservative and Labour Parties." *Political Studies* 53, no. 4 (December): 793–815. https://doi.org/10.1111%2Fj.1467-9248.2005.00557.x.

Quinn, Thomas. 2013. "From Two-Partism to Alternating Predominance: The Changing UK Party System, 1950–2010." *Political Studies* 61, no. 2 (June): 378–400. https://doi.org/10.1111/j.1467-9248.2012.00966.x.

Quinn, Thomas. 2015. *Electing and Ejecting Party Leaders in Britain*. New York: Palgrave.

Quinn, Thomas. 2016. "Throwing the Rascals Out? Problems of Accountability in Two-Party Systems." *European Journal of Political Research* 55, no. 1 (February): 120–37. https://doi.org/10.1111/1475-6765.12118.

Quinn, Thomas. 2019. "The Conservative Party's Leadership Election of 2016: Choosing a Leader in Government." *British Politics* 14, no. 1 (March): 63–85. https://doi.org/10.1057/s41293-018-0071-2.

Rae, Nicol C., and Colton C. Campbell, eds. 1999. *New Majority or Old Minority? The Impact of Republicans on Congress.* Lanham, MD: Rowman and Littlefield.

Raitio, Juha, and Helena Raulus. 2017. "The UK EU Referendum and the Move Towards Brexit." *Maastricht Journal of European and Comparative Law* 24, no. 1 (February): 25–42.

Raju, Manu, Annie Grayer, and Ashley Killough. 2018. "Nancy Pelosi's Freshmen Critics Go Quiet as Major Speaker Vote Looms." *CNN*, November 30 2018. https://www.cnn.com/2018/11/30/politics/nancy-pelosi-freshmen-critics-quiet/index.html.

Rawlings, Richard, Peter Leyland, and Allison Young, eds. 2013. *Sovereignty and the Law: Domestic, European, and International Perspectives.* Oxford: Oxford University Press.

Rawnsley, Andrew. 2015. "Geoffrey Howe, the Close Cabinet Ally Who Became Thatcher's Assassin." *The Guardian*, October 10, 2015. https://www.theguardian.com/politics/2015/oct/10/geoffrey-how-the-cabinet-ally-who-became-thatchers-assassin.

Rawnsley, Andrew. 2019. "The Inside Story of How Boris Johnson's 2016 Leadership Campaign Was Torpedoed by Michael Gove." *The Telegraph*, June 20, 2019. https://www.telegraph.co.uk/politics/2019/06/20/inside-story-boris-johnsons-2016-leadership-campaign-torpedoed/.

Rayner, Gordon, and Steven Swinford. 2019. "Theresa May Loses Brexit Vote by Crushing Margin of 149--and Is Now Expected to Come Out Against No-Deal." *The Telegraph*, March 13, 2019. https://www.telegraph.co.uk/politics/2019/03/12/brexit-vote-latest-news-meaningful-vote-result-theresa-may-deal/.

Reeves, Rachael. 2020. *Women of Westminster: The MPs Who Changed Politics.* London: Bloomsbury.

Rentoul, John. 1995. "Labour Faces Test over Quotas for Women MPs." *The Independent*, December 11, 1995. https://www.independent.co.uk/news/labour-faces-test-over-quotas-for-women-mps-1525198.html.

Rentoul, John, Stephen Ward, and Donald Macintyre. 1996. "Labour Blow as All-Women Lists Outlawed." *The Independent*, January 9, 1996. https://www.independent.co.uk/news/labour-blow-as-allwomen-lists-outlawed-1323046.html?r=91322.

Restuccia, Andrew, and Ted Mann. 2021. "Jan. 6, 2021: How It Unfolded; A Minute-by-Minute Look at the Actions of President Trump, the Capitol Rioters and the Lawmakers Tasked with Certifying Biden's Election." *Wall Street Journal*, February 12, 2021. https://www.wsj.com/livecoverage/trump-second-impeachment-trial-2021-02-11/card/mCT1acVCW0zjKLYztKEJ.

Reuters. "43% of Republicans View Trump as True US President –Reuters/Ipsos." May 24, 2021. https://www.reuters.com/world/us/53-republicans-view-trump-true-us-president-reutersipsos-2021-05-24/.

Riley-Smith, Ben. 2021. "EU Countries Tell UK They Cannot Guarantee Extradition of Criminals in Wake of Brexit." *The Telegraph*, April 13, 2021. https://

www.telegraph.co.uk/politics/2021/04/13/eu-countries-tell-britain-cannot-guarantee-extradition-criminals/.

Roberts, Dan. 2017. "Sweet Brexit: What Sugar Tells Us about Britain's Future Outside the EU." *The Guardian*, March 27, 2017. https://www.theguardian.com/business/2017/mar/27/brexit-sugar-beet-cane-tate-lyle-british-sugar.

Robinson, Eugene. 1993. "Major Survives Vote of Confidence." *Washington Post*, July 24, 1993. https://www.washingtonpost.com/archive/politics/1993/07/24/major-survives-vote-of-confidence/5038d184-f689-4322-bfe2-127e0546fbae/.

Rogers, Katie, and Nicholas Fandos. 2019. "Trump Tells Congresswomen to 'Go Back' to the Countries They Came From." *New York Times*, July 14, 2019. https://www.nytimes.com/2019/07/14/us/politics/trump-twitter-squad-congress.html.

Rohde, David W. 1991. *Parties and Leaders in the Post-Reform House*. Chicago: University of Chicago Press.

Rohde, David W. 2013. "Reflections on the Practice of Theorizing: Conditional Party Government in the Twenty-First Century." *Journal of Politics* 75, no. 4 (October): 849–64. https://doi.org/10.1017/s0022381613000911.

Rosenthal, Cindy Simon, ed. 2002. *Women Transforming Congress*. Norman: University of Oklahoma Press.

Rosenthal, Cindy Simon, and Ronald M. Peters. 2008. "Who Is Nancy Pelosi?" *PS: Political Science and Politics* 41, no. 1 (January): 57–62. https://doi.org/10.1017/S1049096508080086.

Ross, Tim, and Tom McTague. 2017. *Betting the House: The Inside Story of the 2017 Election*. London: Biteback.

Routledge, Paul, and Simon Hoggart. 1993. "Major Hits Out at Cabinet." *The Guardian*, July 25, 1993. https://www.theguardian.com/politics/1993/jul/25/politicalnews.uk.

Rudman, Laurie A., and Peter Glick. 1999. "Feminized Management and Backlash Toward Agentic Women: The Hidden Costs of a Kinder, Gentler Image of Women Managers." *Journal of Personality and Social Psychology* 77, no. 5 (November): 1004–10. https://doi.org/10.1037/0022-3514.77.5.1004.

Rule, Wilma. 1998. "Review of *Women and Power in Parliamentary Democracies; Passages to Power*; and *Political Recruitment*." *American Political Science Review* 92, no. 2 (June): 478–80.

"Rules of the Democratic Caucus, 117th Congress." 2021. https://www.dems.gov/imo/media/doc/DEM_CAUCUS_RULES_117TH_April_2021.pdf.

Rusbridger, Alan. 2017. "George Osborne: From Media Hack to Political Hack, in a Day." *New York Times*, March 29, 2017. https://www.nytimes.com/2017/03/29/opinion/george-osborne-from-media-hack-to-political-hack-in-a-day.html.

Sabbagh, Dan. 2018a. "DUP Refuses to Support May's Brexit Deal for Second Day in a Row." *The Guardian*, November 20, 2018. https://www.theguardian.com/politics/2018/nov/20/dup-refuses-support-may-brexit-deal.

Sabbagh, Dan. 2018b. "May Faces Commons Reckoning over Cross-Border Trade Bill." *The Guardian*, July 15, 2018. https://www.theguardian.com/politics/2018/jul/15/may-faces-commons-reckoning-over-cross-border-trade-bill.

Salm, Christian, and Wilhelm Lehmann. 2020. "Jacques Delors: Architect of the Modern European Union." European Parliamentary Research Service, July 2020. www.knowledge4policy.ec.europa.eu.

Sanbonmatsu, Kira. 2006. *Where Women Run: Gender and Party in the American States*. Ann Arbor: University of Michigan Press.

Sanbonmatsu, Kira, and Kathleen Dolan. 2009. "Do Gender Stereotypes Transcend Party?" *Political Research Quarterly* 62, no. 3 (September): 485–94. https://doi.org/10.1177%2F1065912908322416.

Sandbu, Martin. 2016. "Free Lunch: Know-Nothing Brexit Party." *Financial Times*, June 8, 2016. https://www.ft.com/content/6539258e-2d57-11e6-bf8d-26294ad519fc.

Sandford, Alasdair. 2020. "What Was in Theresa May's Brexit Deal and Why Was It so Unpopular?" *Euronews*, January 29, 2020. https://www.euronews.com/2018/12/07/what-is-in-theresa-may-s-brexit-deal-and-why-is-it-so-unpopular.

Saner, Emine. 2016. "Sayeeda Warsi: Forthright on the Failings of the Tories." *The Guardian*, March 11, 2016. https://www.theguardian.com/politics/2016/mar/11/sayeeda-warsi-former-conservative-chair-interview.

Sargeant, Jess. 2020. "North-South Cooperation on the Island of Ireland." Institute for Government, July 1, 2020. https://www.instituteforgovernment.org.uk/explainers/north-south-cooperation-island-ireland.

Sawe, Benjamin Elisha. 2019. "Shortest-Serving British Prime Ministers." *World Atlas*, May 2019. https://www.worldatlas.com/articles/british-prime-ministers-serving-the-shortest-time-in-office.html.

Sawer, Marion. 2010. "Women and Elections." In *Comparing Democracies*, 3rd ed., edited by Larry LeDuc, Richard Niemi, and Pippa Norris, 202–24. Thousand Oaks, CA: Sage.

Sayer, Zach. 2018. "DUP Leader: No Prospect of Northern Ireland Deal." *Politico EU*, February 14, 2018. https://www.politico.eu/article/dup-leader-arlene-foster-no-prospect-of-northern-ireland-deal-sinn-fein/.

Schleiter, Petra, and Valerie Belu. 2016. "The Decline of Majoritarianism in the UK and the Fixed-Term Parliaments Act." *Parliamentary Affairs* 69, no. 1 (January): 36–52. https://doi.org/10.1093/pa/gsv002.

Schraer, Rachel. 2017. "Have There Been Two Decades of Failure to Reform Social Care?" *BBC*, November 24, 2017. https://www.bbc.com/news/health-42065767.

Scullion, David. 2020. "The Completion of a Revolution." *The Critic*, December 30, 2020. https://thecritic.co.uk/brexit-the-completion-of-a-revolution/.

Seldon, Anthony, and Raymond Newell. 2020. *May at 10: The Verdict*. London: Biteback.

Select Committee to Investigate the January 6th Attack on the United States Capitol. 2022. "Final Report." December 22, 2022. Washington, DC: Government Printing Office. https://www.govinfo.gov/content/pkg/GPO-J6-REPORT/pdf/GPO-J6-REPORT.pdf.

Serhan, Yasmeen. 2017. "Theresa May and the Terrible, Horrible, No Good, Very Bad Week." *The Atlantic*, November 8, 2017. https://www.theatlantic.com/international/archive/2017/11/theresa-may-cabinet-crisis/545168/.

Shipman, Tim. 2018. *Fall Out: A Year of Political Mayhem*. London: William Collins.

Shorthouse, Ryan, Kate Maltby, and James Brenton, eds. 2014. *The Modernisers' Manifesto*. London: Bright Blue Campaign. www.brightblue.org.uk.

Siaroff, Alan. 2003. "Varieties of Parliamentarianism in Advanced Industrial Democracies." *International Political Science Review* 24, no. 4 (October): 445–64. https://doi.org/10.1177%2F01925121030244003.

Siddique, Haroon. 2010. "Profile: Lord Ashcroft." *The Guardian*, March 1, 2010. https://www.theguardian.com/politics/2010/mar/01/lord-ashcroft-profile.

Simons, Ned. 2013. "John Major: I Called Them 'Bastards' Because They Were." *Huffington Post UK*, October 22, 2013. https://www.huffingtonpost.co.uk/2013/10/22/john-major-european-union-conservative-party_n_4142916.html.

Simpson, Fiona. 2017. "MP Sex Pest Scandal: 36 Tories Named over Sexual Misconduct Allegations in Tory Spreadsheet of Shame." *Evening Standard*, October 30, 2017. https://www.standard.co.uk/news/politics/leaked-spreadsheet-reveals-sexual-harassment-claims-against-36-mps-a3670961.html.

Sinclair, Barbara. 1995. *Legislators, Leaders and Lawmaking: The US House of Representatives in the Postreform Era*. Baltimore: Johns Hopkins University Press.

Sinclair, Barbara. 2008. "Leading the New Majorities." *PS: Political Science and Politics* 41, no. 1 (January): 89–93. https://doi.org/10.1017/S104909650808013X.

Singham, Shanker, and Radomir Tylecote. 2018. *Plan A+ Discussion Paper no. 95*. September 2018. London: Institute of Economic Affairs (IEA). Reprinted September 27, 2019. https://iea.org.uk/publications/plan-a-creating-a-prosperous-post-brexit-uk/.

Sjoberg, Laura. 2009. "Feminist Approaches to the Study of Political Leadership." In *The Ashgate Research Companion to Political Leadership*, edited by Joseph Masciulli, Mikhail A. Molchanov, and W. Andy Knight, 149–76. Surrey, UK, and Burlington, VT: Ashgate.

Sjoberg, Laura. 2014. "Feminism." In *Oxford Handbook of Political Leadership*, edited by Paul 't Hart and R. A. W. Rhodes, 72–86. Oxford: Oxford University Press.

Sloat, Amanda. 2019. "Brexit Endgame: A Withdrawal Agreement for Theresa May, But No Clarity on Brexit." Brookings Institution, May 30, 2019. https://www.brookings.edu/blog/order-from-chaos/2019/05/30/brexit-endgame-a-withdrawal-agreement-for-theresa-may-but-no-clarity-on-brexit/.

Smith, Julie. 2017. "The Historical Evolution of EU-UK Relations." European Council, June 2, 2017. https://www.consilium.europa.eu/en/documents-publications/library/library-blog/posts/the-historical-evolution-of-eu-uk-relations/.

Smith, Matthew. 2014. *Policy-Making in the Treasury*. Basingstoke, UK: Palgrave.

Snell, Janet. 2015. "A Quick Guide to the *Care Act*." *The Guardian*, April 28, 2015. https://www.theguardian.com/social-care-network/2015/apr/28/-care-act-2014-quick-guide.

Spangler, Todd. 2018. "Rashida Tlaib 'Probably Not' Going to Support Nancy Pelosi as Speaker." *Detroit Free Press*, August 9, 2018. https://www.freep.com/story/news/local/michigan/2018/08/09/nancy-pelosi-speaker-rashida-tlaib-says-probably-not/946160002/.

Sparrow, Andrea. 2017. "Leadsom Announces Beefed-Up Helpline to Tackle Commons Misconduct Allegations." *The Guardian*, October 31, 2017. https://www.theguardian.com/politics/blog/live/2017/oct/30/commons-sex-abuse-claims-dossier-intensifies-demands-for-ministerial-statement-politics-live?page=with:block-59f7280c5fb4be0730416873.

Spelman, Dame Caroline. 2019. "After Seeing What I've Been Through, My Children Wouldn't Follow Me into Politics." *Times of London*, October 31, 2019. https://www.thetimes.co.uk/article/after-seeing-what-ive-been-through-my-children-wouldnt-follow-me-into-politics-s78fhwx5k.

Spence, Alex. 2018. "The Definitive Story of How a Former Washington Lobbyist Became the 'Brexiteers' Brain." *Buzzfeed News*, May 22, 2018. https://www.buzzfeed.com/alexspence/steve-baker-brexit-meetings-shanker-singham.

Spicer, Sir Michael. 2012. *The Spicer Diaries*. London: St. Martin's.

Sprunt, Barbara. 2021. "7 GOP Senators Voted to Convict Trump. Only 1 Faces Voters Next Year." *NPR*, February 15, 2021. https://www.npr.org/sections/trump-impeachment-trial-live-updates/2021/02/15/967878039/7-gop-senators-voted-to-convict-trump-only-1-faces-voters-next-year.

Stamp, Gavin. 2016. "Who Is Theresa May: A Profile of UK's New Prime Minister." *BBC*, July 25, 2016. https://www.bbc.com/news/uk-politics-36660372.

Stark, Leonard P. 1999. *Choosing a Leader: Party Leadership Contests in Britain from Macmillan to Blair*. New York: St. Martin's, 1996.

Starr, Paul. 1982. *The Social Transformation of American Medicine: The Rise of a Sovereign Profession and the Making of a Vast Industry*. Boston: Basic Books.

Starr. Paul. 2013. *Remedy and Reaction: The Peculiar American Struggle over Health Care Reform*. New Haven: Yale University Press.

Stewart, Heather. 2017. "Bank of England Chief Is 'Enemy of Brexit,' Says Jacob Rees-Mogg." *The Guardian*, October 25, 2017. https://www.theguardian.com/politics/2017/oct/25/bank-of-england-chief-mark-carney-is-enemy-of-brexit-says-jacob-rees-mogg.

Stewart, Heather. 2019a. "May Suffers Heaviest Parliamentary Defeat of a British PM in the Democratic Era." *The Guardian*, January 26, 2019. https://www.theguardian.com/politics/2019/jan/15/theresa-may-loses-brexit-deal-vote-by-majority-of-230.

Stewart, Heather. 2019b. "Teresa May Announces She Will Resign on 7 June." *The Guardian*, May 24, 2019. https://www.theguardian.com/politics/2019/may/24/theresa-may-steps-down-resigns-tory-leader-conservative-brexit.

Stewart, Heather, and Daniel Boffey. 2019. "Theresa May Suffers Historic Defeat in Vote as Tories Turn against Her." *The Guardian*, January 16, 2019. https://www.theguardian.com/politics/2019/jan/15/theresa-may-suffers-historic-defeat-as-tories-turn-against-her.

Stewart, Heather, Rowena Mason, and Peter Walker. 2019. "Brexit: May Vows to Resign before Next Phase of Negotiations if Deal Is Passed." *The Guardian*, March 27, 2019. https://www.theguardian.com/politics/2019/mar/27/theresa-may-to-resign-before-next-phase-of-brexit.

Stolberg, Sheryl Gay. 2019. "'The Squad' Rankles, but Pelosi and Ocasio-Cortez Make Peace for Now." *New York Times*, July 26, 2019. https://www.nytimes.com/2019/07/26/us/politics/aoc-squad-pelosi.html.

Stone, Jon. 2017a. "EU Investment Bank 'Will Owe Britain Money for 35 Years after Brexit." *The Independent*, October 27, 2017. https://www.independent.co.uk/news/uk/politics/brexit-european-investment-bank-eib-britain-alexander-stubb-a8023516.html.

Stone, Jon. 2017b. "Tory MP's Face Being Prosecuted for Electoral Fraud While They Are Fighting the Upcoming General Election Campaign." *The Independent*, April 18, 2017. https://www.independent.co.uk/news/uk/politics/tory-election-fraud-prosecutions-cps-election-campaign-result-overturn-battle-bus-a7689801.html.

Stratton, Allegra. 2010. "Michael Ashcroft's Election Masterplan." *The Guardian*, March 2, 2010. https://www.theguardian.com/politics/2010/mar/02/partyfunding-ashcroft.

Stratton, Allegra. 2011. "David Cameron's Trouble with Women Makes Theresa May Close to Unsackable." *The Guardian*, November 11, 2011. https://www.theguardian.com/politics/2011/nov/11/david-cameron-theresa-may-unsackable.

Streeck, Wolfgang, and Kathleen Thelen, eds. 2005. *Beyond Continuity: Institutional Change in Advanced Political Economies*. Oxford: Oxford University Press.

Studlar, Donley, and Ian McAllister. 2002. "Does a Critical Mass Exist? A Comparative Analysis of Women's Legislative Representation since 1950." *European Journal of Political Research* 41, no. 2 (March): 233–53. https://doi.org/10.1111/1475-6765.00011.

Sullivan, Kevin, and Mary Jordan. 2020. *Trump on Trial: The Investigation, Impeachment, Acquittal and Aftermath*. New York: Scribner.

Sunday Times. 2003. "Focus: Handbags at Dawn for IDS." October 19, 2003. https://www.thetimes.co.uk/article/focus-handbags-at-dawn-for-ids-svjxfn90gdt.

Sundquist, James. 1983. *Dynamics of the Party System: Alignment and Realignment of Political Parties in the United States*. 2nd ed. Washington, DC: Brookings Institution Press.

Swers, Michele L. 2002. *The Difference Women Make: The Policy Impact of Women in Congress*. Chicago: University of Chicago Press.

Swinford, Steven. 2014. "How the European Arrest Warrant Debate Descended into a Shambles." *The Telegraph*, November 11, 2014. https://www.telegraph.co.uk/news/uknews/crime/11222177/How-the-European-Arrest-warrant-debate-descended-into-a-shambles.html.

Syal, Rajeev. 2019. "Tory Official Convicted of Falsifying Expenses in Race against Farage." *The Guardian*, January 9, 2019. https://www.theguardian.com/politics/2019/jan/09/craig-mackinlay-tory-mp-cleared-breaking-2015-general-election-expenses-rules.

Syal, Rajeev, and Alexandra Topping. 2017. "Labour Will Put 10,000 Extra Police on Streets, Vows Jeremy Corbyn." *The Guardian*, May 2, 2017. https://www.theguardian.com/uk-news/2017/may/01/labour-will-put-10000-extra-police-streets-vows-jeremy-corbyn.

Sykes, Patricia L. 2009. "The Gendered Nature of Leadership Analysis: Lessons from Women Leaders as Executives in Anglo-American Systems." In *The Ashgate Research Companion to Political Leadership*, edited by Jospeh Masciulli, Mikhail A. Molchanov, and W. Andy Knight, 219–40. Surrey, UK, and Burlington, VT: Ashgate.

Tamborrino, Kelsey. 2017. "Pelosi Defends Conyers as 'an Icon.'" *Politico*, November 26, 2017. https://www.politico.com/story/2017/11/26/pelosi-conyers-icon-harassment-259832.

Tannen, Deborah. 1994. *Gender and Discourse*. New York: Oxford University Press.

Taranto, James. 2010. "Truth in Advertising: The Case for Nancy Pelosi." *Wall Street Journal*, November 22, 2010. https://wsj.com/articles/SB10001424052748704243904575630533565176688.

Taylor, Mary Anne. 2012. "Madame Speaker, We Have the Votes: Feminist Style and Nancy Pelosi's Personal and Political Roles in the Health Care Reform Debate." *Women & Language* 35, no. 1 (Spring): 127–31.

Telegraph Reporters. 2017. "Who is Theresa May? A Profile of Britain's Prime Minister. June 9, 2017. https://www.telegraph.co.uk/politics/0/theresa-may-profile-britains-prime-minister/.

Thomas, Cal. 2002. "Democrats Writing Their Own Epitaph." *Baltimore Sun*, November 13, 2002. https://www.baltimoresun.com/news/bs-xpm-2002-11-13-0211130360-story.html.

Thomas, Sue, and Clyde Wilcox, eds. 2014. *Women and Elective Office: Past, Present and Future*. 3rd ed. New York: Oxford University Press. https://doi.org/10.1093/acprof:oso/9780199328734.001.0001.

Thompson, Helen. 2017. "Inevitability and Contingency: The Political Economy of Brexit." *British Journal of Politics and International Relations* 19, no. 3 (August): 434–49. https://doi.org/10.1177/1369148117710431.

Timothy, Nick, Kate McCann, and Claire Newell. 2018. "George Soros, the Man Who 'Broke the Bank of England,' Banking Secret Plot to Thwart Brexit." *The Telegraph*, February 8, 2018. https://www.telegraph.co.uk/politics/2018/02/07/george-soros-man-broke-bank-england-backing-secret-plot-thwart/.

Tominey, Camilla. 2017. "Lessons from the Government's Abortion Climbdown." *BBC*, July 29, 2017. https://www.bbc.com/news/uk-politics-40446923.

Tominey, Camilla. 2019a. "Here Come the Girls: The Rising Tory Stars Who Could Be Set for Promotion under Boris." *The Telegraph*, July 22, 2019. https://www.telegraph.co.uk/politics/2019/07/17/come-girls-rising-tory-stars-could-set-promotion-boris/.

Tominey, Camilla. 2019b. "Iain Duncan Smith: From Quiet Man to Boris' Right-Hand Man, Former Tory Leader Continues Comeback." *The Telegraph*, June 25, 2019. https://www.telegraph.co.uk/politics/2019/06/25/iain-duncan-smith-quiet-man-boriss-right-hand-man-former-tory/.

Tonge, Jonathan, Christina Leston-Bandeira, and Stuart Wilks-Heeg, eds. 2018a. *Britain Votes 2017*. London: Oxford University Press.

Tonge, Jonathan, Christina Leston-Bandeira, and Stuart Wilks-Heeg. 2018b. "Conclusion: An Election That Satisfied Few and Solved Little." In *Britain Votes 2017*, edited by Jonathan Tonge, Christina Leston-Bandeira, and Stuart Wilks-Heeg, 267–76. London: Oxford University Press.

Tonge, Jonathan, Christina Leston-Bandeira, and Stuart Wilks-Heeg. 2018c. "Introduction: The Mislaying of a Majority." In *Britian Votes 2017*, edited by Jonathan Tonge, Christina Leston-Bandeira, and Stuart Wilks-Heeg, 1–8. London: Oxford University Press.

Topping, Alexandra. 2020. "Rees-Mogg Accused of Trying to Wreck Parliament Harassment Body." *The Guardian*, June 30, 2020. https://www.theguardian.com/politics/2020/jun/23/rees-mogg-accused-of-wrecking-parliament-harassment-body.

Tracy, Abigail. 2019. "'There Is No Successful Strategy . . . That Involves Casting Them Out . . .': Inside the Struggle between Nancy Pelosi and the Squad." *Vanity Fair*, July 17, 2019. https://www.vanityfair.com/news/2019/07/nancy-pelosi-the-squad-democrats-congress-trump.

Travis, Alan. 2016. "EU Ruling Means UK Snooper's Charter May Be Open to Challenge." *The Guardian*, May 30, 2017. https://www.theguardian.com/world/2016/dec/21/eu-ruling-means-uk-snoopers-charter-may-be-open-to-challenge.

Travis, Alan. 2017. "Tory General Election Manifesto: The Key Points and Analysis." *The Guardian*, May 30, 2017. https://www.theguardian.com/politics/2017/may/18/tory-general-election-manifesto-key-points-analysis.

Triggle, Nick. 2015. "Care Costs Cap Delayed until 2020." *BBC*, July 7, 2015. https://www.bbc.com/news/health-33552279.

Troitino, David. 2013. *Building Europe: European Integration*. Hauppage, NY: Nova Science.

Tumulty, Karen. 2020. "How Nancy Pelosi's Rise Turned Her into the Most Powerful Woman in US History." *Washington Post*, May 25, 2020. https://www.washingtonpost.com/opinions/2020/03/25/how-nancy-pelosis-unlikely-rise-turned-her-into-most-powerful-woman-us-history/.

Uberoi, Elise, Chris Watson, Natasha Mutebi, Shadi Danechi, and Paul Bolton. 2021. "Women in Politics and Public Life." House of Commons Library. Briefing Paper Number 01250, March 4, 2022. https://commonslibrary.parliament.uk/research-briefings/sn01250/.

Ungoed-Thomas, Jon, and Tony Farag. 2021. "Theresa May Zooms to Top of MP's Pay List after Earning 500 K for 'Virtual' Speeches during the Pandemic." *Daily Mail*, July 3, 2021. https://www.dailymail.co.uk/news/article-9753247/Theresa-zooms-MPs-pay-list-earning-500k-virtual-speeches.html.

US Census Bureau. *1980 Census of Population, Volume 1, Chapter B, General Population Characteristics*. https://www2.census.gov/prod2/decennial/documents/1980/1980censusofpopu8011u_bw.pdf.

US House of Reprsentatives. n.d. "Historical Highlights: The House's Decision to Conduct Business During the 1918 Influenza Pandemic." https://history.house.gov/Historical-Highlights/1901-1950/The-House-s-decision-to-conduct-business-during-the-1918-influenza-pandemic/.

US House of Representatives. n.d. "Party Divisions of the House of Representatives, 1789-Present."

US House of Representatives. 2018. "Sick Days." *Whereas: Stories from the People's House*. December 17, 2018. https://history.house.gov/Blog/2018/December/12-14-Flu/.

US Senate. n.d. "The Caning of Senator Charles Sumner." https://www.senate.gov/artandhistory/history/minute/The_Caning_of_Senator_Charles_Sumner.htm.

Usherwood, Simon. 2012. "The Conservative Party and Euroscepticism." *E-International Relations*, November 11, 2012. https://www.e-ir.info/2012/11/11/the-conservative-party-and-euroscepticism/.

V., Jim, and eHei. 2002. "Democrats' Fight for the Future." *Washington Post*, November 8, 2002. https://archive/politics/2002/11/08/democrats-fight-for-the-future/1b87eca3-d89d-45e5-9b64-89a24b2930cww.washingtonpost.com/a2/.

Vernasca, Gianluigi. 2016. "The UK's EU Rebate-Explained." *The Conversation*, June 6, 2016. https://theconversation.com/the-uks-eu-rebate-explained-58019.

Walsh, Deirdre. 2016. "Who Is Tim Ryan? Meet the Man Challenging Nancy Pelosi." *CNN*, November 22, 2016. https://www.cnn.com/2016/11/22/politics/who-is-tim-ryan/index.html.

Walsh, Deirdre. 2022. "Pelosi Is Running for Reelection but Is Silent on a Bid to Retain Her Leadership Post." *NPR*, January 25, 2022. https://www.npr.org/2022/01/25/1075657198/nancy-pelosi-reelection.

Wang, Amy B. 2021. "McCarthy Asks Supreme Court to Overturn Proxy Voting Rules Adopted as Pandemic Precaution and Used by Nearly 100 Republicans." *Washington Post*, September 9, 2021. https://www.washingtonpost.com/politics/2021/09/09/mccarthy-asks-supreme-court-overturn-house-proxy-voting-rules-adopted-pandemic-precaution/.

Warrell, Helen. 2017. "Q & A: Has Theresa May Really Cut the UK's Police Numbers?" *Irish Times*, June 5, 2017.

Watson, Kathryn. 2023. "The Motion to Vacate the Chair and Other Provisions in the House Rules of the 118th Congress." *CBS News*, January 7, 2023. https://www.cbsnews.com/news/mccarthy-motion-to-vacate-rule-speaker/.

Watt, Nicholas. 2012. "Theresa May Takes First Step to Opting Out of EU Law and Order Measures." *The Guardian*, October 14, 2012. https://www.theguardian.com/uk/2012/oct/14/theresa-may-law-and-order-measures.

Watt, Nicholas, and Patrick Wintour. 2014. "Maria Miller Quits as Culture Secretary in Blow to David Cameron." *The Guardian*, April 9, 2014. https://www.theguardian.com/politics/2014/apr/09/maria-miller-quits-culture-secretary-david-cameron.

Watt, Toby, and Michael Varrow. 2018. "The 'Do-Nothing' Option: How Public Spending on Social Care in England Fell by 13% in Five Years." Health Foundation, May 29, 2018. https://www.health.org.uk/blogs/the-%E2%80%98do-nothing%E2%80%99-option-how-public-spending-on-social-care-in-england-fell-by-13-in-five-years.

Watts, Joe. 2017. "Election 2017: Theresa May to Try and Move Campaign Past Police Cuts and Focus on Brexit." *The Independent*, June 5, 2017. https://www.independent.co.uk/news/uk/politics/election-2017-brexit-london-attack-police-cuts-theresa-may-focus-eu-uk-exit-campaign-latest-a7774096.html.

Wauters, Bram, and Jean-Benoit Pilet. 2015. "Electing Women as Party Leaders: Does the Selectorate Matter?" In *The Selection of Political Party Leaders in Comparative Perspective*, edited by William Cross and Jean-Benoit Pilet, 73–89. Oxfordshire, UK, and New York: Routledge.

Wearmouth, Rachel. 2018. "DUP Will Only Back Theresa May if Her Brexit Deal Fails—Boosting Tory Hardliners." *Huffington Post UK*, December 6, 2018. https://www.huffingtonpost.co.uk/entry/dup-brexit-theresa-may_uk_5c083062e4b0bf813ef3b4df.

Weaver, Matthew, Rajeev Syal, Anushka Asthana, and Peter Beaumont. 2017. "Priti Patel Summoned Back to UK as PM Prepares to Sack Her." *The Guardian*, November 8, 2017. https://www.theguardian.com/politics/2017/nov/08/priti-patels-meetings-cancelled-as-pm-considers-sacking-her.

Weiner, Juli. 2010. "Nancy Pelosi, Dejected and Dispirited, Has 'No Regrets.'" *Vanity Fair*, November 4, 2010. https://www.vanityfair.com/news/2010/11/nancy-pelosi-dejected-and-dispirited-has-no-regrets.

Weisman, Jonathan. 2007. "Emerging Grievances within Party Likely to Test Pelosi." *Washington Post*, January 22, 2007, A5.

Weldon, S. Laurel. 2002. *Protest, Policy and the Problem of Violence against Women: A Cross-National Comparison*. Pittsburgh: University of Pittsburgh Press.

Whale, Sebastian. 2018. "The ERG: A Party within a Party?" *PoliticsHome*, September 27, 2018. https://www.politicshome.com/thehouse/article/the-erg-a-party-within-a-party.

White, Michael, and Anne Perkins. 2002. "'Nasty Party' Warning to Tories." *The Guardian*, October 8, 2002. https://www.theguardian.com/politics/2002/oct/08/uk.conservatives200.

Whitman, Richard G. 2013. "On Europe: Margaret Thatcher's Lasting Legacy." *Chatham House*, April 9, 2013. https://www.chathamhouse.org/2013/04/europe-margaret-thatchers-lasting-legacy.

Whittington, Lauren W. 2007. "Stark Gives Apology." *Roll Call*, October 23, 2007. https://rollcall.com/2007/10/23/stark-gives-apology/.

Wickham-Jones, Mark. 1997. "Right Turn: A Revisionist Account of the 1975 Conservative Party Leadership Election." *Twentieth Century British History* 8, no. 1: 74–89. https://doi.org/10.1093/tcbh/8.1.74.

Wilkinson, Peter, and Simon Cullen. 2018. "UK Government Loses Key Brexit Vote." *CNN*, April 18, 2018. https://www.cnn.com/2018/04/18/europe/uk-brexit-vote-defeat-intl/index.html.

Williams, Jordan. 2021. "Greene, Massie, Norman Sue Pelosi Over Mask Fines." *The Hill*, July 28, 2021. https://thehill.com/homenews/house/565212-greene-massie-norman-sue-pelosi-over-mask-fines/.

Wilson, Sam. 2014. "Britain and the EU: A Long and Rocky Relationship." *BBC*, April 1, 2014. https://www.bbc.com/news/uk-politics-26515129.

Wineinger, Catherine, and Mary K. Nugent. 2020. "Framing Identity Politics: Right-Wing Women as Strategic Party Actors in the UK and US." *Journal of Women, Politics & Policy* 41, no. 1 (January): 91–118. https://doi.org/10.1080/1554477X.2020.1698214.

Wintour, Patrick. 2016. "Cameron Accused of 'Gross Negligence' over Brexit Contingency Plans." *The Guardian*, July 20, 2016. https://www.theguardian.com/politics/2016/jul/20/david-cameron-accused-gross-negligence-brexit-contingency-plans.

Withers, Matt. 2018. "Irony Overload as Jacob Rees-Mogg Calls Mark Carney a 'Second-Tier Politician.'" *New European*, November 29, 2018. https://www.theneweuropean.co.uk/brexit-news-irony-overload-as-jacob-rees-mogg-calls-mark-carney-a-36948/.

Wolfensberger, Donald R. 2018. *Changing Cultures in Congress: From Fair Play to Power Plays*. New York: Columbia University Press.

Wong, Scott. 2019. "How Pelosi Is Punishing Some Critics While Rewarding Others." *The Hill*, January 16, 2019. https://thehill.com/homenews/house/425744-how-pelosi-is-punishing-some-critics-while-rewarding-others/.

Woolf, Marie. 2005. "Lib Dems Hold Inquest after Their 'Decapitation Strategy' Misses Targets." *The Independent*, May 7, 2005. https://www.independent.co.uk/news/uk/politics/lib-dems-hold-inquest-after-their-decapitation-strategy-misses-targets-220427.html/.

Yachnin, Jennifer. 2007. "Pelosi Trumps Chairs." *Roll Call*, November 2, 2007. https://rollcall.com/2007/11/02/pelosi-trumps-chairs/.

Yglesias, Matthew. 2019. "The Constitutional Change at the Heart of the UK Parliament's Endless Deadlock." *Vox*, September 5, 2019. https://www.vox.com/2019/9/5/20849086/uk-brexit-fixed-term-parliament.

York, Anthony. 2002. "Harold Ford Crusades to Save the Democrats." *Salon*, November 9, 2002. https://www.salon.com/2002/11/09/pelosi_ford/.

Zanona, Melanie. 2018. "Problem Solvers Dems: We 'Can't Support' Pelosi for Speaker 'At This Time.'" *The Hill*, November 23, 2018. https://thehill.com/homenews/house/418031-problem-solvers-dems-we-cannot-support-pelosi-for-speaker-at-this-time/.

Zhou, Li. 2018. "Congress's Recently Passed Sexual Harassment Bill, Explained." *Vox*, December 20, 2018. https://www.vox.com/2018/12/20/18138377/congress-sexual-harassment-bill.

Index

abortion, 111–112, 133, 145–147
Adams, Gerry, 110
affiliational criteria, 45, 49, 52–54, 85, 93, 98, 186, 193
Affordable Care Act (ACA), 2, 5, 15, 38, 50, 135, 144–149, 154, 167, 187, 192
Albert, Carl, 88, 173
Aldrich, John, 40, 168
Alexander, Danny, 48, 70
Allen, Heidi, 128, 204
ambition, 86–87, 96, 141
Annesley, Claire, 8–12, 16–18, 45, 47–49, 54, 66–67, 73, 85, 93–94, 96–98, 132–133, 183–187, 193
Ashcroft, Michael, 61, 124, 126, 129, 204
Ashe, Jeannette, 57, 60
Atlas Network, 121, 202
attack ads, 152, 157–158, 161, 163, 166, 181, 189–190
austerity, 70, 76, 95, 104

Bachmann, Michele, 152
Backbench Business Committee (UK), 32, 198
Baker, Ross K., 137–138
Baker, Steve, 23, 26–28, 36, 119, 123–126, 196, 201

Bale, Tim, 12, 106
Ball, Molly, 141, 146, 151, 153, 158, 162, 164
Banks, Jim, 176
Barnier, Michel, 108, 122
Bebb, Guto, 120, 123, 202
Beckwith, Karen, 6–12, 16–18, 45, 47–50, 54, 66–67, 73, 85, 93–94, 96–98, 132–133, 183–187, 193
Bercow, John, 82
biases, 7, 15–17, 56, 149
Biden, Joe, 171, 173
Blair, Tony, 21, 31, 51, 59, 196
Blais, André, 17
Blue Dogs, 38, 137, 151
Boehner, John, 152, 158, 167–168
Boll Weevils, 36, 38
Bonior, David, 91
Bradley, Karen, 60, 99, 111–112
Brady, Graham, 26, 196, 203
Brady, Karen, 26, 196
Brexit, 5, 53, 81, 104, 121–123; and farming/fishing policies, 21, 130–131, 205; May's negotiations of, 1–2, 11, 55, 113–114, 117–120, 132–134, 183, 187, 192, 201–212; "no deal," 117, 121–122, 129, 132; Plan A+, 121–122, 202; and Remainers, 5, 10, 68, 105–107, 127–128, 132, 203–204

265

Brexit referendums, 32, 34, 116; calls for a second, 128, 132, 203–204; 2016, 4, 26, 29, 35, 68–69, 96, 99, 105–107, 126, 186, 200–201
Brexit ultras, 27, 67, 125–127
Bright Blue "Modernisers' Manifesto," 51, 54, 99
British Sugar, 126
Brown, Gordon, 30, 52, 196
Bryson, Valerie, 52
Burton, Phil, 83
Burton, Sala, 83–84
Butler, Andrew, 37

cabinet survivors, 10–11, 43–44, 47–48, 69–70, 95–98, 134, 181, 184–185, 193
Cameron, David, 17, 33, 48, 51–53, 58, 61–62, 76, 106, 114, 184, 198–201; Euroskepticism of, 29, 107–108; London "Bloomberg" speech, 34–35, 199; as Opposition Leader, 31, 59; and same-sex marriage, 29, 72
Cameron-Clegg coalition (2010–2015), 24, 32–33, 48, 69–70, 73, 97–98, 131, 198–200
Canada-EU Comprehensive Economic and Trade Agreement (CETA), 119, 132, 205
Cannon, Joe, 40–41, 167–168
Capitol administration, 179–180
Care Act (2014), 101–102
Carney, Mark, 124–125
Cash, Bill, 23–24, 26, 28, 196
Cash, Joanne, 61–62
Celis, Karen, 12, 39–40, 85–86, 183–184
Cheney, Liz, 176
Chequers Conference/framework, 99, 117–121, 123, 208–209
Childs, Sarah, 7–8, 14–17, 44, 50–51, 54–55, 183–184
Churchill, Winston, 20, 195
Cillizza, Chris, 156
Civil Rights Act (1964), 36
"Clare's Law" (2014), 74
Clarke, Ken, 25, 74, 196
Clarke, Mark, 62
Cleaver, Emanuel, 155–156
Clegg, Nick, 32–33, 48, 69–70, 73–75, 77–79, 95

Clinton, Bill, 71, 171
Clyburn, Jim, 151, 159, 166, 168, 180, 189
committee chairs, 2, 40–41, 86, 139, 142–143, 153, 155, 164
common currency (Euro), 23, 34
Common Fisheries Policy, 21, 130–131
conditional party government (CPG), 40, 168
Congress, 39, 60, 143–144, 160–161
Congressional Accountability Act (1995), Reform Act (S. 3749), 161
Congressional Black Caucus (US), 5, 43, 137, 145, 151, 155–156
Congressional Progressive Caucus, 5, 38, 43, 165, 186
ConservativeHome website, 61, 67, 129, 204
Conservative Party (UK), 5, 20, 52–56, 59–60, 115; A-list, 59–62, 95, 132; and the "confidence and supply agreement," 4–5, 10–11, 98–99, 111, 186–187; and diversity/equality, 2–3, 5, 15, 17, 44, 49, 52–53, 56, 58–59, 62; and Euroskepticism, 10–11, 20–25, 29, 32, 52, 54, 60, 66, 79, 96, 191, 198; leadership selection, 8, 65–66; May as chair of, 48, 56–60; modernization attempts, 51, 54, 56–58, 95, 97, 100, 132; Remainers in, 29, 67, 115–116, 128; and social conservatism, 50–53, 55, 71–73, 95; 2017 election, 102, 106
Conyers, John, 160
Corbyn, Jeremy, 70, 104–105, 114, 128, 190, 204
Council of Europe (COE), 20
COVID-19, 135, 175, 177–179, 181–182, 189
Cowley, Philip, 28–29, 198
Cox, Gary W., 40–41
Creasey, Stella, 111–113
critical mass, 13–14, 17
Cross, William, 17
Crowley, Jim, 158, 165
Cruz Lera, Estefania, 166
Cunningham, Sheryl L., 154

Dahlerup, Drude, 12, 14, 18
Davis, David, 23, 58, 66–67, 99, 118–119, 122–123, 126, 132, 196, 201–202

DeLauro, Rosa, 139
Delors, Jacques, 22
Democratic Party (US), 2, 36, 41, 87, 93, 135–138, 149–154, 166; committee chairs, 2, 142–143, 155, 164; and diversity, 2–3, 15, 49; progressive/moderate conflicts, 137, 165–166, 168–169; women in, 39, 86, 91
Democratic Rules, 142–143
Democratic Steering and Policy Committee, 156, 165, 191
Democratic Unionist Party (DUP, Northern Ireland/UK), 106, 108–111, 113, 116, 128–130, 190, 201; allied with ERG, 119, 129; and the "confidence and supply agreement," 4–5, 10–11, 98–99, 111, 186–187; and the customs backstop, 123–124, 129, 133, 203, 209–210
Dingell, John, 142–145, 154–156
"divisiveness," 66
Duerst-Lahti, Georgia, 13, 17–18
Duncan, Alan, 23, 196
Duncan Smith, Iain, 17, 23, 26, 44, 52, 54–58, 60, 71–72, 95, 122, 128, 196

economic conservatism, 52–53, 99
Energy and Commerce Committee, 144–145, 149, 154–157
Equality Act (2010), 59
Equality and Human Rights Commission, 77–78
Escobar-Lemmon, Maria, 9–11, 44–45, 47–49, 85, 90, 95–98, 134, 136, 145, 181, 183–186, 193
Eshoo, Anna, 140, 155–157
EU fiscal stability pact (2011), 33, 107–108, 199
European Arrest Warrant (EAW), 79, 81–82, 95, 117–118
European Coal and Steel Community (ECSC), 21
European constitution, 30–31, 196
European Convention on Human Rights (ECHR), 20, 104, 195
European Court of Justice (ECJ), 20–22, 33, 80–81, 195, 203
European Economic Area" (EEA), 119

European Economic Community (EEC), 21–22, 24, 195
European exchange rate mechanism (ERM), 24
European Parliament, 29–30
European Research Group (ERG), 25, 35–36, 120–123, 131–132, 185, 187, 196, 200, 202–203, 209; and the DUP, 119, 129; and Fresh Start, 35, 120; and Johnson, 55; leadership challenge against May, 123–124, 130
European Union, 25–27, 31, 34, 186, 196; customs union, 116, 129–130, 133–134; and policing/criminal justice reforms, 78–82, 117–118, 131, 196, 199. See also Brexit
European Union Act (2011), 32
Europe/UK relationship 1949-2019, 195–212
Euroskepticism, 24, 31, 114, 196; in the Conservative Party, 10–11, 20–25, 29, 32, 52, 54, 60, 66, 79, 96, 191, 198; and the single market, 27, 34–35. See also specific groups; "Thatcher's children"
experiential criteria, 8–10, 47–49, 66–69, 114, 186, 193

Farage, Nigel, 26, 63, 129
Featherstone, Lynne, 71–72, 76, 95
feminine qualities, 7, 139, 153–154, 176, 179, 181, 190–191, 193
financial sector, 31–35, 199–200, 206. See also London
first-past-the-post electoral systems, 3, 13, 184
Fixed Term Parliaments Act (2011), 24, 100, 124
Fontana, Cary, 23, 196
Ford, Harold Jr., 137–138
Foster, Arlene, 4, 109–114, 116, 210
Fox, Liam, 23, 28, 67–68, 115, 196
Franceschet, Susan, 8–10, 17–18, 45, 47–49, 54, 66–67, 73, 85, 93–94, 96–98, 132–133, 183–187, 193
Franken, Al, 147, 152, 160
Freedom Caucus, 38, 158, 167
Freeman, Jo, 54
Free Trade Institute, 121

Fresh Start, 25–27, 67–68, 78–79, 82, 131–132, 196; "Manifesto for Change," 34, 80, 120, 123, 199
Frost, Martin, 137–138
Fudge, Marcia, 162–164

Gains, Francesca, 12, 16
gender, 16–17, 90, 137–140, 139, 143
gender dynamics, 86–87, 89–94, 136, 138, 141, 143, 150–154, 170, 179
gender equality, 12, 191–192
Geoghegan, Peter, 26, 35–36, 122
Gephardt, Richard, 50, 88, 91, 136–138, 152
Germany, 30
gerrymandering, 37
Gingrich, Newt, 38, 40–42, 84, 89, 143, 173, 193
Good Friday (Belfast) Agreement, 104, 107–108, 110, 117, 201
Gove, Michael, 67–69, 74–76, 99
Greene, Marjorie Taylor, 178–179
Green, Matthew N., 86–90, 92, 94, 136, 141, 154, 163
Grieve, Dominic, 116
Growth Forum (2012), 125

Hague, William, 8, 44, 52, 54, 72
Hammond, Philip, 71–72
Hannan, Daniel, 25–28, 121, 196
Harris, Douglas B., 86–92, 94, 163
Hastert, Dennis, 42, 193
Heath, Edward, 12, 21, 195
Heaton-Harris, Chris, 26–27, 196
Heppell, Timothy, 29, 52, 69–70, 198
Hilton, Steve, 104–105
Hoey, Kate, 120, 210
Home Affairs Committee, 73–74
House, Billy, 152
House Democratic Caucus (US), 5
House Judiciary Committee, 172, 175
House leadership campaigns, 87
House of Commons (UK), 3, 193
House of Representatives (US), 5, 19, 37–42, 137, 167, 193; partisan control of, 37, 40, 167, 169; percentage of women in, 3, 39; as "procedural cartel", 40, 153, 181; Trump impeachments, 169–172, 174–175

House Speaker (US), 3, 39–42, 50, 85–89, 136, 143, 167
Howard, Michael, 24, 55, 58, 204
Hoyer, Steny, 44, 89–94, 137, 140–141, 144–145, 151, 154, 157, 159, 164, 166, 178, 180, 189
Hughes, Melanie M., 12–14

immigration, 30, 35, 73, 81, 104, 196, 200
impeachments, 135, 169–175
"independent" voters (US), 36–37
Institute of Economic Affairs (IEA), 121–122, 125
"institutional care work", 175–181, 191
Intelligence Committee, 172
Ireland, 20, 104, 107–108, 110, 117

Jalalzai, Farida, 18–19
January 6 Capitol attack (2021), 135, 174–176, 175–177, 180, 190
JCB, 126, 128
Jenkin, Anne, 44, 58
Jenkin, Bernard, 23, 26, 28, 44, 196
Jenkins, Jeffery A., 40, 153
Jenrick, Robert, 63
Johnson, Boris, 2, 5, 33, 50, 55, 63, 76, 114, 121–122, 192; and the 2019 election, 6, 119, 184, 212; Chuck Chequers event, 119, 202; deal with the EU, 129–131; leadership campaign, 11, 65, 68, 119, 126, 128, 132, 212; in May's cabinet, 99, 119, 190, 201
Johnson government, 100, 125, 129–130, 132
Johnson, Lyndon, 36
Jordan, Jim, 176
Juncker, Jean-Claude, 108, 113–114, 198

Kanter, Rosabeth Moss, 7, 13
Karteng, Kwasi, 125
Kelly, Rita Mae, 13, 17–18
Kinnock, Neil, 20–21
Krook, Mona Lena, 7–8, 14–17, 44, 50–51, 54, 183–184
Kwarteng, Kwasi, 27

Labour Party (UK), 20, 24, 28, 52, 59, 104–105, 109
Lake, Celinda, 152

Lawless, Jennifer L., 88
Laws, David, 75–76
Lawson, Nigel, 23, 28
leadership, language of, 39, 142
leadership challenges, 136; against McCarthy, 180–181; against May, 123–124, 128, 130, 188, 190, 203–204; against Pelosi, 50, 135–136, 142, 150–152, 162, 168, 170–171, 180, 188–189
leadership PACs, 48, 136, 155
Leadsom, Andrea, 5, 26, 59, 66–68, 99, 107, 114, 196, 201
Legg, Barry, 57–58
legislative institutional norms, 15–16, 50
legislative practices, 16, 51
Lehmann, Wilhelm, 22
Leyenaar, Monique, 12, 14
LGBTQ rights, 5, 29, 71–72, 95, 109–110, 112–113, 192
Liberal Democrats (UK), 31–32, 34, 58–59, 64
Lilly Ledbetter Fair Pay Act (2009), 15
Lipinski, Daniel, 42, 162n8, 167
Lisbon Treaty (2009), 23, 30–31, 34, 197–199; Article 50, 31, 50, 67, 100, 113–114, 116, 126, 130
Little, Marion, 63–65
London, as financial center, 31–33, 35, 43, 125, 200
Lovenduski, Joni, 11–12, 16, 39–40, 85–86, 183–184
Lowndes, Vivien, 12
loyalty, 3, 141, 157, 181

Maastricht Treaty (1992), 22–25, 131, 178, 196–197
McAllister, Ian, 13–14
McCarthy, Kevin, 159, 176, 180–181
McConnell, Mitch, 172–173
McCubbins, Matthew D., 40–41
McGuinness, Martin, 109–111
Macmillan, Harold, 20, 195
McTague, Tom, 103–104, 107
McVey, Esther, 59–60, 123, 203
McVey, Theresa, 132
majoritarian political systems, 3, 6, 40, 94, 133, 167
Major, John, 23–25, 54, 131, 196–197
Marthaler, Sally, 55

masculine qualities, 7, 18, 181, 190–191
mask mandates, 177–179, 181–182, 189
Massie vs. Pelosi, 179
May government, 107, 201–212
Mayhew, Les, 102, 104
May, Philip, 51, 74, 127
May, Theresa, 4, 51–52, 67, 71, 75–76, 169, 182, 192; and the 2015 election, 63–64; and the 2017 election, 104–105, 111; attempts to modernize the Conservative Party, 55, 132; and Brexit negotiations, 1, 11, 55, 113–114, 117–120, 122, 128–129, 132–134, 183, 192, 201–212; as Conservative Party chair, 48, 56–60; experience of, 8–10, 43–44, 47–48, 51–52, 55, 114, 133, 185–186; as home secretary, 2, 15, 35, 71, 73–76, 81, 95–97, 104–105, 186–187; on immigration, 73, 75, 81, 104; Lancaster House speech, 115, 119, 202–203; leadership challenges to, 123–124, 128, 130, 188, 190, 203–204; "Plan for Britain" speech, 115; as prime minister, 19, 96, 99, 133, 184, 186; resignation announcement, 1, 55, 129, 134, 212; on same-sex marriage/LGBTQ rights, 71–72, 95
mentoring, 86, 88, 92–93
Merkel, Angela, 50, 87, 198, 212
metal detector controversy, 179, 181–182, 189
#MeToo, 160–161
Miller, George, 91, 140
Miller, Gina, 113–114, 116, 201
Miller, Maria, 71, 95
Minister for Equalities, 70–72
Mitchell, George, 83
Montgomerie, Tim, 70
Mordaunt, Penny, 27, 196
Morgan, Nicky, 71, 100
motherhood, 139
Moulton, Seth, 162, 163n9, 164–165, 168
Mueller investigation, 170–172
Murtha, John, 84, 93, 140–141, 157

Nadler, Jerrold, 172, 175
national domestic violence bill (2021), 74

"New Democrat" Coalition (US), 5
Norris, Pippa, 11, 16
Northern Ireland, 2, 19–20, 107–114, 118–120, 129–130, 133, 184; customs backstop, 118–120, 122–124, 127, 129, 184, 203, 209–211. *See also* Democratic Unionist Party (DUP, Northern Ireland/UK)
Northern Ireland Executive and Exercise of Functions Act (2018), 112
Northern Ireland Protocol, 132, 184

Obama, Barack, 38, 71
Obamacare. *See* Affordable Care Act (ACA)
Obey, David, 47, 142
O'Brien, Diana, 12, 17–18
Ocasio-Cortez, Alexandra, 165–166
Omar, Ilhan, 165
Open Europe think tank, 27–28, 34, 80, 120, 123, 199
opposition parties, 17–18
"Options for Change" green paper, 27
organizational partisans, 47–49, 97, 134, 185, 193
Osborne, George, 48, 63–64, 68–73, 75–76, 99, 114
Ostrom, Elinor, 8, 16, 49, 98, 183–184, 186, 193

Page, Susan, 167, 170
Paisley, Ian, 108
Pallone, Frank, 155–157
parliamentary research groups, 26. *See also* European Research Group (ERG)
Parsons, Craig, 23, 196
partisanship, growth of, 38–39, 167, 169
party leadership selection (Stark's critera), 67–69
Patel, Priti, 27, 59–60, 100, 125, 132, 196
Paterson, Owen, 122
Paxton, Pamela, 12–14
Pelosi, Christine, 83–84, 92–93
Pelosi, Nancy, 2, 4, 47, 82–85, 93, 143, 183, 187, 192–193; 2010 leadership race, 149–152; 2018 Speaker election,

1, 161–166; and the ACA, 144–146, 148–149; on the Appropriations Committee, 84–85, 90, 94; as California Democratic Party Chair, 83–85; campaigning for whip, 91–94; on the Ethics Committee, 84–85, 90; experience of, 2, 9, 42, 44, 47–48, 83–85, 89–94, 96, 137, 187; as fundraiser, 1, 10, 48–50, 83, 90, 152, 159, 161–162; as House Speaker, 5, 15, 43, 135, 138–141, 167–168, 184–185, 187; and January 6 (2021), 174–176, 180, 190; leadership challenges to, 50, 135–136, 142, 150–152, 157–160, 162, 168, 170–171, 180, 188–189; majority leadership race, 140–142; and #MeToo, 160–161; motivations of, 91–92, 138–139, 190–191; Republican campaigns against, 150, 157, 161, 166, 181, 189–190; step down announcement, 135, 150, 169, 180, 184; support for Eshoo, 155; and Trump, 170, 173–174, 191; and the Trump administration, 172–174; and the Trump impeachments, 169–175
Pelosi, Paul, 83, 93, 180, 190
Pence, Mike, 174, 190
Perlmutter, Ed, 162–163, 163n9
Peters, Ronald M., 40–41, 90–91, 93, 141
Philips, Anne, 14
Pickles, Eric, 62–63
Pilet, Jean-Benoit, 17–18
Poland, 35
police reform (UK), 74–82, 104–105
Police Reform and Social Responsibility Act (2011), 76–77
policy expertise, 47
policy-making processes, 16
"political capital resources" (PCRs), 9
Political Declaration (2019), 130
political leadership selection, 8–10, 13
Portillo, Michael, 23–24, 196, 204
positional power, 15–16, 40, 184
Pressley, Ayanna, 165
primary challengers, and "safe seats," 37
Prime Ministers, 18–19

Problem Solvers caucus (US), 5, 39, 162, 164, 167–168
proxy voting, 178, 189

Quinn, Thomas, 65–67

Raab, Dominic, 26, 120, 123, 125, 196, 203
Rayburn, Sam, 88, 162
Reagan, Ronald, 52
reconciliation process, 148
Redwood, John, 23, 26, 28, 56, 60, 196
Rees-Mogg, Jacob, 11, 24, 27, 124–126, 190, 196
Rees-Mogg, Willam, 24–25
Reeves, Rachel, 59
Reid, Harry, 147
representation, 2, 13, 54; descriptive, 2–3, 6, 8, 12, 14, 49, 56; substantive, 2–3, 6, 12, 14–15, 56; symbolic, 2–3, 6
representational criteria, 8–9, 49, 98, 114, 186, 193
Republican Caucus rules, 40–42, 135–136
Republican Party (US), 36, 39, 52–54, 87, 154; campaigns against Pelosi, 150, 157, 161, 166, 181, 189–190
Republic of Ireland, 73, 107–108, 110, 115, 130, 202
Rice, Kathleen, 162, 163n9, 165
"Road Trip" campaign, 62, 64
Robinson, Peter, 108–109
Rohde, David, 40, 168
Rosenthal, Cindy Simon, 90–91, 93, 141
Ross, Tim, 103–104
Rudd, Amber, 59, 99
Rules Committee, 41–42, 139, 167–168, 178
Ryan, Paul, 159, 167–168
Ryan, Tim, 158–160, 162, 163n9, 165, 168

same-sex marriage, 29, 71–72, 95, 109–110, 112–113. *See also* LGBTQ rights
Sanbonmatsu, Kira, 88
Sawer, Marion, 18
Scalise, Steve, 159, 178
Schiff, Adam, 172, 175
Schlafly, Phyllis, 52

Schleiter, Petra, 19–20
Schrader, Kurt, 162n8, 163
Scottish National Party, 106
Section 60, 77–78
Select Committee on Climate Change, 143
Senate (US), 5, 169–173, 175
Sex Discrimination (Election Candidates) Act (2002), 59
sexism, 83–84, 88, 152, 169, 189–190. *See also* gender dynamics
sexual harassment scandals, 132, 160–161, 191–192
Shapps, Grant, 62–63
Shuler, Heath, 150–152, 159
Sinclair, Barbara, 89
Singham, Shanker, 122
Single European Act (1985), 21–22
Single European Act referendum (1975), 28
single markets, 27–28, 34–35, 130, 199–200
Sinn Fein, 109–113, 130, 133, 184
Slaughter, Louise, 139, 146
Smith, John, 20–21
Social Democratic and Labour Party (SDLP, Ireland), 109, 111
Soros, George, 115–116
Soubry, Anna, 60, 100, 128, 204
Southern Democrats, 40–41
South Thanet constituency (Kent), 64
Spanberger, Abigail, 163
Spelman, Caroline, 58
Spicer, Michael, 25, 27, 56–57, 60, 196
"The Squad," 38, 165–166, 168–169
Stark, Leonard P., 66–67
Stark's Criteria, 66–69, 87
Stewart, Charles III, 40–41, 153
stop and search, 77–78
strategic acting, 54
Stuart, Mark, 28–29, 198
Studlar, Donley, 13–14
Stupak, Bart, 145–147
Sumner, Charles, 37
Swinford, Steven, 82

Tate & Lyle Sugar Company, 126
taxes, 22, 32–33, 101–103, 209–210

Taylor-Robinson, Michelle, 9–11, 45, 47–49, 85, 90, 95–98, 134, 136, 145, 181, 183–186, 193
Tea Party, 167
terrorist attacks, in the UK, 104–105
Thatcher, Margaret, 12, 19, 21–24, 47, 50, 54–55, 131, 182
"Thatcher's children/grandchildren," 23, 25, 27–28, 115, 131–132, 196
Thomas, Cal, 137
Timothy, Nick, 64–65, 100, 103, 116
Tlaib, Rashida, 163, 165
tokenism, 8
Tonge, Jonathan, 100
Treaty of Rome (1957), 21
"tri-committee," 145, 149
Trump administration, 149, 170–174, 177
Trump, Donald, 135, 157–158, 162, 165, 169–177, 191
Truss, Liz, 99, 107, 125
Tusk, Donald, 35, 107, 200
2010 Democratic leadership race, 149–152
2015 election (UK), 29, 63–64, 100
2016 election campaign (US), 157–158
2016 leadership campaign (UK), 5, 65, 68
2017 election (UK), 4–6, 10–11, 29, 50, 64–65, 69, 98–100, 103–106, 111, 186–187
2018 Speaker's race, 1, 161–166
2019 election (UK), 6, 55, 68
2020 election, 173, 175–176; and the January 6 Capitol attack (2021), 135, 174–176, 175–177
2022 Election, 180
2005 election (UK), 29
2006-2007 majority leadership race (US), 140–142
2008 financial crisis, 5, 30–31, 43, 76

Ukraine, 171
Ulster Unionist Party (UUP), 109
UN Declaration of Human Rights, 20
United Kingdom, 15, 21, 28–29, 69, 100, 108; "backwaters," 106; Border Agency, 74–75; campaign finance regulations, 63–64; common-law legal system of, 20; cosmopolitan cities, 106; customs backstop, 118–120, 122–124, 127, 129, 184, 203, 209–211; immigration, 30, 73, 75, 81; pensions in, 102–103; regional divisions in, 19–20; relationship with Europe, 195–212; social care in, 101
United Kingdom Independence Party (UKIP), 28, 30, 34, 63–64, 72–73, 106–107, 196, 205
United States, 14–15, 36–37, 46
United States Constitution, 144n1
Usherwood, Simon, 27–28

Varadkar, Leo, 110, 114
Vickers, Martin, 26, 196

Warsi, Sayeedi, 62
Watergate scandal, 36
Wauters, Bram, 17–18
Waxman, Henry, 142, 145, 154, 156–157
Webb, Paul, 55, 106
Weiner, Juli, 153
Weldon, S. Laurel, 13–14
Whittindale, John, 23, 196
Widdecombe, Ann, 55
Williamson, Gavin, 107
Wilson, Harold, 21
Wilson, Sammy, 123–124
Wineinger, Catherine, 54
Withdrawal Act Bills, 11, 118, 120, 202, 207–208, 211; and Article 50, 31, 50, 67, 100, 113–114, 116, 126, 130. *See also* Brexit
withdrawal Agreement Bill (WAB), 114, 116–117, 119, 122, 124, 127–128, 130, 184, 202, 210–212. *See also* Brexit
Wollaston, Sarah, 26, 128, 132, 196, 204
women, 39, 54–55, 58–59, 88; and ageism, 138, 150, 160, 163, 190; biases against, 13, 50, 56, 73, 169; as committee chairs (US), 2, 86, 187; in the Democratic Party (US), 39, 86, 91, 187; and qualifications, 43, 50, 88
"Women 2 Win" group, 44, 58–59
women-friendly legislation, 13–14
Women's Caucus (US), 5

women's equality, 52–53
women's leadership, 7, 13, 17–18, 46–47; and ageism, 138, 150, 160, 163, 190; attitudes towards, 3, 13, 16, 49–50, 55–56, 73, 85, 94–95, 98, 149, 153–154, 169, 188; barriers to, 6–7, 43; outsider paradox of, 11–12, 50, 188

World Trade Organization (WTO), 117, 121–122
Wright, Jim, 41, 193
Wright, Shaun, 77

Zika virus, 158–159